Our Old Monsters

Our Old Monsters

Witches, Werewolves and Vampires from Medieval Theology to Horror Cinema

BRENDA S. GARDENOUR WALTER

McFarland & Company, Inc., Publishers
Jefferson, North Carolina

LIBRARY OF CONGRESS CATALOGUING-IN-PUBLICATION DATA

Gardenour Walter, Brenda S., 1971–
    Our old monsters : witches, werewolves and vampires from medieval theology to horror cinema / Brenda S. Gardenour Walter.
        p.   cm.
    Includes bibliographical references and index.
    Includes filmography.

    ISBN 978-0-7864-7680-0 (softcover : acid free paper) ∞
    ISBN 978-1-4766-1942-2 (ebook)

    1. Horror films—History and criticism.   2. Monsters in motion pictures.   3. Monsters—History.   I. Title.
PN1995.9.H6G38 2015
398'.45—dc23   2015016044

BRITISH LIBRARY CATALOGUING DATA ARE AVAILABLE

© 2015 Brenda S. Gardenour Walter. All rights reserved

No part of this book may be reproduced or transmitted in any form or by any means, electronic or mechanical, including photocopying or recording, or by any information storage and retrieval system, without permission in writing from the publisher.

On the cover: moon in a forest © 2015 iStock/Thinkstock

Printed in the United States of America

McFarland & Company, Inc., Publishers
  Box 611, Jefferson, North Carolina 28640
    www.mcfarlandpub.com

For the "Munkey," the Man, and
all of the Melancholic Monsters

Table of Contents

Preface   1
Introduction   3

PART I: MEDIEVAL FOUNDATIONS   15

1. Upside-Down and Inside-Out: The Medieval Construction of Earthbound Evil   16
2. Satanic Cinema: His Legacy Is Legion   42
3. Wanton Flesh and Poisoned Breath: Crafting the Satanic Witch   68
4. Wicked Women: Female Flesh, the Satanic Witch and the Horror Film   98

PART II: MODERN PERMUTATIONS   135

5. The Transgressive Monster: From the Melancholic Jew to the Blood-Sucking Vampire   136
6. A Cursed Embodiment: Modernity, Medievalism and the Melancholic Werewolf   166

Epilogue   195
Chapter Notes   197
Bibliography   223
Filmography   234
Index   237

Preface

The modern horror genre is replete with perennially popular monstrous beings coded as evil, including the vampire, the witch, and the werewolf. Blood-hungry and melancholic, each of these "old monsters" share an inverted anatomy and physiology first codified in late-medieval universities. It was there that scholastic theologians such as Thomas Aquinas, William of Auvergne, and Pseudo-Albertus Magnus used Aristotelian cosmology and natural philosophy in conjunction with the authoritative language of medicine to construct the perfect Christian body—rational, ethereal and fundamentally male.

Following the rules of Aristotelian contrariety, scholars likewise constructed the inverted, evil body, which was cold, irrational, earthbound and essentially female. Rapacious with bloodlust, its bowels infested with demons and rife with toxic *pneuma*, the melancholic monstrous body would inform the construction of the wicked witch, the hermeneutic vampire–Jew, and the mournful werewolf.

These old monsters remain popular in horror not only because of their alterity in myriad postmodern contexts, but also because of their essential humanity. Fully human and fully ensouled, they are creatures of the earth who, through their own self-willed weaknesses, have been tempted into damnation and fallen away from the love and acceptance they truly desire. In the post–Cartesian West where soulless zombies and disembodied ghosts haunt popular culture, these old monsters serve as mirrors in which we might observe with *jouissance* our own abjected selves, while suggesting the terrifying notion that our bodies are not merely haunted houses, but inhabited creations of flesh and blood searching for the light.

Introduction

> "What is the flaw of human rationality? It pretends not to see the horror and death at the end of the schemes it builds."—Chief of Theory, *Cosmopolis* (2012)

Over the past twenty years, Western popular culture has witnessed a paranormal renaissance. Ghosts and demons haunt not only movie theaters but also our homes through myriad digital devices. Docudramas such as *A Haunting* (2005–2014) and *Scariest Places on Earth* (2000–2006), as well as paranormal investigation programs such as *Ghost Hunters* (2004-present), *Ghost Adventures* (2008-present), and *Paranormal State* (2007–2011), use POV (point of view) filming techniques, state of the art technology, and the testimony of both eyewitnesses and paranormal experts in their attempts to prove the veracity of the unseen world.[1] Supernatural horror films, from the *Paranormal Activity* franchise (2009–present) to *The Last Exorcism* (2010) and—because it's never the last exorcism—*The Last Exorcism Part II* (2013) all bear witness to our continued obsession with the spirits of the dead, demonic entities, and their power to penetrate the human body. In reference to the body, zombies, too, have achieved celebrity status in recent decades. From *Zombieland* (2009) and *World War Z* (2013) to the incredibly successful television series *Walking Dead* (2010–present), animated corpses stalk the living for no apparent reason other than, perhaps, as an object lesson in what it means to be only half human. These ghosts and zombies form an interesting dichotomy, with one pole being occupied by disembodied mind-spirits, and the other occupied by dis-ensouled and mindless bodies. These binary entities reflect a post–Cartesian, biomedical, and very *Western* view of embodiment—a mechanical body separate and yet somehow still associated with the "thinking stuff" that wafts about within it like a ghost in a machine.[2]

In conjunction with the paranormal renaissance, there has been a resurgence of the preternatural and the monstrous. Alongside post–Cartesian ghosts and zombies, the old monsters—the witch, the vampire, and the werewolf—have revived once again. Once relegated to the dustbins of *Creature Double Features* and midnight schlock, the old monsters are no longer marginalized but at the center of serial programming such as *American Horror Story* (2011–present) and *True Blood* (2008–present), as well as the books and films of the *Twilight* franchise. Some of this is generational; the old monsters are friends from childhood that we pass on to our own children in predictable cycles.[3] As we grow older, these monsters change shape and take on new meanings, in many cases revealing their highly sexualized nature. But there is more to the persistent presence of the witch, the vampire, and the werewolf in Western popular culture than simple nostalgia. Blood-hungry, sexually rapacious, and transgressive, the old monsters speak to our primal fears of penetration and contamination by an abject "other."[4] Although their evil embodiment might give them the appearance of supernatural monstrosity, these creatures are nevertheless fully human, fully ensouled, and well within the bounds of medieval natural law. They are, in fact, *us*—a sort of funhouse mirror reflecting back to our eye a warped, corrupted, and inverted image of our own potential human goodness.

Entangled with the resurgence of monsters in popular culture, monstrosity has become a topic of inquiry in recent scholarship. Discussions of the monstrous are by their very nature multivalent and often interdisciplinary. Scholars such as Timothy K. Beal have sought the sources of monstrosity in the Bible, while Jerome Jeffrey Cohen, Sarah Alison Miller, and Bettina Bildhauer have written about monstrous bodies, births, and blood in medieval contexts.[5] Myriad edited collections, of which *The Ashgate Research Companion to Monsters and the Monstrous* is but one example, explore monstrosity in multiple contexts from the Renaissance through modernity.[6] Stephen Asma's *On Monsters: An Unnatural History of Our Worst Fears* surveys the history of monstrous creatures in Western culture from antiquity to the present, while W. Scott Poole's *Monsters in America: Our Historical Obsession with the Hideous and the Haunting* and David Skal's *The Monster Show: A Cultural History of Horror* explore the relationships between cinematic monsters, politics and popular culture in twentieth-century America.[7] Beyond these historical and cultural approaches, many studies of monstrosity—in particular those related to film studies—rely heavily on discourses from the field of psychology, including Freud's theories of repression, the return of the uncanny, and the resurfacing of "surmounted beliefs" in times of stress, Lacan's theory of the "real and unreal," and Kristeva's theory of abjection and *jouissance*.[8] Postmodernist discourses such as the monstrous "otherness" of Foucault, the alterity of Levinas, and the transgressive leakiness described by Margrit

Shildrick are likewise threaded through scholarly analyses of monstrosity, providing a philosophical foundation for the study of monsters through the lenses of feminism, gender studies, queer studies, and transhumanism.[9]

This book takes a novel approach, finding the sources for melancholic monstrosity in medieval scholasticism and examining the continued power of medieval structures to signify evil alterity in modern horror films. The first part, Medieval Foundations, begins in the learned milieu of the thirteenth and fourteenth centuries. It was then that scholastic theologians reconciled the works of Aristotle and the precepts of learned medicine with the authority of received theology in order to create a single system meant to reflect a consistent divine truth. Chapter 1 traces the construction of divine goodness and Satanic evil found in sources such as the *Summa Theologica* and *De Sententiis* of Thomas Aquinas and the *De Universo* of William of Auvergne. Using Aristotelian cosmology and natural philosophy in the service of theology, scholars argued that the superlunary realm was one of divine perfection dominated by the Christian God who sat upon His throne in the Empyrean beyond the sidereal sphere.[10] This highest heaven was marked by theophanic light, translucence, the color white, weightlessness, warmth and, above all, an obedience to the singular will of God—an obedience observed by the choirs of angels that swirled in perfect circles all the way up to the court of saints and martyrs. In keeping with Aristotelian contrariety, scholastic theologians constructed the sublunary realm as a radical inversion of divine goodness. Evil and chaotic, it was marked by darkness, opacity, the colors black and red, heaviness, coldness, corruption, and disobedience, and dominated by elemental earth, the coldest, driest, heaviest and most corrupt of the four elements.[11]

Farthest from the Empyrean, the melancholic earth was the abode of Satan and his demonic minions who, having been cast down from heaven for their willful disobedience, might fly through the air but never again ascend into the ethereal realms beyond the moon. Weak and disobedient humans often fell prey to the demonic entities who tormented them, possessed them, and seduced them into the service of their dark lord. All those who did not conform to the authority of the Church, including heretics, witches, and non–Christians such as Jews and Muslims, were cast into the category of melancholic evil and imagined to be in league with the Devil. By the fifteenth century, famine, plague, schism, and heretical movements came to signify the strengthening power of Satanic entities, both human and demonic, who appeared to be mounting an organized and successful attack on the Church. It was in this context that Heinrich Kramer wrote the *Malleus Maleficarum* (1486), an inquisition manual that marked the beginning of a textual tradition in which the inverted category of Satanic evil, carrying the weight of theological authority, would be fully conflated with popular ideas about witchcraft.[12] The upside-down world of subversion, inverted rituals, and Satanic worship that was increasingly circumscribed in early modern witchcraft treatises would become a universal signifier for evil alterity in Western culture, and one day serve as the substrate for supernatural horror.

Chapter 2 traces the persistence of inverted evil in modern Anglo-American Satanic cinema. The first section examines the structuring of the Black Masses in *The Black Cat* (1934) and *The Devil Rides Out* (1968), both of which conflate Satanic worship with learned occultism and feature bourgeois Europeans as antagonists. In *The City of the Dead* (1960) and *The Witchmaker* (1969), Satanic rituals conform more closely to witchcraft paradigms and are performed by common folk in the American wilderness. In the discursive realm of horror, as in Western culture more broadly construed, the performance of Satanic rituals is ascribed to subversive "others" who threaten the status quo.[13] For example, *Taste the Blood of Dracula* (1970), *The Satanic Rites of Dracula* (1973), and *The Devil's Daughter* (1973) depict the older generation as Satan-worshipping parasites draining the life from the young, while *I Drink Your Blood* (1970) and *Blood on Satan's Claw* (1971) depict young members of the counter culture as rapacious murderers out to destroy middle-class society. The second section shifts the focus of Satanic inversion and ritual from human society to the human body. A recurring theme in Satanic cinema is the birth of the Antichrist. While medieval scholars were interested in the coming of the Antichrist, it was not stipulated that he be the physical son of Satan. In fact, Aquinas argued that Satan and his demonic minions did not occupy physical bodies, did not possess the vital heat necessary for reproduction, and therefore were unable to conceive children with human women.[14] In a perfect reflection of Aristotelian radical inversion, however, modern films such as *Rosemary's Baby* (1968), *To the Devil a Daughter* (1976), *Prince of Darkness* (1987), *Blessed: Samantha's Child* (2004), *The House of the Devil* (2009), and *The Last Exorcism I* and *II* (2010, 2013)—to name but a few—demand that the Antichrist be the only begotten biological son of Satan and an inconstant woman (or a black dog in the case of *The Omen*, 1976) in mimicry of Christ's conception. In the same vein, possession and exorcism films such as *The Exorcist* (1973) and its myriad prequels and sequels, as well as more recent entries such as *Exorcism* (2003), *The Exorcism of Emily Rose* (2005), *Exorcism: The Possession of Gail Bowers* (2006), *Blackwater Valley Exorcism* (2006), *Chronicles of an Exorcism* (2008), *Exorcismus: La Possession de Emma Evans* (2010), and *The Vatican Tapes* (2015) focus on the female body as a locus for demonic activity and habitation. The depiction of demons, the anatomy and physiology of demon possession, and the processes of exorcism in these films not only conform closely to medieval paradigms, but also reflect salient patriarchal fears about processes of reproduction and the potentiality of the female body to become a vessel for evil.[15]

Building on this theme, Chapter 3 examines the medieval clerical construction of the female body as irrational, wanton, blood-hungry, melancholic, and ultimately evil. According to medieval scholastics, the male body was the paradigm of divine perfection. Qualitatively warm and dry, it was associated with elemental fire and produced the vital heat necessary to balance the four humors—blood, yellow bile, black bile, and phlegm—with minimal superfluities. Fueled by this innate heat, the male heart was able to rarify humoral blood into the Galenic *pneuma* or rational spirits necessary for cognition. Warmed by ardent prayer, the male body was governed by a rational mind, illuminated by heavenly contemplation, and singularly obedient to the will of God. Like a gothic cathedral flooded with light, the categorically good male body stood as a testament to God's continued presence in the chaotic sublunary realm. The female body, on the other hand, was constructed as a radical inversion of divine male perfection. Qualitatively cold, a woman did not have the vital heat necessary to efficiently refine her blood into useful humors. Instead, leftover blood laden with toxins was collected in her uterus and discharged once a month through menstruation—a process that reflected Eve's sinful disobedience and marked her as impure. Her cold nature impeded her heart's ability to rarify humoral blood into rational *pneuma*, leaving her intellectually stunted. The female body, then, was not governed by the lofty spaces such as the brain and heart, but by her lower regions—her bowels and genitals.[16] Irrational and carnal, women were creatures born to chaotic darkness, microcosms of the world below the moon.

The irrational nature of women opened them to invisible spiritual influences, both divine and demonic. Two thirteenth-century Dominicans, Jacques de Vitry and Thomas Cantimpré, wrote the *vitae* of Christina Mirabilis and Lutgard of Aywières, holy women who were transformed through ardent prayer, obedience, and ecstatic union with Christ.[17] Their souls were so inflamed by God's love and their minds so consumed by the divine that their flesh became miraculous. Christina's body floated on air, drawn upward toward the ethereal realm, far from the corrupt and corrupting earth. Lutgard's body ceased menstruation, after which she produced healing fluids from her breasts and mouth. Through the male gaze of their authors, both women were *proven holy* because their bodies had ceased to be truly female.[18] Guided by a purified mind and soul obedient to the will of God, both had taken on resurrected flesh that was warm, dry, buoyant, and qualitatively male. In rare cases, a woman's irrationality opened her to the power of God; more often, it left her susceptible to sin through demonic manipulation or possession. Unlike the male body, which was muscular and tight, or the rarified flesh of the holy woman, which was purified through ecstatic union, the typical female body was loose and spongy—like a mushroom—and contained myriad hidden caverns.[19] These dark spaces, untouched by the presence of God, provided an ideal habitat for demonic entities who preferred to lodge in the fetid bowels. From there, they might rise up through bodily passages to press upon the brain, create phantasies, and incite wicked behavior. A locus for the demonic, the female body was also a source of infectious toxicity. It leaked menstrual fluid that contained corrupting humors with the power to rust metal, cause leprosy, and putrefy male members.[20] In older women, the cessation of menstruation meant that blood collected in her uterus where it decomposed, producing noxious humors that were exuded from her eyes as a poisonous *pneuma* and from her mouth and nose as toxic breath. Perhaps most frightening of all, the demon-prone, irrational and melancholic female body was *hungry*—hungry for warm wet blood and the moisture of sexual congress to balance its humors and to warm its cold and increasingly dry nature. In late-medieval and early modern witchcraft treatises, the female body born under the quills of clerics would be readily transformed into that of the power-hungry, heretical, Satanic witch.

Chapter 4 traces the persistent depiction of the witchy female body—be it young and sexy or old and haggard—as demonic, toxic, irrational, and insubordinate to male authority in modern horror films about witchcraft. Set against the backdrop of the Women's Liberation movement and second wave feminism, films such as *The Devil's Hand* (1962), *The Witchmaker* (1969), *The Brotherhood of Satan* (1971), and *The Witching* (1972) feature female witches in the service of evil patriarchs. *The City of the Dead* (1960), *The Witches* (1966), and *Cry of the Banshee* (1970) depict witchy women who rule others without the close supervision of male authority. The female witches in all of these films are engaged in irrational and ravenous quests for youth, beauty, power, or revenge. Ultimately, these "uppity" women are defeated by either a dominant male or one of his obedient females, each of whom represent a return to traditional and patriarchal control. Films that end with the woman witch triumphant, such as the wicked wives in *Daughters of Satan* (1972) and *Season of the Witch* (1972), argue that the autonomous and self-willed woman is a creature of evil and a danger to male authority and, by extension, the middle-class status quo. Similar anti-woman discourses serve as the foundation for the films *Superstition* (1982), *The Haunting of Morella* (1990), and *The Blair Witch Project* (1999), all of which feature long-dead witches whose earthbound spirits—much like feminism itself—continue to "infect" the living with their melancholic evil. In all of these films, witchy bodies and behaviors continue to operate according to a specific rationality born of Aristotelian inversion and medical theory in the service of a misogynist scholastic theology.

The first part of the book, Medieval Foundations, establishes the inverted structures of Satanic evil and the anatomy and physiology of the melancholic female body. The second part of the book, Modern Permutations, explores the construction of two other monsters, the vampire and the werewolf, both of which would ultimately occupy the same melancholic flesh and inverted ethos as their witchy ancestor, although they arrive there by far more convoluted paths. Chapter 5 links the depiction of the vampire—a modern, not a medieval monster—with medieval constructions of the melancholic Jew. In the early Middle Ages, the hermeneutic Jew played a didactic role in miracle tales as the foolish non-believer who comes to believe in Christ.[21] By the thirteenth century, however, Jews were imagined to be dangerous and potentially demonic outsiders who were responsible for the flagellation and crucifixion of Christ and who continued to pose a threat to His delicate flesh, now clothed in the transubstantiated host. Anti-Jewish authors argued that the Jews' bloodlust did not stop at the stabbing of the Eucharist, but extended to the murder of innocent Christian children.[22] Polemical sources claimed that boys such as Little Hugh of Lincoln and William of Norwich were seduced away from their families, brought to the local synagogue, crucified, and drained of blood. This blood was reportedly consumed by Jewish men both as a mockery of the Eucharist as well as a medicament meant to replace blood lost through male menstruation—a condition brought on because of the Jewish male's melancholic and fundamentally female nature.[23] Irrational and carnal, Jewish men were believed to crave sexual congress at all times; their cold natures, however, prevented them from performing. This frustration purportedly sent them into a rage that overheated their bodies and burned their already-black bile even further, thereby rendering them increasingly toxic.

In the eighteenth century, the first accounts of Hungarian vampires such as Arnold Paole reached Western Europe. Over time, the Eastern vampire was conflated with Western folklore about revenants, the inverted category of earthbound evil, and the character of the blood-sucking Jew—all of which by this point had become deeply embedded cultural constructs.[24] The blood-hungry Eastern vampire was readily associated with elemental earth, demonic agencies, hell, the colors red, pallid gray, and black, the night, autumn, the full moon, wolves, and poisonous creatures such as worms, spiders, and bats.

He was also cast into a monstrous body, dominated by toxic black bile, that forever trapped him in the chaotic cycles of decay, transformation, and regeneration that plagued the sublunary realm. Cold and fetid, his essentially female melancholic body craved warm human blood and passionate sexual congress—carnal desires that were further fueled by a soul willingly given over to demonic forces. Despite his sexual urges, the vampire could not achieve arousal or complete the sex act, and was so consigned to penetrating his female victims with his phallic fangs. Blood-hungry, rapacious, and violent, the modern vampire became an irrational demon-laden "other" with the subtle power to seduce the weak and wanton into his dark embrace and infect innocent Christians with his fetid gaze, breath, and blood. Modern depictions of the vampire remain rooted in medieval constructions of inverted evil and the character of the melancholy Jew, from the rat-like Orlok of in F.W. Murnau's *Nosferatu: Eine Symphonie des Grauens* (1922) and the love-sick Count Dracula of Werner Herzog's remake, *Nosferatu: Phantom der Nacht* (1979) to the gentleman vampires played by Bela Lugosi, Christopher Lee, and Gary Oldman. Like the witch, the abject alterity of the vampire has been used to both challenge and reinforce the patriarchy (*Vampyros Lesbos*, 1971; *Once Bitten*, 1985; *Vamp*, 1986), white hegemony (*Blacula*, 1972; *Queen of the Damned*, 2002) and heteronormativity (*Lost Boys*, 1987, *Interview with a Vampire*, 1994, *True Blood*, 2008-present) of the middle-class status quo.

Like the witch and the vampire, the werewolf has been cast into a melancholic body and has come to inhabit an inverted and Satanic ethos. Chapter 6 traces the development of the werewolf from the medieval world, where his transformation was impossible, to the modern horror film, which demands a pornographic account of his physical metamorphosis. On the transformation of the werewolf, medieval theologians including Aquinas upheld Augustine's assertion, in accordance with Aristotle, that the soul was rooted in the body and could not exist separate from it except by the hand of God. Because the divine principle resided in the soul, and the soul provided a formal cause for the body, and humans were shaped in the image of God, the transformation of a human being into an animal was not only impossible—it was a blasphemy. Like Augustine, theologians did not deny that people either saw werewolves or believed that they became werewolves; instead, they argued that werewolves were the result of demonic phantasy. In medieval literature from Marie d' France's romance *Bisclavret* to Gerald of Wales' *Topography of Ireland*, werewolves are depicted in accordance with these authoritative theological precepts. Medieval literary werewolves are not only pious and honorable, but also retain their fundamental human souls and bodies beneath a wolf-like cloak. They did not truly transform into wolves—even when they appeared to.[25]

The textual transformation of the werewolf from a demonic phantasy into the melancholic monster of modern horror films had its catalyst in witchcraft treatises, beginning with the *Malleus Maleficarum*. After repeatedly invoking the authority of Augustine and Aquinas and acquiescing to the impossibility of human to animal metamorphosis, Heinrich Kramer discusses in detail the power of witches to transform themselves and others into cats and wolves.[26] Almost all subsequent witchcraft treatises, whether written by skeptics or ardent believers, contained sections on lycanthropy; the inclusion of werewolves in this tradition ultimately cast them into the category of inverted and Satanic evil.[27] In his 1580 treatise *Demonmania of Witches*, Jean Bodin argued that the werewolf was a Satanic creature, a human being who had given him or herself over to absolute evil and was physically transformed into a murderous wolf. As evidence he cited the 1573 case of Gilles Garnier, a man who confessed to becoming a werewolf and gleefully devouring children in the local vineyard, as well as a case from 1512 in which two men made a sworn pact with the Devil and routinely sacrificed to him so that they might be transformed into powerful wolves.[28] After lighting a blue- or green-flamed candle or applying an ointment similar to that used by witches before their night flight, the two would sprout fur and fangs, run into the forest, and frenetically copulate with female wolves. They would then seek to satiate another hunger by attacking and eating small children or by poisoning good Christian adults with maleficent powder received at the Witches' Sabbath. In Bodin's imagination, werewolves had made the conscious decision to reject Christ and "worship Satan." As non–Christians, werewolves were cast into the category of inverted evil and became melancholic monsters possessed by an irrational demonic lust for blood and sex.

In modern horror films, the melancholic werewolf, dark and shaggy, continues to be associated with the full moon, autumn, and the chaotic wilderness, as well as a thirst for blood, sexual rapacity, and infectious toxicity—all of which link him or her with Satanic inversion. In films such as *The Curse of the Werewolf* (1961) and *Silver Bullet* (1985), the performance of Christian rituals and the use of holy objects, including silver bullets made from crucifixes and saints' medals, prove as effective against the werewolf as other Satanic entities. As with the witch and the vampire, the modern cinematic werewolf continues to be a creature of evil alterity, serving as a palette upon which Western culture might paint its own warped image. Films featuring male werewolves, such as *The Curse of the Werewolf* (1961), *The Wolf Man* (1941), and *Wolf* (1994), call into question the construct of rational masculinity, while the transgressive female werewolves of *The Howling* (1980), *Company of Wolves* (1984), and *Ginger Snaps* (2000) allow for feminist and queer discourses on gender and othering set against the hegemony of patriarchy. Also questioning the middle-class status quo are films such as *Bad Moon* (1996) and *Dog Soldiers* (2002), both of which locate the source of monstrosity at the very heart of the nuclear family.

Despite the salient themes of inversion, transgression, and alterity, the modern werewolf film breaks from the textual witchcraft tradition in its treatment of human-to-animal metamorphosis; horror audiences demand that a man or woman must be physically transformed into a wolf in order for the werewolf to be real. Accordingly, the transformation of the werewolf is filmed in graphic detail, the sprouting hair and lengthening fangs serving as physical proof for the monster's existence. The fluidity of the werewolf's flesh brings into question Western perceptions of human embodiment. In films such as *Werewolf of London* (1935), *The Wolf Man*, *The Howling*, and *Ginger Snaps*, lycanthropy is infectious, a physical condition contracted through the bite of another werewolf. At the same time, lycanthropy is also linked with an instability of mind rooted in Freudian sexual repression and catalyzed by psychological trauma such as the turbulence of a bad marriage or the horrors of puberty. As a true shape-shifter, the modern werewolf blurs the post-Cartesian boundaries between *psyche* and *soma*, leading us to question whether we are merely ghosts trapped in chaotic flesh beyond our control, or fully ensouled beings bound to nature in tooth and claw.

The witch, the vampire, and the werewolf share a single melancholic body—blood-hungry, rapacious, demon-laden, cold, toxic, and transgressive, that was born under the quills of scholastic theologians. In their attempted reconciliation of Aristotelian natural philosophy and learned medicine with received theology, they codified the category of divine goodness and its inversion, Satanic and melancholic evil. From their premises, those who did not conform to the lofty and largely unattainable ideals of Christian perfection were cast into the only "other" category available—evil alterity. The consequences of this specific rationality as it moved from theory to practice would be terrifying, including the burning of women imagined to be maleficent witches and the persecution of Jews as bloodthirsty monsters. Deeply embedded in Western culture, medieval constructs of inverted evil continue to be used as weapons against those deemed to be dangerous "others," as is evident in Antisemitic propaganda that depicts Jews as vampiric and rapacious, anti-woman discourses that depict women as irrational and power-hungry bitches, and the rhetoric of the Satanic Panic, which depicted all those who did not conform to the middle-class Christian status quo as Satan worshippers.

Like the discourses from which they were born, the old monsters, too, remain with us. Haunting the big screen and the small, the witch, the vampire and the werewolf serve as warped reflections in which we might witness with horror our own feelings of rejection, as well as our own irrational desires, wicked rapacity and bloodlust. They likewise present us with an abject image of our own fleshy dissolution—the return to the melancholic earth that awaits us all—as well as the power of love to persist through the chaos of life and the darkness of death.

Part I
Medieval Foundations

1

Upside-Down and Inside-Out

The Medieval Construction of Earthbound Evil

Diabolus et daemones toto vagantur in orbe.—Saint Jerome[1]

The witch, the vampire, and the werewolf, while each having their own unique folkloric history, share a single theologically constructed monster body—cold, dry and dark. Earthbound and melancholy, these creatures crave warm blood; they stalk their sanguineous prey under the cover of darkness. Primarily nocturnal beings, their powers reach their zenith at midnight under the frigid full moon. Inversions of goodness, they are repelled by the sacraments of the Church and burned into dust by the light of God. To the modern mind, these predictable characteristics and behaviors of old monsters are irrational nonsense, the stuff of horror films and creature features.

And yet the inverted monster body, its anatomy and physiology, as well as the upside-down nocturnal world that it inhabits, are not mere flights of fancy. They are rooted in the specific rationality of the medieval university, where moral and speculative theologians used the works of Aristotle to create an all-encompassing rational system for categorizing visible and invisible worlds.[2] In applying Aristotle's theories of contrariety, hierarchical cosmology, and physics—all of which centered on inverted binaries—to both physical and metaphysical realms, scholastic theologians codified abstractions such as good and evil into rigid and authoritative categories. Divine goodness was marked by light, warmth, weightlessness, and singularity and associated with the heavenly realm beyond the moon. In keeping with Aristotelian contrariety, Satanic evil was marked by darkness, coldness, heaviness, and chaotic multiplicity in the hellish world below the moon. It was this binary codification, validated by both theology and Aristotelian natural philosophy, that would provide the foundation for the worlds of the witch, vampire, and werewolf.

Medieval Aristotle: Contrariety and the Cosmos

The works of Aristotle constituted the curricular core of the medieval university and dominated academic discourse since their initial recovery in the twelfth century.[3] The *trivium* (rhetoric, logic, and grammar) was grounded in Aristotle's *Logic, On Interpretation, Analytics,* and *Categories,* while the *quadrivium* (geometry, mathematics, music, and astrology) was dominated by Aristotle's works on natural philosophy, including his *Physics, Metaphysics, On the Heavens, Meteorology, On Generation and Corruption,* and the *Parva Naturalia*.[4] Students passed through both the *trivium* and *quadrivium* as part of the master of arts program, the prerequisite for advanced study in the graduate programs of law, medicine and theology. By the thirteenth century, students and faculty across the curriculum and across the professions shared a discursive language and a formal understanding of the natural world based on the authority of Aristotle. At the University of Paris, the Dominican scholar Albertus Magnus (d. 1280) translated and commented upon much of the Aristotelian corpus, interpreting Aristotle's natural philosophy through a theological lens. His student and later Doctor of the Church, Thomas Aquinas (d. 1274), took Albert's project a step further, systematically and logically reconciling the works of Aristotle with the *Sentences* of Peter Lombard, Patristic sources, and Biblical authority.[5] The results included the *Summa Theologica, Scripta Super Sententiis,* and *Summa Contra Gentiles,* texts that served as the foundation for theological study and Church doctrine throughout the Middle Ages. In reconciling pagan philosophy with Christian theology, scholastic authors sought to maintain the validity of Aristotelian philosophy without questioning theological authority or falling into heretical error. While scholastic authors readily accepted Aristotle as a handmaiden to theology, other scholars remained committed to the Patristic-based Platonic and Neo-Platonic philosophies of the earlier Middle Ages; these traditionalists saw the scholastic obsession with Aristotle and the conflation of pagan ideals with Christian faith as a threat to theological integrity and a sullying of tradition.[6] In 1277, stalwarts who stood against the "New Learning" at the University of Paris attempted to expunge much of Aristotle from the curriculum there by submitting their *Condemnations* to school authorities.[7] They were, however, a century too late. Aristotle's methods of argumentation and works on natural philosophy had already become the very foundation of the medieval academic enterprise. Likewise, Aristotelian structures—in particular his theory of contrariety, his cosmology, and his system of natural laws—had proven themselves to be effective tools in the theological definition and proof of pure good and corrupt evil, as well as powerful weapons against heretics and other purportedly demonic agents who sought to question the authority of the institutionalized church.

Aristotle's theory of contrariety, discussed at length in his *Categories, Metaphysics,* and *On Interpretation,* provides the central structure of his philosophical system from logical argumentation to cosmic hierarchies and the behavior of the material world.[8] According to Aristotle, for each metaphysical thing that existed, its contrary must also exist; in Aristotelian symbolic logic, this might be expressed as A:~A, which produces a binary of ultimate "A-ness" and ultimate "not A-ness." Aristotle argued that between these two poles there existed a hierarchical gradient, with qualities descending from one extreme and ascending to the other. Aristotle argued that movement between these two poles was not only permissible, but necessary, because this "moving between the contrary poles represented by the possession or privation of some form or forms" was the "basis of generation and corruption in the world."[9] Contrariety was the very subtext of all of nature, for all "that comes to be by a natural process is either a contrary or the product of contraries."[10]

Aristotelian contrariety resonated with scholastic theologians who had mastered an early Christian and Patristic corpus "preoccupied with dualistic themes in its theology, moral philosophy, and historiography."[11] Rooted in Platonic dialectics, sources such as Justin Martyr's *Dialogue with Trypho,* Saint John Cassian's *Conferences,* and Saint Augustine's *City of God* used the comparison of opposites as a method of illuminating truth. The dialectic approach remained a powerful discursive tool throughout the Middle Ages, appearing in scholarly works such as Anselm of Canterbury's eleventh-century *On the Freedom of Choice* and Peter Abelard's twelfth-century *Sic et Non,* as well as hagiographical texts and sermons meant for a less-learned audience. In all of these sources, the didactic approach was almost always the same; through the juxtaposition of opposites, authors and preachers alike demonstrated the absolute goodness and light of Christian belief by casting it against ignorant and heretical darkness. The martyr and the saint shined all the brighter surrounded by pagan unbelievers, their sanctity illuminated by the foul darkness of earthly sin. In the thirteenth century, scholastic theologians following Aquinas applied Aristotelian contrariety to Christian dialectical thought and in the process reduced "all logical opposites to contraries."[12] While Aristotle allowed for the existence of intermediate or neutral categories (*species contraria mediata*) between contrary extremes, "this was not the case for theologians, who maintained contrariety of maximum difference, *species contraria immediata*."[13] Through this process, light and dark, truth and error, orthodoxy and heresy were no longer opposites, but had become absolute inversions of one another.

In addition to a philosophical system dominated by an extreme version of Aristotelian contrariety, medieval scholars inherited an ancient cosmology shaped by Aristotelian paradigms, a closed system in which his laws of physics and metaphysics might function. According to Aristotle, the cosmos was both spherical and bounded.[14] Just beyond its very edge sat the Prime Mover, the eternal, unchanging, intelligent force that set the cosmos into motion through Love.[15] Through the application of friction, the Prime Mover caused the outermost sphere of the cosmos, that of the fixed stars, to move in perfect and unending circular motion. The spinning of the sidereal sphere in turn caused the movement of the planetary spheres nested like matryoshka dolls beneath it, all the way down to the moon which served as a boundary. The realm above the moon was one of perfection and harmony, where intelligences connected to the Prime Mover guided the planets as they glided in unchanging circles of crystalline ether.[16] Below the moon lay a world of chaos and change, a place of shifting elements and violent motion, the very inversion of the perfect world above the moon.[17] Following Empedocles and Plato, Aristotle held that the world below the moon was composed of four theoretical elements, fire, air, water and earth, each of which had its own set of binary qualities and natural place of rest.[18] Directly below the moon burned the ring of elemental fire, which was hot and dry and therefore closest to perfection; below this sat elemental air, which was hot and moist in nature.[19] Because fire and air were both hot, they ascended towards the celestial spheres. They were therefore more pure than the two remaining elements, cold and wet water which was bound to the cold and dry earth, the dead center of the cosmos, the place where Aristotle argued that the heaviest, most corrupt substances of all resided.[20] Following Aristotelian contrarieties and hierarchies, the Prime Mover served as one pole, a point of unchanging, immaterial, eternal perfection, while the earth served as an inverted second pole, a place of ever-changing, material, mortal corruption. The superlunary realm, closest to the Prime Mover, was a place of circular motion and ethereal stability; the inverted sublunary realm, on the other hand, was closest to the earth and dominated by violent linear motion, elemental chaos, and ceaseless material change.[21]

Through reconciling and conflating Aristotelian concepts such as contrariety and categories, as well as his cosmic structure and elemental theories, with theological concepts of divine purity and carnal corruption, theologians created an all-encompassing system that rigidly defined the categorical qualities and fundamental nature of heavenly good and earthly evil. The definition of these two rigid binaries was the first step in creating the inverted, Satanic body—the earthbound flesh of the Old Monster.

Ethereal Good Above

In the thirteenth and fourteenth centuries, scholastic theologians synthesized theological tenets with Aristotelian principles to structure a hierarchical model for holy beings drawn towards God, heaven, and light at one extreme and, simultaneously, a contrary and inverted hierarchy of unholy beings drawn towards Satan, hell, and darkness at the other.[22] The canonical hierarchy of pure and divine goodness ascended toward the *summam bonum*, God, the Christian interpretation of the ultimate Aristotelian universal principle or Prime Mover, a being described by Aquinas as immaterial, immutable, and eternal, the creator of the cosmos and the source of all ordering above the moon and natural law below it.[23] Medieval scholars looked at the Aristotelian model of the cosmos and argued that God must be enthroned in the heavenly extra-cosmic realm, or Empyrean, "which contained within itself the purest light."[24] The Empyrean, like God himself, was immobile and invisible, "resplendent and free of all admixture," completely translucent and composed only of the light of God's love; just as the earth received its light "solely from the sun, the Empyrean should receive its light directly from God."[25] There, in the "heaven of heavens," God reigned with His son Jesus, who was "one in being with the Father" and the enigmatic Holy Spirit. Fully human and fully divine, "begotten not made," Jesus had been sent to the chaotic world below the moon to re-establish his Father's heavenly kingdom, promising those who followed him spiritual redemption, physical resurrection, and a reordered creation at the end of time. After his crucifixion, Jesus was transfigured in preparation for his resurrection and ascension into the "immortal and incorruptible" Empyrean; no longer of this earth, "his face shone as the sun, his garments became white as light" (Matthew 17:2).[26] For Aquinas, the process of transfiguration was the assumption of clarity, translucence and light, the very qualities of the Empyrean itself: "In Christ's transfiguration, clarity overflowed from his Godhead and his soul into his body ... as when the air is lit up by the sun."[27] In his transfigured state, it was "fitting

1. The Medieval Construction of Earthbound Evil

that He should ascend into heaven," because "our dwelling-place is one of generation and corruption" and "the heavenly place is one of incorruption."[28]

The Empyrean, translucent and radiant with ethereal light, was not only "the exterior dwelling-place and kingdom of God," but also of his most blessed creations. Just below the Trinity sat the Virgin Mary, the Mother of Christ, "the august empress of heaven."[29] While theologians such as Aquinas and Bonaventure denied the bodily assumption of Mary into heaven, popular tradition and official iconography placed her there, seated at the right hand of her son, robed in celestial blue and clothed in stars of radiant light. Untouched by earthly corruption, her ever-virginal purity conferred upon her the suave odor of sanctity; she was described as the "lily of the field" and the "rose of Sharon," fragrant with frankincense and myrrh.[30] In the thirteenth and fourteenth centuries, Mary served as a compassionate and maternal figure who might intercede with God on behalf of those who were humbly devoted to her and sought the protection of her heavenly cloak.[31] For many, the most propitious way to Jesus was though his mother, whose implorations he could not, out of love and devotion, ignore. Beneath this holiest of women sat the ranks of the blessed, including the apostles as well as the martyrs and saints—holy men and women who willingly sacrificed their corrupt carnal flesh for heavenly bodies that, according to Aquinas, "shine seven times brighter than the sun."[32] From their theophanic halls of gold, the blessed gazed down upon the earth to observe the sublunary realm of sin and sorrow and await the prayers of the faithful in need of intercession. Like Mary, they brought human requests for miraculous intervention to Jesus and, through their supplication and his divine beneficence, miracles were granted. While it appeared to human witnesses that the Virgin Mary, saints, and their relics performed miracles, theologians argued that they were mere conduits for God's power. Only God might grant miracles, since He alone created the natural laws of the cosmos, and therefore was the only being who might supersede them.

From the throne of God in the Empyrean down to the lunar boundary, the superlunary realm was replete with angelic beings, God's purest of creations. Aquinas combined Pseudo-Dionysus the Aereopagite's fifth-century treatise on angels, *De Coelesti Hierarchia*, with Aristotelian structures in order to develop a "thorough, systematic, comprehensive" angelology that "addressed all of the major natural and metaphysical issues concerning angels."[33] The spherical heavens, Aquinas argued, were a *plenum* of angelic beings, all of whom were incorporeal, immaterial, immortal, a reflection of God's own perfection and plentitude. Aquinas described a heavenly hierarchy of angels which was divided into three major spheres.[34] The first sphere was composed of the *Seraphim*, six-winged angels of pure light who surrounded the Throne of God; so bright was their purity that even other angels could not look upon them. Directly below the Seraphim sat the *Cherubim*, angelic beings each having the face of an ox, lion, eagle, and a man, whose primary function was to guard the way to God's throne; the Cherubim were accompanied by the *Ophanim*, strange wheel-shaped beings terrible to look upon. The second angelic sphere was composed of the *Dominions*, winged angels with scepters, *Virtues*, beings connected with celestial bodies and charged with ensuring the harmony of the cosmos, and angelic warriors called *Powers*. The third sphere contained the Rulers, angels with crowns and scepters, Archangels, God's warriors and messengers to earth, as well as generic Angels who were involved with the daily prayers of human beings. Following Aristotle, Aquinas argued that "the more fully anything corporeal shares in the Divine goodness, the higher its place in the corporeal order, which is order of place"; the same could be said for angels, who descended in power and purity from the Seraphim closest to God down to the cosmic lunar boundary.[35] While angels held "powers surpassing those of all living creatures on earth," these powers were of necessity limited. As the purest of God's creations, angels had no desire or will of their own, but instead followed Him in perfect obedience.[36] At His command, they assumed bodily form and descended below the moon to deliver divine messages and serve as the conduits through which His miracles might manifest.

The ethereal realm of canonical good extended below the lunar boundary not only through the birth of Christ, the intercession of the Virgin Mary and the heavenly saints, and visitation of angels, but also through the hierarchy of the church, the function of which was to draw the faithful into the light and up towards the eternal *City of God*. In a fragmented and chaotic material world, the church was necessarily an imperfect microcosmic reflection of the perfect hierarchy above the moon. Following Aquinas, however, the church was the earthly institution most closely aligned with the Divine; therefore its very structure, including its leaders and rituals, were points of light and true paths to the ethereal realm of clarity and pure good. Like the Kingdom of Heaven, the earthly church was meant to be singular in its leadership under the pope, with the cardinals, archbishops, and bishops acting as a saintly council; beneath the clerical hierarchy, the faithful, like the saints and angels in heaven, were meant to be obedient, unified in God's will through the church. Not only church hierarchies but also church rituals served as conduits for the divine flow of power into the dark and broken earthly realm. Baptism, conferred only once, illuminated an infant's soul and marked it as a child of God and member of the Christian community.[37] Communion, the consumption of bread and wine blessed by the white-clad mass priest and transformed into the true flesh and blood of Christ according to Canon One of the Fourth Lateran Council (1215), illuminated the souls of the faithful from within and offered them a visceral experience of Christ's sacrifice and love. Yearly confession of sins was meant to purge the soul of impurities, clarifying it, so that the light of God might radiate freely. By the thirteenth century, this effusion of ethereal light was made manifest in the architecture of gothic cathedrals such as those at Cologne, Salisbury Chartres, and Notre Dame in Paris, the heights of which seemed to reach up into the divine Empyrean itself. In the dark and opaque sublunary realm, the translucent and light-filled church in all of its manifestations was in theory to function like a glass elevator, fueled by pure love, which "draws the soul toward God," thereby removing it from "more proximate objectives" that might "lead it askew."[38]

Having structured and codified the theoretical category of canonical good using Aristotelian cosmology, linking the Christian God with the single and eternal Unmoved Mover beyond the sidereal sphere and ascribing all things holy with the characteristics of the unchanging and crystal clear-fifth element, theologians turned their attention to the "more proximate objectives" that assailed the church and its faithful in the later Middle Ages. With the "luminous at one end," theologians used contrariety to construct the "opaque at the other," the dark world of Satanic evil.[39] A full inversion of the category of canonical goodness—and just as theoretical and impossible—canonical evil was marked by darkness, blackness, opaqueness, and chaotic multiplicity. Evil beings, unlike their weightless and translucent counterparts, might never ascend beyond the lunar boundary, but instead were doomed to a miserable and sinful existence upon the cursed cold, dry earth.

Earthbound Evil Below

At the center of Aristotle's cosmos sat the terrestrial world, the very core of which was composed of the densest and most corrupt elemental earth. For scholars such as Albertus Magnus, earth was not only "cold and dry" but also "the heaviest among all the elements, not having only a relative heaviness, but heaviness in an absolute sense" because on the scale of creation it was the "lowest in place."[40] The earth, the very dreck of the cosmos, was at the lowest end of the hierarchical gradient not only physically, but also morally; cold and dark, it was the point most distant from the Divine Empyrean and light of God's love. Scholastic theologians argued that God had not intentionally created the earth as a sinkhole of sin, but instead had created a perfect cosmos, with each element comfortable in its natural place of rest and the earth a lush Garden for His innocent creatures. This cosmic balance, however, was shattered by the willful disobedience of Lucifer, who along with his fellow rebel angels fell from the grace of God, rained down through the elemental layers, and set the elements into frenetic motion. This conflation of Aristotelian cosmology and elemental theory with Biblical storytelling is illustrated in a manuscript housed at the British Library, which depicts disobedient angelic beings being cast out of the radiant gold of heaven.[41] (Figure 1.) As the rebels fell from the golden light of the Empyrean, their bodies became dark and misshapen until they crashed to the earth and ultimately to its center where they joined Satan, the first Fallen Angel, flat on his back with his face in the mud in the dark City of Hell.[42] The position of Satan's face, turned away from God and rooted in the earth, is indicative of Lucifer's sin, his egotistical rejection of God's will and pursuit of his own desires. This turning away from the light, according to Saint Anselm, introduced evil into the world and corrupted the earth.[43] From his initial descent into the sublunary realm, Satan's primary goal has been the same: "the destruction of God's harmonious cosmos" through the chaos of human sin and sorrow.[44]

Following the medieval dictum *similia similibus*—that like engenders or is attracted to like—the Devil's body and the corrupt earth to which it was bound were believed to share similar characteristics. Like the earth's core, Satan's body was held to be cold and black, two qualities that were often linked together in medieval color theory, where "black is usually associated with coldness, and white with heat."[45] Blackness, like coldness, was associated with the end-state of decay and the absence of all warmth and light. When light was removed from plants, it was argued, they would turn brown and wither; when light and warmth were removed from humans, however, they first became *pallidus*, or a pasty gray-white, then began to blacken and die.[46] The Devil's cold, black body, then, was merely the physical manifestation of his complete rejection of divine light and his willful desire to dwell in the darkness away from God's love. A shape shifter, the Devil might appear as a voluptuous young woman or a handsome man in dark clothes with a pallid face.[47] By the end of the thirteenth century, Satan more often appeared in his monstrous true form as an inversion of nature with a toothsome mouth, leathery wings, "horns on knees, claves, or ankles, and with faces on chest, belly, and buttocks."[48] In whatever shape he took, Satan's flesh was so black and cold that wicked women who were accused of engaging in sexual congress with him "generally complained of the icy coldness of the devil's sperm and of the painful and bloody lesions caused in their flesh by the subsequent withdrawal of the huge, scaly phallus."[49]

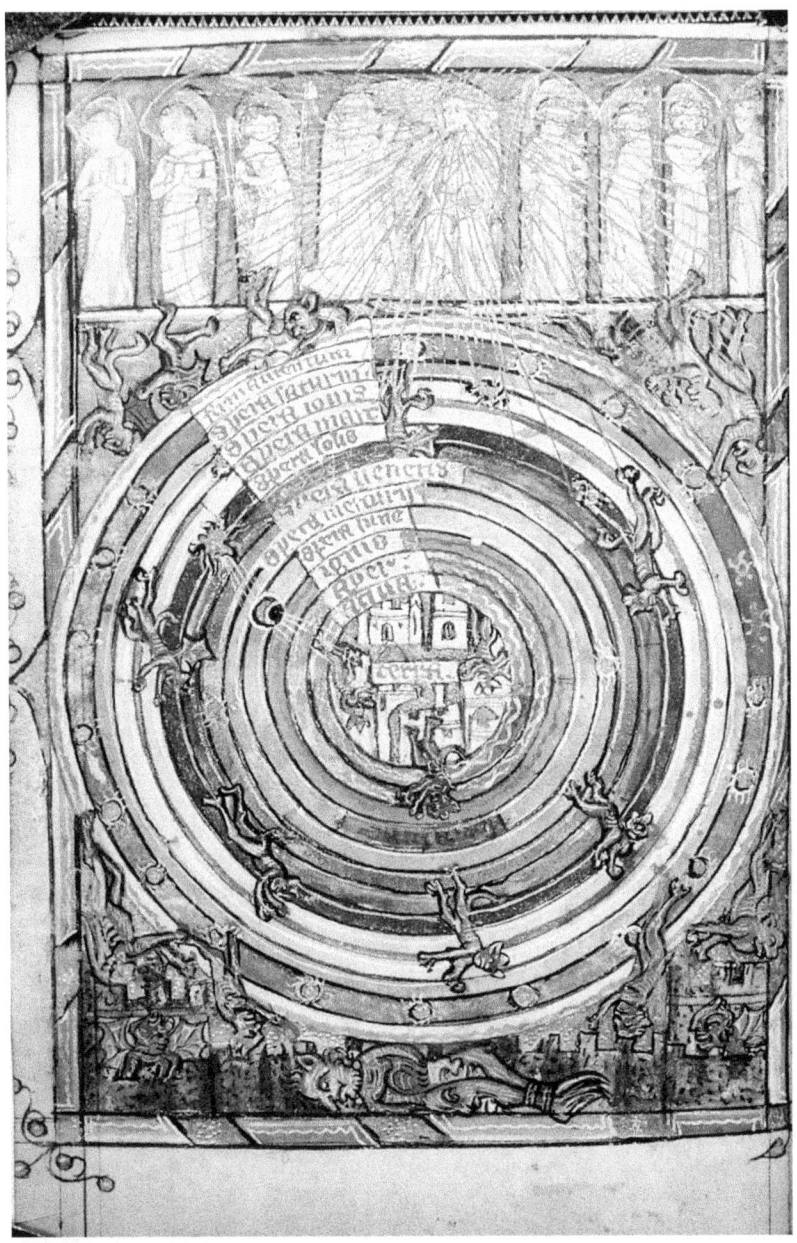

Folio 1v from the Neville of Hornby Book of Hours (London, British Library, Egerton 2781, c. 1340). Rebellious angels are cast from the top register to the bottom of the page, reflecting their fall to the corrupt earth. At the very bottom is Satan, his face turned away from the will of God and buried in the melancholic ground. According to William of Auvergne, Satan's abode in the hellish earth was "the ultimate separation from light and likewise the ultimate of density and grossness." *De Universo Creaturum*.

Satan's body was associated not only with earth's coldness and darkness but also its lowness at the very bottom of the great chain of creation. Unlike the divine, which was linked to the highest heavens and the abstract faculties of pure thought and love that resided in the mind and the heart, earthly evil was linked to the basest of human functions—evacuation and ejaculation—and the lowest parts of the body, the bowels, anus, and genitals. The inverted nature of evil was made manifest in the depiction of Satan's body as having a pelvis and anus composed of voracious mouths. In a motif common to the later Middle Ages, Satan squats down to defecate writhing sinners through his anus while simultaneously ingesting them through his mouth above.[50] In this upside-down schema, Satan's anus likewise becomes a mouth to be kissed by his worshippers, while his mouth is an anus that defecates lies, curses, and the foul stench of flatulence, sulfur, and dead fish.[51] The smell of sulfur, long associated with the Devil and Hell, is linked to the lower body through the Biblical tale of Sodom and Gomorrah, towns that perished in a divine rain of sulfur sent as punishment for "unnatural" sex acts associated with the anus.[52] The odor of fish, too, is linked with the baser functions of the body, this time specifically with female genitalia and the act of sexual congress, both of which have a strong ichthyic smell.[53]

Tied to the functions of digestion and coition, Satan was at times depicted in the form of a goat, the baser appetites of which were legendarily insatiable. Imagined to be a truly horny devil, Satan purportedly sought out sexual contact with as many humans as possible and in as many disguises as necessary. According to Aquinas, Satan's sex drive was linked not to his own sexual pleasure—his lack of a fleshy corporeal body precluded such an experience—but to his delight in tempting weak and fallible humans away from God and trapping them in the shadowy world below the moon.[54] The Devil's knowledge of carnal human desires allowed him to tempt each according to his or her own weaknesses; for most, the sin of lust was most effective.[55] "The devil tempts us with suggestion," Gregory the Great wrote in his *Moralia in Job*, but "we sin by pleasure of the flesh and consent to give ourselves over to it."[56] But how could Satan tempt lustful humans if he had no proper body of his own? According to Albertus Magnus, "The Devil can produce many kinds of forms and set them before the eyes or other senses, and the senses are forced to observe such things."[57] Following his teacher, Aquinas argued that Satan might take myriad forms shaped by the human imagination which was, by its fallen nature, obsessed with the functions of the lower regions of the body.

In his chaotic and destructive work, the cold-bodied Devil was assisted by lesser fallen angels who were in allegiance with him. Satan had diverged from God's singular and unified will in abject disobedience, and "on that account, the Devil was condemned into this darkness, that is into this air, as though into a prison. He fell from the splendor of the angels with his angels." Having crashed through the fiery ring and fallen to earth with their leader, the demons were imprisoned in the world below the moon, locked into a terrestrial realm through which they roamed freely.[58] The bodies of demons, like that of Satan, were tied to the Aristotelian qualities of the cold and corrupt earth.[59] Augustine argued that in their fall, demons assumed bodies of frigid and coagulated air, in part so that they might suffer the torments of fire. The ancient and medieval worlds shared a belief that the atmosphere was swirling with unclean spirits that guided storms, caused hail and plague, and penetrated human bodies.[60] Unwilling to fully reject either this tradition or Augustine's authority, Aquinas argued that demons did not have physical bodies of their own, but instead could assume airy bodies or cold slimy bodies at will in order to tempt and pervert their human prey.[61] Theologians argued that demons, by using their airy bodies and innate intelligence to manipulate the four elements within the bounds of natural law and to cause phantasies in the weak human mind, could manifest in a multitude of forms.[62]

In the manuscript tradition, demons are routinely depicted as inverted angels with black skin, leathery wings, twisted faces, and sharpened fangs and claws. Demonic bodies, however, were not always so outwardly monstrous. In the eleventh century, for example, Raoul Glaber described a pallid humanoid demon that shook his bed violently in the night as having "a slender neck, a thin face, dark eyes, a furrowed brow, a flat nose, a pointed chin, a goat's beard, hair coming out of his ears, thick hair, a stooped back, and dressed in rags."[63] Caesarius of Heisterbach's twelfth-century *Dialogus Miraculorum* included demons that appeared as black hairy worms, sulfurous shadowy beings, as well as a fiendish "gigantic black man."[64] In the late fourteenth century, demons appeared to Ermine of Rheims as monsters, "just like they are in hell," an icy phantom wind that "blows out the candles," "toads the size of dogs," an "incommensurable swarm of flies," snakes, lizards, crows, bats, and owls.[65] All of these manifestations share affinities such as blackness, coldness, and a closeness to the heaviest elements, water and earth; they are all, likewise, creatures of the night.

As inverted angels, demons were not only creatures of the darkness but also masters of the nether parts of the body, the bowels and the genitals.[66] As Martha Bayless argues in her recent book *Sin and Filth in Medieval Culture: The Devil in the Latrine*, demons—like their master—were associated with excrement and the stench of shit. In the early twelfth century, Guibert of Nogent wrote of demons "creeping among the sleeping associates of a bishop and finally retiring into the latrine."⁶⁷ Demons wreaked not only of the bowels of men and their foul bodily soil, their "shameful superfluities," but also of the bowels of the earth, fetid and sulfurous.⁶⁸ In possessing a human host, demons targeted the lower viscera, "the most debased and unclean centers, the coolest and moistest portion of the human anatomy" which provided countless foul internal caverns in which they might lodge.⁶⁹ They likewise targeted the genitals as they tempted weak-willed individuals into unbridled, irrational lust in the darkness of the night. Like Satan, demons were incorporeal and could not experience bodily delight; their pleasure, like their master's, was predicated on their ability to turn the faithful away from God's light and to trap them beneath the moon for eternity. Aquinas argued that since the bodies of demons were made of coagulated air, they could not impregnate the women with whom they copulated; instead, they merely gathered "the seed of men taken for the purpose; as when the demon assumes first the form of a woman, and afterwards of a man."⁷⁰ The children that resulted from demonic congress, then, were fully human in nature—albeit quite difficult to explain.

Icy creatures that rode the winds and assailed the bodies and minds of their human prey, demons in their multiplicity were formidable but not all-powerful.⁷¹ Demons might manipulate earthly elements and cause phantasies in human minds, but they could not perform truly miraculous works. According to Aquinas, "in the strict sense a miracle is something done outside the order of the entire created nature, under which order every power of a creature is contained."⁷² Like all of God's creatures above and below the moon, demons were bound by natural law, which only God might supersede. And while they could affect the human mind and body directly, they could not corrupt the human soul except through human consent and will to sin. In the fifth century, Augustine dismissed demons as nothing more than God's buffoons, loathsome creatures that had been subdued by the power of Christ; furthermore, because of their fallen state, they suffered from a reduced intellect and were therefore even less fearsome. By Aquinas in the thirteenth century, however, demons had gained greater agency against their human prey. In his discussion of the demonic intellect, Aquinas argued that both Satan and his minions had retained their God-given acuity and that, while they did not have perfect knowledge because of their disobedience of God, their intelligence had in fact increased over time.⁷³ Roaming the earth for millennia, the Devil and his demons had acquired a vast repository of knowledge, not only of natural philosophy and the elemental workings of the world below the moon, but also of human nature. As such, they were both cunning and powerful, even if they *were* restricted to natural law.

Against demonic attack, the faithful had recourse to an arsenal of spiritual weaponry. In patristic and hagiographic sources from late antiquity through the later Middle Ages, demons might be set to flight by invoking the name of Christ, reciting the Lord's prayer, or making the sign of the cross, as well as by the presence of saints' relics, holy water, or the body of Christ in the Eucharist. In the thirteenth and fourteenth centuries, theologians and preachers warned of the threats posed by increasingly powerful demonic beings and recommended strict obedience to the dictums and rituals of the church in all things as a form of protection. Where once demons randomly swirled through the crisp night air, lurked in long shadows, and loitered in the darkness of wintry night in order to tempt the unwary, church authorities argued that there now existed terrifying signs that Satan and his demons had become well-organized and were—along with their human followers—planning a physical and spiritual assault against the church and the very Mystical Body of Christ.

Hell Bubbles Up: Satan's Mystical Body

In the thirteenth century, scholastic theologians built on the work of Albertus Magnus and Aquinas, reconciling the works of Aristotle with theological authorities such as scripture, patristic sources such as Augustine, and medieval sources from Anselm to Peter Lombard. Through this process, they created an authoritative and rigid system of binaries for good and evil rooted in an extreme expression of Aristotelian contrariety. Absolute good, they argued, was characterized by unity, flowing downward from the single will of the Godhead. In the superlunary realm, the Virgin Mary, saints, and spheres of angels, bathed in light, submitted to God's will in perfect obedience. In the corrupt, earthly realm below the moon, the Church was meant to be a microcosmic reflection of unified and obedient heavenly perfection, with the pope channeling the will of God, the bishops and archbishops acting as beatific counselors, and the faithful submitting to all of those above them. Through this structure, divine and orderly light might shine down into the dark and chaotic terrestrial world. If absolute good was characterized by singularity, then the hallmark of absolute evil was its multiplicity. Satan and his demons had turned away from the light, each to follow their own disobedient desires, thereby creating chaos all around them. Swirling in the disordered darkness, the legions of the Devil lingered at the edges of the church, working to turn the weak away from God by tempting them into base sin. As theologians defined singular absolute canonical good in increasingly concise terms throughout the thirteenth and fourteenth centuries, they discerned more and more evidence of demonic disorder, at first along the peripheries and later within the hierarchy of the church itself. From the multitudes of so-deemed heretical sects that threatened the unity of the faithful to the Great Schism (1378–1417) in which two and then three men claimed to be pope, evil and chaotic multiplicity had invaded the church, and earthly corruption had contaminated its otherwise luminous body.[74]

As an agent of evil, the idea of heresy had plagued the church since its inception in antiquity. In an attempt to consolidate his own political power as Roman Emperor, Constantine the Great called the Council of Nicaea in 325 CE, a meeting of bishops whose primary goal was to define true Christianity against wrong belief. The bishops at Nicaea debated issues such as the true nature of Christ's body and, deciding against Arius and his theory of adoptionism, asserted that Christ was at once fully human and fully divine, begotten not made, *homousious* with the Godhead.[75] As church leaders and theologians continued to define right belief in ever-tighter circles, heresy—both in its particular forms and as a general category—came to constitute the primary threat to Christendom. Early authors such as Pope Gregory the Great used the image of the pestilent serpent as an allegory for heretical belief. Just as the serpents that infested the Tiber exhaled noxious humors that plagued the citizens of Rome, so too might the foul words of a single heretic pollute the pure belief of the faithful and infect the Christian Body.[76] The trope of the heretical and pestiferous serpent remained a *topos* in medieval hagiography.[77] Saints Hilary, Lifard, Marcel, and Pavacius, as well as the former saint George, all fought dragons whose "very breath ... was pestilential" in order to "rid the country of this plague." Some saints used weapons to slay the heretical beast, while others used the sign of the cross to banish the foul serpent "to the depths of the earth forever."[78]

While a single heretic might be depicted as a toxic, earth-dwelling serpent who must be banished with the rituals of the church, a heretical cohort was often depicted as a diabolical sect who met at night to consume human flesh, drink blood, and engage in licentious behavior. The rhetoric of the cannibalistic night orgy was used as invective against one's enemies in ancient Rome; pagans, in fact, had accused Christians of covering an infant with meal and eagerly licking up its blood and dividing its limbs, as well as "worshipping the genitals of their pontiff" at their "secret nocturnal rites."[79] In the medieval world, authors used this same rhetoric to paint nightmarish portraits of amorphous and theoretical "others" at the edges of society. By the twelfth century, they were lodging these accusations against a specific group of well-organized dualist heretics—the Cathars—that threatened the

1. The Medieval Construction of Earthbound Evil 31

unity of the church.[80] According to Ralph of Coggeshall, the dreaded Cathars not only congregated "in subterranean haunts" in order to consume human flesh and engage in orgiastic activity, but also performed these "execrable sacrifices to Lucifer."[81] While rooted in a familiar rhetorical tradition meant as a general invective against "otherness," such accusations of cannibalism and demonic congress took on a far more literal and fiendish meaning in the later Middle Ages. This shift from allegorical diabolism to a belief that devil worship, night conventicles, and the consumption of infants might be occurring in the flesh can be attributed to the strict binary schema of good and evil elaborated by scholastic theologians as well as the increasingly chaotic and fragmented worlds of the thirteenth and fourteenth centuries.

At the Fourth Lateran Council of 1215, the Cathar heresy was identified as a serious threat to Christendom. Dualists who held all matter to be evil, Cathars believed that Jesus neither could have existed in true flesh, nor could he be truly present in the material bread and wine of the Eucharist. Likewise, the Cathars held the institutional Church to be neither pure nor holy, but instead a carnal manifestation of material evil and its leader, the Pope, the true Anti-Christ. In order to defend itself, prove the beliefs of the Cathars heretical, and put an end to the purportedly evil sect that threatened the unity of the Church, members of the Council demanded that those who refused to abide by "the holy, orthodox and Catholic faith" were to be excommunicated, stripped of their property, and turned over to the secular arm of the law for corporal punishment. Anyone thought to "receive, defend, or patronize" a heretic was to be punished likewise, while secular leaders were admonished to "cleanse" their territories of "heretical foulness" upon pain of censure and excommunication. Those who "girded themselves with the Cross for the extermination of heretics" and defense of the Church were granted the same indulgences and privileges as those who went on crusade to the Holy Land. Through these efforts, clerics believed that the Christian Body might be purified of its heretical corruption and return to its perfect obedience of God's singular will.

Before any penalties or rewards might be meted out, however, wellhidden heretics would have to be uncovered. To this end, members of the newly founded Order of Friars Preacher, or Dominicans, turned to the works of Aristotle, the very foundation of the medieval university curriculum, and found weapons of logical argumentation that were truly indomitable. With Aristotelian paradigms and methods drawn from legal disputation as their primary tools, educated Dominicans worked their way from cities and small towns to the rural hamlets where heresy was likely to hide, delivering sermons, hearing confessions, and asking questions about people's beliefs. In this way, the Dominicans became the eyes, ears, and arms of the papal inquisition set into motion by Pope Gregory IX in 1233.

One such friar was the Dominican Peter of Verona (d. 1252), who was educated at the University of Bologna and steeped in Aristotelian argumentation and law. According to his official life, or *vita*, his arguments against heresy were so persuasive that while he was Inquisitor of Lombardy, many Cathars converted back to right belief. Cathar leaders attempted to silence Peter by beheading him on the road from Milan, but to no avail; Peter wrote the first line of the Nicene Creed in his own blood, orthodox to the end.[82] Unsurprisingly, within a year Pope Innocent IV canonized him as Saint Peter of Verona, Martyr, eternal defender of the Church.

As inquisitors roamed the land providing pastoral care and preaching a unified orthodox faith, they not only confronted the willfully heretical doctrines of the Cathars on the fringe but also uncovered the questionable beliefs of the common faithful in its very bosom, the peasants of the field and the mass priests who tended them. For example, the Dominican friar Stephen of Bourbon (d. 1262) was sent to conduct an inquisition and to preach against heresy in the small town of Villars-en-Dombe in Lyons. Upon repeated questioning, Stephen discovered that the local saint, Guinefort, was actually a greyhound dog who had sacrificed its life to save the lord's infant son from a snake.[83] The healing rituals attending Saint Guinefort's cult were likewise disturbing; sick infants believed to be changelings were purportedly stripped naked and tossed between the fork of a tree festooned with lit candles while the local wise woman chanted. Rituals of natural and sympathetic magic were common in the medieval world; under the scrutiny of learned men, these rituals—which had no correlation within Nicean Christianity or learned medicine—smacked of heresy and perhaps even diabolism. As Dominican preachers like Stephen of Bourbon permeated the countryside, they discovered myriad local beliefs that did not conform with evermore concisely defined Church doctrines and rituals and, likewise, many non-canonical individuals who had to be brought back into the canonical fold, if not by preaching, then by force. Such a reform of the laity was necessary in order to unify and strengthen a church seemingly embattled by a multitude of chaotic and fragmented elements, all of which threatened to obscure it from a distant and heavenly light.

Despite thirteenth-century attempts to reform the church and stabilize its connection to the divine, the fourteenth century brought evidence that these efforts had failed and that demonic chaos would reign in the sublunary realm.[84] What modern climatologists recognize as a temperature shift of two degrees Celsius in 1311 resulted in colder, wetter weather and the failure of

1. The Medieval Construction of Earthbound Evil 33

crops across Western Europe. This climate shift in conjunction with stagnant agricultural practices and monocropping resulted in the Great Famine which began in 1315 and rippled throughout the first quarter of the fourteenth century. In response to food shortages and widespread warfare, many people fled to burgeoning cities in search of relief. This rapid urbanization in combination with malnutrition created an optimal environment for epidemic diseases including the bubonic plague, also known as the Black Death, which spread from Kaffa to port cities and along trade routes across Europe from 1347 forward.[85] Already suffering communities large and small experienced human loss on a horrifying scale and were daily confronted with bloated bodies and the cadaverous stench of decay, visceral reminders of God's wrath and His abandonment of the world to the workings of the Devil.

While human bodies lay suppurating in the streets, the Christian body as represented by the formal Church fared little better. Throughout the fourteenth century, the Church continued to fight the infection of heresy spread by their long-standing dualist enemies in the South, the Cathars, and by newer groups such as the Lollards and the Hussites. Based in England, the Lollards followed the teachings of John Wycliffe (1330–1384), who not only held heretical beliefs regarding the process of transubstantiation, but also argued that the Bible should be translated into the vernacular for general consumption and that priests, prelates, and the entire body of the Church—including the Pope—should aspire to apostolic poverty, humility, and austerity in imitation of Christ.[86] In publicly questioning the authority of the Church, Wycliffe and his followers gave voice to ideas circulating among a laity that was increasingly disgruntled with the shepherds of their flock who had seemingly become wolves and fed upon them in times of need. The Lollard heresy, which infiltrated the Church in the English West, soon infected the Bohemian East through the works of Jan Hus (1369–1415), whose followers were known as Hussites and who, like the Lollards, questioned the nature of the Eucharist and the authority of the Church.

Heretical and rebellious ideas plagued not only the laity in the fourteenth century, but also the ranks of Church elite. The Franciscan order, for example, was rent apart by disputes about the nature of the order itself. Saint Francis had advocated for a mendicant life of poverty and humility among the people, but by the time of his death in 1226 the order had acquired a complex organizational structure, properties, buildings, and vast wealth. Many brothers saw this conventual life as proper to the order's mission; many others argued that the conventual approach violated Francis' third and definitive rule, penned in 1223, which admonished brothers not to accept or even touch money and to live a life of poverty. Adherents to this latter philosophy, known as the Spiritual Franciscans, lived a life of simplicity and suffering among the common people in imitation of the apostles and Christ. Inspired by the apocalyptic works of Joachim de Fiore and the progressive philosophies of Peter of John Olivi, the Spiritual Franciscans questioned the authority of their Conventual brothers, participated in radical activities, and associated with quasi-heretical groups such as mendicant beguines and beghards—all of which would bring them under censure of the Church.[87] By 1317, the Spiritual Franciscans were themselves deemed heretical, and in 1318 several of them were tried and condemned by their Conventual brothers and burned at the stake.[88] As David Burr writes, "It was very much a family affair."[89]

Heretical activities among the laity and schisms within the Franciscan order are only two manifestations of the greater discord within the Church, the chaotic dysfunction of which extended to the very top of its hierarchy. In the thirteenth century, the Church had centralized power in the hands of the Pope through the creation and consistent application of bureaucratic and legal systems. Having consolidated power within the Church, the Papacy looked to extend its sphere of influence over political issues; for example, when the French King Philip IV determined to remove ecclesiastics from participation in secular law and proceeded to tax the Church heavily, Pope Boniface VIII intervened with a bull entitled *Clericis Laicos* (1296), which demanded that the laity might not tax the clergy without express permission of the Pope.[90] In his continued battles against Philip for primacy, Boniface issued yet another bull, *Unam Sanctam* (1302), in which he claimed that the Pope alone held dominion over spiritual and temporal authorities. "This one and only church can have only a single body and a single head—namely Christ and His Vicar of St. Peter (and Peter's Successor)," he argued; "It is not a two-headed monster." Despite his best efforts to commandeer political power, Boniface was effectively deposed by Philip and died beaten and humiliated in 1303. In the following years, the French Pope Clement V not only repealed *Clericis Laicos* and *Unam Sanctam* but also moved the entire papal court to Avignon where it would remain until 1378, the year in which the Italians elected their own Pope, Urban V, to preside at Rome. From 1378 to 1409, the Church was divided between two popes, each of whom had his own curia and papal palace, and each of whom claimed sole authority while denouncing his enemy as an imposter and perhaps even the Antichrist. In response to this ongoing crisis, clerics gathered without papal sanction at the Council of Pisa in 1409 and by their collective authority elected Pope Alexander V, bringing the total number of popes to three.

Meant to be a reflection of the divine perfection, angelic obedience, and luminous harmony radiating from the Empyrean, the Church had by the fifteenth century become a sublunary nightmare of chaotic disobedience populated by heretics and rebellious monks and ruled by three self-willed potentates unwilling to bow to God. Worse than a "two-headed monster" which, like the Devil's forked tongue, might never arrive at singular truth, the church had become a three-headed monster, a mockery of the trinity evocative of the three beasts of *Revelation*, beneath whose leathery wings terrifying chaos reigned.[91] For theologians, the horrors of the plague, the ravages of war, the smoky stench from the pyres upon which heretics were burned, and internal strife within the Church signified God's disapprobation of his earthly flock and His abandonment of his disobedient children to the wiles of Satan as a form of punishment. Deeply wrought, members of the clergy looked to reform the Church from within through increased pastoral care. Drawing upon the chaotic events unfolding around them, preachers frequently used *exempla* about demons and their wicked human followers as a means of educating—and terrifying—the laity. In so doing, they hoped that their horrified listeners would eschew heresy and cleave to the Church and her rituals all the more closely. The didactic purpose of the blackest evil in these tales was twofold: to further illuminate the dazzling and wondrous light of God, and to reform the Christian body so that it might, too, once again shine like a light in a sinful and corrupt world.[92]

While preachers addressed issues of heresy and disobedience among the laity, ecclesiastics once again gathered together, this time at the Council of Constance (1414–18), in order to address issues of multiplicity within the Church. One of the primary goals of the council was the deposition of the three popes and antipopes and the election of a new pope—the only pope—Martin V; the growth of heretical sects was also addressed, and the council ultimately tried, convicted, and had the secular arm execute both Wycliffe and Hus as heretics.[93] The resolution of the Great Schism and the purgation of heretical leaders from the sheepfold should have brought a modicum of relief to ecclesiastics nervous about the chaotic state of affairs in Christendom. Yet even after the conclusion of the Council, fears remained regarding the sources of authority within the hierarchy of the Church. The continued threat of schism as well as the persistence and growth of heretical sects such as the Hussites ultimately brought ecclesiastics to call another council, this one at Basel, which would address the need for reform in the "head and members" of the Church.[94] From 1431 until 1440, church leaders, theologians, and inquisitors from across Christendom not only discussed practical issues such as how to reform the laity and how to combat heresy, but also exchanged stories from their respective regions, many of which involved strange doings, demons, and the activities of heretic-witches.

The Council of Basel acted as a cauldron for the creation of Satanic witchcraft paradigm, in particular the Witches' Sabbath, that would become salient in the Western imagination.[95] There, clerics gathered to discuss deformities in the Church body, in particular the leprous lesions left by heresy. Authorities from the "the Val d'Aosta in northwestern Italy, the duchy of Savoy, the Dauphiné, the area around Lake Geneva, the Bernese Oberland, and Basel itself, generally the dioceses of Basel and Constance" brought their own set of concerns about a "novel sect of heretics"—diabolical witches— "that had appeared only shortly before the council itself formally opened in July 1431."[96] Among this group of men was Johannes Nider, a Dominican prior and advocate of reform, who formally and informally collected stories of demonic heresy recounted by inquisitorial judges and other colleagues throughout the course of the Counsel. In 1437 and 1438, Nider compiled several of these tales in his handbook for preachers, the *Formicarius*, or *Ant Hill*, a text that was widely circulated both in manuscript form and after 1475 in print. The fifth chapter of the *Formicarius* deals specifically with witchcraft, and contains several elements of the paradigmatic Witches' Sabbath, including the belief in an organized diabolical sect that would "come to a fixed meeting place and would see the demon in the assumed likeness of a man."[97] At the Sabbath, the witches would "promise to abjure Christianity, never to reverence the Eucharist, and to stamp on the Cross if they could do so without notice." After renewing their oaths, the Devil's disciples would then cook and eat children as part of their sacrificial feast. Nider's text also includes reference to the flight of the witches through the air to their unholy gathering; following in the tradition of the *Canon Episcopi*, however, he asserts that these witches did not fly in their physical bodies, but instead fell prey to demonic phantasy. The *Formicarius* was not meant merely as an account of witchcraft and its spread through parts of Christendom, but as a handbook for preachers who might use these stories as *exempla* in their sermons. Nider's intent was not the persecution of witchcraft in its nascent form, but the reformation of the Church from its members—the very Body of Christ—to its leadership. For Nider, then, the physical reality and operations of diabolical witches was of far less concern that the illumination of a dark and chaotic Church and its subsequent return to Divine order.

Nider's was not the only witchcraft text to emerge from the culture surrounding the Council of Basel; Bailey and Peters have posited tenuous connections between the Council and the *Errores Gazariorum*, a witchcraft treatise written anonymously in 1430, and Nicholas Jacquier's *De calcatione daemonum* (1452) and *Flagellum haereticorum fascinariorum* (1458). Like Nider's *Formicarius*, these treatises contained the core components of the

Witches' Sabbath, including cannibalism, congress with demons, and the night flight. Unlike the *Formicarius*, which was geared toward preaching and reform, these texts expressed a growing concern that witchcraft posed a very real and organized threat to Christians across Europe. Jacquier, for example, argued that the night flight of the witches was no mere phantasy, but a physical act manifested through the agency of demons. As the fifteenth century progressed and witchcraft trials, tales, and treatises proliferated, learned authors conflated regional particularities into an increasingly standardized and synthetic witchcraft paradigm shaped in part by Aristotelian structures and scholastic methods.[98]

In the *Malleus Maleficarum* (1486), an inquisitor's manual written by the Dominican Heinrich Kramer and, to a lesser extent, Jacob Sprenger, the witchcraft paradigm found its most authoritative and systematic expression.[99] In the *Malleus*, witchcraft was depicted as a very real Satanic conspiracy in which demons and humans were in collusion in their attempt to destroy humanity. Unlike the demons of Augustine, who were mere buffoons, or the demons of Aquinas, which were restrained by natural law, the demons of the *Malleus* were ascribed incredible power in the world below the moon. Having retained their essential intellect, demons were masters of the natural realm, able to manipulate elements and human bodies at will; furthermore, because God had given demons free rein to torment and punish disobedient and sinful humankind, Satan and his minions were granted Divine sanction to perform supernatural wonders as wicked miracles.[100] According to Kramer, demonic attacks were no longer isolated or random incidents but part of an organized and systematic assault against the Church and the Christian body. "The devils deputed to work are not in Hell, but in the lower mists. *And they have here an order among themselves.*"[101] In this work the demons were assisted by their devout human servants, the witches, each of whom could "do nothing without the aid and assistance of the other."[102] For those readers who doubted the possibility of human supplicants aided by dark angels in service of the Devil, Kramer warned, "Would to God that we might suppose all this to be untrue and merely imaginary, if only our Holy Mother the Church were free from the leprosy of such abomination ... we dare not refrain from inquiring into them lest we imperil our own salvation."[103]

Drawing on biblical, theological, and folkloric sources, witchcraft treatises, and his own personal conversations and experiences, Kramer—who as an inquisitor sought and found evidence of *maleficum* all around him—used the basic premises of Aristotelian contrariety to codify the rites and rituals of Satanic witchcraft as a perfect inversion of the Institutional Church. Beneath his quill, once-sporadic incidents of witchcraft became part of a centralized conspiratorial network of demons and witches who functioned within an upside-down anti–Church, in which the Devil served as the Anti-God (sometimes in the form of the Antichrist), demons as his evil angels, and foul witches as his unholy body of wicked disciples. Unlike the translucent and pure Mystical Body of Christ, which offered its members the promise of redemption and entrance to a heavenly kingdom of light, the Mystical Body of Satan offered its co-conspirators carnal pleasures and earthly powers, such as dominion over the weather, corrupt creatures, and human flesh, all of which would guarantee them an eternity trapped in the cold, dark, chaotic hell below the moon.

Initiation into this inverted community of believers mimicked the rituals of the Christian church. Many converts were enticed into witchcraft by someone close to them, almost always a woman, often a wife or mother. The *Malleus* describes the seduction of a husband into witchcraft by his wife's wicked ministrations, which ultimately led him to "deny Christ, his faith, baptism, and the whole Church."[104] Witchy mothers and aunts might likewise offer their daughters and nieces up to Satan as a form of supplication; the young girl's fate was often sealed through a sex act either with a demon, who would become her "little master," or with the Devil himself.[105] Like a heretical disease, witchcraft spread throughout families and infected the larger community. Having been initiated into the sect, the novice would then form a binding and eternal pact with the Devil, sometimes by written agreement, others by mere profession; those whom the Devil did not trust were marked with a sign, often in the exact place of their former Christian baptism. In *Satan the Heretic: The Birth of Demonology in the Medieval West*, Alain Boureau argues that the pact with the Devil, which has its roots in the academic world of the thirteenth century, was an inversion of the sacramental covenants made between the Christian faithful and the Institutional Church.[106] Once initiated, the disciple was then instructed to mock the Church and its rituals at every chance. Kramer writes that "when the priest at the mass blesses the people, saying *Dominus Vobiscum*," the witch "always adds to herself these words in the vulgar tongue, 'Kehr mir die Zung im Arss umb.'"[107] This latter phrase, which translates as "Screw your tongue in my ass," ties this act not only to blasphemy but links it to the bowels and the earth, the hallmarks of the demonic realm.[108] In addition to "fasting on Sundays, eating meat on Fridays [and] concealing certain crimes at confession" against the laws of the Church, the heretical witch also swore "never to adore the Eucharist, and to tread the Cross underfoot"; in her hatred of Christ, she might likewise "beat and stab the crucifix" or desecrate the Host by feeding it to toads—the very embodiment of earthly corruption—for use in her wicked spells.[109]

1. The Medieval Construction of Earthbound Evil

The inverted schema of Satanic witchcraft finds its most perfect expression in the rituals surrounding Witches' Sabbath, or as it has come down to us in the modern world, the Black Mass. Rooted in the ancient trope of the cannibalistic night orgy long ascribed to "others," disparate elements of the Witches' Sabbath were salient features of medieval discourse against heretics and Jews and were featured in discussions of witchcraft from the ninth-century *Canon Episcopi* to the fifteenth-century *Errores Gazariorum*.[110] The *Malleus Maleficarum* makes reference to several ritual components, including the phantasmic night flight of the witches and concomitant use of the magic ointment; the theft, ritual sacrifice, and consumption of infants; baptism and marking by Satan; and the complicated process by which humans might copulate with demons. Building on the authority of the *Malleus* and other works in circulation, subsequent authors would over the next two centuries elaborate upon the Witches' Sabbath, providing evermore detailed descriptions and deepening the level of inversions imagined by their forebears.[111] Open to regional and authorial permutations, the salient elements of the Witches' Sabbath included the mandatory journey of witches, who often traveled by broomstick, branch, or animal familiar through demonic transvection to remote locations. Once they had assembled, the witches and their "little masters" would then summon the Devil through invocation, sometimes under the direction of a Sabbath leader. Upon Satan's arrival, which was most often in the form of a black and shaggy goat, the congregation would venerate him through the *osculum infame*, or obscene kiss, which was placed close to or directly on his anus. Having properly greeted their Lord, the witches then made a sort of profession of faith, renouncing Christ and His Church, trampling or otherwise injuring the Cross, and cursing the Blessed Virgin Mary. New acolytes, including the children of professed witches, came before Satan to be baptized and to take the dreadful oath; other witches were called to confess any evil that they had left undone and were forced to do penance by their Master.[112] The congregation was sprinkled with the Devil's urine, an inversion of the dispersal of holy water at the Christian Mass during high holy days.[113] This business attended to, the congregation of witches gathered around the sacrificial altar or cauldron where infants, baptized and unbaptized, were sacrificed in mockery of the Eucharist, their blood and flesh ritually consumed as part of the Sabbath feast.[114] The infants' bones and other remaining viscera were then concocted into powerful ointments, such as those used for night flight and the transformation of humans into animals, as well as poisons that the witches might use to kill their and their Masters' enemies. At the conclusion of the feast, which also included black bread and black wine—but which never included either white bread or salt—the witches and demons engaged in wild dancing that culminated in a perverse sexual orgy.[115] As the morning light glowed along the horizon, the Sabbath ended with the cock's crow, at which point demons, Satan, witches, and feast instantaneously disappeared as if a dream.

Born of earlier medieval learned and folkloric traditions and organized according to Aristotelian discursive and logical structures, the fundamental elements of the witchcraft paradigm, such as the cold, dark, sulfurous, and earthbound nature of Satan and his demons, as well as their creation of an organized anti-Church with inverted rituals such as the Witches' Sabbath, remained salient features of witchcraft treatises from the fifteenth century forward. Nicholas Remy, the Burgundian judge who wrote *Demonolatry* (1595), Henry Boguet, the prosecutor who composed *An Examen of Witches* (1602), and Francesco Maria Guazzo, the Italian Cleric whose *Compendium Maleficarum* (1608) became an increasingly authoritative reference manual for secular jurists and inquisitors alike, each reinforced and refined Satanic inversion in lavish detail. Devout Catholics, Remy, Boguet, and Guazzo quoted medieval scholastics such as Albertus Magnus and Aquinas as textual authorities. Jean Bodin, a French jurist who was nominally Catholic but leaned toward Protestantism, eschewed medieval authorities in his *Demon Mania of Witches* (1580), relying more heavily on ancient pagan and Patristic sources to support his arguments. Witchcraft treatises by Protestant authors such as the Puritan leader Cotton Mather would follow a similar discursive model while emphasizing the deeper meanings behind witchcraft, in particular the sinful nature of humanity, the righteous wrath of an angry God, and the imminent destruction of the world.

Diabolism also had its skeptics; Reginald Scot, the Anglican author of *The Discoverie of Witchcraft* (1584), dismissed witchcraft as medieval superstition and papist nonsense. Johann Weyer, the Dutch physician and student of Heinrich Cornelius Agrippa who wrote *On the Illusions of Demons and Spells and Poisons* (1563), argued that demons, night flight, Sabbaths and the evil eye were mere phantasy, the natural results of a melancholic complexion and easily explained by reason and learned medicine. In their attempt to refute witchcraft, both Scot and Weyer presented systematic arguments against witchcraft beliefs, in the process reinforcing the very structures that they sought to destroy; Scot's *Discoverie of Witchcraft*, for example, became a compendia of regional and more general witchcraft beliefs organized according to the medieval Aristotelian contrariety. Catholic, Protestant, and Skeptical treaties on witchcraft—no matter their intent—were inextricably bound to the inverted model of Satanic evil constructed in the academic milieu of the thirteenth and fourteenth centuries.

1. The Medieval Construction of Earthbound Evil 41

Post-modernity has yet to shake itself free of the deep structures of inverted evil codified by medieval clerics. In popular culture, inverted crosses, icy and sulfuric entities, nighttime gatherings in remote forests, black-robed supplicants and infant sacrifice remain as potent signifiers of Satanic evil. The melancholic world of upside-down evil forms the foundation of the gothic tradition, from the novels of Horace Walpole (*Castle of Otronto*, 1764) and Matthew Lewis' *The Monk* (1796) to the films of Hammer Horror and the books and films of the *Twilight* franchise. The Devil, too, has remained with us as Mephistopheles from Goethe's *Faust*, the Goat of Mendes from the 1968 film *The Devil Rides Out*, the red-horned beast from *Legend* (1985), the pallid man in black from *Angel Heart* (1987), the dark mist from *Bless the Child* (2000), and Gay Satan from *South Park*. Demons continue to haunt our imaginations through films such as *The Exorcist* (1973), *The Last Exorcism* part one (2010) and two (2013), and the *Paranormal Activity* series (2007-present), and "reality-based" television programs such as *A Haunting* (2005–2007; 2012–present) and *Paranormal State* (2007-present).

Perhaps most terrifying of all, we continue to use the signifiers of Satanic evil to categorize those we fear most, "others" who do not conform to our individually or socially constructed paradigms for acceptability. The Satanic Panic of the 1990s, the McMartin Preschool Trial, the jailing of the West Memphis Three, and the depiction of Muslims, members of the LGBTQ community, Jews, and liberals in post–9/11 America all attest to the persistence of the medieval structuring of the inverted and potentially Satanic "other."

2

Satanic Cinema

His Legacy Is Legion

The inverted signs and signifiers of Satanic Evil codified by scholastic theologians in the thirteenth century and disseminated through witchcraft treatises from the fifteenth century onward did not disappear with the early modern witch hunts. Upside-down evil has persisted in popular culture, inspiring the eighteenth-century gothic tradition and shaping the modern genre of supernatural horror. In the twentieth and twenty-first centuries, inverted and Satanic "otherness" continues to stalk the dream-worlds of visual media, from blockbusters at the multiplex to the streaming of horror films and television programs in the safety of the increasingly elusive middle-class fortress.[1] In films such as *The Black Cat* (1934), *The Crimson Cult* (1968), *The House of the Devil* (2009), and *The Last Exorcism* (2010), television shows such as *The X-Files* (1993–2002) and *True Blood* (2008–present), and "reality-based" programming such as *A Haunting* (2005–2007; 2012–present) and *Paranormal State* (2007–present), the shape of evil "others" and their wicked activities continue to be governed by the specific rationality of medieval scholasticism.

Rooted in Aristotelian contrariety, the upside-down rituals of the modern Black Mass, the melancholic nature of sexually rapacious demonic bodies consumed by bloodlust, and the power of uniquely Catholic objects such as crucifixes, holy water, and the sacraments of baptism, confession, and unction to counter and defeat Satanic Evil would be as eerily familiar to men such as Thomas Aquinas, Johannes Nider, and Nicholas Remy as they are to modern horror fans. Tales focused on the conception and birth of the Anti-Christ and the demonic possession of female flesh operate not only within the constructs of canonical evil as codified in the thirteenth century, but also in accordance with medieval medico-theological paradigms for the anatomy and physiology of the evil feminine. When viewed through these pre-modern lenses, both the structure of Satanism and the strange behavior of Satanic and demon-possessed bodies in modern tales of horror become predictable and disturbingly rational.

Satan's Sabbath in the Cinema

The Witches' Sabbath as imagined by late-medieval and early modern inquisitors continues to be celebrated in movie theaters and in darkened living rooms to the shock and delight of modern voyeurs, many of whom can recognize the inverted signifiers of evil but have no real sense of makes them so.[2] In the 1934 Universal production *The Black Cat* and the 1968 Hammer Horror film *The Devil Rides Out*, the Witches' Sabbath is born again as the Black Mass, with the traditional coven of commoners transformed into a group of bourgeois devotees in the service of a wealthy and powerful male leader learned in the occult arts. *The Black Cat* stars an ashen-skinned Boris Karloff as the impossibly named Hjalmar Poelzig, an Austrian architect-cum-Satanic high priest who has built his Bauhaus on a World War I battlefield. Poelzig's pallid complexion and sunken black eyes are intensified by his tailored black suit, both of which signify death and decay according to medieval color theory.[3] Throughout the film, Poelzig's primary goal is the sacrifice of a white-robed maiden according to the Rites of Lucifer. While we are never told the goals of the ritual, Poelzig's assertion that his doppelganger and familiar—a black cat—is "as deathless as evil" suggests that he must sacrifice virgins in order to extend his own life.[4] The main ritual of the Rites of Lucifer, which Poelzig performs on a windy autumn night during the "Dark of the Moon," takes the form of a highly stylized Black Mass. Garbed in the black robes of a scholarly high priest and wearing a large inverted pentagram about his neck, he intones Latin from a modernist pulpit constructed of inverted crosses and flanked by chrome Egyptian obelisks.[5] Surrounded by his black-robed, wealthy congregation and his brides, each of whom wears the white dress of a debutante, Poelzig lashes his intended victim—an American tourist on her honeymoon—to the altar, subduing her with incantations against a backdrop of organ music. Before the sacrifice can be completed, the ritual is interrupted by Poelzig's nemesis from the Great War, a Hungarian psychiatrist named Dr. Vitus Werdegast (Bela Lugosi), who not only saves the life of the young American, but also captures the Satanic high priest, lashing him to a rack and flaying him alive.

Produced for an American audience, *The Black Cat* reinforced many deep-seated American fears and perceptions of European culture, particularly that members of its intellectual elite were educated to the point of madness.[6] With seemingly limitless time and access to medieval manuscripts and Renaissance incunabula, this imagined European illuminati had discovered ancient secrets—signified in this film by the Egyptian obelisks on either side of the altar—and mastered arcane Black Magic. In their violent lust for personal and political power, many of these illusory men not only practiced the dark arts, but had entered into pacts with the Devil, both of which were conflated into a single category of evil. Like Cotton Mather and his fellow Protestant theologians, many early twentieth-century Americans saw occultism and any form of magic as synonymous with Devil worship; neither were Christian, therefore both were Satanic. Even more terrifying to the American imagination, these power-hungry intellectuals never acted alone, but were organized into an underground network of wealthy Euro-Satanists bent on world domination. The achievement of this goal would necessitate the blood sacrifice of innocent Christian Americans in war should they attempt to interfere in European affairs. In the film, the struggle between Poelzig and Werdegast as well as the use of the American woman as a pawn in their wicked wager were indicative of a much larger danger imagined to be brewing somewhere in the former Austro-Hungarian empire. In its use of Satanic "otherness" to depict distant Europeans, *The Black Cat* reflects American anxieties during a period when the memories of the Great War were still painfully fresh and the fear of another war loomed large in the imagination. Through this lens, the message of *The Black Cat* is clear; instead of girding itself with Christian symbols—which are wholly absent from the film—in preparation for an epic Euro-Satanic battle, America should leave depraved European Satanists and madmen on their own to reap destruction and flay one another alive.

The 1968 Hammer film *The Devil Rides Out*, based on Dennis Wheatley's 1934 novel of the same name, likewise features a wealthy Satanic coven led by a scholarly male priest, this time in the English countryside. Where *The Black Cat* uses inverted signifiers to broadly suggest the presence of Satanic evil, however, *The Devil Rides Out* presents Satanism drawn in exquisite detail and replete with symbols culled from classical Hermetic and alchemical traditions, a reflection of courtly divination and clerical necromancy conflated with the common world of woodland witches.[7] At the center of the tale is young Simon Aron (Patrick Mower), a foil for Simon Magus from the *Apocryphal Acts of Saints Peter and Paul*, who has unwittingly joined a coven of thirteen Satanists in the guise of a bourgeois astronomical society.[8] The Satanists are led by an erudite priest named Mocata (Charles Gray), an "ipsissimus" with the power to control minds, raise icy-cold demons, summon the black horseman of death and conjure "the Goat of Mendes, the Devil Himself."[9] Mocata presides over a Black Mass that conforms in many of its elements to the paradigmatic Witches' Sabbath, including the forest gathering, the use of black candles, the summoning of the goat–Devil, the Satanic baptism of initiates and their prostration before the Evil One, the ritual sacrifice of an innocent lamb symbolic of the Christ child, the drinking of its blood from a sacramental chalice, the feast and the orgy. At a second Satanic rite in the film, Mocata and his coven meet in the basement of Simon's house, constructed as an inverted church, where they attempt to sacrifice a young girl robed in white upon the altar. Added to these traditional Christian inversions are elements taken from Renaissance hermetic traditions: the invocation of Babylon and Osiris at the beginning of the Black Mass, the use of astrological symbols and alchemical signs on the altar cloth and in Simon's observatory, and references to the *Clavicle of Solomon*, a Renaissance grimoire that draws on the Kabbalah.[10]

Mocata's Satanism and learned Black Magic make him nearly invincible and discernibly evil; luckily, young Simon has a protector in the person of the Duc de Richelieu (Christopher Lee) who is himself learned in the occult arts and devout in his Christianity, both of which will be necessary to defeat Mocata and his coven. In his battle against evil, Richelieu uses rituals and symbols drawn from his arcane knowledge of alchemy and hermeticism. Salt and Mercury, which "protect against the Dark Forces," the use of sacred circles, the invocation of Osiris and the raising of dead spirits, and the chanting of the dreadful Susamma Ritual which can alter space and time are all part of Richelieu's occult arsenal.[11] Richelieu likewise uses the Christian cross as a talisman to ward off evil, in one instance placing a silver crucifix around the neck of Simon to be worn as a "symbol of protection" against demonic influences, in another throwing a crucifix at a dark demon and at the Devil, causing them both to disappear into puffs of sulphurous smoke.[12] Richelieu's totemic use of the crucifix is one of the few elements that distinguishes his magical arcana from that of Mocata, since many of their hermetic weapons are drawn from the same texts and traditions. Because he is constructed as evil, Mocata's magic is marked as Black and conflated with Satanism, while the savior Richelieu's magic is deemed White and given a Christian veneer.[13] This transposition of Christian and Satanic themes onto a traditional "magic contest" story about competing wizards illustrates our continued use of structures codified by thirteenth-century scholastics to signify good and evil in modern culture.[14]

Beneath this contest for primacy between two modern-day magi, a second layer of discourse is at work. Mocata and his wealthy coven function as a secret society that maintains its own body of privileged knowledge. Their regal robes, purple and flowing, bear the symbol of their cult, which is a *Magen David* containing an inverted five-pointed star within which sits the Goat of Mendes.[15] The Star of David is a recurring symbol in Freemasonry, as is the five-pointed blazing star, as well as its inversion, which is the primary symbol used by the Order of the Eastern Star, an American group affiliated with the Masons. Freemasonry has long been suspected of Satanic involvement. As small conclaves of wealthy men who gather together after dark to participate in secret ceremonies forbidden to outsiders, their behavior mimics that of medieval heretics and late-medieval witches who were accused of holding their horrid rituals during nighttime conventicles.[16] Further damning in the popular imagination, local Masonic groups do not operate independently, but are part of an international secret society whose organizational headquarters are located in London and Washington, D.C., two centers of political and economic power. This structure echoes late-medieval and early modern suspicions that witch covens were not isolated anomalies, but instead organized into a larger, Christendom-wide conspiracy headed by Satan himself and committed to the destruction of humankind. These suspect characteristics have led conspiracy theorists to imagine that world events have historically been dictated by the Masons and the evil Illuminati at their helm.[17] This fear that a syndicate of influential and evil others—be they Satanists, Jews, or aliens—operates in and among mainstream society, just out of view, has persisted in Anglo-American culture in part because of the deep structure of inverted evil inherited from the medieval world, in part because of our unwavering commitment to the individual as an autonomous agent.[18] In *The Devil Rides Out*, it falls to the Duc du Richelieu, an independent scholar marked by Christian goodness but controlled by no church, to fight the collective evil of Mocata and his followers who mindlessly bow to a wicked man and his Goat-God in their quest for personal power.

In two films set on American soil, *The City of the Dead* (1960) and *The Witchmaker* (1969), the Black Mass and Satanic ritual return to their roots in late-medieval witchcraft. *The City of the Dead*, known to American audiences as *Horror Hotel*, is set in the eldritch town of Whitewood, Massachusetts, where a coven of Satanic witches has persisted since the landing of the *Mayflower*. Nan Barlowe (Venetia Stevenson), a blonde college student who has determined to write a thesis on witchcraft in New England, travels to Whitewood at the instigation of her advisor, Prof. Driscoll (Christopher Lee). En route, Nan meets the mellow-toned Jethro Keene (Valentine Dyall), a dark-suited minion of the Devil, who journeys with her into the fog-enshrouded ruins of a Lovecraftian New England town.[19] There, Nan learns from the local minister that "for three hundred years, the Devil has hovered over this city, made it his own." Having taken a room at the Raven's Inn, a dark and brooding place run by the witch Elizabeth Selwyn (Patricia Jessel), Nan discovers that "a coven of witches whose power came from the Devil" once gathered in the building's earthly bowels "to perform a black mass in the honor of Lucifer." That evening, while Nan is reading a treatise on witchcraft, Selwyn invites her to dance with the other guests in celebration of Candlemas. Finding no one in the lobby, Nan follows the sound of chanting back to her room where she discovers a trap door. Descending into the foul and fetid caverns beneath the inn, Nan falls victim to the witches' Satanic rites which "mock the rituals of the church"; black-robed figures sacrifice her upon the infernal altar in their subterranean chapel, drinking "her blood in the hour of thirteen" as their unholy Eucharist.

Worried about Nan, her boyfriend Maitland and her scientific-minded brother Richard travel separately to Whitewood. In speaking to the reverend, Richard learns that the villagers are "creatures of the Devil," that "they know no other God." Sensing Richard's skepticism, the reverend assures him that "these people have a pact with the Devil, to do his work. In return, he gives them eternal life. To seal this bargain, they must sacrifice a girl on two nights of the year," one of which is Candlemas eve, and the other is the Witches' Sabbath. The only way to stop them, according to the churchman, is to "use the cross ... the shadow of the cross." That night, as the witches gather in the graveyard to sacrifice the reverend's granddaughter and renew their pact with the devil, they are interrupted by Nan's wounded boyfriend Maitland, who lifts an enormous cross from a grave with his dying breath. In a clear *imitatio Christi*, Maitland stumbles beneath its weight toward the coven, saying "I abjure thee in the name of the Living God." As the shadow of the cross touches the black robes of the Satanic supplicants, they erupt into flames—burnt as heretics by God Himself—and dissolve back into the cold, corrupt earth to which they are bound for eternity.

As depicted in *City of the Dead*, Satanic evil and Christian goodness conform to paradigms established in late-medieval and early modern witchcraft treatises. The inverted symbols, signifiers, and perverted behaviors inherent to Satanism are all present, including the color black, the dark of night, the cold and corrupt foggy air, the subterranean coven, the number thirteen (in mockery of the twelve apostles plus Judas), the pact with the Devil, and the ritual sacrifice and consumption of human blood as an unholy Eucharist. Of particular interest, the Sabbath Master and leader of this Satanic coven is a powerful woman, driven solely by her base desires for revenge, youth, and beauty. Following the medieval principle of *similia similibus*,

Selwyn greedily sacrifices that which she wishes to become—young women—drinking their blood as an elixir of life. Cold and dry, emotional and irrational, Selwyn is an embodiment of inverted Satanic evil, a reflection of the chaos below the moon. Like her coven, she dwells within the demon-infested bowels of the earth; heavy with corruption, she will never ascend into the ethereal Empyrean. The only power strong enough to defeat this melancholic and feminine evil is the masculine Christian fortitude of Richard and Maitland. Throughout the film, Richard is depicted as inherently rational, clear-thinking and logical, and demanding of proof before belief. Richard's rationality, however, only goes so far in the destruction of Selwyn's Satanic evil, which requires the selfless Christian sacrifice of Maitland, whose pure death in imitation of Christ cleanses the town and redeems its people of their ancient sins.

One of the primary subtexts in *The City of the Dead* is the demonic continuity between the Old World and the New. We are led to believe that the Satanists of Whitewood originally flourished in early modern Europe, traveled to the Massachusetts Bay Colony with the Puritans, bloomed and spread like a poisonous weed in Salem Town, went underground after the Witch Trials and remained entrenched there, lurking just below the surface, polluting present-day America.[20] In the 1969 film *The Witchmaker*, produced by the small American firm Las Cruces–Arrow, the geographical and temporal linkages between medieval Europe and modern America are made explicit in the strange survival of a Satanic witch cult deep in the Louisiana swamps. The story follows a formula common in horror cinema: a group of young people rent a cabin in the wilderness and encounter evil, be it in the form of ghosts, monsters, demons, or wicked human beings.[21] In *The Witchmaker*, a college professor and his research team have rented a cabin out on the Louisiana bottoms in order to investigate the powers of paranormal psychology. One of the team's key members, Tasha (Thordis Brandt), is a psychic-sensitive whose grandmother was reportedly a "little old witch." Her beauty, blonde hair, and essential witchy powers—which according to the *Malleus Maleficarum* and Remy's *Demonolatry* are passed down through families—make her an object of desire for Luther the Berserk (John Lodge), a Satanist of the highest order and the Sabbath Master of the local parish. In his quest to seduce Tasha and convert her to Satanism, thereby bringing his coven to the required number of thirteen, Luther engages the help of a haggard old crone named Jessie (Helene Winston). In return for her assistance in a series of Satanic rituals, Luther promises Jessie the return of her long-lost youth and beauty. As they "talk like merchants," Jessie agrees to his bargain and they form a pact.

The Satanic realm of Luther and Jessie, as well as the Witches' Sabbath that ushers in the film's conclusion, are distinctly medieval. Both are creatures of the Old World who immigrated to the New World with Acadian settlers and have survived undetected in the impenetrable swamps of the bayou. Luther is depicted as a stereotypical medieval peasant, his enormous frame clad in a sheepskin jerkin and burlap pants, while Jessie wears the long skirt, bodice, and hood of a fifteenth-century matron. Both have pale skin, black hair, and distorted features, which for Jessie includes a hooked nose and warts. Their Satanic rituals require the sacrifice of young women whose blood becomes both a libation for the Devil and a means of ensuring the witches' unnatural longevity. When invoking Satan, Luther dips his finger in human blood and places it in the mouth of his Satanic idol. He likewise uses blood to inscribe a strange sacred symbol on the abdomens of his victims, marking them as offerings to Satan; when their bodies are hung upside down from a tree, the symbol becomes recognizable as an Egyptian ankh, suggesting that Luther is in possession of occult knowledge, that this ritual holds the key to prolonging life, and that it is inherently evil.[22] Sacrificial human blood is also used to sign sacred parchments, just as one signs a Satanic pact. Luther combines these parchments with natural elements such as stones and twigs in order to cast his spells, thereby echoing the late-medieval concern that even seemingly innocent natural magic operated through the agency of demons.[23]

In keeping with medieval inversion, Luther's Satanic lair is located beneath his cabin in a cavern whose fetid darkness is lit by black candles. The configuration of Luther's sanctuary parallels the structure of a Catholic nave, with a sacrificial altar stone in the center and a high tabernacle behind it. In the place traditionally reserved for the crucifix and the consecrated host on the high altar, Luther has a Pan-like statue of Satan and a bowl for collecting blood. In this upside-down sacred space, Luther's ritual actions, including his approach to the tabernacle and his methods of intonation, mimic those of a Catholic priest conducting a Tridentine Mass, a form that had recently been abandoned as part of Vatican II.[24] The Black Mass likewise conforms closely to late-medieval constructions of the Witches' Sabbath as inverted Christian ritual. On Candlemas night, witches from all over the globe, including a voluptuous belly dancer, a cherubic milkmaid from Amsterdam, and a demonic monk, materialize at the command of the Sabbath Master. After an invocation dedicated to Satan, the coven commences the feast, which features plates piled high with meat—as opposed to the transubstantiated bread of Catholic communion—and copious amounts of alcohol. The drunken revelry is interrupted for the accusation, confession, and penitential lashing of one of the witches who has broken the rules of the coven.

As the feast draws to an end and the orgy begins, the Satanic fellowship awaits the arrival of both Tasha, who is to take her final vows to Satan and sign her blood pact with him, and the sacrificial victim, whose blood will be used to baptize the novitiate and to rejuvenate the coven for another year.

Tasha's friends make desperate attempts to save her from Luther and his coven. The professor, who believes in the reality of witchcraft and who is familiar with its history and rituals, uses his arcane knowledge to fight fire with fire. Garlic, he argues, will make them invisible to the witches, while pig's blood will kill the Satanists should they ingest it.[25] Although both of these suggestions prove effective, they are not enough to save Tasha from her fate as the new Sabbath Master of the parish. Likewise, the bravery, self-sacrifice, and love of her friends cannot save her from Satan's grasp, perhaps because she is "tainted in the blood," perhaps because of her own feminine weakness and irrationality. At no point in *The Witchmaker* do Tasha's friends use Christian symbols to fight Satanic witchcraft, nor do they invoke Christianity in any form. From the perspective of conservative twentieth-century mainstream culture, their alliance with paranormal psychology and belief in "New Age" possibilities placed them—along with other members of the Counter culture—in the same non–Christian category as the witches with whom they were fighting.[26] Accordingly, unlike *The City of the Dead*, there is no miraculous intervention in the hour of need, no redemptive *imitatio Christi*, no divine retribution for those who are lost. With Christianity stripped away, Satanic evil—now unchecked—is allowed to spread like an invisible plague, growing stronger and reaping chaos from just below the surface in an increasingly horrific world.

The basic category of inverted evil, the core elements of the Black Mass, as well as the problematic use (or absence) of Christian symbols as weapons against Satanic forces remained salient features of the horror genre throughout the 1970s. In a broad sense, the Satanic came to symbolize all that was wrong in that turbulent decade, including a widening divide between distrustful generations and an increasingly bitter culture war. In the Hammer films *Taste the Blood of Dracula* (1970) and *The Satanic Rites of Dracula* (1973), Christopher Lee as the vampire prince has been transformed into a Satanic high priest who presides over unholy sacraments.[27] In the first film, bitter and bored old men raise Dracula by reconstituting a phial of his dried blood upon the altar of an abandoned church; they then drink Dracula's blood-wine—in which he is fully present—from a chalice in a sacrilegious mockery of the Eucharist. As a consequence of their perverted whimsy, the old men find that they have unleashed a blood-sucking fiend upon the English countryside and endangered their own children who become the vampire's pri-

Lord Courtley (Ralph Bates) mixes his blood with that of Dracula in a chalice upon a black altar. In mockery of the Catholic Mass, Dracula will be born again through the living blood in the cup. *Taste the Blood of Dracula*, Peter Sasdy, Hammer (1970).

mary targets. In the second film, Dracula is the CEO of a Satanic corporation hell-bent on bringing about the end of the world by disseminating a new and extra-virile strain of the bubonic plague. This plot not only draws upon late-medieval connections between the Black Death and the demonic, but also reinforces contemporary conspiracy theories in which organized evil syndicates are responsible for global disasters.[28] The corporation is supported by a network of Satanic covens, their headquarters located at a bourgeois English country house; there Satanic rites are performed for their master, Dracula. In the film's opening scene, an Asian priestess garbed in black robes presides over a Black Mass in which a woman, blonde-haired and naked, lies stretched out upon a sacrificial altar. Familiar symbols abound: the inverted pentagram with the Goat of Mendes in a black circle upon the floor, a black altar cloth and black candles, a cockerel, and a sacred chalice for the collection and drinking of blood. The elderly male supplicants wear robes of red or white; some have inverted crosses drawn in blood on their foreheads, signifying the mark of Cain and parodying the crosses of black ash worn by Catholics on Ash Wednesday.[29] The old men have attended the Black Mass not only to please their boss, but also to convince the "demons of hell" to give them "power over frail mankind" so that they might collectively rule the world. The subtext of both *Taste the Blood of Dracula* and *The Satanic Rites of Dracula* is that society's patriarchs, bound together by their hellishly evil conservative philosophies, are nothing more than Satanic blood-suckers who will feed off of the younger generation in their quest for advancement and power—an understandable assessment when viewed against the backdrop of a disastrous economy and the exposure of corporate greed.

Satanic horror films not only accused the older generation of collaborating with the Devil, but also the younger generation, especially members of the American and British counter culture whose ideals of free love and rebellion seemed suspect in the sobering light of the 1970s. In the American grindhouse film *I Drink Your Blood* (1970), a small band of Satanic and unemployed hippies roams the countryside in their beat-up van. The film opens with the Native American leader of the coven, naked in the firelight, claiming to be the only Son of Satan; surrounded by his nude followers who look like a United Nations of Devil worshippers, he lifts a chalice of blood into which he has sprinkled some street drugs and in mockery of Christ says, "Put aside your worldly things, and come to me. Drink from this cup, pledge yourselves, and together, we'll all freak out."[30] The next day, their sexual urges unsatisfied by the previous night's orgy, they roll into a small town where they terrorize the inhabitants, dosing up a grandfather with LSD, raping young girls, murdering just about everyone else, and drinking their blood. Released one year after the Tate-LaBianca murders and the arrest of Charles Manson and members of his "family," *I Drink Your Blood* reflected conservative middle-class fears about the peace and love generation as an agent for chaotic and Satanic evil.

The British film *Blood on Satan's Claw* (1971) tells a similar tale of dangerous youth, but transports it back to the seventeenth century English countryside.[31] After discovering strange remains while tilling a field, the adolescent Angel is possessed by a Satanic being who uses her to gather skin for his new body. The increasingly hairy and goat-like Angel is assisted in this task by the other children of the village who reject the authority of their parents and follow only her commands to rape, maim, and kill. In *Blood on Satan's Claw*, Satanism and Satanists are imagined to be one and the same with Paganism and nature-worshipping flower children, a conflation of categories consistent with medieval scholastic constructions of Christian good and non–Christian evil.[32] Also consistent with medieval paradigms, Satanic evil in *Blood on Satan's Claw* is distinctly feminine, embodied in a dark, depraved, and irrational female who has allowed a demon to penetrate her. As in *City of the Dead*, the female leader of this young coven can only be destroyed by rational male goodness; Angel's reign of terror is brought to an end by the judge who slays both her and the demon creature with his cross-shaped phallic sword, thereby returning the village to divine order. In both *I Drink Your Blood* and

Blood on Satan's Claw, the message is the same: From the small towns of modern America to the primeval woods of early-modern England, willful young people left to their own devices without patriarchal guidance might easily become agents of chaos and conduits for Satanic evil.[33]

In alignment with late-medieval and early modern fears that witches and heretics were hidden just out of view and corrupting an otherwise pure Christendom, the Satanic films of the 1970s and their prolific descendants present a world in which Satanic "others" have penetrated every part; from the banality of the family home to the barren wilderness to the modern metropolis, there is no place safe from Satanic evil. The American made-for-television movie *The Devil's Daughter* (1973), for example, suggests that established Satanic covens are at work in upper-middle-class suburbs where flower-frocked aunties, doting grannies (Shelley Winters), and even an eccentric uncle (Abe Vigoda) or two worshiped the Devil, performing Black Masses and ritual sacrifices after a game of canasta. *The Devil's Rain* (1975), on the other hand, locates a coven of Satanists originally from seventeenth-century Puritan New England in an old ghost town—complete with a Satanic chapel—in the wild, wild, west. There, in a rugged western wilderness traditionally depicted as uncorrupted and untamed, the coven's high priest (Ernest Borgnine) conducts a Black Mass, raising Satan and thereby defiling nature.[34] Unlike the wholesome American Westerns upon which this film was modeled, the man in the black hat—or in this case the black robe—ultimately wins his battle against white-hatted Christian goodness. The American desert likewise becomes the Devil's playground in the 1971 film *The Brotherhood of Satan*, in which vacationers taking a road trip through the southwestern wastelands discover a coven of elderly Satanists who have sacrificed local children in their quest for immortality.

While *The Brotherhood of Satan* presents a hellish picture of the older generation feeding upon its young, the 1977 film *The Hills Have Eyes* presents the younger outlaw generation feasting upon the multi-generational American family in very literal ways. Captured while driving through the Nevada desert, a vacationing family is tormented by deranged and rapacious cannibals who are inexplicably hungry for infant flesh. Mars, Jupiter, Pluto and their cannibalistic followers are not Satanic *per se*; they are, however, a hellish inversion of the conservative Christian family which they are victimizing, as well as a representation of the wicked others, such as the Manson family and Devil-worshipping hippies, that middle-class Americans feared were lurking along the chaotic edges of society.[35]

Not only has Satanic evil permeated the middle-class suburbs, a signifier for American prosperity, and the rocky western desert, representative of rugged American individualism, but also America's largest metropolis, New York City, an icon for liberty and opportunity. On the big screen, New York has long been depicted as a dark place of danger; in the 1940s it was the perfect setting for *film noir* such as Val Lewton's films *Cat People* (1942) and *The Seventh Victim* (1943).[36] By the 1970s, however, filmmakers imagined New York as a veritable hell mouth and hotbed of Satanic activity.

Less than a decade before the very real "Son of Sam" David Berkowitz purportedly joined the Satanic cult that would drive him to murder helpless New Yorkers in 1976 and 1977, a fictional young woman named Rosemary and her husband moved into the Bramford, a gothic apartment building in the heart of Manhattan, where they would fall victim to a coven of aging Satanists.[37] Released in 1968 and directed by Roman Polanski, *Rosemary's Baby* was only the first in a long line of Satanic movies set in demonic New York apartment buildings and suggested the true dangers of communal living.[38] *The Sentinel* (1977) tells the tale of young model Allison Parker (Cristina Raines) who moves into a church-owned property in Brooklyn, in part because of the reasonable rent. Despite pressure from her boyfriend to move in with him, Allison remains committed to the single life of an independent woman. Too late, she discovers that her neighbors are demonic beings in the service of Satan, and that her apartment building serves as the portal to Hell.[39] In a much lighter vein, Dana Barratt (Sigourney Weaver) of *Ghostbusters* (1984) inhabits an apartment building that is an occult conduit for the quasi–Sumerian demon Gozer the Gozerian. *The Believers* (1987) features a father who moves to New York only to have his son become the target of a seemingly Satanic *brujeria* cult.[40] Both *End of Days* (1999) and *Bless the Child* (2000), drawing on American millennial fears at the turn of the twenty-first century, place the final battle between Canonical Good and Satanic Evil in New York's subways, streets, and slums—a veritable playground for the Devil.

From its construction as an inversion of Christian hierarchies in the Middle Ages to its depiction in the twentieth and twenty-first century horror films, the category of Satanic Evil has remained remarkably salient in its characteristics. The Black Mass, with its mockery of Christian ritual, as well as the belief that powerful and ambitious Satanic others have penetrated "mainstream" society and lurk in the shadowy realm just beneath its surface, remain deep and powerful structures in Anglo-American culture. Like our medieval predecessors, we believe (or want to believe) that "Lucifer and his followers are active everywhere and at all times."[41] In Britain, the Devil lurks along the foggy moors, the deep forests, the cobbled streets of London and the dusty corridors of Bray Castle. In America, Satan resides in suburbs and deserts, church basements and courtrooms, trailers and high-rises, in the imagined Puritan past, the horrors of the twentieth-century experience, the uncertain present, and even the future where he will haunt the deep and dark silence of outer space.[42] Across the Anglo world and across time, then, Satan has a permanent place of residence. The problem, of course, is that the place he desires most is far more fleshy. Satan doesn't need real estate; what he wants is a body.

Satanic Evil in Search of a Body: Conceiving the Antichrist

Much like the medieval learned culture that codified him and the Western culture that has nurtured him, Satan is obsessed with human bodies. In the modern Western imagination, Satan's obsession with human flesh takes many forms, one of which is his desire for a son, the Antichrist, to inherit his evil empire and usher in the End of Days. In ancient and early medieval texts, *an* antichrist might be anyone who denied Christ, such as a blasphemer or a heretic; *the* Antichrist, on the other hand, was imagined as a specific being who was "the summation of all evil"—an "inverse image of Christ's life and deeds" who would come as the Final Enemy to destroy humankind.[43] In the early fifth century, Jerome believed that the Antichrist would be fully human, the "one man in whom Satan will dwell in a corporeal way." In the eleventh century, Hildegard of Bingen believed that he would be a black monster born of the Church.[44] By the thirteenth and fourteenth centuries, the Antichrist was envisioned as a powerful religious or political leader, either an outsider such as the influential heretic Jan Hus, or an insider such as a king, the Holy Roman Emperor, or even the pope himself. Fear of a papal Antichrist ran high during the Babylonian Captivity in Avignon and the resultant Great Schism, periods in which the church became a monster with two and then three papal heads; since only one of the popes might hold the Keys of Saint Peter, the anti-popes could be nothing but abominations, pretenders, and therefore potential antichrists. During the Reformation, Antichrist accusations became a weapon in rhetorical discourse and propaganda between Catholics and Protestants alike. Over time, the character of the Antichrist was meticulously constructed as an absolute inversion of Christ; few texts, however, detailed how exactly he came into the world as a physical manifestation, primarily because authors were far more concerned with *who* and *when* he was rather than *how* he came to be.

In contrast, modern films about the Antichrist focus on his conception and birth and demand that he be physically born of Satan's seed.[45] For medieval scholars such as Thomas Aquinas who spent many a quill theorizing about the ability of demonic beings to engage in sexual intercourse with humans, Satanic reproduction—and in particular the creation of a perfect male child—was simply impossible. Satan and his demons had slimy bodies made of cold coagulated air, and could not produce seed of their own. In the form of a succubus they might steal a man's semen and transfer it to a sleeping woman as an incubus, but the resulting infant, mysterious and inconvenient as it may be, was nevertheless fully human.[46] On the other hand, in the world beyond the intellectual forays of celibate schoolmen, popular belief and folkways long held that copulation with fantastic evil beings was all too possible. If witches held orgies at their Sabbath and copulated with demons, mustn't half-demonic, half-human, and therefore monstrous children result from such unions?[47] And if a woman was impregnated by Satan himself, wouldn't their offspring be the true Son of Satan, the Antichrist, the signal that the world was near its end? Mid-century American and British filmmakers seemed to think so. Satanic reproduction and the coming of the Antichrist were popular cinematic themes in the late '60s through the '80s, a chaotic period in which the Counter culture crashed to the ground, the economy failed, crime rates tripled in major cities, war in the Middle East seemed imminent, terrorism dominated the news, and a New World Order seemed to be coalescing. For members of the Christian right, especially those associated with Evangelical movements that had descended from early–twentieth century Pentecostalism, all of these events were signs of the Apocalypse, the advent of which was to be heralded by the arrival of the Son of Satan and facilitated by an occult and extensive network of Satanic conspirators.[48]

In 1968, imaginary scenarios surrounding the conception and birth of Satan's only begotten son moved from Sunday sermons and conspiracy theories to the big screen with the release of *Rosemary's Baby*, Roman Polanski's interpretation of Ira Levin's best-selling novel of the previous year. The film tells the story of Rosemary Woodhouse (Mia Farrow), a lapsed Catholic who moves with her new husband to the gothic Bramford Apartments in New York City, a building occupied by a coven of Satanists whose *raison d'être* is to facilitate the birth of the Antichrist.[49] In return for a successful acting career, Rosemary's husband, Guy (John Cassavetes), sells both his soul and his wife's womb to Satan. An inversion of the light-filled and sanctified Annunciation of Christ, in which Mary was impregnated without sin through the word of God brought by the Angel Gabriel, the conception of the Antichrist in *Rosemary's Baby* is violent, dark, and impure. On the night that she and Guy decide to conceive their first child, Rosemary is drugged, stripped, and dragged into an empty apartment where she is tossed upon a bare mattress, tied down, and painted with blood as a sexual offering to Lucifer. Surrounded by her naked and chanting geriatric neighbors, Rosemary is mauled and mounted by a black, scaly being with reddish eyes; as he enters her, she seems to enjoy it, tossing her head back, lost in lust, until she realizes that "This is no dream. This is really happening!" The next morning she awakens in her bed and Guy reassures her that it was he who made love to her while she was semi-conscious (quite frankly, a concept as disturbing as non-consensual sex with the Devil).[50] As Rosemary's pregnancy progresses, her physical condition deteriorates; meanwhile, she begins to break down emotionally and mentally, becoming ever more convinced that her neighbors are Satanists who want to sacrifice her child. Drugged once again, she gives birth but is told upon awakening that her child has died. Hearing the cries of an infant in the apartment next door, she meets her son—dark, scaly, and shaggy in his black bassinet. He has his father's eyes.

The success of *Rosemary's Baby* heralded a modern wave of mainstream Satanic horror that eschewed the historical and gothic settings of the past and instead placed events in contemporary context. The emphasis was no longer on what Satan was, but what he is and *still could be*; unsurprisingly, the conception and birth of the Antichrist became popular *topoi* in this new subgenre. One film that plays with these themes, Hammer's *To the Devil a Daughter* (1976), tells the tale of Catherine (Nastassja Kinski), a young woman raised as a nun, and a defrocked Catholic priest, Father Rayner (Christopher Lee), whose sole purpose is the creation of "an avatar ... the personification of the Devil." In order for Catherine to truly become the Daughter of the Devil and bring down the Apocalypse, the heretical Rayner must first channel the demon Astaroth and impregnate a surrogate named Margaret.[51] Upon a darkened altar lit with black candles and surrounded by orgiastic Satanists, Rayner crawls beneath an inverted Crucifix, mounts Margaret, and completes the ritual act. With Rayner's and Astaroth's seed mixed within her, Margaret conceives an unholy fetus that must chew and claw its way out of the womb through her abdominal wall.[52] The result of this monstrous birth is a slimy demonic creature with sharp claws that is kept inside of a darkened incubator and fed human blood. Once it is implanted inside of Catherine's womb, she will be transformed into the Devil re-incarnate. The convoluted and inverse path to Satan's rebirth in this film is muddied by the work of the three screenwriters who diverged from Dennis Wheatley's novel and wrote the script as filming progressed; nevertheless, Wheatley's original vision of the inverted birth of the Devil makes sense within the specific rationality of medieval scholasticism and Aristotelian contrariety combined with elements of medieval medicine.[53] The demon Astaroth possesses Rayner's soul, which is

The defrocked priest Father Reynard (Christopher Lee) looks on while Margaret (Izabella Telezynska) is about to give birth to the demon Astaroth. Unlike a natural fetus, the demon will have to claw its way out through Margaret's abdominal wall to be born, thus her legs are tied. *To the Devil a Daughter*, Peter Sykes, Hammer (1976).

then passed through Rayner's sperm and into Margaret, who serves merely as an impure incubator for the unnatural fetus.[54] Born through matricide, the demon fetus awaits its pure vessel—the sweet virgin Catherine—who will open her birth canal to it and accept it within her so that evil may manifest in and through her flesh. Here, the Devil's rebirth is not merely a reversal of the natural processes of conception and parturition, but also a mockery of the Blessed Virgin Mary and a statement about the fundamentally evil nature of even seemingly innocent female flesh—an unholy and chaotic paradigm that medieval scholars would recognize quite well.

Subsequent films focusing on Satanic reproduction would continue to focus on inversion and unnatural gestation in keeping with medieval paradigms. In John Carpenter's *Prince of Darkness* (1987), an ancient vat of Satanic goo is housed in a church basement and watched over by a secret sect of priests. When the last priest begins to witness bizarre events, he calls in a team of experts in the areas of ancient languages, comparative theology, physics and molecular science to help prevent the Satanic goo's escape and reproduction. As members of the crew come into contact with the evil substance, which is transferred from person to person by regurgitation, they are

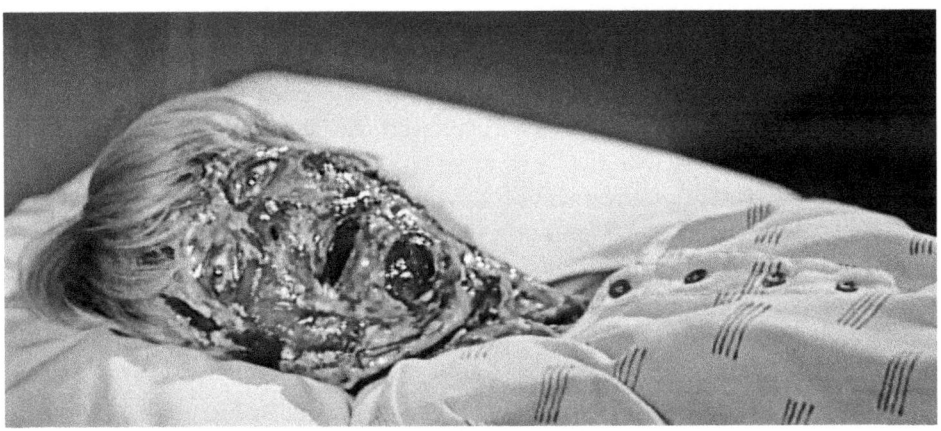

In an inversion of Christ's conception and birth, Kelly (Susan Blanchard) is impregnated through the mouth and eyes by a Satanic goo and becomes an inside-out and decaying vessel for the Antichrist. *Prince of Darkness*, John Carpenter, Universal (1981).

baptized by Satan and become his faithful minions. Two of Satan's converts bring the vat to the bedside of Kelly (Susan Blanchard), a nubile young woman who has been chosen as the vessel for the Antichrist. The lid opens, the goo rises to the ceiling and pools there in opposition to nature, then descends forcefully into the eyes, nose, and mouth of the prone girl—a bastardized inversion of Mary's conception of Jesus through the Angelic word of God.[55] Now that the Antichrist has found "a host in which to live," the unnatural gestation process can begin. Kelly's abdomen swells as if she is pregnant, and her flesh becomes pale, lacerated, and purulent; suddenly, the "fetus" within her is absorbed into her own tissue and she morphs into an abomination with an inside-out body, the inverted Son of Satan made incarnate. The Antichrist then searches for a looking-glass through which he might bring Satan, red-skinned and black-clawed, from the upside-down mirror dimension in which he is trapped and into the right-side-up physical world of humanity. Only the Christ-like self-sacrifice of one of the college students prevents Satan's ultimate return.

Films that take Satanic procreation with humans as their primary subject most often concentrate on the details surrounding the conception, gestation, and birth of the diabolical fetus, and only hint at the horrific consequences of the Antichrist's subsequent arrival. Recent films such as *The House of the Devil* (2009) and *The Last Exorcism* (2010) tell tales of sweet, blue-collar young women captured by underground Satanic covens, one operating under the guise of kindly old astrologers, the other under the auspices of a Lutheran congregation. In *House of the Devil*, Samantha (Jocelin Donahue) is forced to undergo a ritual in which she drinks a demon's blood, thereby conceiving Satan's spawn, while in *The Last Exorcism*, we are led to believe that the farmer's daughter Nell (Ashley Bell) conceives her demon fetus through traditional intercourse with the Devil upon an altar in the forest. Both films end in gestation (the announcement of Samantha's pregnancy) or unnatural birth (Nell delivers a deformed fetus on a bloody altar); in neither case are we told what happens after parturition.

The 2004 film, *Blessed: Samantha's Child* takes a more innovative approach to Satanic embodiment and childrearing. Samantha (Heather Graham) and her husband desperately want a child but are diagnosed as infertile; through a dark miracle, they are offered free in-vitro treatments at an ultramodern research facility where, unbeknownst to them, Samantha's eggs are fertilized with Satan's DNA (isolated from his blood which is kept in an ancient silver device that looks all too much like a *mezuzah*) and implanted in her womb. Throughout her pregnancy, the twin fetuses scratch and kick. Despite the desperate efforts of a rogue priest to kill Samantha and the evil she harbors, the twins are delivered and are absolutely perfect. Even though she knows that they are Satan's daughters, Samantha decides to raise them in an ideal middle-class home. The film ends with the blonde-haired and blue-eyed twins, now about five, at a Halloween party where, dressed as angels and silent as snow, they use their powers to kill a bratty boy dressed as the Devil.

Samantha's desperate desire to become a mother drove her to keep and raise her evil babies; John Carpenter's *Pro-Life* (2006), however, asks what happens when the mother of a demon fetus wants to terminate her pregnancy. The story centers on Angelique Burcell (Caitlin Wachs), the fifteen-year-old daughter of a violent Pro-Life activist. Angelique is violently raped by a demon and is gestating at an unnatural rate. After only a few days, she is rapidly approaching term. For help, she turns to a local abortion clinic; by the time the doctors believe her unlikely tale, it is too late. Her father (Ron Perlman) and brothers break into the clinic, thrust the vacuum-suction device between the lead doctor's spread legs in a mockery of an abortion, and massacre other patrons of the clinic as part of "God's work." Meanwhile, Angelique's demon baby is born. With the head of an infant, the scaly body of a demon, and the legs of a crab, it wails and scurries away into the shadows. It's so hideous, even its mother can't love it; Angelique shoots her offspring in the head and it dies. The demon father, who has been searching for his son, suddenly appears in the delivery room, clearly despondent. Finding the dead infant on the floor, the demon lifts it to his breast, cradling him lovingly, the only character in the film to show either love or compassion. The weeping demon and his dead son descend into hell, while the mother, sitting in a bloody mess, utters, "God's will is done." Angry and misanthropic, this film is a reflection not only of Carpenter's outrage at the abortion debate in American culture and politics, but also of our own fears and revulsion of the human body and the inhuman other, inverted and demonic, that we imagine and create all around us.

Of course, biological conception and birth are not the only options; one might always opt for adoption which, in terms of narrative, helps to sidestep some of the complexities of Satanic reproduction. The Antichrist in *The Omen* (1976), for example, is a child named Damien (Harvey Stephens) who was born of a jackal, making him not only the Son of the Devil but also a son of a bitch.[56] As an infant, Damien serves as a changeling for Robert Thorn's (Gregory Peck) stillborn son who we later learn was murdered. While adopting this orphaned infant at first seems a miraculous way to avoid his wife's grief and proceed with raising a family, Thorn soon learns that bringing up other people's children can present some challenges—especially when the biological father, Satan, is continually intervening on his child's behalf. Picking up where *Rosemary's Baby* left off, *The Omen* asks hard questions about how to raise evil children in general, and how to rear the Antichrist in particular.

The fundamentally creepy and potentially evil nature of children in horror cinema has a long legacy. *The Bad Seed* (1956) explored the idea that evil intentions and behavior might be genetic and be transmitted from parent to child in the act of conception. In the film, the little girl Rhoda (Patty McCormack) is terrifying not only because she is a homicidal psychopath, the grandchild of a serial killer, but also because she is seemingly perfect and yet somehow "off," a cold, calculating adult trapped in the purportedly innocent body of a child.[57] Unlike the fully human Rhoda, Damien's hidden and supernatural genetic background makes him far more subtle; with "the looks of a sheep but the heart of a demon," Damien does not need to act upon his evil impulses, but merely will them into reality through the adults who serve him.[58] Perhaps most terrifying of all, Damien can't be stopped by either human or supernatural means. In consultation with a Catholic priest, Thorn is told, "You must take communion, you must drink the blood of Christ and eat his flesh, for only if He is within you can you defeat the son of the Devil." These signifiers of Canonical Good, long effective against all forms of inverted Evil, are useless against this little Antichrist who, innocent and beautiful, survives both of his parents; at his father's funeral, he turns towards the audience and smiles sweetly—and with that, seals our doom.

Fallow Flesh: Demon Possession and the Satanic Body

The Satanic obsession with human flesh does not stop with the desire for progeny; if creating new hybrid flesh is complex and theologically tenuous, there still exits a sea of human bodies ready for demonic occupancy. The idea of demonic possession, both ancient and medieval, is facilitated by a belief in the invisible world and the conception of a primarily unbounded human body open to visible and invisible forces. For physicians such as the fourth-century BCE Hippocrates of Cos and the second-century CE Galen, the human body was susceptible to humoral changes due to dietary intake, exercise, sexual activity, and other forms of physical and therapeutic regimen. Likewise, the body lay open to less tangible forces such as the movement of stars, the changing of seasons, and the blowing of winds potentially laden with demons, all of which might penetrate the body through porous openings in the skin, called *stoma*, as well as through the very act of breathing.[59] Once inside the body, the actions of the heart converted environmental air into *pneuma*, which then became the vital spirit that influenced the mind and imagination and, according to Aristotle and later Aquinas, the very shape of the physical body.[60] Spirit possession, demonic and otherwise, was not merely a function of popular superstition or learned theology in the ancient and medieval worlds, but a very real and medical possibility.

In the thirteenth and fourteenth centuries, spirit possession came under the close scrutiny of scholars concerned with the categories of canonical good and inverted evil. That possession was *possible* was not in question; the real issue was discerning what type of spirit was possessing an individual. This concern was especially acute in the case of women who were constructed as cold, moist, and irrational, and therefore open to possession by both divine and demonic forces.[61] To this end, scholars focused on the body as a locus of possession and asked how different spirits might enter and occupy our inner architecture. Where did spirits go and how did they function within a possessed individual? In the aggregate, scholars' responses fell into a familiar bipartite schema. The upper region of the body, the dwelling place of the heart and the soul within it, belonged predominantly to divine spirits; since the soul was a reflection of God, it was sealed against demonic transgression. According to Nancy Caciola in *Discerning Spirits: Divine and Demonic Possession in the Middle Ages*, academic theologians held that the Eucharist taken into the body through the mouth did not descend to the stomach to be digested with grosser matter but instead was absorbed directly into the heart, the holy of holies within the body.[62] Once possessed of the Holy Spirit through the Eucharist, divine revelation, or ecstatic union, the mind of the holy woman was filled with warm ethereal light that radiated from the holy tabernacle of the heart; the balance of her body melted away, transformed into purified flesh.

While divine spirits dwelled above, demons dwelled in the lower regions of the body, in the viscera, "the most debased and unclean centers, the coolest and moistest portion of the human anatomy."[63] Women, being qualitatively cold and moist, made perfect targets for demonic beings in search of a home. Because of their sluggish intellect and carnal natures, women were easily tempted into sin, opening a pathway to demonic invasion; likewise, the spongy nature of the female body provided numerous moist openings through which demons might penetrate and countless internal caverns in which they might lodge.[64] Once inside, demons could travel through the blood and into the cool moist brain, causing visual and auditory hallucinations and encouraging sinful behavior on the part of their host. Having corrupted the *pneuma*, demons could cause the voice of the possessed to change, forcing them to speak in strange tongues, grunts, or growls. This demon-laced fetid bodily air was emitted through the eyes, ears, nose and mouth and was toxic to those who came into contact with it. Demons not only polluted the *pneuma* and mind but also the body that it suffused, contorting its flesh, causing spastic fits and mania, frothing at the mouth, convulsive vomiting, urination, and defecation. Pale and twisted inversions of canonical goodness, the bodies of the demon possessed became warped reflections of their formerly human selves. Trapped within this hellish torment was the soul which, peering out through the heart and witnessing the horror just beyond the tabernacle, could do nothing but await divine help.

In the medieval world, demon possession was healed through contact with the divine. Early miracle tales recount the expulsion of demons through the prayers of the afflicted, their families, clerics, and even saints who might actively intercede on the part of the suffering.[65] Contact with holy relics, including the corporeal remains of saints (bones, hair), their belongings (staffs, capes, girdles), or objects that had touched them (*brandea, aqua loto*) might also cause a demon to flee from a human body. Similarly, the sign of the cross, the application of holy water, the recitation of the Mass, and contact with or consumption of the Eucharist were effective in the expulsion of demons.[66] Like the human heart which is sealed against evil by the presence of the Holy Spirit, these relics, rituals, and sacred objects were imbued with the divine and therefore intolerable to demonic entities which often fled from them with explosive force. In hagiographical accounts, the flight of a demon from human flesh was often marked by radical purgation, such as vomiting, defecation or the emission of a foul sweat, all of which served as visible and disturbing signs that a healing event had taken place. The expulsion of demons, long the provenance of local saints, had throughout the Middle Ages become a formalized process under the auspices of a highly organized and bureaucratic church increasingly embattled by heretics and others who questioned its authority. Just as the power to canonize saints was removed from local purview and centralized in the papacy, so too was the power to cure demon possession taken from local saints and healers, codified in text as the rite of exorcism, and placed in the hands of authoritative members of the clergy.[67] In this form of demonic expulsion, the male priest with his book of Latin rites serves as a conduit for divine power that forces the demon to flee from the possessed individual who—in this paradigm—is almost always female. The male priest is warm, dry, celibate, and therefore a perfect vessel for the warm light of the divine; the female is cold, moist, weak and corrupted, the perfect abode for the cold darkness of the demonic.[68] If pure of heart, the warm male might counteract the cold demon within the female body and liberate her from demonic pollution, rendering her tenuously sweet and innocent once again.

Late-medieval paradigms for demonic possession and exorcism, as well as the binary categories of warm-male-divine and cold-female-demonic, have persisted in modern horror films such as *The Exorcist* (1973) and the legion of imitators that continue to follow in its wake. *The Exorcist*, based on William Peter Blatty's 1971 novel of the same name, tells the story of Regan (Linda Blair), a rosy-cheeked and innocent girl on the edge of puberty, and her demonic transformation into a melancholic monstrosity, the paradigm of earthbound evil.[69] Regan's metamorphosis begins when she plays with a Ouija board in the basement of her Washington, D.C., home while her mother is busy on the set of her new film.[70] Through the witch board, Regan meets the seemingly harmless Captain Howdy, a name reminiscent of children's shows such as Captain Kangaroo and Howdy Doody; in truth, Captain Howdy is an ancient demon named Pazuzu who has recently been liberated from a cavern within the dark, cold earth to which he is elementally connected.[71] When Regan experiences powerful emotional reactions to her father's rejection, her mother's relationships with men, and her own burgeoning sexuality, the cold demon seizes his chance to own her, initially clouding her mind with perverse words and thoughts and causing erratic behavior. The demon then infects her lungs and *pneuma*, the internal bodily air which according to medieval medical theory was responsible for sense perception, intellection, and motion; the breath rising from her foul mouth becomes a fetid and icy air that fills her room with toxic fumes. This same infected *pneuma* allows the demon to manipulate Regan's voice, now deep and rasping, now imitating the voice of her exorcist's dead mother, now speaking backwards.[72] Regan's demonic *pneuma* is likewise exuded from her dilated pupils and fetid ears, facilitating her preternatural vision and hearing. Traveling through her inner architecture, the demon suffuses the young girl's physical being, allowing her body to contort into impossible positions, causing her once-pink flesh to become pale and grey, stinking and ruptured with fissures. From its hiding place in her dark and moist digestive tract, his favorite resting place, the demon causes the ceaseless vomiting of impossibly green bile and dribbling of yellow mucous; from her groin, he directs her to violently masturbate with a crucifix and grind her mother's face into her bloody pudenda.

From deep within this contorted, inverted, and unholy vessel—which conforms to medieval structures of feminine and Satanic evil—the untouched soul of little Regan, trapped in her pure heart by the power of the demon and her own horrendous flesh, sends out a desperate plea etched on her abdominal skin: "Help Me."[73] Help comes in the form of Damien Karras (Jason Miller), a young priest wrestling with his own sort of demon—his wavering faith—and Lankester Merrin (Max von Sydow), an old priest of great faith and familiar with Pazuzu.[74] Both men use the Roman Rite, ardent prayer, the sign of the cross, and ritual objects, such as the crucifix and holy water, in their battle against Satanic evil. Through the arduous process, Merrin's faith remains strong, but his physical heart is weak and he perishes from his efforts, leaving Karras to finish the exorcism. Karras, trained as a psychologist and skeptical of the Roman Rite, is unable to finish the ritual by formal means; to save Regan, he offers himself up to the demon, who willingly jumps from one sow to another. As it enters Karras' body, his flesh is immediately subsumed by the demonic presence, turning gray and black; his eyes widen, his voice changes and he begins to choke on the fetid fumes rising within him. In an act of self-sacrifice, he jumps out of the window to his death on the staircase below, where he receives Last Rites from his friend, Father Dyer.[75] Regan, liberated at last, has no recollection of what happened to her. Her body returns to its former flush of innocence and youth, and with almost all evidence of her former trauma erased, she journeys into young adulthood.[76]

The medieval constructions of male-coded canonical goodness and female-coded Satanic evil made manifest in *The Exorcist* are salient features of its numerous prequels (*Dominion*, 2005; *Exorcist: The Beginning*, 2004), sequels (*Exorcist II: The Heretic*, 1977; *Exorcist III*, 1990) and exploitations (the Blaxploitation film *Abby*, 1974; the German softcore film *Magdalena: Possessed by the Devil*, 1974; Italy's Giallo version *L'Anticristo*, 1974; the Spanish entry *Exorcismo*, 1975; *Cathy's Curse*, 1977).[77] In the twenty-first century, possession and exorcism films continue to be an extremely popular and profitable sub-genre of supernatural horror, including films of varying quality such as *Exorcism* (2003), *The Exorcism of Emily Rose* (2005), *Exorcism: The Possession of Gail Bowers* (2006), *Blackwater Valley Exorcism* (2006) *Chronicles of an Exorcism* (2008), and *Exorcismus: La Possession de Emma Evans* (2010). Each of them tells the familiar tale of a troubled young woman who transforms into a demonic being. Many of these films use the "based on true events" trope to enhance the frightening possibility that demons might exist and able to penetrate vulnerable female flesh.[78] This sense of "reality" is emphasized in films that utilize documentary style, found footage, and point-of-view filming techniques. For example, *Anneliese: The Exorcist Tapes* (2011), like *The Exorcism of Emily Rose* (2005) and *Requiem* (2006) before it, purportedly tells the tale of Anneliese Michel, a young woman from Bavaria who suffered from convulsions, heard voices, saw strange visions, and believed that she was possessed by demons. When physicians were unable to treat her, she was placed in the care of a priest whose efforts to exorcise her ultimately contributed to her death at the age of twenty-four. Unlike its cinematic predecessors, *Anneliese: The Exorcist Tapes* uses a documentary format and "real footage" woven throughout the narrative to support its "true to life" claims. *The Last Exorcism* (2010), *The Last Exorcism II* (2012), *The Devil Inside* (2012), and *The Vatican Tapes* (2015) likewise capitalize on this format, weaving narrative, found footage, and interviews to create a sense of reality. In the *Paranormal Activity* series (2009, 2010, 2011, 2012), a family whose ancestor signed a pact with the Devil is stalked and possessed by a demonic entity; safe in their own homes, voyeuristic viewers witness these events through security cameras, digital hand-held cameras, cell phones, and the like. The films of *Paranormal Activity* are made all the more terrifying because of their setting in the family home. The audience, as the narrator, must weave their way through the otherwise familiar lives of the family on the screen, piece together the evidence, and make meaning of the demonic events unfolding before their eyes.

The use of POV and documentary film styles is prevalent in paranormal investigation programs, "reality shows" in which the specific rationality of canonical evil in general and demonic possession in particular play fundamental roles.[79] The team in *Paranormal State*, for example, encounters many traditional and non-traditional homes that are haunted by the angry or sad spirits of the dead who are detected by the use of modern "scientific" equipment and good old-fashioned mediums; having been contacted, these spirits are encouraged to cross over into the next life, to move into the light, and to leave the afflicted family in peace. The worst cases, however, are not those of haunted houses, but haunted people. In the *Paranormal State* episode "I Am

Six," for example, the team is called into "the age-old battle between heaven and hell" when they are contacted by the family of Laura, a twenty-six-year-old tormented by a demonic force. She has been physically beaten, sexually assaulted, drowned in the tub, and stalked by black shadows that bring with them icy cold air. Words have materialized on her stomach "as if written from within," just as claw marks have been scratched into her walls and pentagrams burned into her flesh. In between bouts of vomiting and convulsions, during which she is spritzed with holy water that burns her, Laura reveals that she might have unleashed the entity when she conducted an informal EVP session, during which she engaged a disembodied female voice in conversation. The team leader, Ryan Buell, realizes that he is dealing with a demon and calls in the assistance of the psychic Chip Coffey (who hears the demon say, "Get rid of all of this fucking religious stuff") and an Episcopal priest. In the course of the investigation, the demon's name is revealed to be Six, or "legion"; accordingly, the priest approaches Laura, weak and weeping in her childhood bed draped with a pink chiffon canopy, and says with paternalistic machismo, "This thing is not going to leave of its own accord. It's going to have to be removed by force." The balance of the episode deals with the exorcism itself, all of the elements of which are familiar to the audience who already knows exactly what is going to happen, and how.

From the later Middle Ages to the horror films of the twentieth and twenty-first centuries to "reality-based" paranormal television, the depiction of Satanic evil as an inversion of Christian goodness is remarkably consistent. The Black Mass is conducted by powerful "others" who have made Satanic pacts in their quest for personal power and world domination; just out of view, these evil covens, robed in black, sacrifice innocents, drink their blood, and participate in inverted Christian rituals. The Satanic Body is melancholic, cold and dark, foul and poisonous, hungry for sex and violence. Satanic forces swirl through the air seeking vulnerable female flesh, weak and malleable, either to incubate the Antichrist or to possess as a plaything. Against these forces and those who worship them, only the traditional rites and symbols of the Catholic church, and in rarer cases faith in the Christian God, can prevail. Transported through time and space, medieval scholars such as Thomas Aquinas, Psuedo-Albetus Magnus, Johannes Nider, and Heinrich Kramer would find much in our supernatural horror films to be frighteningly familiar. Sitting beside us in a darkened theater, they would recognize all of the codes and anticipate what was hidden around every corner. Would they mistake us for a culture of faith? Or would they recognize us for what we truly are—obsessed by the devil?

3

Wanton Flesh and Poisoned Breath

Crafting the Satanic Witch

> *"Governed by a good spirit, [women] are the most excellent in virtue ... governed by an evil spirit, they indulge the worst possible vices."—*
> *Malleus Maleficarum*

In the thirteenth and fourteenth centuries, theologians such as Thomas Aquinas and William of Auvergne used Aristotelian modes of thought and natural philosophy to codify the realm of pure goodness and its inversion, corrupt evil. Divine goodness found its source in the unified will of God and the Empyrean beyond the bounded cosmos, a realm of light, translucence and weightlessness populated by angelic beings all the way down to the lunar sphere. Satanic evil was rooted in the chaotic and Hellish realm of the corrupt earth, a place of darkness, opacity, and density populated by melancholic devils and the sinful humans who justifiably served as their prey. If divine goodness was linked with the incorporeal and spiritual, then Satanic corruption was interminably linked to the material and the fleshly—an inverted paradigm that caused theological discomfort in light of the Church's ongoing war with dualist Cathar heretics for whom matter was inherently evil and unredeemable. Faced with this intricacy, theologians argued that nature itself was not evil; it was, however, subject to demonic forces that had corrupted an inherently good creation through their own willful disobedience.

In this chimerical sublunary realm where things were never quite what they seemed, theologians sought to discern between that which was truly miraculous and that which was mere demonic illusion. The need for discernment was especially acute when dealing with malleable female bodies that might serve as vessels for either divine purity or Satanic corruption. In defining the qualities of holy female flesh, theologians constructed the saintly body, which was warm, dry and humorally balanced. A conduit to the ethereal realm, the holy woman not only experienced ecstatic union with God but also radiated light, levitated, and had the power to heal. Theologians likewise codified unholy flesh in alignment with the inverted qualities of earthbound and demonic evil. This maleficent body, which would eventually become that of the Satanic witch, was cold, dry, and humorally imbalanced; a willing channel for the demonic, she could fly through the air, hungered for human blood, emitted poison through her eyes and mouth, and had the power to harm or heal at the Devil's pleasure. Scholars attributed the preternatural powers of both the holy woman and the witch to their unique anatomy and physiology; in support of their theologically based arguments, they used the authority of Aristotle, the language of learned medicine, and select elements of learned medical theory. When viewed through the lens of scholasticism, phenomena such as the evil eye and the rapacious nature of witches carried the weight of unquestionable authority and appeared both logical and provable by physical means. The same rational and medical foundations used to construct the maleficent woman in the later Middle Ages would be used to elaborate the anatomy and physiology of the Satanic witch through generations of witchcraft treatises and witch trials, and would influence cultural perceptions of feminine evil from the early modern to the postmodern period.

Fundamentals of Learned Medieval Medicine

The medieval academic medicine that would serve as a handmaiden to theologians as they constructed holy and unholy flesh was rooted in the ideas of Greek Hippocrates and his chronologically distant Roman disciple, Galen. Their works had been collected and preserved along with myriad other medical texts by eighth-century Muslim scholars at the Bayt-al-Hikma, or House of Wisdom, in Baghdad, the capital of the Abbasid Caliphate.[1] There, Muslim scholars translated medical treatises from Greek and Latin into Arabic, and wrote learned commentaries on them. Muslim and Jewish scholars augmented the ancient medical corpus by composing original treatises such as the *Almansoris* of Rhazes, the *Qanun* and *Poem on Medicine* of Avicenna, the *De Melancholia* of Ishaq Ibn Imran, the *Viaticum* of Al-Jazzar, and the *Pantegni* of Al-Magusi.[2] These texts were copied and translated from Arabic into Latin by twelfth-century scholars such as Constantine the African, a Tunisian monk of the Benedictine monastery at Monte Cassino, and disseminated to learning centers such as the medical school at Salerno, Italy.[3] Similar translations were taking place on the Iberian peninsula as Latin scholars arrived in the newly conquered cities of Toledo and Cordoba. Working alone, as Gerard of Cremona, or in translation teams composed of a Muslim, a Jew, and a Christian, Greco-Arabic medical texts were rendered into Latin and ultimately disseminated to the newly founded universities of Bologna, Montpellier, and Paris.[4] There, along with Aristotle, medical texts became a part of the university curriculum, and by the twelfth century both Paris and Montpellier had faculties of medicine that taught in the doctoral program alongside the faculties of theology and law.[5] Thirteenth-century scholastic theologians such as Albertus Magnus, Thomas Aquinas, Jacques de Vitry, and Thomas Cantimpré shared an academic language of discourse rooted in the works of Aristotle, which were the very foundation of the masters curriculum, and in the learned medical texts that circulated among scholars in the graduate programs.[6] Thomas Cantimpré, for example, not only wrote theological treatises such as *De Bonum Universale de Apibus* and the hagiographies of several holy women, including Lutgard of Aywières, but also an encyclopedic work, *De Natura Rerum*, which contained a section on medicine and pharmacology.[7]

According to medieval medical theory, the human body was a microcosmic reflection of the macrocosmic world of which it was an integral part. Like all matter, the body was composed of the four elements—fire, air, water, and earth—each with their attendant qualities, and each in different proportions. The four elements were likewise expressed in the four bodily humors: yellow bile, which was warm and dry and therefore aligned with both elemental fire and Summer; blood, which was warm and wet and therefore aligned with elemental air and Spring; phlegm, which was cold and wet and linked to elemental water and Winter; and black bile, which was cold and dry and linked to elemental earth and Autumn.[8] Every human body contained these four humors in different proportions, with one humor generally predominating, leading to the concept of a humoral complexion, temperament, or disposition. A person in whom blood was the dominant humor, for example, was said to have a sanguine complexion characterized by ruddy skin and disposed toward carnality and the consumption of red wine.[9] While each body had its own unique state of humoral balance, resulting in general health, allostasis was rarely if ever achieved, nevermind maintained. Like a porous clay vessel, the medieval body was open to environmental and cosmic forces that had the power to engender or impede humoral production and alter the shape and appearance of the body itself.

According to Galen and his medieval commentators, the natural humoral balance of the body might be disrupted by five binary pairs of "non-natural things," including: air and environment, food and drink, motion and

3. *Wanton Flesh and Poisoned Breath: Crafting the Satanic Witch* 71

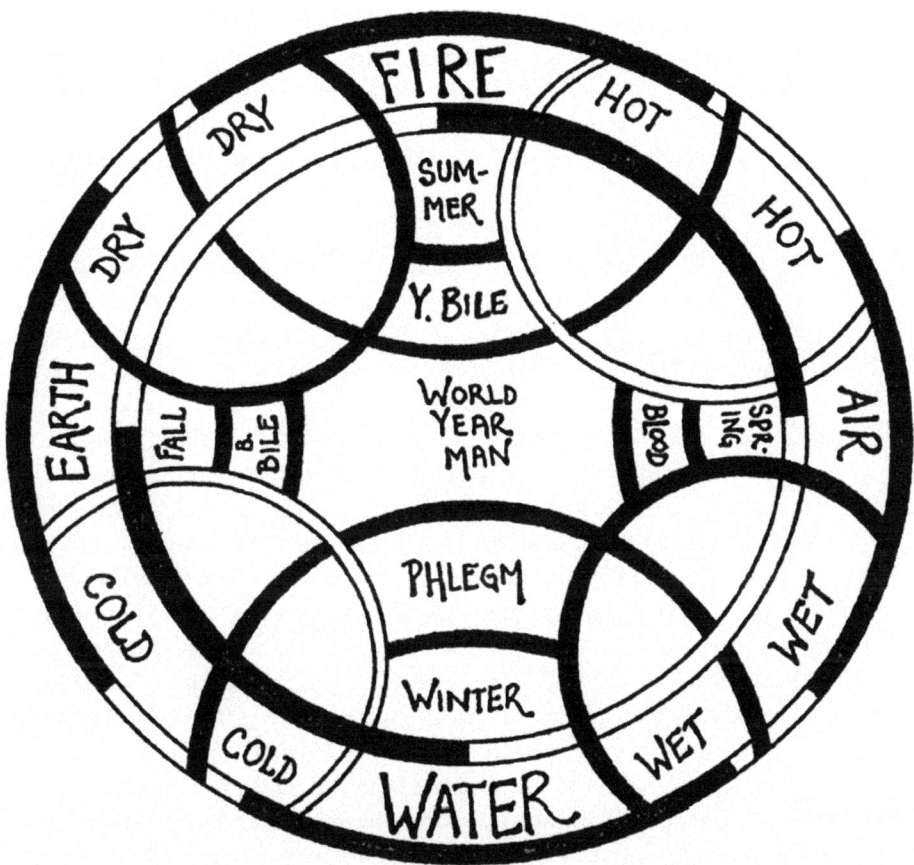

Author's line drawing and translation of the "Mundus, Annus, Homo" roundel from Isidore of Seville's *De Rerum Natura* (Munich, Bayerische Staatsbibliothek, clm 16128, folio 16r, seventh century).

rest, sleeping and waking, retention and excretion, as well as the passions of the soul.[10] The belief that environmental air played a critical role in the etiology of illness can be traced back to the Hippocratic corpus upon which much of Galen's work was based. According to Hippocratic treatises such as *Airs, Waters, and Places* as well as the *Epidemics*, a working knowledge of an individual patient's regional atmosphere, including the direction of the prevailing winds and seasonal weather patterns, was vital to the practice of medicine since these environmental factors were among the root causes for humoral imbalance. In *Airs, Waters, and Places*, for example, Hippocrates argued that through shifts in the winds and the weather, "the digestive organs of men undergo a change."[11] Digestion was the central process through which the body used vital heat to break down food into blood; this blood was then refined through "cooking" into phlegm, yellow bile, and black bile.[12] *Airs, Waters, and Places,* the *Epidemics,* and *On the Sacred Disease* all warn that shifts between the cold and dry north wind, called *Septentrio,* and the warm and moist south wind, called *Meridies,* as well as the corresponding transitional seasons of spring and fall were particularly dangerous to human health.[13] When exposed to the winds of *Septentrio,* the body was robbed of vital heat and became chilled, a process that restricted digestion and produced an excess of black bile. Those exposed to the excessive moisture of the southerly "plague" winds of *Meridies,* on the other hand, were likely to have heads "of a humid and pituitous constitution, and their bellies subject to frequent disorders, owing to the phlegm running down from the head."[14] The invisible movements of the air and the seasons—and even the stars—might lead to physical changes in the human body and its humoral processes.[15]

Just as macrocosmic forces might disrupt humoral balance, so too might more quotidian microcosmic elements and activities cause physical change. Both Hippocratic and Galenic medicine in its ancient and medieval permutations emphasized the importance of diet for the maintenance of health. Food and drink, like all matter below the moon, had inherent binary qualities of coldness or warmth, dryness or moisture, in varying degrees. Foods that were warm and moist, such as red meat and red wine, engendered the production of the warm and moist humor, blood; "wine is by nature hot, and new wine is warmer and more nutritious than old. Dark wines (*vina negra*) nourish the blood."[16] Drinking water, on the other hand, encouraged the excessive production of cold wet phlegm and might lead to a condition called *hydropsy* in which the body became morbidly tumescent, especially in those whose constitutions were naturally phlegmatic to begin with. The consumption of eels was particularly dangerous, since they were believed to have "melancholy flesh" and "black blood" that might produce an excess of black bile and the effects of *melancholia* once assimilated into the body.[17] In the *Isagoge,* an eleventh-century Latin translation of Hunayn Ibn Ishaq's Arabic commentary on Galen's *Tegni,* Johannitius not only classifies foods as "good and bad according to the humors they produce" but also as either "heavy" or "light." To these classifications, Constantine the African's eleventh-century Latin translation of Isaac Israeli's Arabic treatise, *On Diets,* adds "thinness" and "viscosity," and classifies food and drink as hot-cold, dry-moist, heavy-light, and thin-viscous according to the inherent nature of the foodstuff in relation to the environment that it once inhabited.[18] From the perspective of medieval medicine, anything that was introduced into the body—either through the local environment or through the ingestion of substances—influenced its humoral composition and, in some cases, the very structure of the body itself.

In order to practice good medicine, the medieval physician required an intimate understanding of each of his patients as unique individuals. He not only had to be familiar with the patient's fundamental humoral temperament, dietary habits, and living environment, including the orientation of the winds that blew into both home and body, but also his or her bodily regimen, including levels of physical activity and amount of rest, how much time was spent sleeping and how much awake. Physical exercise caused the body to produce heat and, in healthy moderation, encouraged digestion and humoral balance. In men, excessive exercise in the summer could cause a cooling of the stomach and restrict digestion; in women, excessively strenuous activity on a routine basis could cause the cessation of menstruation and the development of male features, such as large muscles and a beard.[19] Like exercise, sleep was vital to humoral balance, for "food is digested optimally during sleep, not in the stomach alone but in the whole mass of the animal."[20] During sleep, food was broken down in the stomach and passed to the liver where it was converted to blood, then to the organs where nutriments were absorbed and superfluities released; upon completion of this process, a person awoke to start the cycle anew.[21] It was also during sleep that the coolness of the brain and the heat of the stomach became balanced, the brain became bathed in moisture, and the vapors that had accumulated in its cells dissipated through dreams.

Medieval medical practice required that a physician be aware not only of his patient's vaporous excretions, but also his or her physical waste products as well. According to a late thirteenth to early-fourteenth century scholar and physician, Arnau de Villanova, the process of diagnosis entailed a consideration of the "things excreted from the body, first of the animate parts [associated with the head and the brain], as what flows from the nose and ears and mouth, then the spiritual ones [associated with the lungs and chest] like what we spit out, finally from the nutritive members [associated with the digestive tract and reproductive organs] like urine and *secessus*, or from all, like sweat."[22] The rate, quantity, and quality of such excretions were critical to the diagnosis of humoral imbalance and the prognosis for cure, for "things given off are all changed in quality and quantity by damage to the natural operations or by a bad quality of the body or both."[23] Urine that was cold, thin, and watery was a sign of excessive phlegm, while cold, blackish and thick urine suggested an excess of black bile.[24] Male and female seed were considered as bodily effluvia and, like urine and feces, were monitored in relation to their retention, excretion, quality, and quantity. A patient's sexual regimen, therefore, was a vital element of a physician's assessment.

According to medieval medical theory, humoral fluctuations disrupted not only physical but also mental health. Galen argued that the body contained a substance known as *pneuma*, a sort of rarified air produced through respiration. Air was drawn into the lungs and close to the heart where it was refined into the *vital spirit*, which then traveled to different areas of the body: *vital spirit* existed in the brain and nerves as rational or *psychic pneuma*, in the heart as *spiritive pneuma*, and in the liver as *appetitive pneuma*. Using this tripartite schema, Galen charged the brain (because it contained the purest rational spirit) with governing the lower spirits that resided in the heart and base animal instincts that resided in the liver and lower regions. By managing the flow of blood and *pneuma* through the vessels or "nerves," the rational brain could control the irrational spirits that dwelled in the lower members.[25] In his *Passions and Errors of the Soul*, Galen argues that the rational mind must govern emotions and physical desires in order to maintain bodily health; to give in to gluttony, for example, is to disrupt the body's humoral balance and to risk illness.[26] Because material causes such as humoral fluctuations could disrupt the production and flow of rational *pneuma*, Galen argued that the state of the body might influence the mind's ability to control the lower spirits.[27] Physical imbalances might cause increases in appetite and irrational behaviors, just as irrational behaviors might increase physical appetites. For the ancient or medieval Galenic physician, intemperate emotional responses from patients could be considered a symptom or cause of bodily illness and were assessed accordingly.[28]

The treatment, if not the cure, of illness was elicited by a rebalancing of an individual's bodily system. One therapeutic approach was the physical removal of excessive or corrupted humors through purgation. Two of the most common methods for purging humors such as yellow bile and phlegm included the use of emetics such as hellebore and radishes, which were taken orally and induced immediate and violent vomiting, and the use of medicated clysters, or enemas, which caused peristalsis and diarrhea. In either case, the experience of acute evacuation would provide a catharsis for the patient, an abundance of humors for the physician to analyze, and visual evidence for the otherwise invisible processes of healing.[29] Another more generalized therapy used as both prophylaxis and treatment was phlebotomy, or bloodletting, which was performed through surgical venesection or, less commonly, the application of leeches. Since blood contained an admixture of all four humors, each of which might become corrupt and therefore toxic, its purgation constituted a form of humoral cleansing. While the manual act of blood-letting was often performed by barber-surgeons, physicians prescribed the location of the cut and the time of day and year (in cases of prophylaxis) at which it should occur based on a medical textual tradition extending from Galen, through Ibn-Jazzar, Abulcasis, and Avicenna. "A general rule has it," according to this tradition, "that for humoral excess from the neck up, the *cephalic* vein is opened; from the neck down, the, *basilic* or *hepatic* vein; and for either sort of excess, the median or cardiac vein."[30] Medieval treatises on phlebotomy contained charts called "vein men" that depicted specific sites for cutting according to disease state; impotence, for example, was cured by venesection behind the knee, while melancholia was alleviated with a cut to the forehead.[31] Cautery, a process that entailed the application of burning hot instruments to specific areas of the body, as well as cupping, in which glass cups were heated and applied to the skin to draw noxious humors to the surface of the body, served as two more vehicles for the purgation of noxious humors and internal cleansing. In all of these cases, purgation constituted physical evidence for otherwise invisible therapeutic processes.

Against the fluidity of the humors, physicians also prescribed therapies such as changes in sexual regimen, which would lead to either the retention or expulsion of seed, and changes in physical exercise, which would lead to an increase or decrease in vital heat. Medicinal baths, had the potential to warm or cool the body and carry away toxins. In addition, physicians recommended simple and compound medicines, all of which were prescribed according to each patient's unique humoral constitution.[32] Physicians determined drug therapy according to the theory of "similars," in which like engendered like, and "contraries," in which opposites countered one another. For example, a hot and dry substance taken into the body would both facilitate the production of the hot and dry humor, yellow bile, and counter the production of its opposite, the cold and wet humor, phlegm. Cordials were taken to nourish or moisturize the brain, the heart, or the liver, the three areas of the body central to Galenic medicine. Antidotes, such as those against poisons, operated on the principle of *similia similibus curantur*, or like cures like; the introduction of small amounts of a toxic substance into the body might render that same body completely immune to the original toxin.[33] Of all of the antidotes, "the most famous and sought after was theriac," which was "believed to possess virtually magical powers."[34] Made from the flesh of vipers, it was not only an antidote against the bites of snakes, insects, and rabid animals, but also a panacea that could "cure fevers, prevent internal swellings and blockages, alleviate heart problems, treat epilepsy and palsy, induce sleep, improve digestion, strengthen limbs, heal wounds, and ... even prevent and cure the plague."[35]

The authoritative lens of medieval medicine reveals an unbounded human body very different from its modern biomedical counterpart; like a porous clay vessel, the medieval body was a microcosm open to both visible and invisible forces that might penetrate its viscera, disrupt its humoral balance, and even alter its fundamental shape.[36] This fluidity of form allowed for bodily transformation through physical and spiritual agents, thereby rendering medical concepts useful to theologians who sought connections between the human body and invisible beings, be they angelic or demonic. At universities such as Paris where theology and medical faculties operated within the same curriculum and shared languages of discourse, theologians borrowed freely from learned medicine and natural philosophy in their quest to rationalize and prove what had once been of necessity taken on faith alone. In this process, ecstatic union with God, celestial visions, teleportation and levitation, miraculous healing, demonic possession, copulation with incubi and succubae, and the toxic power of the evil eye—as well as the strange anatomy and physiology of virginal holy women and wanton witches—would no longer exist solely in the realm of faith and folklore, but would become theoretically possible and physically provable.

Warm as Fire, Cold as Earth: The Codification of Holy and Unholy Female Flesh

Scholastic theologians culled select theoretical elements from learned medicine and used them in conjunction with Aristotelian natural philosophy to support the construction of the sanctified body and its categorical inversion, the Satanic and evil body.[37] All bodies below the moon were earthbound, inherently corrupt and subject to decay. In his thirteenth-century treatise, *De Misera Condicionis Humanae*, Pope Innocent III said that a human being, when alive, "brings forth lice and tapeworms; dead, he will beget worms and flies. Alive, he produces dung and vomit; dead, he produces rottenness and stench."[38] According to a fourteenth-century preacher's handbook, the body not only produces filth, but is itself composed of "the worst and most fetid kind of earth," cold, heavy, and born to decay.[39] While all flesh was corrupt, not all sublunary flesh was created equal.[40] Following Aristotle, scholastic theologians argued that the warm and dry male body was the paradigm for perfection. The male body was characterized by a powerful innate heat that facilitated the proper digestion of food into blood and blood into humors.[41] Through cooking, the humors were concocted into useful bodily products such as hair, hard muscles, and sperm; the efficiency of the healthy male system meant that few toxins were produced and none stored.[42] The male body was not only qualitatively warm, but also dry in proportion to age, with the bodies of young men being naturally warmer and moister than those of older men. While age brought about cooling and desiccation, these processes were in no way harmful to the rational and balanced male system; in fact, according to Augustine, age tempered the destructive fires of lust and brought wisdom and a mindfulness of God.[43] Following Galen, the male body's innate heat and dryness allowed for the proper digestion and concoction of humors, and also for the production and circulation of his *pneuma* and attendant vital spirits. Galen taught that environmental air was inhaled into the lungs and warmed by the heart, which transformed it into the rational, vital, and appetitive spirits, as discussed above. Through the lens of Aristotelian male perfection, theologians posited that the balanced bodies of Christian men produced a rational *pneuma* so rarified that it was able to effectively control the lower spirits of emotion, which resided in the heart, and carnal desires, which resided in the lower torso.[44] Through its continual association with warmth, the perfect Christian male body shared a theoretical association with elemental air and fire, the lightest and purest elements in Aristotle's schema. Just as maleness was allied with all things furthest from earth and closest to the lunar boundary, so too was the male body governed by the organs most distant from the earthly corruption, the brain and the rational spirits in the head.[45] A pious man's rational *pneuma* was further warmed and rarified by his continual and ardent prayer, which thereby fortified him against irrational sin, the wiles of devils, and the plague of heresy.[46]

In alignment with Aristotelian contrariety, theologians argued that if the perfect male body was marked by warmth, essential dryness, firmness, rationality, and all things that rise toward the divine and ethereal, then the female body was its wicked and earthbound inversion.[47] Predominantly cold and marked by excessive moisture in youth and excessive dryness in old age, women lacked the vital heat necessary to refine blood into tight muscles. Unlike the compact bodies of men, women were categorized as having spongy glandular flesh and pendulous bodies filled with a variety of passageways, called *phlemes*, which linked the cavernous abdomen and its myriad compartments to various parts of the head.[48] A woman's inability to produce vital heat likewise meant that she could not digest food into blood or rarify blood into humors with any efficiency, resulting in an excess of toxin-laden blood in her system. This superfluous and fetid blood was stored in her uterus which was flushed out once a month through menstruation. A woman's essential coldness also impeded the production of rational *pneuma* that might rise to the head and fuel cognitive processes; because of this, theologians argued, women were more likely to give in to the appetitive spirits that dwelled in the liver and the lower abdomen.[49] Irrational creatures, women were susceptible to sin not only through their own bodily cravings for sensual warmth, but also at the suggestion of demonic entities that might lead them into temptation.[50] Chastity and ardent prayer were necessary to warm women's hearts and preserve them on the path to God.[51] Unlike male bodies, which were associated with the buoyancy and warmth of elemental fire and air, female bodies were associated with coldness of elemental water and earth, neither of which could ascend into the upper regions because of their essential corruption and decay. Correspondingly, where maleness was correlated with the upper regions of the body, femaleness was allied with the bodily regions farthest from the lunar boundary, the lower abdomen, the bowels, and the gross functions of generation and excretion.

In the thirteenth and fourteenth centuries, the human body—and in particular the female body—became a locus of intense interest for scholastic theologians, many of whom were Dominican friars trained at the University of Paris. Using Aristotelian paradigms bolstered by medical theory, men such as Jacques de Vitry, Thomas Cantimpré, and Pseudo-Albertus Magnus sought to codify two distinct female bodies: the saintly and miraculous body that served as a vessel for the divine and had the potential to heal those around it, and its inversion, the wondrous and wicked female body that was possessed by the demonic and potentially harmful to the bodies and souls that came into contact with it. The thirteenth-century clerical male obsession with the codification of female flesh had a multifactorial genesis, one key element of which was the rapid growth of women's religious orders.[52] In the twelfth century, the Cistercian Order had founded numerous female convents which were quickly filled with women in search of spiritual nourishment and the relative peace and safety of the *vita contemplativa*.[53] The founding of the Franciscan and Dominican orders in the thirteenth century opened further opportunities for women to participate in conventual religious life. While Franciscan and Dominican men were called to mendicant lives of learning, teaching, and preaching, their sisters were cloistered behind high walls and locked away from society. These segregated all-female houses posed serious problems for the mendicant brothers who were ultimately responsible for their pastoral and sacramental care. Written in 1215, the canons of the Fourth Lateran Council reinforced the requirement that those who had reached an age of majority must go to confession and take communion at least once a year.[54] For laypeople, confession and communion might be received either from a parish priest or from an ordained member of a mendicant order; cloistered women, however, required an ordained priest from within their order to serve as their confessor and to consecrate and distribute the bread that became the transubstantiated flesh of Christ. This necessitated the entry of

3. Wanton Flesh and Poisoned Breath: Crafting the Satanic Witch   79

a male cleric into a female microcosm that, for him, must have seemed strange and fraught with temptation.

As male clerics entered into these sealed communities and worked among their female charges, they encountered women with seemingly miraculous physical powers, including the ability to fast for long periods and to survive on the Eucharistic wafer alone.[55] Some women claimed to be transported from one place to another so that they might witness distant events; others levitated, contorted their limbs into impossible configurations, and produced bodily oils and tears that had the power to heal the sick. Holy women such as Marie d'Oignies (d. 1213), Lutgard of Aywiéres (d. 1246), and Christina Mirabilis (d. 1224) steadfastly attributed the miraculous nature of their female flesh to their devout love for God and their ecstatic communion with Jesus.

Despite these claims of divine congress, academically trained confessors such as Jacques de Vitry and Thomas Cantimpré were acutely aware of the weak intellectual and physical nature of women which rendered them open to unseen forces. Believing that women were susceptible to demonic temptation and invasion and faced with behaviors that on the surface could easily be construed as signs of demonic possession, male confessors sought to prove the sanctity of the astonishing women in their care. Because the verbal testimony of these women could not necessarily be trusted, their male confessors looked to the female body for physical evidence to discern whether they were holy or unholy vessels.[56] In the process, these men codified the anatomy and physiology of the holy woman; using Aristotelian schema and learned medicine as their tools, they transformed corruptible female flesh into a male-oriented paradigm of resurrected perfection.[57]

The male clerical construction of the sanctified female body is evident in the works of de Vitry, including his *Life of Marie d'Oignies* and his sermons, as well as those of his protégé, the Dominican friar Cantimpré. Educated at the University of Paris, de Vitry took a master's degree in 1210 and that same year was ordained into the priesthood. During his time at Paris, he befriended a holy woman named Marie d'Oignies who lived the ascetic life of a hermit in the diocese of Liege. After his ordination, he travelled to Liege to become Marie's confessor as well as to minister to the sacramental needs of the *mulieres sanctae*—be they conventual women religious or beguines—who lived there.[58] In writing his hagiographical account of Marie's life, de Vitry contributes several critical elements to the construction of the holy female body as seen through the male clerical lens. Unlike typical women who were spiritually weak, physically cold and moist, and given to intemperate behaviors because of their fundamentally carnal natures, Marie d'Oignies is depicted as being so rarified through prayer that her spirit had unified with Christ and her body had become dry, warm, aromatic, and filled with light.[59]

De Vitry writes that, at a young age, Marie was "set on fire with a great ecstasy"; wishing to dwell not in her flesh but in the "tabernacle of her heart," her sanctified and purified soul "chose suspension," and flew close to the ethereal light of the Godhead, through which "all the humors of her senses were dried out."[60] In describing Marie's soul as warm and dry, De Vitry aligns it with elemental air and fire, both of which are ascendant and share qualities with superlunary ether, as well as Aristotle's paradigm for masculine perfection. The ascent of Marie's soul went hand in hand with the rejection of her body, which she saw as "filth and foulness," a view that led her to punish her flesh through a variety of ascetic practices, including fasting to the point of starvation.[61] De Vitry writes that Marie was so "overflowing with spiritual food" that "refreshment from corporeal food" was rendered unnecessary and impossible.[62] Through a lifetime of subsisting mainly on the Eucharist, which she described as being surrounded by a light whose brightness exceeded that of the sun, her physical body became "constricted and all dried up."[63] Marie's body was not only dry but also marked by a "glowing heat generated in the spirit" so pervasive that "she did not even need physical fire to ward off the winter cold."[64] De Vitry assures his reader that Marie was compensated for "the corporeal delights she had given up for the sake of Christ." Her preternaturally dry and warm body was no longer plagued by the "stirrings of lust" so common to cold and moist women; likewise, where the cold and moist bodies of natural women were imagined to produce foul odors and toxic fluids, Marie's mouth miraculously tasted of "a precious aromatic wine ... a very sweet fragrance which seemed like burning incense" and her "aromatic sweat even made her clothing smell sweet."[65] Marie's body could not help but to exhibit the continued marks of purity and sanctity—including a postmortem brightness and clarity of the face and the ability to detect and repel demons—because of the radiance of the soul dwelling in her heart.[66] Under the quill of Jacques de Vitry, the Divine illumination of Marie's soul was reflected in a sanctified female body rendered as warm and dry, masculine in nature, and no longer wanton or toxic.

The rarefication of female flesh exhibited in the de Vitry's account of Marie's life is echoed and intensified in the hagiographical works of Thomas Cantimpré, who would ultimately become de Vitry's successor as confessor at Liege. Trained at the University of Paris, steeped in Aristotelian modes of discourse and familiar with learned medical theory, Cantimpré authored several influential works, including *De Natura Rerum* (1230), a compendium of "natural science assembled as a preaching aid," and his *Bonum Universale de*

Apibus (1256–63), a collection of exempla, demonstrative stories purportedly taken from real life and used by preachers as didactic tools.[67] Following in the quill marks of de Vitry, Cantimpré would compose the *vitae* of several miraculous women under his care, including Christina of Sint-Truiden, also known as Christina Mirabilis, and Lutgard of Aywiéres. In writing the lives of both of these women, Cantimpré emphasized their somatic experiences, recording in detail the miraculous nature of their warm, dry, resurrected bodies as physical evidence of their sanctity and proof against demonic possession.

In his *Life of Christina Mirabilis* (1232), Cantimpré writes that as a young girl, the future holy woman and mystic experienced divine communion with God in her heart, and through intense devotion her corrupt female body withered away and died.[68] Christina's pure soul ascended to the Empyrean where it was rarified in the light of God, who gave her the option of staying with Him or returning to the fetid and corrupt earth to "undergo there the punishment of an immortal soul in a mortal body without damage to it." In this new and miraculous flesh, Christina would suffer both for her love for Christ and the redemption of sinful souls from purgatory. Having agreed to resurrection, Christina awakened during her funeral mass. Her corpse "rose up and, like a bird, immediately ascended to the rafters of the church."[69] Throughout the text, Cantimpré associates Christina's body with elemental air and fire, the purest of earthly elements, both of which naturally rise toward the ethereal realms of the divine beyond the moon. Buoyed up by the purity of her soul, her body often flew "to the tops of castle or church towers, to any lofty structure."[70] Cantimpré writes that "her body was subtle and light that she walked dizzy heights and like a sparrow hung suspended from the most slender branches of trees."[71] Warm and dry, her body was unharmed by flames when she "crept into fiery ovens"; like elemental fire itself, she floated above the water and walked across the Meuse River.[72]

Christina's resurrected and miraculous flesh was a reflection of divine male perfection, constructed in opposition to the cold and earthbound nature of female and demonic corruption. Cantimpré writes that while Christina was impervious to most pain, she routinely complained of human stench, a reference to the sulphurous emanations of earthly sin; the cold earth so disgusted her pure body that "it was very painful for her to touch the ground while praying."[73] Christina likewise held the fruits of the earth in contempt, eating only the coarsest bread; if she was offered food that was tainted with sin, she felt as if she was "swallowing the bowels of frogs and toads or the intestines of snakes," all of which had the Aristotelian qualities of coldness and moisture and were traditionally associated with poison and evil. Unlike the natural bodies of women which were either cold and moist like toxic mushrooms or cold and dry like the fetid earth, Christina's warm, dry, and qualitatively masculine body was not plagued by base menstruation or lactation, and instead produced only rarified substances. When she was starving in the forest, she was miraculously fed by her own "virginal breasts [which] were dripping with milk against the very law of nature"; likewise, her breasts dripped with the "dearest oil" which she not only consumed as food but also "smeared on the wounds of her festering limbs as an ointment." In constructing Christina's wonderful body as qualitatively male and dry, and repeatedly asserting that her impossible deeds were truly miraculous—"against nature" and therefore beyond the powers of the demonic—Cantimpré made her a pure vessel for the divine by stripping her of any toxicity that might come through her female flesh.

In his *Life of Lutgard of Aywiéres* (1246–48), Cantimpré follows a similar pattern: In constructing a fundamentally male resurrected body for Lutgard, he cleanses her of any carnal female corruption and counters any accusations that her miraculous flesh might be demonic in nature. Unlike Christina who was a lay woman, Lutgard lived a conventual life, first with the Benedictine sisters at Liege and later in a Cistercian house in Aywiéres. As her confessor and friend, Cantimpré looked to Lutgard as both a spiritual mother and a true vessel for the divine. In proving her sanctity, Cantimpré constructed Lutgard's body according to the paradigms of canonical goodness: weightlessness, light, purity, and masculine warmth. Like Christina, Lutgard levitated towards heaven, "for her soul had already become more exalted than the world."[74] Where foul earthly sinners were "lying in their own filth," Lutgard hovered "two cubits" above the ground, floating towards the ethereal realms, and radiated flames of light from her head and mouth that pierced "the upper air." "So filled up inwardly with super-abundant grace," Lutgard's body not only levitated but also produced miraculous substances, such as healing oil that dripped from her fingers and saliva that "tasted mellower than the sweetest honey" and had the power to cure illness and exorcise demons.[75]

Like Christina, Lutgard engaged in ascetic practices such as continual fasting in an attempt to control her wanton female flesh; in rejecting the carnal pleasures of the corrupt physical world, Lutgard prepared the "tabernacle of her heart" to receive Christ. Desiring martyrdom such as that suffered by Saint Agnes, Lutgard prayed so feverishly that "one of the outer veins opposite her heart burst, and so much blood flowed from it that her tunics and cowl were copiously drenched."[76] The flow of blood from her side was not only symbolic of her *imitatio Christi*, but also of her radical purification, a process that began with the holy communion of Lutgard's spirit with Christ and exploded outward through her physical being. At this moment, Lutgard was born anew into a resurrected body, one so rarified that she no longer suffered "the nuisance with which God tamed pride in the sex of Eve." Reborn into perfectly-balanced warm and dry flesh, Lutgard was purified of cold and moist female corruption and therefore ceased menstruation.[77] With the lower "feminine" regions of her body cleansed and subdued, Lutgard dwelled solely with Christ in the "male" upper regions of her body, the mansions of her pure heart and mind.[78]

In the *vitae* of both of these women, Cantimpré emphasizes their somatic experiences as proof of their sanctity. Christina and Lutgard both die to their corrupt female bodies, which centered on the toxicity of the uterus, genitals, and bowels, and are reborn into warm, dry, essentially male bodies centered on the pure upper regions of the mind and heart. The cessation of menstruation and the purging of the lower abdomen signified that these women were no longer potential vessels for demonic entities that might hide in the spongy moist caverns of earthbound female anatomy. The pure nature of these miraculous women was reinforced in their command over cold and fetid demons that possessed the bowels of their associates. Lutgard, for example, cleansed a sister "wearied by a demonic incubus ... who had vexed her and polluted her body with such filth that ... she would have offered herself as a public prostitute."[79] While this sister was "liberated through Lady Lutgard's prayers," others were exorcised when Lutgard applied her suave saliva to their flesh or when she made the sign of the cross over their tormented bodies. In all cases, demons fled from her pure presence which, like the Eucharist itself, radiated the divine light of God.

The authoritative command over demons remained a salient feature of male clerical discourse on the bodies of holy women throughout the Middle Ages. In the later thirteenth century, for example, Peter of Dacia wrote the *Life of Christina of Stommeln*; Christina was continually afflicted by demons who "defecated repeatedly on her" as she and her sisters kept vigil.[80] Once Christina demanded the demon depart, the "fetor" was replaced by the "sweet smell" of sanctity. On another occasion, several priests attempted to exorcise the demon from Christina, believing that he was possessing her; as the priests laid hands on her, "new excrement materialized beneath their fingers."[81] The demon only ceased his flinging of excrement at Christina's command, proving that the demon did not dwell within her but around her sanctified flesh, and that she—the holy vessel of God—had greater authority in such matters than the male priests who ministered to her.[82]

Christina Mirabilis, Lutgard of Aywières, and Christina of Stommeln were not typical thirteenth-century women; they were, however, typical of the thirteenth-century male clerical imagination, one that demanded that in order for a woman to be truly sanctified, she must first be rendered safe, her humorally imbalanced and potentially toxic system marked by menstruation remade into warm, dry, balanced male perfection. Associated with elemental air and fire, the resurrected flesh of these women became weightless and pure, holy tabernacles that radiated the divine light of God. As such, the bodies of these imaginary women were rendered impervious to earthbound demons and carnal temptations that might corrupt those around them. Unlike their cold, moist sisters, their flesh had the power to heal, to cleanse, and to repel the demonic elements that swirled about the dark world below the moon.

University-trained scholars such as Cantimpré used Aristotelian paradigms and elements culled from learned medicine to construct the sanctified body of the holy woman which, like a bee, flew through the summer air and "turned all to sweetness." Cantimpré's colleagues used these same tools to construct her inversion, the body of the earthbound, demon-infested, evil woman which, like a spider creeping about in the moist darkness, "turned all to poison."[83] The concept of woman as inherently wicked and potentially toxic was not new to the thirteenth century, of course; misogynistic views had informed Christianity through its earliest authors, including Paul, Augustine, and Isidore, and were reflected in medieval exempla and sermon literature. In the sermons of Jacques de Vitry, for example, women are not only referred to as spider-like and poisonous, but also as over-sexed adulterers whose depredations cause even devils to flee.[84] Commenting on Ecclesiastes, de Vitry describes women as fickle, wicked, and "more bitter than death," for it was "through woman that death entered the world."[85] While preachers delivered sermons expounding upon the toxic and evil nature of women, several scholars sought to prove the wickedness and carnality of women by examining their physiology. One such scholar was Pseudo-Albertus Magnus, whose quasi-medical treatise, *De Secretis Mulierum*, purported to reveal the hidden workings of the female body. Through the selective and non-systematic use of learned medical theory and Aristotelian natural philosophy, Pseudo-Albertus Magnus provided an authoritative model for wicked female anatomy and physiology, one that would not only reinforce theological beliefs in feminine evil, but would inform the discourse on witchcraft that would ripple through the later Middle Ages and into the early modern era.[86]

Written some time in the late thirteenth or early thirteenth century by a man claiming to be Albertus Magnus, perhaps one of his pupils, *De Secretis Mulierum* or *The Secrets of Women* is replete with examples of female toxicity. One of the core themes of *The Secrets of Women* is the poisonous nature of female anatomy and physiology, in particular that of her womb and menses.

Unlike medical authors such as Hippocrates, Galen, Soranus of Ephesus, and Avicenna, who saw a woman's menstrual cycle as natural and healthy, Pseudo-Albertus followed in the theological tradition of the seventh-century Father, Isidore of Seville, who wrote that menses had the power to cloud mirrors, rust metal, dissolve glue, and cause rabidity in dogs.[87] Like Michael Scotus in his thirteenth-century *Tractatis de Secretis Naturae*, Pseudo-Albertus argued that because women do not have "enough innate heat" to refine blood into useful humors, they produce "bad humors" in abundance, which are then collected in the uterus.[88] If conception takes place, the fetus is "nurtured in the maternal uterus in menstrual and fetid blood"; if conception does not occur, then the blood, which continues to decompose, is collected in the womb until the appropriate phase of the moon when it is discharged through menstruation.[89] Pseudo-Albertus and his commentators warn that men must avoid contact with menstrual blood during sexual intercourse, because its "venom" will cause injury to the penis, perhaps even cancer or leprosy, and the "stink will corrupt a man's insides" for at least a month.[90]

The *Secretis Mulierum* warns that avoiding contact with menstrual fluid was not enough to protect oneself; while the epicenter of female toxicity was located in the womb, it nevertheless radiated throughout her entire body, infecting her breath, skin, and hair. In healthy women, blood stored in the womb decomposed and became increasingly fetid until menstruation; in older women whose "natural heat is so deficient that the menses collected in them cannot be expelled," the blood was stored longer and decomposed to such an extent that it produced noxious fumes.[91] Because of the porosity of the womb and the cavernous nature of loose and spongy female flesh, these vapors traveled throughout the body. Rising upward, they pressed upon the heart and brain, causing wild thoughts and phantasies; moving into her lungs, the "venomous" fumes were exhaled, allowing her to "infect the air by her breath." Men who inhaled this fetid air might themselves become corrupted and suffer severe illness; children and infants might die.[92] Toxic menstrual fumes might also be exuded through a woman's cold and moist eyes, "because the eye is a porous part of the body," and injure others through the act of vision.[93] According to medieval medical theory, psychic *pneuma* left the brain through the optic nerve, came into contact with physical objects, and returned to the brain to form an image.[94] In toxic women, noxious uterine vapors were intermingled with the *pneuma* that served as the matrix for vision; because the process of vision was an intimate one, involving physical contact between the viewer and the object viewed, spiritual and physical contagion by poisonous *pneuma* was a terrifying and very real possibility. For this reason, Pseudo-Albertus argues that parents of young children must exercise caution around old women who might "poison the eyes of children lying in their cradles."[95] The reason, one of his commentators elaborates, is that an old woman's "menses are venomous" and therefore "continually borne to the eyes. Because of the porosity of the eyes, they infect the air, which reaches the child, for he is easily infected because of his tenderness."[96]

Throughout the text, Pseudo-Albertus and his commentators draw parallels between the poisonous nature of women and serpents. Following misappropriated medical theory, women were either cold and moist, which led to a phlegmatic humoral complexion, or cold and dry, which resulted in a system dominated by black bile and a melancholic complexion. These humors linked her body with elemental water and earth, both of which engendered corruption, decay, and the birth of horrid creatures through spontaneous generation. For example, Pseudo-Albertus writes that during menstruation a woman's "cold and humid" hair becomes so "venomous" that if strands are buried beneath "manure during the winter, then in spring or summer when they are heated by the sun a long, stout serpent will be generated." His commentator explains, "[T]he reason for this is that hairs are made from vapors that have risen to the cerebrum, and these humors are undigested in women, and they are poisonous because of the cold that remains in them; therefore, from this type of rotting, a serpent is generated."[97] Creatures considered cold and wicked, including serpents, lizards, toads, mice, and flies, were all believed to generate spontaneously from fetid earth and, as such, were considered "extremely venomous, for the matter from which [each] was produced was exceedingly putrid." Lizards, like women, were held to be poisonous enough to die from their own reflections; "since women are naturally poisoned," however, "they do not poison themselves."[98] The ability of women to serve as poisonous vessels without succumbing to their own toxicity has precedent in other "poisonous animals, such as spiders and snakes."[99] In this way, the *Secretis Mulierum* repeatedly draws connections between the heaviness and base toxicity of the cold elements, earth and water, venomous creatures, and the poisonous nature of lower female anatomy and physiology.

Unlike the idealized bodies of men or the rarified flesh of holy women, both of which were warmed by an innate heat so strong as to produce a pure rational *pneuma*, the corrupt bodies of wicked women were too cold to refine gross air into the very substance of rational thought. Without the governance of a rational mind or a pure heart—the very tabernacle of God—to guide the body, it became irrational and wanton, willing to give in to mental phantasies and the desires of chaotic flesh.[100] Pseudo-Albertus attributes the insatiability of a woman's sexual appetite to the "tickling" of her menses and her uncontrollable desire for genital pleasure; women craved sexual intercourse, he argued, because the vigorous thrustings of the male member and the nature of his sperm provided her with the vital heat her body so desperately needed.[101] Women's bodies were so humorally imbalanced and sexually hungry, apparently, that their vulvas attracted penises and sperm like lodestones. Theologians concurred, adding that a woman's irrationality, her concupiscence, and the cold and fetid nature of her toxic bowels made her an ideal plaything and a dwelling place for demons. Aquinas argued that demons might tempt women by coming to them in the guise of men, appealing to their female vanity, and seducing them into sexual sin. In some cases, demons might appear in corporeal forms, having formed false bodies out of coagulated air; in other cases, demons entered the body and pressed upon the brain, causing the powerful illusion of a corporeal presence. While Aquinas allowed that a demon could enter the body of such a woman, he argued that demons could not penetrate the heart or the soul, both of which belonged to God alone.[102] In wicked women, however, the demonic presence in her bowels had the power to "alienate" her from her own "heart and soul." Prevented from dwelling in the contemplative regions of the body, she was unable to engage in the ardent prayer that might rebalance her system and—with the permission of God—allow her to return to the rational purity of Christ.[103]

Because of their natural corruption, all women were susceptible to demonic possession, a process that began with the entrance of a demon or demons through the mouth, eyes, or ear and their descent into the bowels.[104] Once inside, the demon could move "the inner perceptions and humors," thereby effecting "changes in the actions and faculties, physical, mental, and emotional, working by means of any physical organ whatsoever." The symptoms of demon possession included swellings in the abdomen—sometimes in the uterus in mockery of the conception of Christ—which might be provoked into fetus-like movements through the application of sacred objects and rituals.[105] From their fetid roost in the woman's bowels, demons released a foul stench, be it ichthyic or sulphuric, which was emitted from the eyes and ears as well as through the mouth.[106] If the woman suffered from an unnatural retention of the menses or was post-menopausal, the demonic hellstench was mingled with the already fetid toxic fumes rising from her womb. Because the demon could travel through the body as infected air, he was able to operate his host's vocal chords, making it seem as if she was speaking in a guttural voice, grunting, or growling. Pressing upon her brain, the demon caused hallucinations that might lead to convulsions and sexual behaviors such as the waggling of the tongue and the thrusting of the hips. The bodies of the possessed sometimes levitated; unlike the bodies of holy women who ascended toward the ethereal realms because of the overflowing sanctity of their hearts, however, the bodies of possessed women floated through demonic agency, in mockery of the Divine. Demons dwelling in the bowels naturally wreaked havoc on the digestive system, causing vomiting, diarrhea, and incontinence—physical manifestations of a loss of bodily control.[107] Their miraculous departure was likewise marked by a traumatic somatic act, whether they fled through a woman's genitals, jumped from her mouth or anus as a cloud of black-winged demons, or emerged in vomit as a "toad, blood, frozen coal, black smoke, [or] a hairy worm"—all of which were associated with earthbound putrefaction.[108] Through the male clerical lens, the possessed female body was qualitatively associated with not only the cold and black demons that inhabited it, but also the melancholic and chaotic earthly realm within which it was forever trapped because of its humoral complexion and fundamental corruption.

From Toxic to Satanic: The Maleficent Body in Later Medieval and Early Modern Witchcraft Treatises

Through the chaotic fourteenth and fifteenth centuries, scholars and theologians became increasingly concerned that Satanic evil had permeated European society. The Great Famine and the Black Plague in the early fourteenth century were followed by the Avignon Papacy and the Great Schism, during which two and then three men claimed to be pope. Abroad, generations of crusaders had repeatedly failed to oust the Muslims from the Holy Land, while at home, heretics multiplied and infected an already beleaguered Christian body. Even the steadfast academic world of scholasticism was being challenged from within by Augustinianism and thinkers such as William of Occam.[109] For many theologians, it seemed that demonic chaos had penetrated and infected the Christian body at God's command as a righteous punishment of his sinful and wicked children. This increased awareness and fear of demonic disorder shaped learned discourse on women's bodies, in particular those of saints.[110] Gone were the *vita* and *miracula* of holy women like Christina Mirabilis whose chaotic behavior—including levitation, contortions, ecstatic fits and palsies, all of which had been offered as proof of her sanctity—might now be confused with demonic possession.[111] In their place stood the hagiographies and autobiographies of women such as Catherine of Siena (d. 1380) who were calm and well-ordered, much like the Empyrean realm itself.[112] With the passage of time, theologians increasingly came to believe that the essentially corrupt female body could never truly attain the

3. Wanton Flesh and Poisoned Breath: Crafting the Satanic Witch

saintly zenith of dry, warm, and orderly masculinity no matter how sanctified her flesh might appear. In her recent book *The Bride of Christ Goes to Hell*, Dyan Elliott argues that by the fifteenth century, clerical authors became suspicious of women who claimed to have supernatural lovers, in part because it was impossible to discern between a woman possessed by Christ as her bridegroom and a woman possessed by the Devil; in fact, for many theologians, both forms of possession had become one and the same thing.[113] Through the male clerical lens, *all* women were hopelessly imprisoned by their cold and imperfect carnality and susceptible to demonic attack, and therefore all women were dangerous. By the end of the fifteenth century, witchcraft treatises such as the Malleus Maleficarum would cast women as the foulest of melancholic creatures—women so wicked that they were not mere victims of their chaotic and corrupt flesh but willing collaborators with demonic and Satanic evil.[114]

In writing his 1486 inquisitorial handbook, the *Malleus Maleficarum*, Heinrich Kramer—a mendicant friar and inquisitor active at the Counsel of Basel—drew upon a variety of sources, including folklore, legal procedure, Aristotelian natural philosophy, *exempla*, and scholastic sources on demons and the nature of feminine evil.[115] His primary goal was to persuade his colleagues that maleficent witchcraft was a pervasive threat to Christendom and should be persecuted through the sacred and secular arms of the law. In his elaboration of the witchcraft paradigm, Kramer reinforced the fundamentally toxic nature of women codified in the thirteenth century and conflated it with the explicitly diabolical structures of inverted Christianity. For example, according to the *Malleus*, poisonous women no longer existed as random and natural events, nor were they mere victims of demonic attack, but instead were linked together into a conspiratorial network of maleficent witches who sought out demonic consorts and signed pacts with the Devil.[116] As part of this pact, witches were abjured "to profanely renounce the Catholic Faith," to "devote themselves body and soul to all evil," to "offer up unbaptized children to Satan," and to indulge in every kind of carnal lust with Incubi and Succubi and all manner of filthy delights."[117] They were likewise called to convert others, often family members, to join the Devil's network of followers. In return for their devotion, witches purportedly believed that they would be given power over other human beings, the weather, and the base creatures of the earth, including toads, bats, wolves, frogs, snakes, mice and cats. While the rewards themselves seem hardly worth the price of one's soul, the *Malleus* led its readers to believe that witches did not think out their bargain with the Devil; instead, they acted as irrational creatures on the irresistible impulses of their own wanton and wicked flesh.

In the *Malleus Maleficarum*, the melancholic and phlegmatic bodies of unholy women were wed to diabolical forces to produce the strange anatomical and physiological hallmarks of the Satanic witch. Founded in deeply held misogynistic beliefs inherent to Christianity and built on the theologized medical theory of treatises such as the *De Secretis Mulierum*, the witch and her wicked powers as codified in the *Malleus* would have been familiar and completely rational to its fifteenth-century male readers. And because the *Malleus* became an authoritative source on witchcraft—either despite or because of its official censure by the Church in 1490—the maleficent female body depicted in its pages would haunt generations of witchcraft and anti-witchcraft treatises, right through the Reformation.[118] While sixteenth- and seventeenth-century protestant authors on witchcraft typically rejected medieval authorities such as Aquinas in favor of biblical and patristic sources, they nevertheless continued to use the fundamental argument structures of the *Malleus* as well as its construction of the witch body—all of which were stitched together from medieval parts—in writing their treatises. In both protestant and Catholic sources on witchcraft, the anatomy and physiology of the diabolical witch remained remarkably consistent, not only because authors continued to draw on medieval paradigms, but also because the maleficent body reinforced deeply ingrained male cultural and theological assumptions about the corrupt and weak nature of women and functioned logically according to the specific rationality of humoral medicine, the basic precepts of which had not changed.[119]

As conjured in the male imagination and depicted in witchcraft treatises, the salient features of the maleficent female body included her physical toxicity and her subsequent association with the concoction and administration of poisons, her bloodlust, which made her a particular danger to children, and her sexual rapacity, which made her a danger to men. In the *Malleus Maleficarum*, as in the *De Secretis* of two centuries earlier, fetid humors retained in the uterus had the potential to decompose and produce noxious fumes; these in turn might be exuded from the eyes as toxic optical *pneuma* and exhaled from the mouth and nose as poisonous breath. All women were naturally cold in humoral complexion, be they phlegmatic in their youth or melancholic in their old age, and therefore potentially venomous. According to the *Malleus*, however, the bodies of witches were far more lethal than their non-maleficent sisters because of their willful collusion with demons and their purposeful manipulation of their own toxicity for the destruction of Christian others. The *Malleus* makes reference to the power of witches to injure humans and animals through "a touch and a look, or by a look only."[120] The glance of a wicked woman is compared to that of a basilisk which can kill a man with a glance because "owing to its anger, a certain terrible poison is set in motion throughout its body" which it can then "dart from its eyes, thus infecting the atmosphere with deadly venom."[121] The witch's power to kill with the evil eye was rationalized through medieval theories of vision, according to which optical *pneuma* left the eye, mingled with the physical world, and reported its findings back to the brain; because vision was a physical act, contamination through sight was theoretically possible.[122] Witches not only exuded poison through their eyes, but also their breath.[123] The *Malleus* recounts a tale from Constance in which a woman contracted leprosy after a "warm wind came from the house" of a witchy woman with whom she had quarreled.[124] Likewise, as a woman from the Black Forest was being burned for heresy, she blew into the face of her jailer and said, "I will pay you...." "And he was at once afflicted with a horrible leprosy all over his body, and did not survive many days."[125] In both of these *exempla*, the foul breath of the witch is metaphorically conflated with the southerly plague winds of Meridies from Hippocrates' *Airs, Waters, and Places*,[126] the toxic breath of serpents from earlier hagiographical texts, and the pestiferous nature of heresy that threatens to contaminate the Christian body. In *Demonolatry* (1595), Nicholas Remy tells the story of a witch named Catharina who wanted revenge on a pregnant woman named Lolla. At the signal of her demon, Catharina "blew her foul breath upon Lolla, who at once was attacked by the most violent labor pains and only with the greatest difficulty reached home in time."[127] In his *Compendium Maleficarum* (1608), Francesco Maria Guazzo argued that the noxious vapors produced by a witch not only aided her in poisoning her enemies, but also allowed her to see distant events, for "by some devil's work, they send a thick vapour from their mouths, in which they can see all that is done as if in a mirror."[128] A witch's *pneuma*, then, was both poisonous and demonic, a danger to innocent bodies and souls.

Witches could produce poisonous substances from their own bodies and also concoct them from natural ingredients, often with the help of devils. The maleficent use of poisons, alluded to in the *Malleus Maleficarum*, is drawn in greater detail in subsequent treatises. In *Demonolatry*, Remy describes two different types of poison: powders and unguents. Powdered poisons came in three colors, the actions of which corresponded with medieval color theory.[129] "The powder which kills is black; that which only causes sickness is ashen, or sometimes reddish in color"; a third powder, which was white, created the illusion of miraculous healing, but was really a trick of the Devil meant to mock the power of the saints.[130] In his *Demonmania of Witches* (1580), Bodin adds that Satan himself distributed jars of poisons to the witches at the Sabbath; at their next meeting, they would be forced to testify as to how the poison was used.[131] Witches administered poison to their victims by sprinkling it upon them while they slept or pouring it forcibly into their mouths "by the light of a candle burning with a sulphuric flame."[132] Both Remy and Guazzo claim that witches could also kill by touching poison to the clothes of their intended victim—an inverted mockery of the gospel story in which Veronica is healed of the bloody flux after touching the hem of Christ's garment.[133] Toxic unguents such as the famed "flying ointment" were made from corrupt creatures (toads, slugs, snakes) as well as the boiled flesh from "murdered children."[134] Witches not only smeared this ointment on the bodies of those they wished to harm, but also on the doors, thresholds, and window sills of their homes. Theoretically, the poisoning of these apertures would have been effective because of their frequent use by the intended victim, during which he or she might come into contact with the poison; these openings likewise served a metaphorical purpose as representations of the body's many orifices, through which toxins were exhaled and inhaled—reminders of the fundamentally porous nature of the medieval body. While lethal to others, these poisonous unguents were harmless to the witches who applied it to their skin in preparation for the night flight to the Sabbath. Because they were themselves poison maidens, witches were not harmed by any of the toxic potions or ointments that they readily handled, but instead were fortified by them.[135]

A poisonous witch was not only a danger to the specific individuals who crossed her path, but to entire communities which might be infected by her pestiferous evil. In the Latin hagiographical tradition, noisome heretics and wicked serpents had long been accused of poisoning the Christian body with their foul beliefs and diseased air. In 1574, the Calvinist author Lambert Daneau argued that serpentine and heretical witches spread disease in a similar manner, by using both their breath and their potions to poison the "air and water," which because of their fluid natures were easily rendered "pestiferous and hurtful."[136] Like a "pestilent smell or vapour," a witch could "infect a whole region" and engender the "most grievous and infectious diseases."[137] Writing in 1602, the Catholic Henry Boguet likewise stated that witches might "cause the plague by means of their ointments.... [T]hey most usually poison and infect the air and the water.... And if the air is sometimes corrupted by the odor from a dung-heap so as to cause a plague throughout a whole district, why should we not believe that witches can infect it by the heavy and loathsome stenches which they draw from a poison that they know to compose with the help of their master?"[138] Because of the body's porous nature, a witch's environment became an extension of her odiferous demon-infested toxicity. Her poisons, bodily and manufactured, might travel unseen upon the winds like demons and penetrate the vulnerable flesh of the innocent.[139]

The witch targeted the most innocent members of the community through her insatiable hunger for warm human blood, particularly that of infants and children. In the *Malleus Maleficarum*, for example, a man went in search of his missing infant and "finding a congress of women in the nighttime, swore that he saw them kill his child and drink its blood and devour it."[140] Witches were also reputed to throw children into ovens[141] and to boil infants dead and alive in large cauldrons so that they might be eaten as soup.[142] Remy and Bodin both recount tales of witches who crept into the homes of young families in order to steal, murder, and consume their infants.[143] In Pierre de Lancre's full elaboration of the Black Mass, children "both baptized and unbaptized" were "served and eaten" as part of the ritual feast; others were "cut into quarters at the Sabbath" and distributed widely "in order to have several parishes partake of them." In the male imagination, witches not only ate infants and children as an unholy foodstuff, but also used their bodies as the main ingredient of several concoctions, including a potion that imparted diabolical knowledge and the ointment used by witches in their flight to the Sabbath.[144] For these purposes, witches procured the corpses of infants—those who died of natural causes as well as those murdered by "diabolical midwives" through abortion or infanticide—and stored them in great pots.[145] Bodin states that when searching a witch's hovel, the inspector should look for "toads, lizards, communion wafers, strange bones, ointments ... and human members, especially those of little children."[146]

That the witch's bloodlust would be directed primarily at infants and small children made sense within the scholastic rationality that had given birth to the witchcraft paradigm. Following a bastardized interpretation of humoral theory and the natural philosophy of Aristotle, the bodies of the young were the warmest and moistest; the consumption of their flesh and blood, therefore, would be most effective in rebalancing a cold and corrupt female system.[147] Wicked witches—in particular melancholic old witches whose cold and dry bodies craved warmth and moisture—were biologically driven to drink blood and eat red meat, preferably the perfect blood and flesh of innocent Christians. From a theological perspective, the consumption of infants conformed to a familiar and authoritative ancient trope; accusations of cannibalism had long been used as rhetorical invective against heretical sects from Arians and Pelagians in the early medieval world to the Albegensians, Lollards, and Hussites in the high and later Middle Ages. In the case of diabolical witches—the most heinous of heretics—the supposed sacrifice of infants and the ritual consumption of their flesh and blood also represented an extreme inversion of the Christian Eucharist; instead of reverently consuming Christ's miraculously transubstantiated flesh-bread and wine-blood to nourish their souls, witches ravenously glutted themselves on the actual bodies of children in order to feed their carnal desires. That witches abducted, tortured, and killed a family's most vulnerable members had the added benefit of making a mockery of Christian motherhood. Good mothers nourished their children and kept them within the protective folds of the Christian church; witches, on the other hand, either killed and consumed their own young or infected them with the heresy of diabolical witchcraft, offering their daughters to the devil and damning their offspring for all eternity.[148] Constructed as an inversion of the Blessed Virgin Mary, the most perfect mother of all, witches reviled the Blessed Mother and went into a frenzy at the mere mention of her name. The witches' hatred of the Mother logically extended to her Son; in one episode from the *Malleus*, witches gather around a statue of baby Jesus and stab it with arrows, causing it to bleed human blood.[149] From the misogynistic viewpoints of skewed medical and theological traditions, the torture, sacrifice, and consumption of fetuses, infants, and children by maleficent women was not only possible but woefully predictable.

The bloodlust of the witch was equaled only by her sexual rapacity and hunger for penetration. All women were imagined to have insatiable sexual appetites, in part because of an anti-woman biblical tradition extending back through the epistles of Saint Paul to Genesis. In the Middle Ages, scholars such as Pseudo-Albertus Magnus rationalized and reinforced the theological paradigm of the libidinous woman using elements of learned medical theory; because of their fundamentally cold and corrupt natures, they argued, phlegmatic young women and melancholic old women craved bodily contact with men and the warmth generated through the friction of intercourse.[150] Through ardent prayer and obedience to male authority, some women were able to keep their carnal desires under control; diabolical witches, however, gave in to their insatiable lust because of a "natural madness, a rabid concupiscence, a wanton fancy, as is seen from their spiritual sins of pride, envy, and wrath."[151] The demands of her hungry womb drove the witch to use a "natural dog" and "consort with even the devils" in order to satisfy her lust, which in turn led her to practice diabolical witchcraft.[152] Even before making their Satanic pact, witches tended to be women who were "more hot to satisfy their filthy lusts."[153] For example, the *Malleus* recounts the tale of one young woman propositioned by the Devil while on her way to fornicate with her lover. Not satisfied with human carnality, she accepts his offer and for eighteen years practices "diabolical filthiness with him, together with a total abnegation of the faith as a necessary condition."[154] All witches were accused of practicing "carnal copulation with devils" who have condensed bodies for themselves out of the "gross vapors raised from the earth."[155] The goals of this "abominable coitus" were "venereal pleasure on the part of the witch" (although many treatises discuss the unpleasant nature of demonic copulation), the engendering of child witches,[156] and the utter destruction of the witch's soul.[157]

The witches' demonic and frenzied sexual rapacity posed a powerful threat to unwitting men who fell into their snares. Sexual desire was a weakness for men as it was for women; because of their warm and rarified rational *pneuma*, however, men were theoretically better able to control the base desires of their lower organs.[158] Through the cunning realization that his power "lies in the privy parts of men," the Devil often approached them in the form of a seductive woman, of which Adam and St. Antony's temptations are but two examples.[159] The *Malleus* describes a pious young man who was "tempted by the devil in the form of a woman to copulate." Terrified, he threw Blessed Salt at her, at which she "looked fiercely at him and, cursing whatever devil had taught him to do this, suddenly disappeared."[160] The witch, like her master the Devil, could appear as an alluring and lovely woman. For example, a young girl in the *Malleus* is taken by a beautiful woman to meet a handsome man who wishes to be her husband; having been tempted by the promise of romance and trusting in the woman's beauty, the young girl does not suspect subterfuge until the woman warns her not to make the sign of the cross. Instinctively, the girl crosses herself and at that moment, her lovely guide is revealed to be an ugly old hag in the service of Satan.[161] Whether she was truly young and beguiling or an old hag using potions to appear so, the witch's beauty was a false veneer that hid a festering soul with the power to contaminate and kill. For this reason, a woman was always to be regarded as a Chimera, a "monster of three forms ... beautiful to look upon, contaminating to the touch, and deadly to keep."[162]

The unwitting man who fell into the witch's snares was doomed in soul and body. The *Malleus* recounts the tale of a man whose beautiful wife seduced him into drinking a vile potion and practicing witchcraft; both were burned at the stake, the man with contrition, the woman un-absolved and destined for hellfire. Witches were not only terrible wives, but deadly lovers who compromised a man's soul by enticing him to commit lust and fornication, thereby sinning against God. In taking a witch as his lover, a man became forever enslaved to her sexual demands, jealous behavior, and vengeful wrath, the latter of which was focused on the punishment and torture of his male member. Like frigid demons, witches could "freeze" a man's desire for sex and "prevent the erection of that member" necessary for copulation.[163] For example, a handsome young man had fallen into the trap of a beautiful young witch but eventually jilted her and married another. The witch sought revenge by causing impotence in the man, thereby preventing him from consummating his marriage. Only when he discovered "a pot in the well in the middle of [his] yard containing certain objects evilly bewitched" was he able to break her spell and engender children.[164] Even if the man was able to achieve an erection, the witch could still "prevent the flow of the vital essence to the members in which lies the motive power, by closing as it were the seminary ducts, so that it does not descend to the generative channels," thereby preventing ejaculation and conception. Witches also had the power to spirit away a man's genitalia, making it appear to him as though it had vanished completely. Although this was merely a demonic phantasy, "it is no illusion in the opinion of the sufferer."[165] The *Malleus* contains a unique adaptation of the penis theft paradigm, arguing that witchy women not only stole men's members but kept them in birds' nests where they were fed oats like hungry little chicks.[166] While the nest of penises appears only once in the textual tradition, the power of witches to penetrate and control male sexual anatomy remained a salient feature of the witchcraft tradition.[167]

In late-medieval and early modern witchcraft treatises, all women were fundamentally toxic, and all had the deadly potential to be diabolical witches. What did the witch look like? How might she be recognized? The young witch might be beautiful, but her body remained cold and moist, a corrupt vessel for fetid toxins and the perfect abode for demons. Like bait, the Devil used such willing women to lure men to their doom. While the young witch was dangerous, the old witch was far more so. With age, her body became increasingly cold and dry until it ceased to menstruate completely. Unlike holy women, this cessation of menstruation did not signify a purified body, but instead instigated the creation of a radically toxic creature whose body continued to produce superfluities which now had no monthly means of escape. Accustomed to sexual intercourse and the release of female seed through orgasm, the aged witch body produced a superfluity of female fluids which decomposed and produced further noxious fumes. The old hag, driven by desperate sexual desire but unable to seduce men because of her ugliness, was driven into the arms of demons who fornicated with her and helped her dupe unwitting humans into satisfying her. The old crone's contact with demons made her all the more frigid, causing her to become intensely cold, dry, and humorally imbalanced.[168] Dominated by black bile, infested with demons, the physiognomy of the aged witch reflected her warped and toxic interior.[169] Her skin was pockmarked and pallid, the color of impending death; in some cases she bore the devil's mark as a sign of her baptism. Her body was haggard and bent, crooked like her misshapen soul. Her eyes, ears, nose

3. Wanton Flesh and Poisoned Breath: Crafting the Satanic Witch

and mouth—all of which were apertures for the poisonous gasses escaping from her leaky body—were large and foul-smelling.[170] Her poisonous hair, black and gray, hung all about her face like long serpents.[171] Because of her melancholic complexion, the witch came to be associated with autumn, death and its corresponding colors, gray and black, and elemental earth, the dross of the cosmos, to which it was forever bound. Earthbound and corrupt, the witch shared a body with serpents, toads, worms, slugs, cats, and flies, all of which were believed to be pestiferous and prolific, and generated spontaneously from excrement and decay.[172] Stitched together according to the specific rationality of medieval scholasticism, the melancholic and inverted body of the witch would serve as the foundation for all non–Christian "others," including Jews, and would inform anatomy and physiology of the vampire in the modern period.

4

Wicked Women

Female Flesh, the Satanic Witch and the Horror Film

In late October, when frosty winds twist through gnarled branches and jack-o'-lanterns are alight, one can almost imagine the silhouette of an old woman clad in tattered black rags riding on her broom across the harvest moon. With her black cat at the helm and pointy black hat, she is readily recognizable as the wicked witch. Her physiognomy, too, is familiar; her large, hooked nose, warty pallid-green skin, deep-set black eyes, unkempt salt-and-pepper hair, and crooked frame all mark her as a toxic and evil creature. At home in her woodland hovel, the witch stirs her bubbling cauldron of "hell-broth," adding "Eye of newt and toe of frog, Wool of bat and tongue of dog, Adder's fork and blind-worm's sting, Lizard's leg, and owlet's wing" as she casts her evil spells in search of love and revenge.[1] The one ingredient the witch desires most, of course, is a child that she and her sisters might stuff into the oven as a meal or drop into the pot to enhance their potion. As an old crone, the wicked witch is the terror of small children who imagine they hear her cackling on quiet autumn nights.

Children, however, are not the witch's only target, for she has yet another face—that of the sexy young vixen with mountainous breasts, red lips, and fishnet stockings who rides through the air with a phallic broom clenched between her supple thighs. The sex-witch serves as a temptress for men, luring them away from their humdrum lives with promises of lustful adventure. While the old crone and the young vixen appear as nearly opposite characters, they are nevertheless one and the same—a single creature of feminine evil, born under the quills of male clerics, on an endless flight through our imagination.

4. Wicked Women: Female Flesh, Satanic Witch and Horror Film

From Shakespeare's *Macbeth* and nineteenth-century fairy tales to the Wizard of Oz, Harry Potter and the wonderful world of Halloween, the wicked witch has become a nostalgic character, a reminder of childhood innocence re-imagined, a sweet vehicle for feminine flirtation. Beneath its seeming benignity, the romanticized image of the witch as maleficent old crone or sexy young vixen hides a horrible history, the roots of which extend back into the Middle Ages when male clerics used Aristotelian natural philosophy and learned medicine to support anti-woman theological beliefs about the wicked nature of female flesh. Using these tools, scholars sculpted the female body as the inversion of Christian male perfection. Unlike men who were typically warm and produced enough vital heat to properly digest food and blood into bodily humors, women were predominantly cold and unable to refine their humors through digestion. As a result, women produced an abundance of toxin-laden blood that collected in their wombs and was discharged once a month through menstruation. While the bodies of old and young women alike were deemed potentially poisonous by male clerics, older women who had ceased menstruating were most lethal. The body of the old hag was acutely melancholic, radically cold and dry like the corrupt elemental earth to which she was bound for eternity. Because she no longer menstruated, she could not purge herself of toxins; instead, the corrupt blood lingered in her body, decomposed, and produced fetid menstrual vapors that exuded from her eyes and mouth. The aged woman's bodily fumes were so toxic that she had the power to poison grown men and small children by merely breathing upon them or gazing into their eyes. Women young and old were not only toxic, but carnal and wanton, craving the heat of sexual intercourse and the consumption of warm red meat and wine in order to rebalance their humoral systems. Unlike the ideal Christian man who produced strong rational *pneuma* and could resist these temptations, irrational women were unable to control their bodily desires and sought to drag others down into carnal sin with them. Once again, the old hag was more dangerous than her younger counterpart: Ugly and undesirable, she was unable to seduce men, and therefore unable to satiate her sexual appetite. Her lust having turned to sexual frustration and rage, the melancholic old woman was imagined to vent her wrath on all those who, like flies, strayed too close to her deadly and inescapable web.

The weak and corrupt bodies of women were toxic vessels with the power to poison the innocent both spiritually and physically; the irrational nature of female flesh likewise left them susceptible to invasion by invisible forces, both divine and demonic. In the thirteenth century, scholars such as Thomas Cantimpré believed that holy women might be possessed by God and dwell in rarified flesh that was warm, dry, and essentially male.[2] Vulnerable women might also be possessed by cold demons who dwelled in their cavernous bowels and caused physical contortions and maniacal behaviors.[3] In these cases, only the rational male authority of the priest or the power of a saint might, with God's permission, expel the demon from the powerless and chaotic female flesh objectified beneath their gaze.[4] By the fifteenth century, male clerics were less inclined to see women as pure vessels for the divine or naïve victims of demonic attack; instead, women who exhibited unusual behavior—no matter how holy or innocent they might seem—were potentially wanton and willing collaborators with demons and their master, Satan. According to the late-medieval paradigm for diabolical witchcraft, a wicked woman's desire for sexual satisfaction drove her to intercourse with demons, which immediately brought her into the service of Satan. With his evil blessing, the witch might then copulate with anyone she could beguile, including family members and other witches, during the Sabbath orgy.[5] Her desire to consume red meat and wine became an insatiable bloodlust for infants and children who were sacrificed to the Devil in mockery of the Eucharist and used in wicked potions. Her *pneuma* was no longer merely toxic and dangerous to physical bodies, but laden with infectious demons and dangerous to souls. Mistress of the winds, carried through the air by demons, the witch spread her heretical poison like a plague; like the worms, snakes, frogs, and mice with which she was closely associated, the phlegmatic young witch and the melancholy old witch multiplied like spontaneously generated vermin within an imperiled Christian body. The only remedy against these earthbound and toxic creatures was the confession of their crimes to male authorities and the commission of their pestiferous flesh to cleansing fire.

Modern horror films about Satanic witches and witchcraft are rooted in an anti-woman discourse that has changed little since the *Malleus Maleficarum*. The British and American horror traditions in particular feature witchy bodies and behaviors that continue to operate according to the specific rationality of medieval scholasticism. The physiognomy of the wicked old witch conforms to that of the toxic hag, with her stringy hair, pallid, warty skin, and toxic eyes, nose, and mouth. Even when the witch on film is depicted as a sexy young temptress, she retains her haggard and demonic form just beneath the façade of her rosy porcelain skin. In modern horror cinema, as in the fifteenth century, even the loveliest of women are potentially demonic and cannot be trusted. Satanic witches continue to be driven by their sexual rapacity and their insatiable bloodlust. Desperate for youth and beauty, the wicked witch consumes human blood and the flesh of the young in order to feed her vanity and live forever. Hungry for male attention, the witch pursues men so that she might satiate her own sexual desires, tempt him into sin, and destroy his previous relationships. The destruction of loving couples and happy families is central to the witch paradigm in modern horror; many films emphasize this element by portraying the witch's nemesis as the "good woman," a chaste, modest, devoted and obedient counterpart to the chaotic and sex-hungry witch. Embedded in this discourse is the belief that these two naughty daughters—one weak and helpless and the other wicked and devious—require governance by paternal authority.

Like her early-modern sisters, the cinematic wicked witch is routinely depicted as a threat to male authority and patriarchal structures. Films with purportedly happy endings show the defeat of the chaotic Satanic witch and a return to the blissful order or Christian male authority, while films that end on a wicked note feature the witch triumphant—an act meant to send shivers through an audience terrified of an irrational woman's power to overthrow a rational patriarchy. Horror films about witchcraft are generally conservative not only in their gender politics but also in their adherence to traditional religious systems, most often mainline Protestant Christianity. Just as all empowered women are collapsed into demonic witches, all non–Christian practices are conflated into a single, organized, underground Satanic sect that threatens the patriarchal white Protestant status quo. Feminism, Judaism, Islam, Hinduism, Buddhism, Occultism, Atheism, New Age religions, Voodoo, and especially Catholicism are all cast into the inverted category of feminine and heretical evil and depicted in collusion with the Devil.[6] While the construction of the inverted female body, the repeated use of binary categories, and the signifiers of the Satanic in horror films about witchcraft are rooted in medieval scholastic paradigms, the depiction of witchcraft on film is an artifact of modern culture, and is therefore also open to postmodern and feminist critique. Foucault's discourses on objectification and "othering,"[7] Mulvey's theory of scopophilia, Clover's and Creed's discussions on voyeurism and the phallic penetration of the male gaze,[8] and Kristeva's theory of abjection and *jouissance*[9] will serve as useful interpretive tools in contextualizing the following dissection of the witch, her evil body, and its multiple meanings in Anglo-American horror films.

In the Flesh: Anglo-American Witches

Witchcraft makes for a scintillating story. Women's bodies and their sexual desires, their power to manipulate nature for their own evil purposes, and their associations with the demonic and Satanic—all set the stage for a terrifying tale, especially one told through visual media. From the earliest days of cinema, the witch has been an object of visual consumption, from documentary-style films such as Benjamin Christensen's *Häxan* to the American family classic *The Wizard of Oz*. The Swedish *Häxan* (1922), a feature length exposé of the history of witchcraft, begins with a teleologically structured school lesson on witches in the ancient and medieval worlds. Later parts of the film recreate the tale of a medieval European village infested by witches, most of whom are older and inexorably filthy, with stringy hair, missing teeth, and tattered rags. Rooted in late-medieval and early modern witchcraft treatises such as the *Malleus Maleficarum* (1486), *De calcatione daemonum* (1452), and *Demonolatry* (1595), the film depicts witches compounding the magical ointment, flying to the Sabbath on broomsticks, desecrating the cross, consuming infant flesh, drinking human blood, and having sex with demons. The film's final scenes explain the phenomenon of witchcraft through the lens of modern psychiatry, arguing the witch's nightly transportations, raptures, and terrified mannerisms were merely symptoms of female hysteria and neurasthenia. Christensen suggests that modern-day "witches"—forgotten, misunderstood, locked up in institutions and subjected to torturous therapies—fare little better than their medieval ancestors who were tortured by wicked clerical inquisitors. Throughout the film, Christensen is sympathetic towards the plight of women cast as witches in both the medieval and modern worlds. Despite this—and despite his rejection of gods, devils, and the purportedly backwards beliefs of superstitious Catholicism—Christensen adheres to medieval constructions of the feminine, including a woman's intellectual and physical weakness, her susceptibility to invisible or psychic forces, and her inability to resist temptation. Furthermore, while attempting to redeem women, Christensen routinely depicts them as scintillating objects of desire. Whether flying naked in the moonlight, whipped on the buttocks by Satan, copulating with demons, or forcibly stripped, tortured, and probed by the phallic instruments of inquisitors and physicians, the female body is repeatedly penetrated by the male gaze both within and beyond the film's frame.[10] Unlike his medieval sources, which ascribed a terrifying occult power to women through witchcraft, Christensen's witches are rendered utterly helpless, pitiful souls requiring male patience and protection.

In early twentieth-century Sweden, Christensen saw the witch as an innocent and dispossessed victim; in the United States, however, the witch remained a wicked and warty agent of evil. The paradigmatic American witch is immortalized in the 1939 film *The Wizard of Oz*. Based in part on the Frank

L. Baum novel *The Wonderful Wizard of Oz*, Victor Fleming's film features Judy Garland as Dorothy, a rosy-cheeked adolescent with blood-red lips who plays the role of an endangered child, and Margaret Hamilton as the Wicked Witch of the West, whose purpose is to capture Dorothy, steal her sanguine-colored shoes, and avenge her sister's death.[11] While only a minor character in the original novel, the Wicked Witch is the lynchpin of the film's narrative; without her, Dorothy's journey would be uneventful at best. In *The Wizard of Oz*, the physiognomy of the Wicked Witch correlates with the medieval construction of the witch as an earthbound and melancholic creature. Her green skin, warty chin, spindly frame, desiccated black hair, deep-set eyes, and bony fingers reflect a humorally imbalanced body dominated by black bile and shaped by a sinful and disfigured soul. Her long nose, a trait common to witches and vampires, likewise links her with medieval inversion and anti–Judaism.[12] The dryness of her body manifests in her harsh voice and arid cackle; in the book, Baum states that the Wicked Witch does not bleed when bitten by Toto "for she was so wicked that the blood in her had dried up many years before."[13]

The Wicked Witch is not only a black-clad creature of cold, dry melancholia, but also of great demonic power. Like her medieval predecessors, she flies through the air on her broom and uses her scrying glass to see future events, witchy abilities traditionally attributed to the assistance of demons. She is likewise mysteriously transported from place to place, ascending and descending in plumes of fiery-red sulphurous smoke that signify hellfire and brimstone.[14] From her sunken castle built of earthbound stone, the Wicked Witch commands her demonic familiars, the Flying Monkeys, to do her bidding. Perhaps most tellingly, water is the only way to destroy the Wicked Witch. According to Aristotelian physics, elemental water has the power to smother dry and cold elemental earth; according to Christian theology, baptism in water has the power to wash away the black stain of sin and protect against Satanic evil. Both physically and spiritually, our melancholic and demonic witch is in trouble.[15] The Wicked Witch of the West conforms closely to medieval paradigms for inverted and Satanic evil and is in alignment with late-medieval and early modern witchcraft treatises. In designing her on-screen character, her creators did not consult medieval sources, nor were they necessarily aware of Aristotelian theories of matter. Instead, they drew upon signifiers that are rooted in deep and invisible discourses of power—signifiers of evil that speak an unspoken language to audiences young and old about the malignant and terrifying nature of women.

Häxan and *The Wizard of Oz* present two opposing cinematic constructions of the feminine, one in which women are palpably human, innocent, and helpless victims, and another in which women are demon-infested monsters with maleficent powers. In the first of these binary categories, the intellectually weak woman is a mere child in need of paternal authority to guide and protect her from invisible forces that might take control of her. In the second, the wicked woman answers to no human power; unconstrained by male authority, she gives free rein to her irrationality and unleashes unmitigated chaos on all those who dare to deny her desires. These two sides of a single imaginary female coin cast by medieval male clerics have remained salient features of feminine evil as depicted in Anglo-American witchcraft films, a genre that became increasingly popular in these regions from the mid-twentieth century forward.

The proliferation of films about witches and witchcraft in the 1960s and '70s can be attributed in part to the development of a youth culture that delighted in horror films, particularly those that promised moments of sexual titillation. The primary catalyst for the production of witchcraft films during this period, however, was the rise of the feminist movement, in which liberal-minded women advocated for equality and challenged male hegemony and privilege. Women demanded the power not only to participate in politics, the workplace, and the household as equals, but also to control their own bodies through reproductive rights, including access to the contraceptive pill and clinical abortion. By the late sixties, branches of the feminist movement became increasingly radicalized and potentially violent. In 1967 Valerie Solanas, for example, published her S.C.U.M. (Society for Cutting Up Men) Manifesto, a blueprint for creating a feminist world in which men were no longer needed—not even for reproduction.[16] The late sixties also saw the Stonewall Riots and the subsequent rise of the Gay Liberation Front, both of which empowered lesbians, bisexual and transgendered women to live openly as independent individuals who did not need men for sexual satisfaction or social validation.

Through the lens of conservatism, feminism and its discontents were not catalysts for long-overdue social change but the abrogation of a natural order, constructed by God, in which men held power over women in the social, political, and domestic spheres. Male dominance extended to control over the bodies of women, who were far too irrational to understand things like anatomy and physiology or the importance of motherhood to the broader social order. For conservatives, a woman's place was in the home where she was to obey her husband and serve as a good mother and moral mentor to her children. In return, she was protected from the dangers of society and from her own stupidity by the dominant and rational husband-father to whom she legally married in holy wedlock. At first, members of conservative culture saw the Women's Liberation Movement as a phase of hysterical irrationality so common to the female sex, one that would soon pass. Feminism, however, continued to gain ground and as it did, more and more "good" daughters and wives were lost to its "deviant" agenda. As they stared on in abject terror at the empowered and sexually liberated modern woman, many Christian patriarchs began to see the hand of the Devil in feminism's success. First of all, there was no way that women were strong or smart enough to have achieved these things on their own without the help of some malignant force. Secondly, there was a deceptive element to feminism; even the prettiest and most delicate of women might turn out to be a wanton vixen on birth control or a lipstick lesbian looking to challenge male authority. Lastly, feminism and the other liberal ideals to which it was bound appeared to be suspiciously infectious, traveling through underground channels much like heresy, Devil worship, and witchcraft.

The culture wars surrounding Women's Liberation and the feminist movement emerge in the horror cinema of the 1960s and '70s. In these films, the witch remains either the wicked old crone who feeds on the young and the innocent in her quest for youth and beauty, or the young and deceptive temptress who hides the festering evil witch beneath her firm young flesh. In both forms she is emotional, irrational, often hysterical, and never to be trusted. Her coven might be patriarchal, in which case she was part of an inverted and Satanic family—or more appropriately a commune—headed by a wicked father who had led his multiple wives and daughters astray. Her coven might likewise be matriarchal and therefore without any rational guidance, a clear damnation of the single-mother or lesbian household. As alternative models of the family, both of these coven structures represented a threat to the white middle-class status quo as it was imagined in mid-century America and Britain. Events in 1969 (including the Altamont Free Concert, which was meant to be a peaceful gathering of hippies but ended in murder and rioting, and the Tate-LaBianca murders, which were committed by members of the free-thinking Manson Family), called into question the liberal agenda of the counter culture, its effects on American youth, and the future of the traditional family. For conservatives, these events were a tangible validation of the Satanic horrors that had befallen society.

The collective fear that Satan and his wenches had somehow destroyed Anglo-American family values by infecting the young and penetrating the middle-class home was made manifest in the horror cinema of the 1970s, when demon-possessed adolescent girls joined the rank and file of witches and Satanists.[17] Released in 1973, William Peter Blatty's film *The Exorcist* spoke to cultural angst about female sexuality and the empowerment of young women in American culture. In the film, Regan's liberated mother is a successful actress who spends the bulk of her time working and networking with colleagues. Divorced and a single parent, she does her best to spend what time she can with her daughter. Young Regan is left to her own devices much of the time, however, and entertains herself with a Ouija Board, through which she befriends a demon in the guise of Captain Howdy. Unsupervised in the basement with this purportedly male entity, Regan—on the very edge of puberty—opens herself up to him, either consciously or unconsciously, and becomes possessed. Regan's mood swings become violent, her language offensive, her sexual impulses unhidden; her body is transformed into corrupt and melancholic flesh, cold and ashen, that emits foul vapors and uncontrollable mucous, vomit, and urine. Once a sweet and innocent girl, the pubescent Regan has become a creature of abject horror. Her transformation reflects a cultural fear of sexually awakened and liberated female bodies as potentially toxic, corrupt, demon-ridden, and deadly. While *The Exorcist* drew viewers from a broad range of constituents, it was particularly popular with conservative, evangelical, and charismatic Christians. For these groups, the film confirmed many of their beliefs, including the need for paternal management within the family, the irrational nature of women, the dangers of female sexuality, the increasing presence of Satanic evil in modern America, and the ability of demons to use the young generation for wanton evil Furthermore, *The Exorcist* seemed to reveal the perversity of Catholicism and the limited effectiveness of Catholic Ritual—both of which were held under suspicion by many Protestant groups as potentially Satanic.

The success of *The Exorcist* spawned a whole new genre of supernatural horror film that focused on possessed female bodies. Along with official and unofficial sequels to *The Exorcist* came the exploitation films *The Antichrist* (1974), Blacksploitation films such as *Abby* (1974), and the Nunsploitation films *Satanico Pandemonium* (1975) and *Guardian of Hell* (1981).[18] In each of the subgenres, female flesh is constructed as irrational, wanton, weak and in desperate need of control by white male authority. Nunsploitation films carried the further message that women should not live alone as a community without close male supervision; to do so is to risk hysteria, lesbianism, demon possession, and Satanic witchcraft. Throughout the '70s and into the twenty-first century, possession films have proliferated alongside those centered on witchcraft, and the two subgenres have often been conflated. Through the persistent lens of male hegemony and anti-feminism, there is little difference between the self-possessed woman, the woman possessed by the Devil, and the witch that straddles them both.

Patriarchal Evil: Women Witches in the Service of Wicked Men

Several witchcraft films from the 1960s and '70s, including *The Devil's Hand* (1962), *The Witchmaker* (1969), *The Brotherhood of Satan* (1971), and *The Witching* (1972), feature wanton witches young and old who worship together in covens led by patriarchal figures. In each of these films, the irrational body of the melancholy and Satanic witch is subject to an inverted father-husband who uses his authority to lead his female ward into perdition. Although she is often cast into a more modern form, both the body of the witch and the inverted family structure in which she operates conform to the paradigms of Satanic evil crafted by late-medieval theologians. Just beneath the modern veneer of each of these films, there lurks a suppurating feminine evil, dark and primal, aching to be unleashed.

In the American film *The Devil's Hand*, directed by William Hole, Jr., Rick Turner (Robert Alda) is torn between his frowsy girlfriend Donna Trent (Adriana Welter) and a blonde vixen (Linda Christian) who appears to him in his dreams. Night after night, she floats into Rick's imagination wearing a filmy white robe and dancing seductively through storm clouds.[19] "Shall I sing until your head throbs with the sound of my voice?" she sings, "Shall I dance for you, until the blood races through your veins? Do you find me desirable? Would you kiss me if you could? Would you hold me close?" Unable to resist her, Rick determines to visit her the following evening. When he arrives at Bianca's apartment, she greets him at the door wearing a sheer white negligée that allows him to see every curve of her voluptuous body. When Rick asks her why she has been entering his dreams, his flirtatious hostess tells him, "I saw you, I wanted you. That's what makes you special." He responds like a father scolding a spoiled child, telling her, "We can't always have what we want." Confidently, she replies, "I can." When he explains that he is engaged to be married, she laughs at him: "There you are then. I had to condition you. Wear down your resistance. Make you want me. So I visited you through mental projection." She then demonstrates her ability to penetrate his mind, much like a medieval demon that can manipulate the rational *pneuma* and cause lucid sexual phantasies.[20] In a haze of thunder and lightning, against a backdrop of howling storm winds, Bianca—like a night-flying witch—crosses the room and enters his thoughts. As she materializes, Rick says, "You cast no shadow, no reflection. What are you? A she-devil?" Laughing, Bianca says, "Don't you know? A witch!" Rick pulls her close, gives in to her power. "You are evil," he whispers, "but beautiful and fascinating."

Bianca, like a late-medieval sex witch, is a creature of deception. On the surface, she appears to be young and beautiful; beneath her radiant veneer, however, she is corrupted by an infectious evil. Having cast her spell on the otherwise-rational Rick, Bianca tells him that if he wants her physically, he must first join her coven, which worships "Gamba, the devil god of evil." To become one of them, Rick must "take an oath to Gamba," just as medieval witches and their victims were believed to sign a pact with the Devil. Bianca brings him to the coven's temple behind a doll shop run by a European man named Francis Lamont (Neil Hamilton). When they arrive, the members of the coven, many of whom are vaguely foreign and all of whom are wealthy, are gathering for the "midnight sacrifice" of a human, according to the devil god's decree. The room is filled with iconography from Buddhism, Hinduism, and African Animistic traditions; a statue of a Roman mother goddess, perhaps Venus, holds a prominent position.[21] In pairs, they sit on Oriental carpets and sway back and forth while a zombie-like black man drums a Voodoo beat and a black woman named Mary gyrates in ecstasy. Francis, the high

Bourgeois members of the Gamba Cult gather in their secret chamber, complete with Buddhist, Hindu, and African iconography, while Mary (Gere Craft) dances wildly to "Voodoo" drums. *The Devil's Hand*, William J. Hole, Jr., Crown International (1962).

priest and authoritative father figure of the coven, ascends to his pulpit and says, "Tonight is the first night of the full moon. The tides rise to their highest level and vibrations fill the air. It is a time for restlessness and madness. It is a time for death." At the conclusion of the ritual, Rick and Bianca kneel before Francis as if they are getting married, and Rick takes his oath to follow Gamba. At home, Bianca says, "You still don't realize it yet, do you, darling? You've renounced goodness, forsaken virtue. You'll never escape me now." Through the power of one wicked woman, Rick has left his fiancée, enslaved himself to a witch, and sold his very soul to "the devil god of evil."

Medieval inversion dominates in *The Devil's Hand*, particularly in its treatment of women as fundamentally corrupt. The women of the film form a trinity, each of them having a name—Mary, Bianca, and Donna—that connotes purity and holiness. Despite their appellations, the first two of these women are irrational and best governed by male authority. Beneath her calm exterior, the servant girl Mary, whose name might be a reference to the Blessed Virgin or the Magdalene, is an agent of evil, dancing for Gamba's pleasure and serving the needs of the coven at Francis' command. While Mary is quietly obedient to Francis and his evil god, the witch Bianca is not. Bianca, or "white," at first appears to be a liberated creature of power in full command of her own fate; her ability to manipulate Rick, however, is nevertheless governed by the male coven leader, Francis, who is also revealed to be her husband. Francis indulges his beautiful wife's irrational desire for other men but always maintains financial and spiritual control over her, forcing her to curb her appetites when they endanger the coven. When Bianca pouts after being told to exterminate Rick, Francis reminds her that she is "an amazing woman, but a *woman nonetheless*." If she does not obey him, she will lose everything. The third woman, Donna, an abbreviation of Madonna, is the most innocent of the three. Plain and humble, she is aware of her own emotional and intellectual weaknesses; at one point, she reminds Rick that she is jealous, but she is just "being a woman." Even though he has abandoned her romantically, Donna remains kind, patient, and obedient. For example, Rick tells her that she must leave town for her own safety; although she does not understand the circumstances, she obeys him and agrees to uproot her entire life and start over somewhere new. Ultimately, Bianca and Francis capture Donna and demand that Rick sacrifice her like an innocent lamb upon the altar in order to prove his fidelity to Gamba and the coven. Instead, Rick kills Francis, sets the temple on fire, and escapes with Donna. Since the evil heretics have been burned, Rick believes that he is now free from their corruption. As he and Donna drive into the sunset, however, Bianca's voice can be heard from the clouds mocking him: "That's what he thinks!" The ending reinforces the toxic nature of sexually desperate women, their ability to destroy sacred relationships in the past, present and future, and the necessity that men be wary of them and vigilant against their chaos at all times.

The Devil's Hand speaks to medieval inversion not only in its depiction of feminine evil but also in its structuring of the Gamba coven, which is led by an evil man in parody of a Christian congregation. Like the imaginary covens of the later Middle Ages, the acolytes gather in a secret place, in this case hiding behind the innocence of a doll shop, and perform midnight rituals involving human sacrifice and blood pacts with their evil god.[22] Just as medieval theologians cast any group that did not conform with Christian orthodoxy into the inverted category of Satanic evil, so too does this film conflate all non–Christian traditions into one sinister cult. The Gamba temple looks less like a Satanic ritual space and more like a meeting place for a local theosophical society—both of which, from a conservative Christian point of view, may appear to be one and the same thing. Of all of the religions represented, Voodoo has the most influence on the cult's practices, including their use of drums, wild dancing, and effigies to control those who cross their paths.[23] The use of dolls and pins has long been associated with witchcraft in the West; in the twentieth and twenty-first centuries, however, it has likewise become a signifier for Voodoo, both African and Haitian, as imagined by terrified whites.[24] During the American occupation of Haiti between 1915 and 1934, Americans developed a primal terror of Voodoo as an expression of Black Power, and this fear manifested in horror films such as *White Zombie* (1932) and its myriad descendants. Voodoo was quickly conflated with Satanism and witchcraft, and since the early twentieth century has become a salient feature in films about occult evil. *The Devil's Hand* is replete with African and Haitian motifs, from the bongo drummer and Mary the quasi-possessed dancing servant to the use of masks, dolls, and the evocation of Gamba, who is not only evil but also, apparently, black in multiple senses. In this context, the white Francis' service and obedience to a black deity sets up yet another layer of inversion for mid-century conservative audiences discomfited by the burgeoning Civil Rights Movement. The conflation of blackness in *The Devil's Hand* not only conforms to medieval inversion, but also speaks to racial dynamics that are unfortunately still prevalent in modern America.[25]

Released seven years after *The Devil's Hand*, Bill Brown's *The Witchmaker* (1969) shares several of the previous film's themes, including the wicked power of irrational women and the necessity for patriarchal control. Unlike *The Devil's Hand*, however *The Witchmaker* speaks directly to the tradition of late-medieval Satanic witchcraft as imagined by theologians and jurists and suggests that it has permeated modern America, just beyond the view of mainstream society.[26] In this film, Professor Ralph Hayes (Alvy Moore), his student assistants from the college, the clairvoyant Tasha (Thordis Brandt), and reporter Victor Gordon (Anthony Eisley) rent a dilapidated cabin in the Louisiana swamps where they plan on conducting research related to electromagnetism and psychic energy.[27] Professor Hayes, who serves as a father figure for the group, and Victor, who is romantically interested in Tasha, are aware that several young women have been the victims of a ritual murderer who frequents the bottom lands around their cabin. Hayes is unconcerned and believes that he will be able to protect his brood against whatever might be lurking out on the bayou; unfortunately, he does not realize that their cabin is in close proximity to a five-hundred-year-old witch named Luther the Berserk who functions as the Sabbath Master of a Satanic Parish, and that they have arrived three days before Candlemas, the night of the Witches' Sabbath.[28] Upon seeing the blonde and beautiful Tasha, Luther determines that she will join his coven, which stands one witch short of the required thirteen members, and be his evil bride-companion. The balance of the film centers on the battle for the possession of the objectified Tasha's body and soul, with the professor-father and Victor-husband on one side and Luther-father-husband and his coven on the other.

In both his physical appearance and role as Satanic coven master, Luther conforms in almost every detail to late-medieval paradigms for inverted evil. He is an ugly and melancholic creature, large and lumbering, with shaggy black hair, deepset eyes, and an enormous unibrow, long considered the sign of a shape shifter. Realizing that he will need help seducing Tasha into the coven, Luther conducts a ritual invoking Satan's help; through the agency of demons, a second witch arrives to assist him, announcing, "I have come a great way." Jessie, like Luther, is an embodiment of melancholic evil. As she emerges from the shadows, she appears in the guise of a paradigmatic witch, with black stringy hair, pale and pendulous flesh, warty skin, hooked nose, and unibrow. Like Luther, she is wearing medieval garb, including a long peasant skirt, tattered shirt, and shawl, all of which are filthy. Jessie and Luther sit down at the Sabbath table and eat greasy meat washed down greedily with thick red wine. Looking at him intently with her watery red eyes, Jessie says usuriously, "Let us talk like merchants." Luther wants Tasha to take an oath to Satan and join his coven. In order to seduce her, he needs Jessie to perform a Satanic ritual with a young woman's blood under the full moon. In return for her assistance, Luther promises to rejuvenate Jessie so that she might once again seduce and manipulate attractive men. Their covenant sealed under the watchful eyes of Satan, Luther slaughters another young woman and uses her blood to transform Jessie into a voluptuous vixen with flowing black hair and firm breasts. Despite her transformation, Jessie's appearance—like that of all irrational women—is deceptive; beneath the false veneer of youth and beauty lies the same old toxic and melancholic creature, the continued presence of which manifests in the raspy and aged voice that emanates from her otherwise demure throat. Glaring seductively at Luther, she says, "It's been a long time since a man has looked at me like that," and he drags her into his arms and kisses her roughly. With Luther having kept his part of the bargain, Jessie uses her demonic powers to penetrate the mind of our third witch, the blonde and lovely Tasha.

In *The Witchmaker*, Tasha plays the most deceptive and cunning role of all of the witches. Luther and Jessie are unquestionably evil, and their wicked natures are written in their flesh, voices, and actions. Unlike Luther and Jessie, Tasha is not outwardly dark or melancholic, nor is she a subterranean creature of the Middle Ages. Instead, she is a paradigm of mid-twentieth century youth and beauty, blonde and tan, fond of sunbathing in a bikini. Tasha also gives the impression of being innocent and vulnerable, in part because of her clairvoyant powers. For example, Hayes tells Victor that Tasha is so highly suggestible that he can hypnotize her almost instantly. At several points in the narrative, Tasha's clairvoyance is attributed to her family lineage: We learn that her grandmother was reputedly a witch who cast vengeful spells on all those who maligned Tasha as a child. When Victor questions the professor about the existence of witches, Hayes confirms that not only did they once "cast spells and sign pacts with Satan," but that they still do. By this estimation, all witches—including Tasha's grandmother and, through her, Tasha—are in league with the Devil. According to witchcraft treatises including Nicholas Remy's *Demonolatry*, the Satanic stain of witchcraft is carried in the blood from one generation to the next.[29] Tasha's New Age psychic powers, then, are in no way innocent, but a sign that she is marked for evil. Her suggestibility and hereditary wickedness make Tasha an easy target for Jessie's mental manipulations, and she is quickly brought under the control of the coven. She begins wearing a filmy red negligee as she wanders mindlessly through the swamps, ultimately joining Luther and Jessie and making her pact with Satan.

Tasha appears to be an innocent victim of circumstance; however, she is in truth a toxic creature who is impossible to stop. Irrational and daft, Tasha nevertheless defeats every man in the film and reigns as an evil queen at its conclusion. Despite the professor's best efforts to thwart Luther, which include the use of garlic as protection against the witches' powers, Tasha slips from his control and, like a rebellious daughter, becomes his enemy. She uses her newly awakened sexual prowess to seduce a sweet college boy assigned to stand guard; she likewise manipulates her suitor, Victor, into doing her bidding. As Luther chases Tasha and Victor through the swamps, the viewer is led to believe that Luther will be defeated and the young couple will escape and live a blissful middle-class life. In reality, Tasha destroys both Luther and Victor, each of whom hoped to control her as her husband, and she becomes the head witch and Sabbath Master of the Parish. Like Bianca in *The Devil's Hand*, Tasha is not only impossible to kill but also increases in her evil power with the destruction of the patriarchal forces put in place to control her. In both films, the message is the same: men must be wary of their wives and daughters, no matter how seemingly sweet and pure. Every woman is tainted in the blood, and even the nicest of girls harbor evil tendencies which might be exacerbated by external forces such as feminism and New Age beliefs. Fathers and husbands must maintain control over their irrational female charges. If not, the chaos of feminine evil will permeate a society turned upside down.

The Devil's Hand and *The Witchmaker* both feature wicked men who lose control over the evil women in their Satanic families; *The Brotherhood of Satan* (1971) and *The Witching* (1972) feature Satanic witch covens who are ruled by absolute patriarchs who dominate the women and children within their domains with unwavering power. Bernard McEveety's *The Brotherhood of Satan* follows a single father named Ben (Charles Bateman), his girlfriend Nicky (Ahna Capri), and Ben's daughter from his first marriage, K.T. (Geri Reischl), as they travel across the Inland Empire of Southern California to visit Ben's mother and celebrate K.T.'s birthday. What begins as an idyllic trip quickly turns to dysfunction and terror as the young family is lured into a small desert town plagued by a Satanic witch cult from which they cannot escape. As events unfold, Ben, the sheriff (L.Q. Jones), and the priest (Charles Robinson) discover that a coven of elderly witches led by the town doctor (Strother Martin) are capturing the town's children in order to steal their young bodies and live "one more lifetime in the Brotherhood of Satan." The desire of the wealthy and wicked elderly to feed on children and thereby regain their own youth is in alignment with the blood-hungry body of the melancholy witch as constructed in the later Middle Ages.

The dominant theme in *The Brotherhood of Satan* is fatherhood, with the failure of Christian patriarchy and the destruction of the traditional nuclear family on one side, and the success of Satanic patriarchy and the creation of the alternative family from wicked women and stolen children on the other. The film features several broken families, including that of Ben, a single father trying desperately to nurture and discipline his daughter while having a steamy relationship with his young and self-willed girlfriend.

Another single father in the film suffers from manic depression and alcoholism; because of his helplessness and self-loathing, his son Joey is abducted by the coven. Other failed paternal authorities include the sheriff, who is powerless to prevent the death and disappearance of his citizens, and the priest, who can't to stop the coven despite his specialized knowledge of the occult and the holy powers with which he was ordained.

The impotence of the priest is not only a failure of paternalism, but also an indictment of Christianity's power to offer guidance and protect against evil in modern society. The failure of traditional family structures and Christian values is further evidenced in one of the town's most devout families. The unnamed father is a hard-working man whose wife stays home and cares for their young son and daughter. Upon returning home from work, he disciplines his wife and children, warns them of the dangers lurking beyond their home, and demands that they remain indoors and not leave without his permission. After telling his wife that her sister has been slain by the coven, he orders her to control herself, to mind her emotions in front of the children. Later that evening, after the children are in bed, he reads to his wife from the Bible as she does needlework. Despite his best efforts to impose Christian order on his family, the coven enters this man's home, steals his daughter, strangles his wife, and slaughters him while he is in the very midst of prayer. With strong fathers and Christian values becoming scarce, the small town sits defenseless in the sight of the Devil.

While Christian men have lost control of their flocks, the coven leader Doc Duncan dominates his Satanic family without mercy. Duncan, who is both a doctor and a Satanic witch, is a delightfully duplicitous character. As a physician, he is a trusted individual within the community, a man above reproach. He has authority over the bodies of his patients, all of whom must follow "doctor's orders."[30] As the Patriarch of a Satanic coven, he is similarly all-powerful, in control of the lives and bodies of the men and women under his wicked pastoral care. All of the coven members are wealthy, old, grasping, and gnarly; one of the female witches, Dame Alice (Helen Winston), is particularly desperate.[31] Arriving late to one of the Sabbath meetings, she is mocked by hissing, gossipy women. Accused of having her baby baptized in the Christian church, Dame Alice—who is also Duncan's wife—is condemned by her husband for her disobedience and beaten to death by the members of the coven.[32] While Duncan may be a stern and merciless patriarch willing to sacrifice his own wife for her willfulness, he nevertheless provides the coven with the children that they require, performs all of the sacrifices and inverted Catholic rituals necessary for their rebirth, and even delays his own transformation until he is assured that the rest of the members of his brood have safely passed

4. *Wicked Women: Female Flesh, Satanic Witch and Horror Film* 115

In this underground Satanic chapel, dominated by gothic arches and the colors red and black (both of which signified death, decay, and earth-bound evil in medieval color theory), the patriarchal high priest, Doc Duncan, transfers the souls of his elderly congregation into the bodies of stolen children. The ankh behind the altar indicates the conflation of the New Age with the Satanic. *The Brotherhood of Satan,* **Bernard McEveety, Columbia (1971).**

over. The film's conclusion makes it clear that Duncan's Satanic family, albeit inverted and evil, will survive well into the future because they respect and obey his patriarchal authority. For conservative Americans, this small desert town with its failed Christian fathers and successful Satanic coven was merely a microcosm of American life at mid-century. From their perspective, American culture was under siege by liberated women, flower children, and New Age religions, all of which had compromised the sanctity and security of the Christian patriarchal family and allowed a Satanic New World Order—strong and hierarchical—to emerge on the edge of the Apocalypse.[33]

Like *The Brotherhood of Satan*, Bert I. Gordon's *The Witching* (also known as *Necromancy*, 1972) features a megalomaniacal father figure as the leader of a Satanic coven of California witches. The film centers on a young woman named Lori (Pamela Franklin) who has just given birth to a stillborn child, and her husband Frank Brandon (Michael Ontkean), who has taken a job in the small town of Lilith. Despite her recent trauma and her fear of leaving Southern California, Frank tells Lori to relax and demands that they relocate immediately. Witnessing a gruesome car crash as they approach the gated community of Lilith, Lori has a vision of a dark-haired woman who warns her that the town is "filled with slime and evil" and that she should be wary of Mr. Cato (Orson Welles), owner of the toy company where her husband will work. The apparition likewise warns Lori to "beware of their bitter waters" in Lilith because they are deadly. After their arrival, Lori is skeptical of everyone she meets, aggressively questioning Cato and his associates much to her husband's embarrassment. Upon their first meeting, Cato asks Lori if she believes in the Black Arts and offers her a Renaissance grimoire called the Clavicle of Solomon. At their second meeting, she is offered a cup of bitter liquid to drink—in fact all of the water in the town is bitter like gall.[34] Upon drinking from the goblet, Lori looks at Cato and his true visage, that of a goat-headed Devil, is revealed. At an orgiastic party held by the town doctor-psychic, Lori and her husband see naked women fondling grapes and stroking the horns of a goat, a man being whipped by a leather-clad dominatrix, and people getting drunk in monastic robes as they wander through a house filled with black candles and pentagrams. The doctor informs Lori that the town is not only dedicated to Satanic witchcraft, but that it has been given over to absolute pleasure—as long as Cato's rules are followed.

One of Cato's strictest rules is that children are not allowed within Lilith's boundaries, and women who become pregnant while living in Lilith meet a sudden death.[35] Like their medieval counterparts in the *Malleus Maleficarum*, the witches of Lilith have the power to interrupt the processes of conception and to kill fetuses in utero by using spells, potions, and effigies.[36] Despite Cato's injunction, Lori is stalked by a blond-haired little boy who leads her to confront Cato about his hatred of children and his intentions in bringing her to Lilith. Cato confesses that he knows about Lori's power to bring the dead back to life—an ability that the film wrongly calls necromancy—and that he has brought her to Lilith to revivify his dead son. It was his young son's death that served as the catalyst for his revival of "the old religion" of Satanism and the reason he cannot bear to look upon children. In a dreamlike sequence of events, Lori learns that the coven invoked Satan and used an effigy to kill her baby, that her husband is having sex with the other women of Lilith, and that her mother—the dark-haired woman in her visions—was a powerful witch who cursed Cato and caused his son's death. These revelations in combination with the bitter and corrupting waters of Lilith place Lori under Cato's power; his spirit enters her helpless body and she is led to his house where she is forced to stand naked before a Satanic altar, complete with flaming red candles and a huge painting of Baphomet. Placing a black robe on her, Cato commands her to make her pact with the devil and to accept Lucifer as her only god by saying, "That other god and his church, I here renounce, all its laws and sacraments I refuse." After making her pact, she sacrifices her lecherous husband upon the altar and offers his blood to Satan.[37] Having joined Cato's Satanic family, Lori is brought to the cemetery where she raises Cato's son from the dead and is herself cast into the casket. In her dying scene, she sees images of a Catholic church and witnesses herself killing her husband and stabbing a doll-like effigy, all of which suggests that she is truly responsible for the deaths of her husband and child. Her final vision only confirms her guilt as she watches herself burn at the stake like a heretical witch, tainted in the blood and wicked as hell despite her efforts to be a good wife and mother.

A deeply misogynistic film from beginning to end, *The Witching* conforms closely to medieval paradigms in its construction of all women, no matter how well-intentioned, as evil. Descended from witches, Lori is doomed as a daughter of Eve, who through no fault of her own is stained by the sins of previous generations. Like late-medieval mystics and witches, Lori is a weak and irrational vessel open to both good and evil spirits; she is likewise easily manipulated by the powerful men in her life, including her adulterous husband, the omnipotent Cato, and perhaps even Satan himself. While the film begins with her rational attempts to question male authority and unravel the mysteries that surround her, Lori becomes increasingly irrational as her husband abandons her and she is dominated by Cato, who abuses her, treating her like a bad daughter who must die so that his good son might live. Despite her efforts to rebel against Cato and her husband, she is unable to break free. She kills her husband at Cato's command, yet feels remorse at what she has done; she signs a pact with Satan under Cato's influence, yet still perishes in flames as a witch. Unable to become a mother, Lori's primary function in the film is to serve the needs of men, first her husband, then the paternalistic Cato. When Cato no longer needs her, he tosses her melancholic body into the ground like a piece of garbage, returning it to the cold and corrupt earth from which it came.

Wicked Power: The Woman Witch Ascendant

At the height of the Women's Liberation Movement in the 1960s and '70s, witchcraft films emphasized the need for patriarchal control over unmitigated female empowerment. Films such as *The City of the Dead* (1960), *The Witches*

(1966), and *Cry of the Banshee* (1970) explored the terrifying consequences of allowing women, with their irrational and fundamentally evil natures, to rule others without the close supervision of male authority. Each film features a wicked female coven leader engaged in a ravenous quest for youth, beauty, power, or revenge for anti-woman violence; these witches are ultimately defeated by either a dominant male or an obedient female, each of whom represent a return to traditional and patriarchal control. *The City of the Dead* opens with black-hooded figures moving through dense fog, carrying lit torches, and chanting Latin in low and somber voices. The object of their journey is the execution of Elizabeth Selwyn (Patricia Jessel), a pale woman with wild and stringy black hair who stands accused of being a whore and sacrificing young girls to Satan in order to attain youth and beauty. As a man named Jethro looks upon her helplessly, saying, "Lucifer, please help her," the rest of the townsfolk shout, "Burn the witch!" In response, the local minster intones her fate: "May the flames cleanse thy soul of His Evil, of His lust for blood." Disregarding the minister's authority, she calls out to her true master, screaming, "I have made my pact with thee, Oh Lucifer. Hear me!" Like a spoiled child caught misbehaving, Selwyn demands that her father, Satan, avenge his righteous daughter. As she does so, a shadow, cold and dark, moves across the village, sealing its melancholic doom.

When next we meet Selwyn she is the sole proprietor of the Raven's Inn, a business that operates in the cursed town of Whitewood, Massachusetts. Set in a sea of fog, the Raven's Inn obscures the subterranean meeting place of a coven of Satanic witches, over which the duplicitous Selwyn rules as Head Witch and Sabbath Master. While she is managing the Inn, Selwyn appears as a prim and proper business woman, her suit closely fitted, her hair in a spartan bun, her thin and pale face calm and serious in its expressions. As a professional, it is her responsibility to see to the needs of her guests, including Nan Barlowe, a college student who has come to Whitewood to research witchcraft. Below ground, however, Selwyn is an inversion of herself; as leader of her coven, she wears a flowing black robe, her hair is unkempt and wild, and her eyes and face express a tempest of frenetic emotions. In this, her true and irrational form, Selwyn drags Nan Barlowe down into the bowels of the Inn where she is sacrificed to Satan and her blood consumed by the witches, including Jethro, so that they might live forever.

Like her medieval European ancestors, Selwyn is driven by her melancholic female flesh to consume the warm wet blood of the young to rebalance her bodily system. Through the agency of Satan, this blood restores her youth and beauty, thereby ensuring that she will be able to seduce men and, like a spider, extract their vital heat and fluids and bind them in her web. Jethro, for example, is spellbound by Selwyn, sees her as an unquestionable authority, reveres her as an evil goddess, and obeys her every command. Jethro's emasculation by Selwyn's evil power is in conformity with medieval texts such as the *Malleus Maleficarum*, which discusses the ability of female witches to prevent erections and to abscond with the penises of their enemies.[38] Despite the potency of Selwyn's feminine evil, she is ultimately defeated by Nan Barlowe's boyfriend, a young man from outside of Whitewood, who raises a cross against Selwyn and her coven and burns them alive. The warmth and light of his male rationality coupled with the fortitude of his Christian self-sacrifice are the remedy required to defeat the melancholic Selwyn's 200-year reign of feminine terror. Only in the world of inverted and Satanic evil can a woman hold power over men and dictate their actions; in the realm of goodness and light, it is the strong Christian man who must lead women and contain their potential to wreak havoc.

The intelligent and liberated woman's quest for youth, beauty, and power are at the very heart of Hammer's *The Witches*. Released in 1966, *The Witches* tells the tale of Gwen Mayfield (Joan Fontaine), who teaches at a missionary school in Africa. Her African assistants explain that a local priest has cursed her and that he will send a spirit to "eat her soul." As she assures the young men that their belief in witchcraft is irrational, a ritual object is thrown into the hut and Gwen becomes so terrified that she has a nervous breakdown.[39] We next see Gwen, timid and delicate, as she accepts a job as headmistress in the small English village of Heddaby, which strangely enough does not have a local church. As director of the school, Gwen answers to the town's wealthy nobles, a man named Alan Bax (Alec McCowen), who has a penchant for dressing up as a priest and studying theology, and his sister Stephanie (Kay Walsh), a journalist known for her intelligence, cutting wit, and willingness to brashly question authority. Gwen attempts to get closer to Alan, but his shy nature makes a relationship nearly impossible; Stephanie, however, is extroverted and charming, and the two immediately strike up a friendship. In a tree, Gwen discovers a doll that has been stabbed with pins. When she confronts Stephanie with her discovery, Stephanie tells her that she is not surprised, and that such simple witchcraft is the sort of thing that old women do as they feel themselves losing power. She claims that it's harmless and suggests that they do research and collaborate on an article about local witchcraft for publication. Several events convince Gwen that this witchcraft is not so innocent: a young man who resembles the doll unexpectedly falls into a coma and his father is drowned in a pond after confronting a local old woman named Granny Rigg, who many claim is a witch. Slowly, Gwen's mind unravels, and she is once again committed to a mental hospital.

Upon her return to Heddaby, Gwen is welcomed into Stephanie and Alan's home and returns to work at the schoolhouse. One of her students, Granny Rigg's granddaughter Linda, has disappeared. Playing detective, Gwen is lured into one of the Bax family tombs where she is stunned to discover Stephanie wearing monastic robes, a chasuble bearing a dark and demonic face, and a headdress with two skeletal hands in the shape of antlers with lit candles at the tips.[40] Stephanie, pleased to have her secret discovered, takes Gwen back to the house and shows her a Renaissance grimoire containing alchemical recipes and learned spells which she has studied and mastered. Through this elite magic, which Stephanie claims is superior to the false witchcraft of the foolish peasants, she has found a solution to prolonging her own life.[41] Driven mad by her irrational desire to be the most intelligent and powerful woman alive, Stephanie has determined to become young again by sacrificing young Linda Griggs, who is merely a peasant and therefore disposable. Why should a noble woman with such mental prowess and potential be wasted in the grave? Despite Gwen's apprehension and disgust, Stephanie explains that she must guide young Linda into the sacrifice and ensure that no blood contaminates the altar before the appropriate time. In the film's

The highly educated Stephanie Bax (Kay Walsh), whose study of Renaissance grimoires and her own lust for power have led her to found a witch cult in the small hamlet of Heddaby. Notice the headdress with its skeletal hands alight, representing pagan images as well as the Hand of Glory from the *Malleus Maleficarum*. *The Witches*, Cyril Frankel, Hammer Horror (1966).

concluding scenes, Gwen and Linda, both of whom wear white, and the red-clad Stephanie descend into the subterranean sacrificial womb-chamber where the townsfolk, inexplicably wearing rags and writhing in ecstasy on the floor to the beat of bongos and asynchronous horns, begin engaging in orgiastic behavior.[42] Linda enters the room, her body is possessed, and she dances seductively towards the altar. While Stephanie prepares to penetrate Linda's virgin body with her steely knife-phallus, Gwen slices into her own arm and her motherly blood splatters onto Linda and Stephanie, saying, "At the moment of sacrifice, let no blood be spilled!" Gwen's redemptive blood not only destroys Stephanie, whose old and contorted body is cast to the cold dry ground, but also redeems the life of the innocent lamb Linda, whose beauty, innocence, and youth are preserved.

Wealthy, irrational, and greedy for superiority, Stephanie is a manifestation of feminism as seen by its detractors. Her hunger for knowledge and a command of elite magic has led her into a realm traditionally reserved only for men. Manly in her appearance, Stephanie is unmarried and apparently uninterested in either men or motherhood, perhaps because of her self-obsession, perhaps because she is more interested in Gwen and the company of women. Her objectification of and desire for Linda's body, be it through possession or phallic penetration, further suggest a lesbian interpretation of this witchy character. Lesbian or not, Stephanie's voracious hunger for domination has led her to subordinate her pathetically weak brother Alan and an entire village of people entrusted to her care, making her not only a bad potential wife, but also a horrible sister and wicked mother. This voracious feminist nightmare is held in check by the traditionally oriented Gwen, whose primary impulses are maternal, evident in her protection of the schoolchildren in her care, and wifely, evident in her nurturing and deferential treatment of Alan. Domesticated and meek, obedient and kind, Gwen sheds her own blood in order to defeat Stephanie's evil and protect young Linda. Her sacrificial act likewise liberates Alan, who can now prevail as the town's Christian authority; together, he and Gwen will serve as proper parents for their village family now that the wicked stepmother-sister is dead.

Like *City of the Dead* and *The Witches*, Gordon Hessler's *Cry of the Banshee* (1970) features a powerful matriarch, this time named Oona (Elisabeth Bergner), as the leader of a coven of witches. Unlike her predecessors, however, Oona and her coven only turn to Satan when they have been raped and tortured by the true source of evil in the film, the tyrannical patriarch Lord Edward Whitman (Vincent Price). Following on the success of the harrowingly misogynist film *Witchfinder General* (1968), *Cry of the Banshee* centers on the male members of the Whitman family and their repeated victimization of women. In the opening scene, a haggard woman is accused of witchcraft. Stripped to the waist, she is whipped through the village, put into stocks and tormented by men who call her a "dirty witch." Later, at Whitman's banquet, two young villagers are thrown before the magistrate as "heathens" accused of subversion. The brother is made to watch while several men rip the clothes from his pubescent sister as they kiss her mouth and nipples. In this simulated gang rape, it is Whitman who ultimately throws himself upon the young girl, kissing her savagely as she begs for mercy—all while looking back at his disgusted wife in triumph. After the youths are slain by Whitman and his "bully boy," his angelic wife Patricia (Essy Persson) bends down and touches their blood to her hands; holding them up as if marked by the stigmata, she glares at her husband and says meekly, "Murderer." Her stepson Sean Whitman (Stephan Chase) then warns her, "Take care, woman. He can soon find a third wife." After escorting his stepmother to her room, Sean abuses her, telling her, "My real mother raised me, and she was a *wife* to him! Without him, you are nothing." He then proceeds to rip open her bodice and rape her. Again, in the local tavern, Sean and his thugs brutalize the serving wench, ripping open her dress and savagely attacking her, all while the bar's patrons—and through the camera's lens, the audience—look on, feeding their scopophilia, fully entertained. A beautiful redhead is then discovered to be selling "acorns, shells, and feathers," and is accused of witchcraft, her breasts exposed, and tormented until she reveals the leader of the coven to be an old woman named Oona.

While the first half of the film focuses on the victimhood of women, the second half features vengeful women who summon Satanic forces against their male oppressors. When we first meet the coven leader Oona, she is wearing a black robe beneath a white chasuble, a sign of her duplicitous nature. In the ruins of a medieval church deep in the forest, Oona leads her scantily clad followers, all of whom wear white and have flowers or leaves intertwined in their hair, in a fertility dance. Upon a stone altar, a naked woman lies prone, awaiting her male companion. While much of this scene echoes elements of Satanic worship as imagined in late-medieval and modern popular culture, including the orgiastic dancing, the nude sacrifice upon the altar, and the forest setting, it is presented as an innocent pagan ritual conducted openly in daylight.[43] When they are discovered by Whitman and his men, Oona and her followers are savagely attacked; two men are garroted, the nude woman is penetrated by an enormous phallic sword, and several others are ensnared in a net and hacked to death, all while Oona cries out, "My children!" Whitman decides to spare Oona and thirteen of her coven as a testimony to his authority over life and death. Driven to darkness by Whitman's cruelty, Oona transforms into a black-cloaked priestess; in a subterranean chamber beneath the graveyard, she chants: "Lord Satan, god of miracles and wonders, on this evil day, I curse Lord Edward Whitman ... I conjure you, Lord Satan, send me an avenger!" Satan's vengeance manifests in Roderick (Patrick Mower), the Whitmans' groom, who is not only a foundling, but also a changeling—a soulless *sidhe* who transforms into a wolf and does Oona's bidding by killing the Whitmans, one by one.

Whitman, desperate to maintain authority, routinely denies that witchcraft is involved in either the misfortunes of his household or his failure as a patriarch to protect his family. After his son's death, his men hunt and slaughter an enormous black dog and place its head on a pike in the banquet hall. With the bitch dead, Whitman believes that he has won. When his frail wife sees the piked head, she goes mad, raving about curses and blaming Whitman for the family's demise. Whitman cannot believe that his submissive wife is suddenly strong through her own inner fortitude, and believes instead that Oona has "possessed" and "bewitched" his charge. In abject terror of losing his power and being victimized by a woman, he speaks of Oona's believers: "If they should believe that she still has power, if I should lose my authority..." In order to locate Oona, a young woman is brought into Whitman's torture chamber and forced to confess. At first she claims that Oona is good, "Oona heals"; like her late-medieval sisters, however, she quickly figures out what her inquisitors want to hear, and tells them that a "black man" came to her bed and promised her a "silver dress," and adds, "When I fly, I can shoot down any Christian who does not cross himself."[44] The young woman dies before revealing Oona's location; Whitman has failed yet again. His wife then dies at the fangs of the werewolf, and her corpse turns gray-green and her hair white, thereby taking on a truly witchy and melancholic appearance. This transformation further convinces Whitman that Oona, like all women, must be destroyed so that he may regain control. However, even after his son Harry discovers Oona's lair and slices her throat, her power continues to work from beyond the grave; her *sidhe* not only kills his remaining children, but kidnaps him and forces him on a hell-ride through eternity.

In *Cry of the Banshee*, male authority is neither granted the power to quell evil, as we saw in *City of the Dead*, nor is it redeemed by a "good woman," as we saw in *The Witches*. Instead, an aged woman confronts an abusive and misogynist patriarchy and utterly defeats it. The film is sympathetic toward Oona and the plight of all women[45]; it is, however, far from a feminist success story, and continues to promulgate deeply held anti-woman constructs born in the Middle Ages. Women young and old remain delicate beings subject to invisible forces; even the most apparently innocent of women contain the seeds of Satanic evil just below the surface of their skin. Perhaps most terrifyingly, a woman scorned will irrationally destroy both the guilty and the innocent in a fiery and uncontrollable blaze of emotions that are "born in fire" and must "die by fire."

As irrational vessels open to Satanic forces, witchy women threaten all patriarchal authority, including that of the good husband within the domestic sphere. In films such as *Daughters of Satan* (1972) and *Season of the Witch* (1972), unstable wives are the conduit by which Satanic and evil feminist forces enter into the home and quite literally murder male authority. In *Daughters of Satan*, a well-educated art dealer, Jim Robertson (Tom Selleck), and his frail young wife Chris (Barra Grant) have settled in the Philippines for the sake of Jim's career. While on an art-buying trip at Chang's Antiques, Jim finds a seventeenth-century painting of an inquisitor burning three witches at the stake in a Manila plaza. One of the witches looks exactly like his wife, so he buys it and brings it home to her. When Chris sees it, she is not only disturbed by the image but also knows the exact date of the burnings: 1592. Dumbfounded that his sheltered and clueless wife could know anything about the painting, he asks her in a patronizing tone, "Now how would you know an obscure thing like that?" She looks at him vapidly and says, "I have a funny mind ... sometimes I think I have a mind full of meringue." Throughout the course of the film, the characters in the painting come to life, including a rabid black dog named Nicodemus, a Filipina witch named Juana Rios (Paraluman), and an American witch named Kitty Duarte (Tani Guthrie). Chris, Juana, and Kitty are each linked to the painting through their witchy ancestry; so, too, is Jim, whose ancestor was the inquisitor who slaughtered the women in colonial Manila. The balance of the film follows the three witches in their attempt to kill Jim in retribution for his ancestor's actions, a quest that is finally fulfilled by his seemingly innocent and loving wife Chris.

The three women have duplicitous natures. Chris transforms from a frail and loving wife into a conniving woman committed to murdering her husband. Juanita, a selfless registered nurse, becomes a violent handmaiden of Satan in the guise of a domineering housekeeper. Kitty, a wealthy American jet-setter adventuring in the Orient, becomes a mentally unstable and sexually rapacious widow who leads the Manila Assembly of Lucifer, an underground Satanic coven.[46] Despite their varied backgrounds, the three women share the same paradigmatic body—inverted, corrupt, tainted in the blood, prone to irrational behavior, and open to invisible forces. Just as their bodies conform to medieval paradigms of inverted evil, so too does the construction of their Satanic coven. The group gathers in a subterranean chamber, invokes Satan, and punishes those who do not obey his will as heretics; novitiates are forced to desecrate the cross and deny the Christian God, and also to recite Satan's prayer, which is the Lord's Prayer backwards. In the most terrifying inversion of all, Kitty—who wears a red-flamed purple leotard with coordinating cape—subjugates her entire coven, male and female, to her unbending feminine and evil power.

The inverted world of these three Satanic witches speaks not only to deep structures and medieval paradigms but also to twentieth-century concerns about liberated women and the pestiferous nature of feminism. Juanita and Kitty are single women, self-sufficient and financially independent; Chris, however, is a traditional woman who works in the home and is dependent upon her husband for protection and financial survival. Through the power of Satan, Juanita and Kitty befriend Chris and attempt to liberate her from the subservience of housewifery and bring her into the modern world.

In the final scenes, the three women believe that they have finally killed Jim and meet at a bar. Chris mentions that she has never been there without her husband, a sign of her sheltered lifestyle; now that he is presumed dead, however, she is free to drink in historically male spaces with her newfound lady friends. Despite her freedom, Chris returns home and discovers that Jim has survived the accident that was meant to take his life. At first relieved to see him, she suddenly reverts into her evil self and stabs him as they nuzzle lovingly on the couch—one of the most domestic pieces of furniture in existence. Despite his rationality and intelligence, Jim's fatal flaw was his blind love for a woman who has joined forces with other liberated women and escaped his control. His death, then, can be interpreted as a microcosmic representation of mid-twentieth century fears that outwardly docile women were murdering male authority and destroying the traditional family under the influence of feminism.

The toxic nature of a disgruntled housewife empowered by witchery is at the heart of George Romero's *Season of the Witch* (1972).[47] It opens with a dream sequence in which Joan Mitchell (Jan White), a frowsy and tired-looking older woman in a house frock, follows her well-appointed husband Jack Mitchell (Bill Thunhurst) through an autumnal forest.[48] As they walk, he reads a paper, never looking back at her or noticing anything around him, including images of his wife as a younger woman, or their daughter who is present both as an infant and a young child. Branches repeatedly lash Joan's face and cut her skin, as if she was being abused. She then awakes to her husband looking at her disgustedly and saying, "Bye, hon." Joan falls back asleep and dreams that her husband forces her into a car, beats her with a newspaper, places her on a leash, and kennels her so he can go on a business trip. In a third dream sequence, this time brought on by boredom and Valium, Joan is with a real estate agent who is showing her around a house that comes with a handsome young handyman and a series of televisions with programming meant "to give you ideas." Other rooms are filled with women shopping, playing bridge, and having empty conversations. In this desultory house where "anything goes," Joan sees herself reflected in a mirror and again prone on the bed; in these moments of Kristevan abjection, she sees a revolting and haggard old woman with pallid wrinkled skin and gray and brittle hair. In a fourth dream vision which is repeated three times throughout the film, Joan is chased through her house and raped by a man wearing black clothes and the mask of a demon. These dream sequences establish Joan as a depressed, dissatisfied, and sexually frustrated older woman who feels trapped and tormented in a loveless, empty, and potentially violent marriage. To counteract the emptiness of her life and the powerlessness she feels within it, Joan sees a psychiatrist, who repeatedly assures her that "Joanie is the only one imprisoning Joanie." That very evening, Joan finds two paths to empowerment: witchcraft and sex, both of which are intertwined throughout the film.

Joan first learns of witchcraft while at a cocktail party where her friends are gossiping about a woman named Marion (Virginia Greenwald) who claims to be a witch. Her friend Shirley (Ann Muffly) jeers, saying she can see Marion "running around naked killing goats" and "dancing in a circle. How's the moon tonight?" Despite her skepticism, Shirley agrees to take Joan out to see Marion; on the way, Joan confesses that she wants to have an affair. Arriving at the house, Shirley warns Joan, "If the mousse tastes chalky, don't eat it!"—a clear reference to *Rosemary's Baby* (1967). After Marion reads Shirley's tarot, the three women have tea; Marion talks about her mother, who was also a witch, and how much easier it is to practice in "today's culture of 'everything goes.'" Despite easier access to spells and supplies, she warns Joan that the old magic is extremely powerful and not to be played with. Ignoring Marion's injunction, Joan begins to practice witchcraft as a source of personal empowerment by gaining sexual control over Gregg (Raymond Laine), a very young and hyper-liberated college professor who is having sex with her daughter, Nikki (Joedda McClain). After discovering her mother masturbating while listening to one of her sexual encounters with Gregg, Nikki runs away from home in anger and disgust.[49] As both a means of revenge and sexual satisfaction, Joan determines to seduce Gregg and possess him as her slave. On Ash Wednesday, she uses her own blood, a cauldron, and passages from the Bible to invoke "the power of earth, the resplendent angel (Lucifer)" by the light of the moon. As if by magic, Gregg appears and makes violent love to her. On a second occasion, Joan calls Gregg over to do a "conjuration" of "Virago." "We're gonna call up the Devil, aren't we?!" he says, accusing her of making excuses for what's really going on: "It's ballin', lady. That's all it is. Ballin', lady. You're getting balled." After another round of violent sex, Joan tells Gregg that she never wants to see him again. She has come to realize that using her wicked powers to seduce men leaves men in power; instead, she will live an empowered life that is focused on herself and the feminist art of witchcraft.

The final barrier to Joan's true freedom is removed after her final vision, during which she is once again chased by the masked demon. In her delirium, she shoots the demonic intruder, who turns out to be her husband returning early from a business trip. There, on the threshold of his own home, Jim lies dead, never to penetrate the family fortress—or violate his wife—ever again. As policemen examine Jim's bloody corpse, they complain that Joan will get away with murder; women, they argue, "get everything from us, they get everything. Poor bastard." Despite his violent self-centeredness, Jim is imagined as a martyr, an innocent victim of an irrational and evil woman thirsty for his money and power. Acquitted of her husband's murder, Joan is at last free to live the life of a feminist witch.[50] No longer bound by any male authority, she is initiated into Marion's coven. In a darkened space complete with ankhs and cauldron, Joan is lovingly stripped, blessed in all of her parts by Marion, tied to the altar, and ceremonially whipped while the old witches chant, "So mote it be"—a phrase that draws parallels between the all-female witch coven and the all-male secret fraternity, the Freemasons.[51] Unlike the film's opening scene, where Joan is beaten, chained, and subjugated by her husband, she offers herself up willingly to the coven, both to the benefit of her liberated sisters and herself. After the ceremony, Joan attends one last cocktail party and seems confident, centered and self-possessed. Despite her escape from patriarchy into a self-willed matriarchy, those around her continue to speak of her as "Jim's wife" or "Mrs. Mitchell," a comment on the limitations placed on women in their own attempts to define themselves as free individuals. Likewise, she is forever labeled a man-killer, a woman who has found liberation and moved beyond her *proper place* by killing her own husband and destroying the family unit.

Out on her own and living beyond the patriarchal precinct, the empowered and Satanic witch becomes a toxic threat to society, one that might unleash chaos on the innocent if her desires are not fulfilled. In Bert I. Gordon's *Satan's Princess* (1990), for example, a young and beautiful European woman, Nicole St. James (Lydie Denier), owner of a modeling agency, is a demonic daughter of Satan. Her modeling scouts, all of whom are male, double as her worshippers; it is their job to bring young women into the company;

some of them become her lesbian lovers, some become sacrifices in Satanic rituals. In this masterpiece of post-feminist misogyny, women are routinely objectified; for example, as policemen examine the mutilated body of a female victim, one says, "Too bad. Nice piece of ass." Just as the men in the film treat women as meat, so too does Nicole; she not only serves women up as a visual feast for both consumers of fashion and voyeurs within and beyond the film's frame, but also feeds upon women as carnal prey. In this inverted Satanic realm of female sexual power and domination, she likewise feasts upon men who become subservient to her supernatural power. In one scene, her driver tells her that he must have her; she allows him to touch her breast, then burns him savagely with a cigarette. Despite her cruelty, he obediently brings her to a bathhouse where a naked man presents himself to her for inspection. Licking her lips, she sprouts black talons and slaughters him phallus first, a scene that might once have been included in the *Malleus Maleficarum*.[52] When she is ultimately confronted by one of the cops, whose family she has destroyed, he asks her "What *are* you?" She replies playfully, "Just a bad girl." After she confesses to having killed "a thousand men," the cop sets her alight with a blowtorch, a historically appropriate punishment for wickedly "bad girls." Unwilling to die complacently in the flames, Nicole reaches up with her clawed left hand and rips away her once-beautiful skin to reveal her true inner self, a cold, slimy, rapacious demon with gray hair and a poisonous glare. This melancholic creature, inverted and earthbound in its corruption, unable to ascend to male perfection, conforms in depressing ways to the late-medieval construction of the witch and the misogynist belief that all women, no matter how lovely on the outside, have essentially evil natures lurking just below their soft and tempting surfaces. Perhaps most frightening to the patriarchal order, this rapacious woman won't die, but instead returns again and again, like feminism itself, to feed on male power.

Crypt Mothers: Witches, Ghosts and the Return of the Past

With her penchant for questioning, raping, and murdering male authority, the Anglo-American witch became a staple character in the horror films of the mid-twentieth century, a time when women lashed out against patriarchy as part of the Women's Liberation Movement. In these films, the witch might appear as a sexy vixen, an innocent wife, or a wicked hag; to the terror of conservative audiences, the witch could also manifest as a specter that preyed upon the living long after her own bodily death. As a ghost, the witch

4. Wicked Women: Female Flesh, Satanic Witch and Horror Film

functions as a repressed memory, one that has been locked safely away in the mind crypt where it will do no harm.[53] Typically, the witch remains stored in a dusty corner of the mental attic with nearly forgotten memories of childhood until some external stimulus, be it an individual or event, causes her memory to resurface. This return of the uncanny unleashes the witch's true power, reminding us not only of our deep cultural fears of empowered feminine evil, but also of the abject mother-figure who has been violated and abused and who drags us back into her womb, kicking and screaming.[54] This return of *and to* the hungry mother serves as a recurring theme in films featuring phantasmic witches who rise up from feminism's smoldering embers to haunt the modern imagination.

One such film, *Superstition* (1982), centers on the ghost of a seventeenth-century witch and the haunted New England house that serves as an extension of her toxic body. In the opening scenes, two adolescent boys break into the house in order to play pranks; after penetrating a hymen-like barrier, they run through its slick marble halls, up into its spider-infested attic, and down into a kitchen left abandoned and in disarray. Both boys are attacked by the witch's ghost in the kitchen, a space deeply coded as feminine, motherly, and domestic. The first boy is beheaded and his decollated head is cooked in the microwave. The second boy initially escapes the witch's "motherly" embrace but is ultimately sliced in half by a window as he attempts to crawl out of the womb-tomb and is left flaccid and dangling, much like an aborted birth or a severed male member.[55]

Despite these murders and the house's reputation for consuming all those who enter her, the Protestant Church that owns the property determines to renovate it so that an alcoholic reverend and his dysfunctional family will have a place to live. During construction, a senior reverend is jugulated by a saw blade; a younger reverend, David Thompson (James Houghton), dismisses his colleague's death as a horrible accident and determines the house to be safe for occupancy. The balance of the film follows the ghost witch as she devours the vulnerable family, as well as all those who come their rescue, dragging her victims down into her fetid bowel-basement.

After several strange events, the Reverend David finally becomes convinced that supernatural forces are at work and turns for help to the wise old woman who acts as the property's caretaker. Warning him that his "twentieth-century mind" is a liability, she tells him to look into the past, to check the records of the Catholic Church, specifically those of the seventeenth-century St. Luke's Parish. (This is historically problematic because Puritan anti–Catholic legislation ensured that there *was* no seventeenth-century Catholic Church in New England.) The reverend makes his way to St. Luke's, gains access to the archives and finds a copy of the "Maleficorum (sic)," erroneously described as "the book of the Spanish Inquisition," to which is appended the church's history, a further link between Catholicism and inverted evil. As he opens this textual memory crypt, he witnesses the trial of a woman with black wiry hair, crazy eyes, and seductive lips; she is accused of giving "service to the unholy forces of hell" and sacrificing a small child to the Devil. Like a woman possessed, she cries out in a gravelly and deep voice, "I am the daughter of Satan. He is my lord and salvation. He will protect me. He will bring you all to death!" As she screams, monks chanting Latin tie her to a large beam and hoist her above a fire, causing her skin to bubble and boil. Calling on Lucifer, she condemns all the generations who come near "this place" and says "I *will not die*! You do not have the power to destroy me!"[56] Horrified, Father Andrew Pike takes pity and refuses to burn the young woman, although this is the only way to truly destroy the witch's power. Instead, he drowns her in the pond behind the now-haunted house, throwing a silver crucifix in after her, believing that "a holy relic from Rome will be the seal" that prevents her escape. His leniency with this disobedient woman proves to be the community's undoing; the Church is burned, a tempest destroys most of the village, leprosy infects the people, and a young girl named Mary is dragged into the pond by the wicked witch, now a voracious and black-clawed demon. The witch comes for Pike last, attacking him in the church's cellar. He is forced into a grape press and his blood becomes the sacrificial wine of communion.

In *Superstition*, the return to the past through the text explains the return of the past in the present. The house is not haunted by former occupants; instead, it serves as an extension of the toxic female body floating at the bottom of the adjacent pond. Like a rotting fetus, the witch is tied to the house through an umbilicus of evil that remains uncut because of the repeated failure of men to discipline "wicked" women. In the seventeenth century, Father Pike was too gentle with the accused witch and failed to burn her according to the law; as a result, she destroyed him and the flock in his care and has continued to feed on those who cross her path.

In the twentieth century, several weak men unwittingly facilitate the witch's vengeance. The caretaker's son becomes the slave of the witch, subordinating his masculine authority to her feminine power. The alcoholic reverend is a failure both as a shepherd for his flock and as a father in his own household. He is drunk and weak and his wife has no respect for him; she is left to act as the true leader in the family. When his family is being attacked by the witch, he lets policemen do the work for him, following them around impotently like a helpless boy, a mere shadow of a man. He is likewise powerless to control his two daughters, one of whom is blonde, angelic, and obedient, the other brunette, overtly sexual, and disobedient. Representations of the binary nature of the feminine, the angel and the vixen routinely argue about their father. When the vixen speaks honestly about their father's impotence and hypocrisy, the angel lashes out at her: "Shut your bitchy mouth!" Without a rational male force to curb the chaos, the female principle spins out of control. The witch slays the mother in the kitchen and the father as he stares into a mirror; the slutty daughter has a phallic stake thrust into her head as she runs through the attic, while the good daughter is killed as she hides in the Reverend David's van. With the destruction of the nuclear family, the witch's work is nearly complete. She then turns to the reverend, who attempts to destroy her festering evil at the source by setting the pond on fire. As the gasoline burns atop the surface, a blonde little girl wearing a white dress appears behind him and lies, saying that the witch really should have been hanged. Realizing that she is the witch in the sweet and innocent guise of a daughter-figure, he thrusts a silver cross through her heart and she bursts into flames. Despite his efforts, he is nevertheless dragged down into the pond by a black-clawed hand. Like all those before him who have attempted to subdue the chaos of the witch's feminine evil, he has failed and she remains in control, awaiting her next human meal. From a conservative perspective, the true sin of the fathers was to allow feminism to progress and to fester. Had they been stronger and burned it when they had the opportunity, then the present generation would not be faced with feminism's lingering evils, including the subordination of men and the destruction of the American family.

Nearly a decade later, male impotence and the uncanny witch-ghost returned as core themes of Roger Corman's *The Haunting of Morella* (1990). Corman had already adapted the Poe story "Morella" as part of his 1962 anthology horror film *Tales of Terror*.[57] The two films tell the same essential tale, that of a witch named Morella who returns from the dead to possess her eighteen-year-old daughter as a means of killing her (Morella's) husband. While both films feature the power of an evil wife-mother to destroy her family from beyond the grave, the 1990 version is far more graphic in its depiction of the witch and her lesbian sisters as Satanic, sexually voracious, and hell-bent on the obliteration of male authority. At the wicked heart of the film is Morella, a beautiful and intellectually hungry young woman. Like the much older Stephanie Bax in *The Witches* (1966), Morella is obsessed with immortality and power. Following a set of rituals written in a grimoire, she slaughters one of her household wenches—who happens to be a virgin—in the bathtub. After she slices the young woman's throat, Morella strips naked and bathes in the girl's blood, much like we see in the Elizabeth Bathory myth. After rubbing the blood across her naked breasts (this is a Corman film, after all) and thereby "invoking the powers of darkness," she takes her infant daughter Lenora out into the woods where she will complete the ritual upon an altar. Flanked by her red-robed sisters and a bubbling cauldron, Morella raises her daughter into the air, suggesting that she will slaughter her own offspring to live forever. The ritual is interrupted by the townsmen led by her husband and his best friend, the town doctor. The men warn each other, "Don't look into her eyes. She has the power to control men's minds"; because of this, they crucify her and put her eyes out with a red hot poker, so that "after death she will be able to cast no more evil spells."[58] Morella calls out to her husband, "Mark well our daughter; I will live on in her." With this promise that their daughter is tainted in the blood and that she will one day serve as a vessel for her mother's vengeance, Morella is left to die.

True to her witchy word, Morella returns seventeen years later with the help of her lesbian lover and fellow sex-witch, Miss Deveraux, who is a servant in Morella's old house and a governess to her daughter Lenora. In order to revive her dead lover, Deveraux performs rituals in Morella's tomb upon an stereotypical Satanic altar, featuring a grimoire, black candles, and inverted cross with a crucified infant. "Arise my love," she chants, "a fresh young body awaits you." Key to her resurrection is Lenora. Possessed by her dead mother, Lenora is forced to have sex with a stable boy and Deveraux, thus destroying her virgin purity. With each act of debauchery and blood sacrifice, Morella's flesh is reconstituted on her earthbound bones.

Throughout the film, Lenora is torn between her desire for her fiancé, a young lawyer from town who promises a traditional middle-class life of wedded bliss, and her mother, who drags her ever further into the Satanic abyss, promising her empowerment and eternal life. Like all women in these films, Lenora is bifurcated. Obedient to her weak and pitiful father and faithful to her future husband, she is at the same time a disobedient whore under the influence of her irrational feminist mother's ghost. "Can't you feel it, Lenora?" Deveraux chants. "Her blood in your veins, her spirit in your body, her thoughts in your mind?" "I don't want to be like you!" Lenora cries. Pulled ever closer to evil, unable to resist her mother's influence, Lenora must be protected by the film's triad of male authority figures: the doctor, the lawyer, and her father.[59] In the end, it is her father who goes to the tomb of his domineering wife, embraces her animated corpse, and sacrifices himself so that his daughter may live. At first it appears that he has finally controlled the bad wife who has destroyed his home and family; feminine evil, however, never dies. As the smoke from the witch's fatal embrace clears, Lenora clutches her abdomen; over a faint heartbeat, a voice whispers "I still *live*!" The message born of male terror is clear: Chaotic and feminine evil, much like the witchcraft paradigm itself, is reborn in each generation of women.

"I Will Not DIE!"

As the fires of feminism cooled in the last decades of the twentieth century, and mainstream culture became more superficially conservative in its values, movies featuring truly *terrifying* wicked witches became less prevalent. One exception, *The Blair Witch Project* (1999), capitalized not only on pseudo-documentary, found footage, and POV filming techniques, but also on the traditional signifiers of evil and wicked female inversion. The dwelling place of the Blair Witch is the dense woods surrounding the small town of Burkittsville, Maryland. Construed as a liminal space of potentiality and chaos, the forest becomes an extension of the witch's body; those who penetrate it lose all direction and are repeatedly brought back to the fetid womb-house at its core. Partly filmed in black and white, the haunted woods appear as a melancholic body-scape: devoid of all life, an inversion of nature's otherwise thriving fecundity, a barren womb where nothing surivives. The description of the Blair Witch, who is never shown on camera, likewise conforms to medieval paradigms. One woman, an eccentric with a hooked nose, long scraggly hair, gray wrinkly skin, and wearing almost witchy garb herself, describes the Blair Witch as floating in the air, wearing a wool shawl, and covered with "dark, real dark, almost black hair." Like her medieval sisters, the melancholic Blair Witch craves the warm blood of young children and enslaves a weak man to harvest them from their homes, drag them into the woods, and slaughter them in her house-womb. As a wicked mother and bad wife, she feeds on children, manipulates men, and lives beyond male authority, thereby posing a threat to the patriarchal families of the well-ordered, conservative town of Burkittsville. Heinrich Kramer, the fifteenth-century author of the *Malleus Maleficarum*, would find much familiar here.

The Blair Witch Project is only one film in a sea of witchy late-twentieth and early twenty-first century films that draw on medieval constructions of witchcraft. Although most of them are not meant to truly frighten, their depiction of witchy women, be they harlots or heroines, continue an anti-woman discourse codified in the medieval world. Sexploitation films such as *Virgin Witch* (1971) open the witch body to penetration by the male gaze while reinforcing the medieval paradigm of the irrational, sexually rapacious woman driven to chaotic licentiousness with demons, married men, and other women. Films such as *The Craft* (1989), *Practical Magic* (1989), and the

X-Files episode "Syzygy" (1996) focus on teen angst and the pubescent female body as a conduit for chaotic evil. These narratives suggest that young women might only become liberated and powerful through devilry, and that they must be closely monitored lest they ascend too far beyond the subjugated role that society has assigned them. At the close of each narrative, "normalcy" and "order" are only reestablished through the cleansing and subjection of the maleficent vixen's flesh. Even seemingly harmless programs featuring good witches as role models, for example *Sabrina the Teenage Witch* (1996–2003), are rooted in anti-woman dialogue, suggesting that families composed solely of women are somehow supernatural, if not wicked, and that young girls might only truly be clever and popular through the aid of witchcraft. Likewise the good-witch sisters of *Charmed* who serve as protectors might only do so with the aid of supernatural forces.[60] Does a woman truly require "super" powers to rise above her "natural" corruption and earthbound ineptitude?

The witches in children's films fare no better. Both Ursula of Disney's *Little Mermaid* (1989) and the Sanderson Sisters of *Hocus Pocus* (1993), for example, are delightfully spooky characters; nevertheless, they are each manifestations of misogynist medieval constructs. Old, ugly, overweight, and single, Ursula the Octopus feeds upon souls and attempts to destroy a human hetero-normative relationship in the realm of purity and light beyond the cold and dark sea. Winnie Sanderson, old, buck-toothed, and homely, worships Satan and feeds on children in an attempt to become beautiful and live forever. Each of these witches is ultimately defeated, ushering in the return of warm, rational, and patriarchal order. Despite the witch character's repeated burnings, she returns again and again. She wears many different masks; beneath the surface, however, sits the melancholic and bloodthirsty hag—sculpted from fetid clay under the hands of medieval clerics—that haunts the modern imagination and refuses to die.

Part II
Modern Permutations

5

The Transgressive Monster

From the Melancholic Jew to the Blood-Sucking Vampire

The vampire, with his dark clothes, pallid skin, and lust for blood, did not enter into the Western European imagination until the late seventeenth century, when cases of purported vampirism traveled from Eastern lands and into the courts of the Hapsburg Empire. The sensational accounts of Arnold Paole and Peter Plogojowitz, whose corpses were accused of terrorizing small villages and drinking the blood of the living, spread rapidly through Europe, inspiring both fear and wonder in those who heard them.[1] Discourse on vampirism became so intense that Augustin Calmet, a Benedictine monk, began an in-depth inquiry into the possible existence of vampires that would eventually be published in 1746 as *A Treaty on the Apparition of Spirits, and on the Vampires and Revenants of Hungary, Romania, etc.* Structured as a theological treatise and written for a learned audience, Calmet's work argued that vampirism as it appeared in Eastern Europe was theoretically possible. This authoritative approbation in combination with the myriad stories of *strigoi* emerging from the East catalyzed an obsession with the bloodthirsty undead in Western culture, one that would inspire works of gothic horror such as John Polidori's *The Vampyre* (1819), Sheridan Le Fanu's *Carmilla* (1872), and Bram Stoker's *Dracula* (1897). In the twentieth and twenty-first centuries, the cinematic vampire has taken on a variety of forms, from *Nosferatu*'s (1922) rat-like Count Orlok and the debonair aristocrats portrayed by Bela Lugosi and Christopher Lee to the sex-hungry vixens of *Vampiros Lesbos* (1971), the handsome gentlemen of *Interview with a Vampire* (1994), and the Mormon-esque boyfriends of Stephanie Meyer's *Twilight* series. While all of these modern and postmodern vampires reflect cultural fears and biases against transgressive "others" at different historical moments and from divergent perspectives, they each share a common body—melancholic, blood-hungry, and toxic—that is rooted in medieval constructions of evil alterity.[2]

The Western vampire shares a monstrous body with his medieval cognates—the witch and the Jew—both of whom existed beyond the theologically delineated category for warm, male, Christian perfection and were therefore constructed as cold, female, and evil. Born of Aristotelian structures and the authority of learned medicine in the service of anti-Judaism, the character of the transgressive Jew as seen through the lens of Christian theology and medieval scholasticism provides the foundation for the physiology, physiognomy, and aesthetics of the modern vampire. Jews had long served a discursive role in Christian theology, but by the thirteenth century they had become a paradigm of abject otherness. Throughout the later Middle Ages, the "hermeneutic Jew" came to be portrayed increasingly as a blood-hungry, sexually rapacious monster who dwelled in the shadows and was doomed to wander the earth along with his demonic brethren.[3] Plagued by black bile, he was believed to be cold, dry, toxic, and essentially female, all of which gave rise to the myth of the Jewish male menses.[4] Some Christian authorities argued that in order to compensate for this monthly loss and to satiate his melancholic cravings, a Jew might sacrifice a Christian child and drink its warm wet blood.[5] Driven solely by the demands of his chaotic bowels, the feminized Jew was a creature of carnality, craving not only sanguine but sexual gratification. Despite his desires, his melancholic nature mitigated his attempts to achieve an erection and ejaculate, all of which caused him to fly into fits of frustrated rage. Unable to control the envy, greed, lust, and wrath roiling within him, his irrational system overheated, causing the combustion of his blood and the production of more black bile. The Jew's melancholic body then became a smoldering cinder, a lump of earth so fetid that it emanated corruption and decay, infected the air and water, and spread leprosy and plague within the Christian body.[6] According to medieval scholastic constructs, the Jew was not only toxic but also terrifyingly transgressive; behind a dark, brooding, purportedly masculine façade lurked a leaking and irrational woman, a blood-hungry monster clothed in human form that at any moment might lash out or infect the unwary.[7]

Blowing into the eighteenth-century West, Eastern vampire stories found fertile ground, ultimately spawning a hybrid creature, a strange amalgamation of popular and learned elements. When Westerners heard of the bloodsucking corpses reportedly stalking remote Eastern villages, they conflated these stories with indigenous folklore about revenants, the inverted category of earthbound evil, and the character of the blood-sucking Jew—medieval constructs that by the eighteenth century had become invisible structures deeply embedded in Western culture.[8] The vampire was readily associated with elemental earth, demonic agencies, hell, the colors red, pallid gray, and black, the night, autumn, the full moon, wolves, and poisonous creatures such as worms, spiders, and bats. He was also cast into a monstrous body, dominated by toxic black bile, that forever trapped him in the chaotic cycles of decay, transformation, and regeneration that plagued the sublunary realm. Cold and fetid, his melancholic body craved warm human blood and passionate sexual congress—carnal desires that were further fueled by a soul willingly given over to demonic forces. Despite his sexual urges, the vampire could not achieve arousal or complete the sex act, and so was consigned to penetrating his female victims with his phallic fangs. Blood-hungry, rapacious, and violent, the vampire became an irrational demon-laden "other" with the subtle power to seduce the weak and wanton into his dark embrace and infect innocent Christians with his fetid gaze, breath, and blood. As a source of contamination and contagion, the modern Western vampire came to be associated with infectious conditions such as the plague, the pox, cholera, and syphilis.[9]

The modern vampire, like the hermeneutical Jew with which he shares multiple affinities, is above all a creature of transgression, a being that crosses over the boundaries of structural categories, ultimately coming to reside in the spaces between.[10] For example, the bourgeois vampire born in the nineteenth century appears to be a debonair and civilized gentleman, but he secretly commands animals, such as wolves and rats, and controls forces of nature such as the demon-laden winds. Barred from the harmonious unity of heaven, the vampire is a master of earthly multiplicity; using his knowledge of the elements in conjunction with dark forces, he can shape-shift between human, animal, and mist. Formally male yet qualitatively female, the vampire transgresses gender boundaries, penetrating both male and female victims alike, sucking their necks in a sensual embrace.[11] While male vampires embody emasculated evil, female vampires take on authoritative and powerful male roles, often dominating their victimized male subordinates and preferring the sexual attentions of their female companions. These slippages place the vampire in a liminal position between culturally constructed gender categories, making it a powerful creature for questioning the status quo.

The vampire's unbound body is likewise transgressive in its leakiness. In feeding, it exchanges its own fluids with those of its victims. It seeps infected blood from its mouth, transfixes its victims with toxic *pneuma* from its eyes, and emanates foul odors from its flesh that poison the atmosphere. Most profoundly, the vampire crosses the boundary between life and death, hovering somewhere between light and dark, known and unknowable. At once familiar and unspeakable, the vampire's body is an animated representation of our own future corpse-selves, a powerful locus of fear, and an object of intense Kristevan abjection. Our initial revulsion at seeing the rotting, rapacious, and blood-hungry self-other stimulates a sense of *jouissance*—an inability to look away coupled with an obsessive desire to become one with the horror before us. It is perhaps because of this that the vampire, both horrifying and seductive, has persisted in the Western imagination. Not only does the vampire represent our collective and very palpable fears of embodiment and disembodiment, but also our longing to become one with the discursive melancholic other—to finally embrace the ensouled monster who dwells within us all, searching for communion, aching to be fed.

De Melancholia: Body and Soul

The foundations of the modern Western vampire can be traced back to the medieval university, where scholastic theologians appropriated the authoritative languages of Aristotelian philosophy and learned medicine to create a categorical and biophysical template for those who did not comply with Christian dictums. Because monstrous "non–Christians" and obstinate heretics were imagined to be perpetually bound to the corrupt earth, theologians argued that their melancholic bodies were dominated by black bile, the heaviest and most fetid of the four humors, which was associated with elemental earth and processes of decay. According to medieval medical theory, which was primarily Galenic, black bile occurred naturally in the body as a "sediment of the blood." In its natural form, it served several functions, including the feeding of the spleen, the stimulation and control of hunger in the stomach, and the removal of toxins through excretion. Non-natural black bile was a byproduct of blood, yellow bile, or natural black bile that had been burned through exposure to extreme heat. Warm foods, hot weather, and intense emotions such as rage, jealousy, or lovesickness might serve as a catalyst for the combustion process, which produced a colder, heavier, and more concentrated precipitate of black bile. Venomous in nature, these toxic cinders were the "cold and dry opposite of life itself, which is warm and moist," and their presence in the body caused myriad conditions associated with decay, stench, and slow death.[12] Galen and Avicenna attributed the horrifying condition of *lepra*, or medieval leprosy, to the presence of "black bile that had been overcooked or burned."[13] During the fourteenth century, black bile melancholy came to be associated with the plague, the symptoms of which included "blackish lips," "black nails," a "black tongue" and an eventual blackening and putrefaction of the entire body.[14]

According to Avicenna, the black bile melancholiac was marked by "a powerful blackness" and "dryness," qualities that extended beyond the physical and into the mental and spiritual. In the medieval body, mind, body and spirit were interconnected, and each played reciprocal roles in shaping health and illness. For example, the presence of excessive non-natural black bile caused inflammation of the spleen, which in turn stimulated uncontrollable appetites, including "increased cravings" for warm foods such as red wine and red meat.[15] The immoderate consumption of these substances, however, caused damage to a stomach whose "coldness" and "melancholic condition" compromised its ability to properly digest food.[16] The patient's inability to satisfy his hunger not only caused acute physical discomfort, but also elicited emotional responses such as despair and anger. A body already overheated by the introduction of hot substances and subject to fiery emotions raged like a furnace; the result was the further combustion of black bile, one byproduct of which was a "sooty or smokelike vapor" that rose to the brain and obscured rational thought.[17] The clouded mind-body was at one moment calm, despairing, or lethargic, the next irrational, frenetic, and filled with a maniacal rage.[18] Unable to regulate its own emotional and physical responses, tossed between terror, sorrow, and hatred, the untreated melancholic body experienced repeated episodes of humoral combustion, yielding a system that was increasingly "dried, concentrated, opaque" and above all "black."[19]

In their discussions of black bile melancholy, plague, and leprosy, learned medical authorities focused primarily on physical and emotional etiologies of disease and eschewed theological discourse.[20] For scholastic theologians, however, the melancholic mind-body dominated by black bile was not merely suffering from a humoral imbalance that led to physical degradation, but a deformity of the entire being that was connected to a much larger and complex cosmological system. Chaotic and corrupt, the melancholic body was a microcosmic representation of a sublunary realm coded as inverted and evil. Black bile was in qualitative alignment with elemental earth; both were cold, dry, and heavy with corruption and associated with processes of death, putrefaction, and decay, as well as toxic substances such as sulphur and mushrooms, and venomous creatures, such as spiders and snakes. Cats, rats, worms, and flies were likewise signifiers of earthly corruption because they were believed to have been generated spontaneously from the heat of decomposing matter.[21] Because of these universal characteristics, theologians argued that the melancholic body was fetid and toxic.[22] Cold, sluggish, and earthbound, it was also cast as primarily female, a radical inversion of the warm and buoyant perfection of the Christian male. Like the female body, the melancholic male body was driven by its lowest regions, its stench-ridden bowels, which craved bloody red meat and wine, and its lustful genitalia, which were hungry for the heat and moisture of sexual congress. Without the Christian temperance of the rational male mind, the female-coded melancholic body satiated its carnal desires at every opportunity. Driven to feed on others for its own survival, it preyed upon the innocent and brought vulnerable bodies into contact with its blackening feminine poison.

Through the lens of scholasticism, black bile melancholia and its attendant symptoms not only signified a corrupt body, but also a disfigured soul given over to willful alterity, demonic evil, and utter damnation. The blackened blood-hungry body was shaped by a dark and heavy indwelling soul that had been drawn downward towards the earth and away from the ethereal realms of the divine.[23] Like Satan and his black angels, the melancholic soul was self-obsessed and self-willed; in its desperate quest for power and authority, it became opaque, no longer able to receive or reflect heavenly light. Obscured from all rational guidance, the darkened soul fed the body's carnal desires, making it easy prey for demonic phantasies and infestations. It likewise led the mind into all manner of wrong belief, including heresies such as dualism, witchcraft, and pacts with the Devil.[24] Such heretical beliefs questioned the authority of the church and threatened to corrupt the unity and purity of the communal Christian body from within. Theologians compared the corrosive and toxic nature of heresies to leprosy and plague, arguing that they were all inherently evil and emanated from blackened points of contagion allied with Satan. Partly in response to the dialectic argumentation of scholasticism, which sought to discern singular truth out of multiplicity and thereby codify good and evil, church authorities became increasingly concerned with the melancholic bodies and infectious ideas of evil "others" and their corrosive power within the sheepfold from the twelfth century forward.[25]

The Evil Other: Constructing the Melancholic and Blood-Hungry Jew

Concerns over alterity and hidden evil were at the core of the Fourth Lateran Council (1215), which sought to establish concrete doctrine and to uncover those who did not uphold it. Heretical groups such as the Cathars were targeted for inquisition and reconversion. While many of the Cathars were open in their rejection of church authority and willing to engage in public debates with Dominican inquisitors such as Peter of Verona, many other lurked in the shadows.[26] These unseen Cathars were of great concern, in part because their invisibility masked the extent of the heretical corrosion that was taking place just beneath the skin of the Christian body. The Fourth Lateran Council not only advocated the discovery and destruction of wrong believers within the church, but also condemned non–Christians such as the Jews, who had long existed in Christian lands as worlds within worlds.

Separate from any physical existence, the character of the Jew occupied the Christian imagination in multiple ways. In the early-medieval hagiographical tradition, the hermeneutical Jew was often cast in the role of the foolish and somewhat wicked non-believer whose didactic purpose was to prove the veracity of Christianity, the miraculous nature of given saints, and the merciful grace of Christ and His mother, the Virgin Mary.[27] By the eleventh century, discursive otherness had given way to organized physical violation. One year after the Council of Clermont and Pope Urban's call to crusade against Christ's enemies in the Holy Land, Count Emicho of Leiningen and his followers took it upon themselves to attack the Jews in the Rhineland.[28] Preying upon popular anti–Jewish sentiment, Emicho argued that the Jews were the true enemies of Christ and all Christians and should be vanquished; accordingly he and his false crusaders marched on Worms and Speyer in 1096, demanding that the Jews either convert or die. Most chose death by their own hands, with fathers killing their wives and children before committing suicide. Scholars such as Israel Yuval have argued that the events of 1096 not only reflected the increasing culture of hostility between Christians and Jews, but also served as a catalyst for the ritual murder, blood libel, and host desecration myths that would proliferate in the twelfth and thirteenth centuries and beyond.[29] While the church in no way sanctioned the crusaders' violence against the Jews in the late eleventh century, the canons of the Fourth Lateran Council reveal a shift in official attitudes. Canons sixty-seven through seventy decreed that Jews must be publicly identified as such through unique styles of dress and the wearing of badges, banished from Christian sight during Easter week, prevented from obtaining public office, and limited in their financial power over the church and its flock.[30] While the canons of the Fourth Lateran Council did not advocate the eradication of the Jews, they did attempt to isolate and suppress them as dangerous outsiders who had penetrated the Christian body and posed a threat to its purity.

The Fourth Lateran Council not only ratified the anti–Judaism inherent in medieval Christian culture, but also served as a catalyst for its future growth through the elaboration of the doctrine of transubstantiation. In its discourse on the Nicene creed, Canon One states that Christ's "body and blood are truly contained in the sacrament of the altar under the forms of bread and wine, the bread being transubstantiated by divine power into the body and the wine into the blood."[31] While the idea of transubstantiation extended back into antiquity, the term itself was first used by the eleventh-century theologian Hildebert of Tours and made popular by twelfth-century scholars such as Stephen of Autun and Peter of Blois.[32] Established as dogma in the thirteenth century, transubstantiation and its inner workings became a topic of discourse for speculative theologians such as Thomas Aquinas. In his *Summa Theologica*, Aquinas discusses the nature of consecrated bread and wine in terms of Aristotelian hylomorphism, arguing that the substance of the sacrament is transformed into the true body and blood of Christ, while the accidents remain those of bread and wine.[33] Despite these miraculous metaphysical changes, "the presence of Christ's true body and blood in this sacrament cannot be detected by sense, nor understanding, but by faith alone, which rests upon Divine authority."[34] Dominican confessors, mendicant preachers, and parish priests communicated the doctrine of transubstantiation to the laity, teaching that Christ's true flesh was concealed within the Host. While all Christians might receive Christ through communion, only the most faithful of God's children would be granted a *vision* of His miraculous physicality in the bread and wine.

Christian responses to the idea of transubstantiated flesh-bread and blood-wine were complex. Holy women such as the Beguines received the Eucharist with reverence and joy; believing it to be an opportunity for ecstatic union with the divine, Eucharistic worship became central to their unique spirituality.[35] Through the work of one devout woman, Juliana of Liege, a Praemonstratensian canoness, Eucharistic devotion spread beyond the cloister and into the lives of the laity. In 1264, Pope Urban IV acquiesced to Juliana's demands and instituted the feast of Corpus Christi as a holy day of obligation dedicated to the sanctity of the Eucharist.[36] From the perspective of the official Church, the transubstantiated host and wine—the very body and blood of Christ—had become the physical glue that bound all Christians into one unified, purified, and redeemed entity.

The doctrine of transubstantiation and the development of Eucharistic devotion, however, brought with them concerns about the divine flesh dwelling within the consecrated host. The Fourth Lateran Council had made yearly confession and communion mandatory. While Aquinas had argued that the substance of the Eucharist went straight to the sealed tabernacle of the human heart where it might warm and edify the soul, many individuals were nevertheless disgusted by the idea of digesting and excreting Christ's flesh and fearful of the consequences.[37] These fears were heightened as the Eucharist came to be associated not only with the Crucified Christ, but with the adorable baby Jesus. Just as the Beguines received visions of the Christ child during communion and nurtured baby dolls in His image as a form of devotion, so too were the cult of Mother Mary and her infant Son conflated with Eucharistic worship.[38] The precious and vulnerable baby concealed within the consecrated host caused great anxiety about its endangerment and the need to protect it from those who would do it harm, most notably "heretics Jews, and other unbelievers."[39]

As a reflection of these anxieties, Christian polemic throughout the thirteenth and fourteenth centuries increasingly portrayed the character of the Jew as a malicious malcontent whose ancestors were responsible for the death of Christ and who remained intent on attacking Him and his Mother in the form of the Eucharist.[40] In 1290 Paris, fears about Jews and the Eucharist coalesced in the elaboration of a host Desecration narrative that would permeate Christian culture for centuries to come. According to the tale, a Jewish man convinced a weak Christian woman to steal a consecrated host from Easter mass and deliver it to him. Once it was in his possession, the Jew stabbed it with a knife, purportedly to disprove the doctrine of transubstantiation, upon which it began to bleed. Blind to the miracle before him, he went on to hammer it with nails, throw it into boiling water, and cast it into a fire. "Indestructible, changeable, full of mystery," the bleeding host rose up and transformed into a crucifix, a miraculous vision granted to the Jew's wife and children who were summarily converted; the Jew himself, however, remained stubborn and was led to destruction.[41] The host desecration narrative established in Paris disseminated quickly through thirteenth-century Europe, spawning accusations in Laa (1294), Rottingen (1298), and Vienna (1299), a trend that continued through the fourteenth century.[42] Tales of Host Desecration proliferated rapidly not only because they played upon Christian anti–Judaism and fears of child endangerment through the Eucharist, but also because they traveled along the same paths as earlier ritual murder tales originating in England and centering on two Christian children purportedly tortured and killed by Jews.[43]

Thomas of Monmouth's *Life and Passion of Saint William the Martyr of Norwich* (1155) tells the story of a twelve-year-old boy whose mutilated corpse was discovered in Thorpe Wood outside of Norwich on the day before Easter, 1144.[44] According to Monmouth's account, William had been seduced away from his mother by a Jew in disguise who offered the poor woman money, promising that her son would be employed as a cook. William was then taken to the house of Eleazar, the leader of the Jewish community, where he was gagged with a teasel, lacerated about the head and neck with knotted cords and thorns, crucified "in mockery of the Lord's passion," lanced in the side, boiled, and left for dead in the forest.[45] Monmouth's hagiography insists that miraculous rays shone down upon the boy's body, which led to its discovery and ultimate identification by his uncle, Godwin. Convinced that his nephew had died at the hands of the Jews, Godwin went to the sheriff and lodged an accusation against them, but his claims were rejected by secular authority. Despite the official vindication of the Jews in this case, Godwin had William's body translated to a local monastery where he would ultimately be venerated as a martyr and saint who had died innocent at the hands of Christ's enemies.

One hundred years later, in 1255, a similar tale was told of Little Hugh of Lincoln, a nine-year-old who was purportedly tortured, forced to drink gall, and crucified by Jews in mockery of Christ.[46] In this version related by Matthew Paris, the Jews went on to disembowel the child, perhaps "for the purpose of their magic arts," and dump him into a well.[47] Unlike the Norwich Jews who were protected by secular authority, those in Lincoln were arrested and executed, in part because the crown was interested in obtaining their property, in part because of an increasing fear and hatred of Jews. Both of these forces would contribute to the expulsion of the Jews from England in 1290, after which visual and literary anti-Jewish narratives would continue to proliferate into the early modern period.[48]

In England and on the Continent, late-medieval anxieties about the Eucharist, child endangerment, defilement of the vulnerable and sacred, and the penetration and pollution of the Christian body—especially during the Black Plague of the mid- to late fourteenth century—coalesced and were conflated in the polemical character of the blood-hungry Jew. According to a narrative dating from 1236 in the region of Fulda, Jews tortured and killed Christian children not only as a mockery of Christ and the Eucharist, but also for the express purpose of drinking their blood. In this new elaboration of the ritual murder tale, the Jews of Fulda were accused of slaughtering five boys while their parents were at Christmas mass and draining them of blood for use as a "remedy" for their melancholic illnesses. By the fifteenth century, Jews were commonly believed to need Christian blood for myriad reasons, many of which are elaborated upon in a document from Tyrnau dating from 1494. In it, the Jews were reputed to consume blood as an "alleviation of the wound of circumcision," as an aphrodisiac, as a remedy for male and female menstruation and other symptoms of melancholia, and as a "blind obedience to cruel tradition" that demanded the annual slaughter of a Christian child. The paradigm of the blood-hungry Jew was not only stitched together in popular anti-Judaic tales that circulated among clerics and laity alike, but also carefully constructed and defended in learned literature, with the two genres often informing each other in formal and informal ways. As with the development of the witchcraft paradigm, scholastic theologians used Aristotelian structures and learned medical theory in order to shape and rationalize popular discourses about evil "others." In so doing, they crafted a text-based biophysical construct for the stereotypical melancholic Jew, including his physiognomy, femininity and carnality, irrationality and sexual rapacity, bloodlust and infectious toxicity.

The existence of a uniquely Jewish physiognomy in the Middle Ages has been the subject of much recent scholarship. Both Joseph Ziegler and Irven M. Resnick have argued that medieval Jews were indistinguishable in their physiognomy from their Christian neighbors.[49] Because of this, the Fourth Lateran Council mandated that Jews wear badges and distinct forms of dress to prevent accidental mixing of Christians and Jews through sexual contact.[50] Despite the physical similarities between these two groups, Christian texts from the thirteenth century forward increasingly depicted Jews with a unique physiognomy, one in conformity with scholastic constructions of inverted and melancholic evil.[51] For example, both the Chichester Psalter (1250) and the Luttrell Psalter (1325–35) contain images of monstrously misshapen Jews tormenting John the Baptist and Christ. In these texts, the Jews have skin that is either blackish or pallid—colors that associated them with black bile melancholia, processes of death and putrefaction, and earthbound evil. Unlike the flushed skin of Christian figures which indicated their vital heat and ardent faith, the pallid or dark skin of the Jew indicated his essential coldness and the corruption of his blind soul that dwelled in darkness, away from heavenly light. The blackened soul of the Jew made his body not only dark, but also crooked and out of proportion, his face disfigured by a beaklike nose or animalistic snout, a creature of the wilderness.[52] This theme is particularly evident in the Luttrell Psalter's crucifixion scene, in which a Jewish high priest wears a bifurcated hat giving him the appearance of having goat's horns. The monstrous physiognomy ascribed to medieval Jews can be correlated with contemporary depictions of humanoid demonic entities, which often had "a furrowed brow, a flat nose, a pointed chin, a goat's beard, hair coming out of his ears, thick hair, [and] a stooped back," as well as animalistic demons, which were marked by black skin or scales, bulbous eyes, beaked noses, snouts, horns, leathery wings, and misshapen and inverted bodies.[53]

Theologically constructed as absolute inversions of male Christian perfection, the Jewish body shared characteristics with all other beings in that category, including demons and women.[54] Like women, Jewish men were

5. The Transgressive Monster

imagined to be cold and corrupt, devoid of the vital heat common to their prototypical Christian male counterparts, a condition that left them pallid and timid.[55] Unable to fully digest food into blood, blood into humors, and humors into muscle tissue through physical activity like Christian men, the Jewish male body experienced a build-up of polluted and toxic humoral blood that was purged every month through menstruation.[56] Unlike the female body, in which corrupt blood collected in the uterus and was discharged through the shameful *pudenda*, or vagina, the melancholic male body collected blood in the anus and discharged it through rectal hemorrhoids. This purgation from the filthiest and basest area of the human body served as a signifier of the Jew's gross carnality and earthbound orientation—a sign of damnation that Caesarius of Heisterbach argued became more acute at Easter.[57] The menstrual organ of the Jew, much like that of the witch, was a barren womb, a fetid and toxic vessel that leaked corrupt substances that poisoned all who came into contact with it. The transgressive nature of the Jewish male body was coded by medieval scholastics and written in his very flesh, making of him a monster with the power to penetrate and infect the bodies of unsuspecting others, a liminal creature who was at once externally male and qualitatively female, menstrual and yet unable to generate life.

The Jew's noxious menstrual vapors were responsible, in part, for his fundamental irrationality, yet another characteristic that he shared with vapid women. Due to his inability to produce vital heat, he was plagued by an abundance of black bile, the fumes from which might press upon the diaphragm, float to the brain, and cause confusion and illusions, much like drinking "too much wine."[58] Wandering through this dark mental fog, the Jew at times lashed out in fits of anger and rage, quaked in fear of retribution for the death of Christ, or trembled from his own simpering idleness.[59] Theologians argued that the Jew's irrationality was bound not only to his physical corruption but also to his spiritual weakness, a deformity that manifested in his unwillingness to see the logical truth of Christianity when he and his people had been the very ones for whom Christ had come. This blindness had been "revealed" in the twelfth century, when Christian theologians engaged in verbal and textual debates with Jewish scholars. Using newly acquired Aristotelian tools of argumentation and proof, they sought to reason with the Jews and prove the veracity of Christianity. Repeatedly they found themselves at an impasse against Jewish scholars with an acuity and theological tradition far deeper than their own. Instead of conceding defeat, Christian theologians concluded that the real problem stemmed not from their own faltering premises, but from the irrationality and blindness of the Jews who were stubborn in their faithlessness and in denial about the truth of Christ's message. Christian scholars argued that the Jews, like Satan, were self-willed and disobedient, their faces turned from God's grace to face the craggy and chaotic earth that they claimed as their dominion.[60] Not only were the Jews disobedient like Lucifer, they maintained, but also envious and avaricious like Judas Iscariot who had irrationally denied Christ for a mere bag of silver, a further affirmation of their carnality and greed. With stony hearts, the Jews had rejected Christ's love and instead sought the fulfillment of their own irrational desires here in the realm below the moon. As such, there was no point in engaging them in logical discourse.[61]

According to this rhetoric, the Jew's irrational and carnal nature in combination with his melancholic and inverted physiology made him a slave to his basest desires. Where the Christian body was governed by its loftier regions, including a devout heart and an intellectual head, the Jewish body was a slave to its lower regions, the generative organs and bowels, which dominated its entire being. Because the Jew was ruled by the bodily regions closest to the earth, he was captive to carnal desires such as sex, consumption, and defecation. Like irrational women and animals such as goats and hyenas, the Jewish man was believed to be sexually rapacious. Melancholic, his cold and dry body ached for warmth and moisture—a craving that quickly turned to an insatiable desire for sexual contact and release. Driven mad with sexual urgency, he ultimately sought to satiate his carnal needs with the warmest of bodies—those of young Christians. Despite these desires, the Jew's humoral composition and lack of vital heat prevented him from attaining an erection and achieving ejaculation.[62] Repeated attempts at sexual satisfaction and subsequent failure led him into a sexual frenzy, a madness and desperation for release that could in no way be achieved. With each repeated episode of lust and failure, the Jew's melancholic body underwent a process of emotional and physical combustion. As yellow bile was burned into black bile and further reduced to burned black bile, his body became over-heated and subsequently chilled until it became an ashen cinder, a toxic lump of coal that could never be reconstituted by physical means.[63]

The Jew's melancholic desire for warmth and moisture not only drove him to sexual madness and potential violence, but also to bloodlust. The Jewish body craved sanguine substances as a counter to its acute melancholia. Levitical law, however, prohibited the consumption of blood in any form; red meat was even salted in order to absorb any interstitial blood remaining in the flesh. While Jews were prevented from eating sanguine foods, their diet was dominated by products that engendered black bile, which only exacerbated their melancholic conditions. Weighted down with black bile, Jewish blood purportedly sank to the lower regions of their body and accumulated

5. The Transgressive Monster

in the rectum, thereby facilitating the monthly flux of blood from that area.[64] Starved of foods that would stimulate the production of humoral blood and regularly losing blood though menstruation, the Jewish male body was theoretically dominated by a powerful need to rebalance his system through the consumption of blood. By the thirteenth century, Christian theologians used a twisted version of learned medical theory to argue that Jewish men, because of their acute melancholia, were driven to a bloodlust so intense that they consumed the purest and warmest blood of all—that of innocent Christian children—as a panacea.[65] Hot with youth and rich in vital *pneuma*, the blood of these children was purportedly extracted during perversions of Christian rituals and consumed in chalices upon the altar. Christian blood was also rumored to be baked into the Passover matzo and Purim cakes; used as an aphrodisiac and a cure for erectile dysfunction so common to melancholics; applied to the skin as a preventative for *lepra* related to black bile; and worn as a perfume whose sweet odor of sanctity might hide the Jew's foul stench.[66] Within the context and specific rationality of medieval scholastic anti-Judaism, pure Christian blood meant life both for the faithful and for the inverted monsters who walked among them.

In the Christian imagination, Jewish men were not only dangerous to women and children because of their sexual rapacity and primal blood lust, but also to the Christian body as a whole. Their melancholic flesh exuded fluids and vapors that were malodorous, poisonous, and infectious to those who came into contact with them.[67] Jews were reputedly susceptible to disfiguring conditions such as black morphew, cancer, varicose veins, elephantia, and leprosy, the latter two of which were feared not only as signs of sin and divine wrath, but also as sources of contagion.[68] During the fourteenth century, Jews likewise came to be associated with the Black Plague, a disease that caused the body to first become red, then white, then black, all signs of putrefaction according to medieval color theory. The blackening of the flesh began with swelling lymph nodes which appeared to contain blood thick with black bile. Over its course, the Plague caused its victim to sweat profusely, vomit blood, and ooze fetid humors, transforming the body into a leaking and transgressive mess.[69] As the Plague spread throughout Europe, several intertwined theories as to its causes began to emerge. Some believed that it was the wrath of an angry God, a prelude to the Apocalypse. Others believed that the plague traveled as a foul-smelling poison that floated on the air, a subtle spirit that entered the body and stole the blood.[70] In 1338 and '39, rumors circulating in German cities blamed the Jews, claiming that they were part of an organized conspiracy to destroy Christendom.[71] The plot was imagined to have its source in Toledo, from which orders came to a Rabbi Peyret in Savoy, who distributed poison to Jewish merchants. When brought before the inquisition, Jews confessed under torture that they were instructed to contaminate wells frequented by Christians as they traveled through France, Switzerland, and Italy. Each forced confession brought about accusations in new towns, the result of which "was that they were burnt in many cities, and wherever they were expelled they were caught by the peasants and stabbed to death or drowned."[72] By the fourteenth century, Jews were not only imagined to be blood-hungry and toxic monsters dangerous to all who came near them, but also to have joined together in an organized conspiracy, an upside-down and inside-out perversion of the Christian Church that operated as a Synagogue of Satan.[73]

Back from the Grave: The Melancholic and Transgressive Vampire

Cast into the same inverted category as the maleficent witch and assigned the same evil and transgressive body, the character of the blood-hungry and melancholic Jew codified in the Middle Ages has become a persistent figure in Western discourse—one used as a universal signifier for monstrous alterity. During the Reformation, Protestants and Catholics created propaganda defaming their respective "others" as monstrous creatures.[74] In early modern France, Huguenots and Catholics described their enemies as blood-sucking leeches responsible for draining the life of the Christian body politic and spreading corruption within it like a plague.[75] Stuart Clark has argued that witchcraft persecutions were in part a manifestation of social fears about disorderly others lurking within a tenuously ordered communal body; on the continent, likewise, both Protestants and Catholics accused each other of subversive maleficence in the service of the Antichrist in his war against the true Christian faith.[76] Also in collusion with Satan's dark army were the Jews, demonized by both groups as the wicked killers of Christ who continued to feed on His Christian children. Jews received the disapprobation of Protestants such as Martin Luther in his *On the Jews and Their Lies* (1543); they were likewise targeted by the Catholic Church through the resurgence of the Blood Libel and the concomitant resurrection of the medieval cults of Little Hugh of Lincoln and William of Norwich as well as the later cults of Simon of Trent and Anderl von Rinn.[77] Two points of contention in Reformation debates included the transubstantiation of the Eucharist and the cult of saints. In reconfirming the beatitude of children purportedly murdered by melancholic and blood-hungry Jews, the Church proved that the precious child Jesus dwelled within the consecrated host, reaffirmed its power over the miraculous transformation of the Eucharist, and argued that the saints were squarely in their court. The concomitant result was an intensified hatred of the Jews as inverted and toxic monsters who sought the destruction of Christian children as part of their organized plan to suck the life from Christendom.[78] This paradigm would enjoy a long life, shaping Antisemitic discourses into the modern and postmodern periods.[79]

The rhetoric of the other as an inverted and melancholic monster—the child-eating witch or blood-sucking Jew with the power to spread poison throughout the non-monstrous body—provided the core structure around which the ethos of the vampire would eventually coalesce. The vampire did not enter Western consciousness until the early eighteenth century, when stories of hungry corpses rising from the grave to stalk the living emerged from Eastern Europe and penetrated the literate circles of Western Europe. One of the most famous cases was that of Arnold Paole, a Serbian man who claimed to have been harassed by a vampire and who had smeared blood and soil on his skin as a prophylactic. Despite his efforts, he broke his neck in a wagon accident, was buried, and shortly after began to terrorize his neighbors, who fell ill and died. Afraid of an outbreak of contagion, an Austrian detail was sent to conduct an inquest into Paole's case; the military surgeon Johann Flückinger examined Paole's corpse and, observing its postmortem condition closely, determined it to be in a state of vampirism. His findings were published in a 1732 report entitled *Visum et Repertum*, which supported the viewpoint of the local peasantry—that Paole was a vampire and that vampires, in fact, did exist.[80]

Flückinger's account brought detailed medical observations in conjunction with popular beliefs about vampires from the rural areas of the East to the intellectual circles of the more urbanized West; there, theologians and medical men set about proving or disproving the vampire's existence with their specialized knowledge applied through the lens of Enlightenment reason. One such scholar was Dom. Augustin Calmet, a Benedictine exegete who not only wrote a troubling diatribe on the foolishness of rabbinical literature, but also a lengthy discourse on eastern vampires entitled *Dissertations sur les apparitions des anges, des démons et des esprits: Et sur les revenants et vampires de Hongrie, de Boèeme, de Moravie et de Silésie*.[81] Published in 1746, Calmet's authoritative treatise argued that the Eastern vampire was unique from Western revenants in its postmortem quest to feed on blood.[82] His voice was only one in a sea of arguments for and against the existence of vampires reflected in publications such as *Dissertatio de Vampyris Serviensibus, Disserationes de Masticatione Mortuorum*, and *Dissertatio de Cadauveribus*

Sanguisugis, all of which fueled both learned and popular fascination with Eastern vampires and the blood-sucking undead.[83]

In the West, eastern tales of vampirism were interpreted through several lenses, including indigenous popular lore about revenants and inverted constructions of melancholic evil that extended back to medieval scholasticism. Belief in revenants, or animated corpses that returned from the dead, pre-existed stories of Eastern vampirism. In the medieval world, theologians argued that bodies could not come back to life without the miraculous intercession of the divine. Should corpses *appear* to rise from the dead, they did so through the agency of demons who used the human body as a puppet. In his thirteenth century treatise *De Apibus*, Thomas Cantimpré argued that the animation of a dead body by a demon "is not possible for long, for the body is fluid in nature, and cannot preserve the necessary vigor without an enlivening spirit. The body corrupts swiftly when its humor slows down."[84] The corpse is only available for demonic animation, then, when still fleshy, and it is not rendered completely inert until it is in skeletal form.[85] Popular belief held that those who had died violently or unbaptized or who had been wicked in life were most likely to become revenants, either through the agency of demons or through the volition of their own evil souls, although this latter theory did not receive the approbation of learned theology, which relegated such beliefs to the realm of *superstitio*.[86]

For protection against revenants, in particular those animated by melancholic demons, holy water, prayer, and confession of one's sins were all believed to be effective. Once subdued, the corpse could be dismembered, and preferably decapitated as a final step.[87] To prevent a revenant's return, suspected corpses, including the unbaptized, were staked to the ground in their coffins.[88] When Westerners heard reports of Eastern vampires who rose from the grave in order to feed upon human blood—and whose escape from the realm of the dead and penetration of the realm of the living caused plague-like contagion and death—they conflated these creatures with their own demon-infested revenants who might be warded off by the sacramental power of the Church. Likewise, the descriptions of vampires in reports such as *Visum et Repertum*, including their nocturnal activity and preference for fall and winter, their reddish, blackish, and pallid appearance and foul stench, as well as their blood lust and pestilential nature, likewise coded these creatures as inverted, melancholic, and evil for Western audiences.[89] The vampire's association with the corrupt earth, death and decay bound him even closer to the deep structures of melancholia, inversion, and Satanic alterity—all of which were uniquely Western constructions, born in the Middle Ages, and had little to do with Eastern vampirism.

Throughout the eighteenth and nineteenth centuries, the Eastern vampire was conflated with the deep structures of the medieval revenant and the melancholic and blood-hungry "other" to create a whole new, fully ensouled creature that would stalk the Western imagination in perpetuity. Born of double-coding, the Western vampire became an amorphous figure, a being upon which we might inscribe our fears of alterity and evil.[90] Over time, the shape-shifting vampire has morphed into myriad forms, each of which serves as a distorted mirror in which we might see our own abjected selves reflected in a darkened glass. A vast corpus of scholarship has been dedicated to the study of the vampire in literature and film from a variety of perspectives, including political and economic history,[91] literature,[92] psychoanalysis,[93] gender studies,[94] post-colonialism,[95] and post-modernism.[96] The balance of this chapter will focus on a theme that is absent from much of this scholarship: the persistence of medieval paradigms for melancholic evil and the blood-sucking "other" in European and American vampire films of the twentieth and twenty-first centuries. When seen through the lenses of medieval medicine, natural philosophy, and theology, the vampire's anatomy, physiology, and the ordering of his ethos not only make rational sense, but reveal a salient system of signifiers, born in the medieval academy, that continue to shape our perceptions of evil alterity in a multi-contextual and dynamic postmodern world.

Persistence of the Discursive Blood-Sucker

A vampire is a slippery thing. An enduring creature of liminality, transgression, and alterity, he exists in the interstices, in the shadows between culturally constructed categories; he is dead but alive, rapacious but impotent, repulsive but appealing. The vampire has become a darkened glass upon which society might inscribe its fears and witness in horror its own inverted image. From the moment of his literary birth under John Polidori's quill, the vampire has shifted through many forms, from Sheridan Le Fanu's blood-hungry vixen Carmilla to the pitiful and penny-dreadful *Varney the Vampire* to Bram Stoker's *Dracula*, which has become a sort of Ur text, the foundational vampire narrative that would spawn myriad others across space and time.[97] In its nineteenth-century incarnations, the vampire is shadowy, buried within the dark forest of words on a page. With the advent of modern cinema, however, the vampire has risen from the undead letter to become a ghostly projection, an amorphously alive incarnation that has haunted the imaginations of moviegoers for decades. No longer confined to movie houses, the vampire and his kin have now penetrated the middle-class fortress, infiltrating our living rooms and bedrooms through digital media; like Lucy, our visual windows are always open, our necks awaiting the vampire's sanguine kiss.

In the West, the vampire is legion, enjoying perpetual undeath through countless remakes of remakes.[98] In each filmic adaptation, the vampire is reconstructed to reflect the concerns of contemporary culture while retaining the salient elements of the melancholic vampire and its inverted ethos. The following analysis traces the persistence of medieval paradigms in modern vampire films and examines the ways in which these deep structures shape perceptions of self and otherness in a variety of historical contexts. Because the proliferation of vampire cinema over the past century makes an exhaustive survey nearly impossible, I will analyze thematic elements of select films in three broad categories. The first section explores the vampire cast as the melancholic Jew in F.W. Murnau's *Nosferatu: Eine Symphonie des Grauens* (1922); Werner Herzog's remake *Nosferatu: Phantom der Nacht* (1979); *Salem's Lot* (1979), a made-for-television miniseries adapted from Stephen King's bestselling novel; and Roman Polanski's *The Fearless Vampire Killers* (1969).[99] The second examines the vampire's transformation into the debonair black-caped count whose seductive charms lure his victims to an ecstatic and horrifying death. Films such as *Dracula* (1931), *Horror of Dracula* (1958), *Dracula: Prince of Darkness* (1966), *Dracula Has Risen from the Grave* (1968), *Taste the Blood of Dracula* (1969), *The Satanic Rites of Dracula* (1973), and *Bram Stoker's Dracula* (1992) reveal the persistence of inverted evil—now embodied in the gentleman vampire—and provide multiple perspectives on its proliferation in the modern world. The third section analyzes postmodern adaptations of the vampire from multiple perspectives, including: feminism in *Maschara del Demonio* (1960), *Vampyros Lesbos* (1971), *Twins of Evil* (1971), *Once Bitten* (1985) and *Vamp* (1986); exploitation/alterity in *Blacula* (1972) and *Queen of the Damned* (2002); queer theory in *The Lost Boys* (1987), *Interview with a Vampire* (1994), and *True Blood* (2008-present); and the reassertion of patriarchy and Christian conservatism in *Twilight*. Across all of these categories, the upside-down world of melancholic and Satanic evil constructed and codified by medieval scholastics serves as the foundation for the vampire and his ethos. While these signifiers remain the same, the evil "others" that they are meant to signify are ever-shifting, much like the character of the vampire itself.

Nosferatu: The Melancholic Vampire-Jew

In F.W. Murnau's *Nosferatu: Eine Symphonie des Grauens* (1922), the vampire manifests in the guise of the melancholic and blood-hungry Jew, a product of medieval discourse on evil alterity. Medieval inversion, in fact, provides the subtext for the film's narrative. Hutter, a young and rosy-cheeked clerk flush with love for his beautiful wife Ellen, must leave the well-ordered and civilized world of Western Europe for the forested Eastern wilderness in order to complete a legal transaction. His entire journey is one of moving from the rational and masculine light of day into chaotic feminine darkness. There, in the upside-down world of the East, Hutter meets his inverted self, Count Orlok, an undead creature of the night who sleeps in fetid earth by day, moves about under the cold light of the moon, recoils from the symbols and rituals of Christianity, and is doomed to wander the earth for eternity.[100] As he emerges from the shadows of his ruined castle, the vampire's frail and crooked frame, bundled beneath layers of dusty black wool, reveals a familiar physiognomy: that of the melancholic Jew. His pallid skin, desiccated flesh, and baldness signify his lack of male vital heat, rendering him cold and feminine.[101] Perverting an already horrid visage, the vampire's dark sunken eyes, enormous beaked nose, and pointy ears mark him as a foul and poisonous creature. Just as the Jew's body was once believed to emit a "fetid odor" that might only be masked through the application of sweet-smelling Christian blood, the vampire's *pneuma* reeks of the tomb.[102] Like the wicked witch, with whom he shares a body, Orlok emits toxic *pneuma* from his eyes, thereby mesmerizing his prey, as well as from his enlarged nostrils and ears—pestiferous openings that have become salient elements in the depiction of Jews in modern Antisemitic propaganda.[103] Orlok's rat-like teeth link him with vermin once believed to generate spontaneously from corrupt earth and decaying corpses. For generations, rats, like the imagined Jew—and through him, the vampire—have been associated with contagion, including the Black Death. Orlok's arrival in Bremen signifies the penetration and subsequent infection of the Christian body by a corrupting foreign plague—unseen as it sleeps in a coffin of fetid soil, surrounded by rats and growing like a poisonous mushroom—that will drain it of life and drag it down into the melancholic tomb.[104]

The vampire's cold dry flesh makes him irrational, rapacious, and hungry for blood. In Murnau's *Nosferatu*, Orlok is consumed by greed. At the dinner table, the vampire crouches behind an enormous legal parchment, his black close-set eyes only inches away from the page, a cantor's hat perched upon his head. In his counting house, Orlok sits hunched at his desk, surrounded by bags of money and obsessing over the real estate contracts that would eventually bring him to Bremen. In both of these images, Orlok conforms to the stereotype of the grasping, usurious Jew embedded in Christian Western culture since the Middle Ages.[105] The only forces powerful enough to distract Orlok from his monetary obsession are his hunger for warm Christian blood,

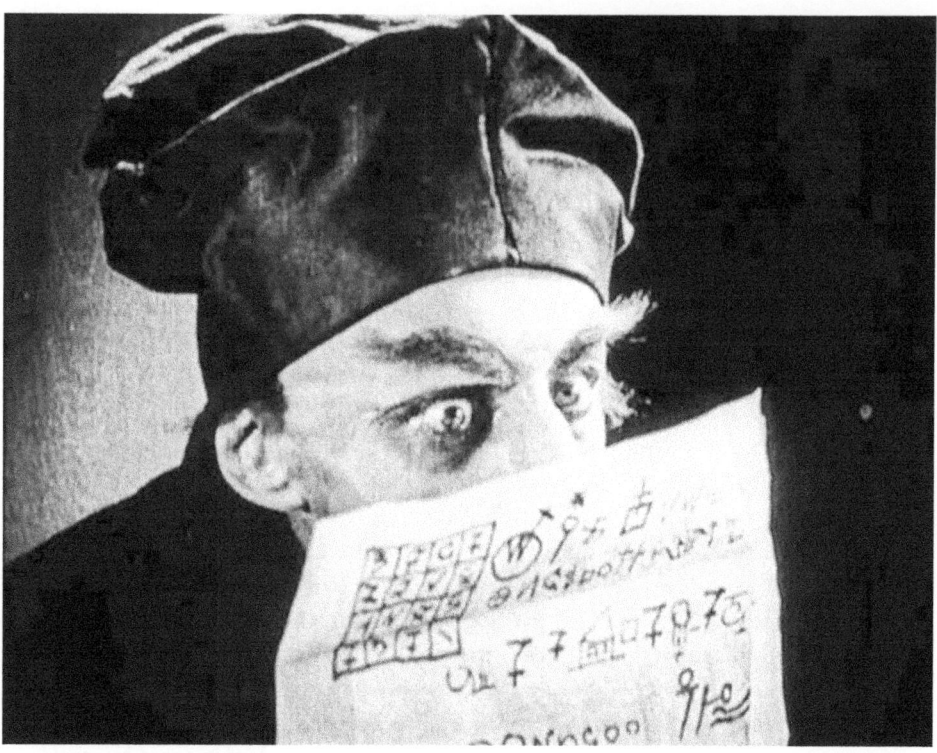

Count Orlok (Max Schreck) as the Jewish Vampire; his hooked nose, bushy eyebrows, deep-set eyes, pallid skin, baldness, dark clothes and cantor's hat, as well his grasping and rapacious nature, all bind him closely to Antisemitic stereotypes born of medieval inversion and anti-Jewish discourses. *Nosferatu: Ein Symphonie des Grauens*, F.W. Murnau, Film Arts Guild (1922).

evident when Hutter cuts his thumb with a breadknife, and his lust for Christian women, which is revealed when he discovers Ellen's picture among Hutter's belongings. Suddenly consumed with desire, the vampire drops his legal parchment, snatches her photograph with nimble pointed fingers, and gives voice to his double-edged hunger: "Is this your wife?" he asks. "What a lovely throat!" Like the melancholic Jew, the vampire is driven by his own uncontrollable urges to drink human blood, in part to replace those lost through his leaky and transgressive body. Similarly, his melancholic physiology drives his sexual rapacity, his need for warmth and moisture through intimacy. Like the medieval character of the Jew, the vampire does not generate the male vital heat necessary for erection and ejaculation; instead, in his bloodlust the vampire must penetrate his victims orally. Determined to sexually possess Ellen, Orlok is forced to enter her bedroom through an alternative opening,

5. The Transgressive Monster 157

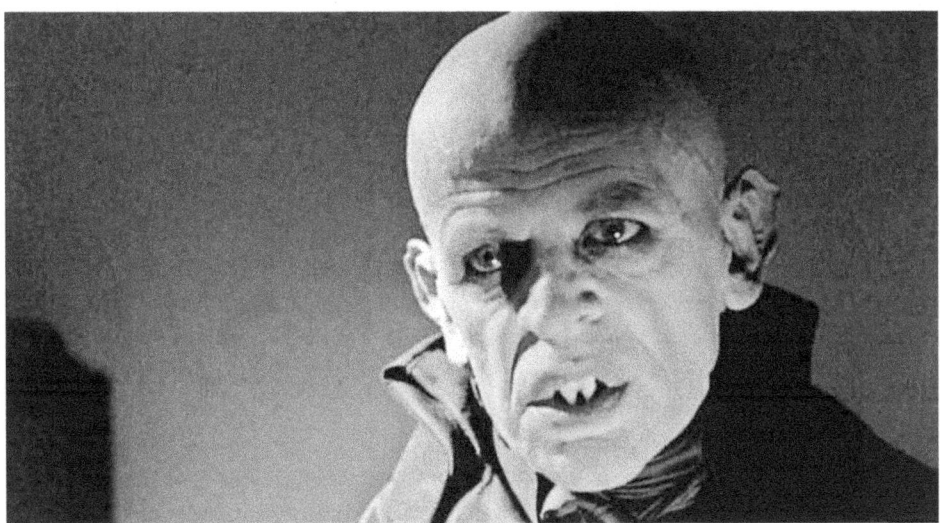

Klaus Kinski as a nihilistic Count Dracula plagued by lovesickness exacerbated by black bile melancholy. *Nosferatu: Phantom der Nacht*, Werner Herzog, 20th Century–Fox (1979).

using her window rather than the door used by her husband. Falling upon her in bed, he rapes her "lovely throat" with his fangs in lieu of a true husband's virile member.

Werner Herzog's remake, *Nosferatu: Phantom der Nacht* (1979), builds upon Murnau's vampire–Jew, adding another dimension to his primal melancholia, that of lovesickness. As played by Klaus Kinski, Herzog's vampire, painted in hues of blue and gray, is consumed by an insatiable desire for wholeness, an uncontrollable longing for love that moves beyond mere carnality.[106] The "constant melancholic anxiety" of lovesickness was known in the medieval world as a medical condition affecting both body and soul. In Ibn-Jazzar's *Liber de heros morbo*, translated by a student of Constantine the African, Johannes Afflacius, lovesickness is attributed to an "intense obsessive desire" for a beloved that remains unfulfilled.[107] This irrational and uncontrollable passion corrupts the humoral balance of the patient, thereby facilitating the over-production and retention of black bile, the vapors from which press against the diaphragm, causing the patient to sigh uncontrollably. Should this desire go unrequited, these corrupt vapors will rise to the brain where they first cause sleeplessness and lethargy; following a sustained period, the patient will experience a full episode of black bile melancholy.

Kinski's vampire is a creature of lovesick despair; ashen and gaunt, he feels the "absence of love" acutely, and longs for death, which is "not the worst." "Dying is cruelty for the unsuspecting," he tells Lucy, the object of his desire, "but death is not everything. It is more cruel not to be able to die." He then tells her of his longing to "partake in the love" that she shares with her husband, Jonathan. Sensing his rapacity and desperation, she spurns him, taunting him with soft breasts barely concealed beneath a filmy tunic. His response to her is primal; denied, he writhes with sexual rage, shudders, and retreats to his ruined manse. At the film's conclusion, Lucy opens her window, calling to the vampire, inviting him in. With an affect of longing, desire, and sorrow, the vampire enters her bedchamber and kneels beside her as she reclines on her bed. Surveying her female topography, he slowly runs his clawed hand up from her shins, exposing her legs and the shadowed region between them, where his fingers come to rest. As her arms reach to encircle him, his hand rests on her breast as his hungry mouth descends on her exposed neck; his fangs penetrate her, and he possesses her at last. It is, of course, his much longed-for doom. Inverted evil cannot withstand the piercing rays of divine sunlight, rational and masculine; in that pure light, the vampire becomes a blackened husk, curled up in the corner like the fetid carapace of a long-dead insect, consigned to the earth at last.

The vampire that dominates both versions of *Nosferatu* is a creature sculpted from medieval clay, his body an inversion of Christian male perfection. In modern cinema, the vampire's pestilent evil is not confined to the crumbling cities of the old world, but has crossed oceans of time to infect small American towns like Salem's Lot. Based on the novel by Stephen King, *Salem's Lot* (1979) tells the tale of an idyllic middle-class New England town, a place where time stands still, that is corrupted by the arrival of two European outsiders, the effete British Richard Straker and his vampiric Austrian partner, Kurt Barlow. The two men—in the absence of women—have purchased a haunted mansion on the forested crest overlooking the town and opened an antique shop. Having settled in Salem's Lot, they begin feeding upon the good Christian blood of its citizens. As the vampire, Barlow conforms to medieval structures; his skin is bluish gray and hairless, his breath is icy cold, he emits fetid vapors, has a crooked nose, pointed ears, and enormous rat-like fangs which he uses to exsanguinate his victims. Unlike the vampire–Jew of *Nosferatu*, however, Barlow is enormous in size, towering over his victims with preternatural strength. The arrival of this unstoppable homosexual, decadent, European bloodsucker signals the end of Salem Lot's heteronormative and blue collar idyll, as young and old begin to penetrate each other in a frenzy of transsexual and trans-generational feeding. The inverted monster has brought foreign chaos to the once-orderly Christian town, now an epicenter of vampiric infection that will spread outward to destroy middle-class American culture and shatter all delusions of the American dream.[108]

Medievalism in Stoker's Gentlemen

Roman Polanki's 1967 film *The Fearless Vampire Killers* features two seemingly paradoxical vampires. On the one hand is Yoine Shagal, a Jewish innkeeper turned vampire who not only sucks the blood of the living but continues to pursue a sexual relationship with his former maid, a buxom young Christian named Magda. Entering her bedroom as he once did in life, Shagal the vampire approaches the plump blonde with rapacious desire; terrified of his grotesque visage, Magda holds up a crucifix, to which Shagal chuckles through a Jewish brogue, "Oy, for you've got the wrong vampire!" Against this vampire–Jew, at once comedic and horrifying, stands the film's other vampire, Count Krolock, who is wealthy, debonair, and popular with the ladies. He is above all attractive, with a symmetrical face, balanced features, and even complexion; tall and straight, he seems to be a novel creature, one who does not conform to medieval structures of inverted alterity. As the noble gentleman vampire, however, Krolock has merely changed his Aristotelian accidents, and not his formal substance; beneath his charming façade, his fundamental physiology remains that of the melancholic blood-sucking "other" whose ethos conforms in every detail to the structures of inverted evil codified by medieval clerics.[109] His preferred environments, habits, powers, and weaknesses belie his true—if hidden—nature as a melancholic monster.

In 1931, Universal Studios introduced American audiences to the world of *Dracula* and the gentleman vampire as played by the Hungarian actor, Bela Lugosi.[110] Lugosi's Dracula is handsome, a mysterious and wealthy stranger wearing the garb of a long-perished nobility as he moves through the well-ordered, bourgeois, and urban culture of modern England. Despite his arrival in modernity, Dracula is a creature of the Old World, a being born of the distant past who carries within him an upside-down nocturnal domain of inverted evil. In Transylvania, Dracula sleeps by day in a coffin of corrupt earth hidden within the moist basement of his crumbling castle; there, he is joined by possum-rats, spiders, and other melancholic monsters, including his three moldering wives.[111] By night he stalks the fog-laden forests, becoming one with "the children of the night," shapeshifting into a wolf or bat. Like the medieval witch, Dracula has a toxic gaze, his glowing eyes having the ability to mesmerize his prey with a mere glance. Witch-like, he commands the fog and wind, raising the tempest that brings the ship carrying his earth boxes and its cargo of corpses to Whitby.[112] Safely in England, the vampire takes up residence in a ruined abbey, a sacred building slowly returning to the corrupt earth. There, he lodges his earth box in its subterranean chambers, its fetid basement-bowels serving as an inverted, rat-like nesting place. In late-medieval witchcraft treatises, the sign of the cross has the power to drive out Satanic entities and return them to the sulphurous pits of hell; similarly, Dracula cannot abide the crucifix, the Eucharist, or holy water. Nor can Dracula tolerate mirrors, perhaps because it might reveal his own inversion and the negation of his true Christian self which he so irrationally denies. All of these signifiers belie the otherwise-attractive gentleman Dracula as an inverted and melancholic monster, damned to wander the earth and never ascend from the corruption that manifests in his fleshly being.

In keeping with medieval paradigms, the irrational realm of the vampire is hidden from the rational Christian men who surround him. To the sober young Harker and the scientifically minded Dr. Seward, Dracula's ways are merely odd, the mark of his foreign and somewhat backwards culture.[113] For them, vampires cannot exist except as silly superstitions in the minds of little old ladies and uneducated peasants. Of the male characters in the film, it is only Van Helsing who understands the specific rationality of the vampire. A foreigner himself, he is not only a physician who holds pre–Cartesian ideas about the body, but also a scientist and scholar of esoteric subjects, including theology. Familiar with both learned treatises and folklore, Van Helsing makes meaning from the seemingly chaotic events unfolding around him. When his colleagues initially reject his theory that Dracula is a vampire, he warns them that "the strength of the vampire, is that people will *not* believe in him."[114] The women in the film, of course, believe in the vampire immediately without the need for rationalization. As in medieval discourse, the women of *Dracula* are irrational creatures, susceptible to unseen evil forces that tempt them into sexual sin and drag them to their doom. Cold and wanton, Lucy and Mina stand little chance against the voracious sexual predator who longs to possess their bodies and drink their inspirited blood. Desire for desire, both possessor and possessed are drawn into a whirlwind of emotion and feeding, sucking and being sucked, and through this are doomed to the melancholic world of the flesh for all eternity.

The vampire's transgressive nature proves to be a danger to the patriarchal order. Outwardly male and rational, he is fundamentally female and irrational, all of which allows him to pass in the world of men while controlling women and imperceptibly undermining erstwhile male power. In *Dracula*, for example, the submissive Mina becomes willful and defiant of male authority under the influence of the vampire, rejecting both her father and fiancé as protectors and instead rushing into the arms of her undead beloved. In this context, Dracula becomes at once Mina's rapacious husband and controlling father, an inverted figure so powerful that it takes three men to defeat him. Having secured Mina's "liberation" from the vampire's irrational power, she is returned to a place of safety under their own control.

The gentleman vampire's ability to challenge and destroy the patriarchal status quo becomes a central theme in the films of Hammer.[115] In *Horror of Dracula* (1958), for example, Christopher Lee plays a handsome, aristocratic vampire whose goal is sexual domination. A polygamist, he has several brides imprisoned in his castle. All of them appear young and beautiful but they are in reality moldering corpses—a fact revealed when Harker penetrates one of them with a wooden stake and she dissolves into her true melancholic form.[116] Unsatisfied with the wives that he has, Dracula seduces Lucy and Mina, both of whom in this film are constant, Christian, and obedient to male authority. Despite their best efforts, Van Helsing and Holmwood are unable to protect Lucy, who works against them and becomes one of Dracula's brides; their only recourse is the impale her with a phallic stake, thereby forcing her back under their God-given patriarchal power. Even though they now understand the nature of their enemy, the men are still unable to prevent Dracula from entering their house and penetrating Mina, the woman in their care. Dracula's rapacity, however, is once again his doom; having absconded with Mina, he is repelled by a cross and forced into the rational sunshine, radiating down from the Empyrean itself, which destroys him, rendering his melancholic flesh dust.

Like all vermin, the vampire never stays dead for long. In *Dracula: Prince of Darkness* (1966), the vampire is revivified by mixing his cold and dry ashes with the blood of a young man sacrificed for this purpose. The use of living blood to sustain an inverted monster is rooted in medieval rhetoric about the libelous bloodlust of melancholic Jews. Throughout the Hammer series, Christopher Lee's vampire returns again and again, always in the form of the gentleman vampire; true to his shape-shifting nature, however, the parasitic and power-hungry "other" that he signifies morphs with the historical context of each film. In *Dracula Has Risen from the Grave* (1968), for example, the vampire goes to war with the Catholic Church. When a monsignor arrives in the village near Dracula's castle, he finds a faithless priest in a community too terrified to enter the local church because of the vampire's power. In attempt to return this flock to the papal enclosure, the monsignor exorcises Dracula's castle and leaves, believing that he has vanquished the evil. In retaliation, Dracula enslaves the local priest and kills the monsignor as he attempts to protect his beautiful niece, who has now become the vampire's sexual fixation. The girl is ultimately saved by the faithless priest and her atheist boyfriend Paul, who impales Dracula with a crucifix and, apparently, regains his faith in Christ—all without the intervention of Catholic authority. Released just three years after the conclusion of the Second Vatican Council, the film uses the vampire as a foil for an equally irrational, impotent, and perhaps evil Catholic Church. One year later, Hammer released *Taste the Blood of Dracula* (1969), which features two bored and wealthy old men raising Dracula for fun and thereby exposing their own children to the vampire's wrath. Although set in the sempiternal gothic nineteenth century, the film links the evil of Dracula with a reckless older generation willing to feed off of its own young—who only wanted peace and love—in order to continue its decadent lifestyle. *The Satanic Rites of Dracula* (1973) continues this discourse, arguing that the older generation has attained its financial and political power through membership in an elite Satanic cult that worships and sacrifices to Dracula as its dark lord. These rituals are held in a gated mansion where innocent victims are slaughtered and their blood consumed by the faithful, a construct born of medieval anti–Judaism. The narrative of the wealthy gentleman who is in reality an inverted bloodsucker in disguise is not only in alignment with medieval discourses on the demonic, but also reflects the Satanic Panic already brewing in mid-twentieth century Anglo-American culture.[117]

The Dracula narrative, much like the vampire itself, never dies. Stoker's gentleman vampire, that strange amalgamation between medieval melancholic monstrosity and aesthetic pleasure, continues to be one of the most-told tales in Western culture.[118] His power lies not only in his sexual prowess, as evident in Louis Jourdan's rendition of the vampire in *Count Dracula* (1977), or in his tragic and romantic ethos, a key element in the popularity of Francis Ford Coppola's *Bram Stoker's Dracula* (1992), but also in his elusive nature. Everpresent yet unreal, tangible yet ethereal, he is a chimera, ever-changing to suit our cultural need for a desired and reviled "other." In this way, the gentleman vampire not only reveals the persistence of medieval paradigms for inverted and Satanic evil and provides a lens on contemporary fears about its proliferation in the modern world, but also reveals to us our own inverted selves, and in so doing illuminates who we believe ourselves to be—and who we believe we are not.

Postmodern Vampires: Other Others

Through the lenses of postmodernism, the blood-hungry vampire is no longer simply and passively defined by dominant culture as a reviled "other," but a dynamic entity who actively uses melancholic monstrosity as a means of questioning the status quo and achieving self-empowerment. For example, throughout the twentieth century and in concert with second wave feminism, female vampires underwent a drastic transformation from Dracula's brides or daughters, demure and obedient to his commands, to independent operators who fulfilled their own desires and founded their own matriarchal clans. For example, Mario Bava's *Black Sunday* (1960) features a female vampire named Katia Vajda who feeds upon the warm blood of the young in order to assume her previous beauty.[119] In her quest for rejuvenation, Katia manipulates the weak men who fall in love with her, penetrating them, feeding upon them, and using them as slave-like servants. Unlike earlier female vampires, Katia did not become a bloodsucker through congress with a male vampire, although she gladly infects all those who come into contact with her. Instead, her vampirism is a natural outgrowth of her primary role as a Satanic witch—the paradigm around which almost all female vampires are constructed.

Rooted in stories of *lamias*, such as those recounted in John of Salisbury's *Policraticus*, as well as the melancholic witches that haunted witchcraft treatises, the female vampire's desire to drink the blood and eat the flesh of children makes her the worst of all mothers.[120] This theme is echoed in films based on the mythologized life of Elizabeth Báthory, who purportedly bathed in the blood of sacrificed virgins in order to become young once again. Despite recent historical works such as Tony Thorne's *Countess Dracula* and films such as *Báthory: Countess of Blood* (2008) and *The Countess* (2009) that have attempted to debunk the Bathory legend, popular culture continues to regard her as a vampire who drained the blood of children to serve her irrational vanity.[121] The persistence of this myth can be attributed to the strength of the vampire-witch paradigm in Western culture and the continued perception of women in power as both aberrant and evil.[122]

The female vampire's witchy nature extends beyond bloodsucking and into sexual rapacity, making her not only a bad mother but a wicked wife. In Hammer's *Twins of Evil* (1971), for example, Frieda is obstinate, sexually adventurous, and impious, the radical inversion of her sister Maria, who is compliant, conservative, and devoted to Christianity. Anton, a young man from the village, courts the sweet Maria but finds himself entranced by her sexually charged sister; despite their binary natures, he cannot tell the innocent sister from the evil one. Frieda is uninterested in Anton, preferring instead the Satan-worshipping bad boy Count Karnstein, who has been transformed into a vampire by an ancestor named Marcilla. The count spreads his vampiric infection to the wanton women who submit to him, including the all-too-willing Frieda. Ultimately Frieda pays for her irrational desires and sexual voracity with death by beheading—effectively putting an end to her headstrong ways. The film's conclusion leaves Maria and Anton—an embodiment of the patriarchal and Christian status quo—intact.

In *Twins of Evil*, both Frieda and Maria are enslaved by men, be they Christian patriarchs, abusive vampire lovers, or future husbands. The second half of the twentieth century, however, saw a new type of female vampire, the fully empowered and sexually liberated bloodsucker who mercilessly fed on men while maintaining absolute control over them. While vamps such as the Countess Nadine Carody of Jess Franco's *Vampyros Lesbos* (1971) and the transgressive vampire women of Jean Rollin's films might enjoy men as sexual playthings, they do not wish to become wives, nor do they require access to a penis for sexual satisfaction.[123] As a creature of power, the lesbian vampire hisses with a forked tongue, on one hand claiming that women are powerful enough to satisfy each other without men, while on the other pandering to a male gaze that objectifies the female body and finds pleasure in female coupling. In the same vein, female vampire films such as *Once Bitten* (1985) and *Vamp* (1986) at first appear to subvert the patriarchal order by objectifying male bodies, fang-raping them, impregnating them, and forcing them to transform as they breed more members for a wicked matriarch.[124] Beneath this veneer of liberation, however, all of these female vampires remain enslaved by medieval discourses of inverted evil, once again reinforcing the age-old Western belief that powerful women are wicked and must be destroyed.[125]

The vampire has not only been used to challenge patriarchal authority, but also white hegemony and heteronormativity. Films such as the "fangadelic" *Blacula* (1972), *Scream Blacula Scream* (1973), *Vamp*, and *Vampire in Brooklyn* (1995), all of which feature powerful black vampires, prey on white fears of penetration and possession by African Americans.[126] While such films offer white audiences the opportunity for an abject contemplation of slavery, the African American postcolonial experience, and the vampiric nature of a socio-economically imbalanced capitalist system, they do so while hiding behind the mask of humor. From the campy to the openly comedic, these films problematically suggest that black hegemony—while interesting as entertainment—could never really exist. Likewise the African American female vampires in *Vamp* and *Queen of the Damned* (2002), while powerful creatures of great beauty, merely reinforce persistent stereotypes and suggest that an African American woman who has power over white men is an unnatural and monstrous inversion.[127]

A similar contorted paradigm prevails in programs such as *True Blood* (2008-present), which uses vampires as a metaphor for, among other groups, the LGBTQ community. Because of its transgressive nature, the vampire has always been suspected of being queer; producers at Universal Studios were so sensitive to the subversive ways that the penetration and sucking of male victims by Bela Lugosi (and, in the sequels, Lon Chaney and John Carradine) might be interpreted that the act itself was never shown. *The Lost Boys* (1987) features ambient gay themes, while *Let the Right One In* (2008) addresses issues of "slippage" and transgendering. In both films, a liberated younger generation questions the moral economy of its conservative elders. *True Blood* takes this liberal agenda even further, depicting a familiar world in which queer vampires must fight against the heteronormative and middle-class status quo for equal human rights. In casting these social issues through the lens of monstrosity, *True Blood* serves as a mirror in which modern society might see its own horrific constructs reflected back at it; in our discriminatory practices, it is we who are vampires, and the vampire "other" who is truly human.[128]

Despite its liberal values, in framing issues of alterity through the lens of medieval inversion and monstrosity, *True Blood* comes under the sway of deeply rooted discourses of power. The fifth season of the show introduces a character named Roman Zimojic (Chris Meloni) who serves as the leader of a rabbinic-like council called the Vampire Authority. They meet in a subterranean space with a Mediterranean style reminiscent of a Spanish synagogue; tablet-shaped structures line the walls, a wooden door bears two stars similar to the Mogen David, and there is a pool reminiscent of a mikveh. Within this space we witness a strange communion ritual in which members of the council kneel down to receive the blood of Lilith, the heroine of the Vampire Bible that predates and serves as the basis for the Hebrew Bible, while Hebrew-like chanting can be heard in the background. Later, a vampire named Drew is sacrificed at the table and his heart-blood consumed by Roman. Although he is five hundred years old, Drew takes the form of a small, blond-haired and blue-eyed boy, a spitting image perhaps of Anderl von Rinn or Little Hugh of Lincoln, both of whom were rumored to have been killed by blood-hungry and rapacious Jews in the service of their dark lord.

Ironically, the title of this particular episode is "Authority Always Wins." In using medieval discourses on inverted evil, this is exactly what happens and continues to happen unless we are ever-vigilant in our mindfulness of its horrifying and seductive power.

6

A Cursed Embodiment

Modernity, Medievalism and the Melancholic Werewolf

> "The people of this country ought to know as much as any others about werewolves; for they have always been known here."—
> Boguet, *An Examen of Witches*

> "Everyone knows about werewolves."—
> Gwen Conliffe, *The Wolf Man*

The story is an old one. A man, either through his own culpability or as the victim of a tragic curse, falls under the sway of the full moon. As its rays fall upon him, he begins his transformation from a rational human being into an irrational, ravenous wolf. Beyond the bounds of morality and reason, he is free to feed upon warm wet flesh, be it human or animal. The melancholic werewolf stalks forests and villages until the cock's crow and the first rays of sunlight, or until he is slain by a huntsman, at which point his body transforms once again into its human form.

The modern horror film emphasizes the physicality of the werewolf's transgressive nature. The afflicted man does not merely *appear* to be transformed, but fully *becomes* the wolf-monster in every part of his being. The prioritizing of physical over metaphysical metamorphosis is made evident in the werewolf film's lavish depiction of the creature's transformation; the camera's steady gaze holds fast as now-fluid human flesh sprouts fur, fangs, and snout and eventually returns into its original, bipedal, and far less furry frame. The question of whether such physical transformation is possible, as well as the meaning of human embodiment and the nature of the rational soul, are at the heart of the werewolf's long shape-shifting history.

In ancient Rome, authors such as Petronius, Ovid, Pliny the Elder, and

Apuleius told horrifying and humorous tales of men who through their own agency or that of others had been physically transformed into beasts. For many pagans, including Platonists and Pythagoreans, metamorphosis and metempsychosis were natural in a world where everything was interconnected and in flux. This fluidity of form—in particular as it pertained to the relationship between humans and animals—posed a philosophical and theological problem for Christian apologists such as Tertullian, who argued that to believe in such things not only went against the belief in a single, unified, and fundamentally good creator God, but also contradicted natural philosophy as elaborated by Aristotle.[1] Two centuries later, in *City of God*, Augustine articulated what would become the orthodox Christian view on human-to-animal transformation, including the existence of werewolves. Such metamorphosis, he argued, was impossible within the bounds of nature, for only God, the author of natural law, might supersede it and transform one type of matter into another. Just as human flesh could not become animal flesh, so a rational human soul—a very reflection of the Deity Himself—could not become an irrational animal soul. To believe such a thing was to make a mockery of God's creation and to question the nature of humanity, including that of Jesus Christ. For if a human could transform into a base animal, where did the rational soul, which was rooted within the body itself, go? Confronted with a plethora of authoritative pagan texts that detailed human metamorphosis into animals and aware that such stories were prevalent in Roman culture, Augustine did not dismiss these creatures out of hand. Instead, he conceded that people may indeed *appear* to become wolves. Such werewolves, however, were merely phantasms, illusions created by demons in the minds of their victims. Werewolves in fur and fang, however, could not physically exist.

In medieval Europe, Augustine's works bore the weight of unquestionable textual authority, and his ideas on the impossibility of human metamorphosis outside of the miraculous were echoed in legal texts, such as the *Canon Episcopi*, wonder tales, such as those of Gerald of Wales, and romances, such as Marie de France's *Bisclavret*. In each of these sources, the werewolf character is either a demonic delusion, in which case he does not exist, or merely dons a wolf-like skin while retaining a rational soul, in which case he or she remains fundamentally and tragically human.[2] With the introduction of Aristotle into the Latin West and the concomitant flowering of scholasticism, the transformation of matter once again fell under learned scrutiny. Scholars Albertus Magnus, William of Auvergne, and Thomas Aquinas questioned the nature of material change in the sublunary realm, exploring its processes and potentialities through the lenses of Aristotelian natural philosophy and

Christian theology. Like Augustine before them, they concluded that substantial material transformation, such as the transubstantiation of the Eucharist, was possible only through the suspension of natural law by God; in short, it was a miracle. All other transformations were non-substantial and, although they may seem wondrous, were within the bounds of nature. Standing in Augustine's shadow, William of Auvergne and Thomas Aquinas reaffirmed the impossibility of werewolves based on the incongruity of the human and animal soul, arguing that werewolves were the products of phantasy in which demons either manipulated the humors of their human victim, thereby imprinting false images in their minds, or used airy substances in order to form monstrous bodies that seemed real to the human eye. Drawing from learned medical treatises, including the *De Melancholia* of Ishaq Ibn-Imran, scholars argued that those suffering from black bile melancholia were most susceptible to such delusions of transformation.[3] With its cold brain clouded by dark and toxic vapors, the melancholic body became a warped vessel open to penetration by demons and other superlunary forces, such as Saturn and the moon. For theologians, the blackened body was not only humorally and spiritually vulnerable, but also categorically associated with inversion, earthbound corruption, and feminine evil.[4]

The scholastic assertion that shape-shifting between human and animal forms was physically impossible within the bounds of nature would be challenged in late-medieval and early modern witchcraft treatises. At first, Heinrich Kramer's *Malleus Maleficarum* (1486) appears to reinforce the orthodox views of Augustine and Aquinas, arguing that the flight of witches and the transformation of werewolves are merely glamors created by demons. Once Kramer has paid lip service to textual authority, however, he veers into his main argument that witches and by extension werewolves are very real and must be hunted down and eradicated. The conflicting views that haunt the *Malleus* became a characteristic of future witchcraft treatises on the continent, such as Jean Bodin's *Demonmania of Witches* (1580), Henry Boguet's *An Examen of Witches* (1602) and Pierre de Lancre's *On the Inconstancy of Witches* (1612), all of which incorporated discussions on werewolves and shapeshifting.[5] Unable or unwilling to reject the authority of medieval theologians and the findings of earlier writers, these authors were bound to incorporate skeptical viewpoints into their own work, even if they believed in the possibility of witchy levitations or the physical transformation of the werewolf. Boguet and de Lancre, for example, ultimately dismiss the possibility of human metamorphosis, although they both discuss werewolves in lavish details that hint at their belief that such creatures may in fact exist—a belief that was likely to be shared in some part by their readers.[6] Among these authors, it is Jean

Bodin who unapologetically argues for the existence of werewolves, claiming that through demonic agency, a man might light a blue-flamed candle, sign a pact with Satan, rub a foul ointment on his flesh, and transform into a wolf who eats children and engages in orgiastic sex with other wolves. In Bodin, we see the full elaboration of the werewolf as an inverted and melancholic monster. Cast into the same category as the witch and, by extension, the hermeneutic Jew, the werewolf was transformed from a mere phantasy that cloaked and clouded fully human beings into a blood-hungry and rapacious Satanic other who had given himself over to evil and was beyond redemption.

Despite the attempts of church fathers such as Augustine and medieval authorities such as Aquinas to reason away the belief in human metamorphosis beyond the power of God, and despite the arguments of early modern skeptics Johann Weyer (*De Praestigiis Daemonum*, 1563) and Reginald Scot (*Discoverie of Witchcraft*, 1584) that witchcraft and werewolves were preposterous superstitions, the evil werewolf—hungry, hairy, and truly transformed—has persisted in Western culture. No longer the topic of theological discourse, the modern werewolf remains a salient character in the horror genre where it haunts comics, popular novels, manga, and moving images on the large screen and small. The cinematic werewolf in particular is a strange amalgamation of codes and signifiers drawn from its own chimerical history and shaped by multiple postmodern lenses. Omnipresent are the inverted structures of melancholic and Satanic evil, including the werewolf's dark and shaggy appearance, his association with nighttime, the full moon, autumn, and the chaotic world of the forests, as well as his thirst for blood, sexual rapacity, and infectious nature—all of which link him with the stereotypical witch and the vampire–Jew. The cinematic werewolf not only reveals the persistence of inverted structures, but also serves as a palette upon which modern culture might paint its own warped image. Through the lens of Freudian psychoanalysis, the werewolf character is interpreted as the primal self, released from the constraints of civilization, a mere illusion created by a disordered mind. Using retrospective diagnosis, some scholars have argued that the werewolf of modern horror is a product not of the mind but of the body—that historical werewolves were merely victims of hypertrichosis, a medical condition that ancient and medieval people were too foolish to understand.[7] Rejecting both of these paths as reductive, postmodernists have seen the werewolf character as the Foucauldian other who lives on the edges of human society and collective morality, a source of Kristevan abjection in which we see our own base natures written in the flesh, a representation of male power and a signifier through which gender roles might be deconstructed.

At the heart of our fascination with the werewolf and the proliferation of werewolf films is our desire to understand what it means to be embodied as human in an increasingly liquid modernity.[8] Are we fully ensouled, our bodies inspirited and therefore unable to be other than human? Are animals ensouled and are we, one of them, a part of nature or apart from it? Or are we, as Descartes taught, bifurcated, our souls merely ghosts in a machine that might operate beyond our own wills as we, trapped inside the monster, watch helpless and alone?

Immutable and Ensouled: The Theologians and the Werewolf

The Greco-Roman literary tradition is rife with tales of material change, hybridity, and human-to-animal metamorphosis. Homer's *Odyssey*, for example, recounts how Odysseus, lost on the storm-tossed wine-dark sea as a punishment for his disrespect of Polyphemus, becomes stranded on Circe's enchanted island where his men are transformed into swine.[9] In the Roman poet Ovid's (d. 17 CE) *Metamorphoses*, Lycaon, king of Arcadia, tests the power of Zeus by serving him the flesh of a murdered man made "tender in seething water" and roasted over a fire.[10] As punishment, Zeus turns Lycaon into a wolf, a physical transformation that reflects his inner beastly self: "His clothes became bristling hair, his arms became legs. He was a wolf, but kept some vestige of his former shape. There were the same grey hairs, the same violent face, the same glittering eyes, the same savage image." His metamorphosis complete, the werewolf runs out to slaughter sheep, "still delighting in blood," just as he did in human form.[11] Written half a century later, Petronius' *Satyricon* features a different type of werewolf—one that transforms through his own free will, perhaps through the agency of magic.[12] In a tale recounted at Trimalchio's Funerary Banquet, a man was seen walking through a graveyard while "the moon shone bright as mid-day"; removing his clothes, he pissed in a circle, "turned into a wolf, started to howl, and then ran off into the woods."[13] While a wolf, he was speared through the neck by a woodsman; the next day, he was discovered in his apartments, back in human form, and under the care of a physician for his tell-tale wounds.

Such stories, drawn from mythology and folklore, were set against a philosophical milieu fascinated with processes of material change, the nature of the human soul, and their relationship to one another. In the sixth and fifth centuries BCE, the Ionian philosophers Pythagoras and Empedocles sought to understand the underlying nature of matter. For Pythagoras, all matter was driven by mathematical principles, or *archas*, and these were responsible for change in the natural world. Empedocles, however, argued that there were four "roots" (fire, air, water, and earth), later labeled by Plato as elements, that were present in all matter in different proportions. The shifting of these elements resulted in material change; because these elements could not be created or destroyed, nature was in a continual state of flux and transformation. In accordance with their theories of material transformation, Pythagoras and Empedocles argued that the human soul is immortal "and that it transmigrates into other animated bodies." A soul might not only experience metempsychosis, but also metensomatosis, or body-hopping, allowing for all manner of human transformation.[14] In the fourth century BCE, Plato followed his forbears in believing that the human soul was immortal. According to his theories, the soul was incorporeal in the truest sense; because it was completely immaterial, and did not occupy space, the soul was unbound from the world of corruption and change below the moon. Free from the world of shadowy matter, Plato argued, the soul was able to see into the superlunary realm of the perfect and immaterial forms.[15] In his *Meno*, *Cratulus*, *Phaedo*, *Gorgias*, and the *Republic*, Plato asserts that the immortal soul could not only exist outside of the body, but also experience metempsychosis.[16] Ever at odds with his teacher, Plato's star pupil Aristotle argued that the soul, like all other matter below the moon, was material, even if it was made of such thin matter as to be insensible, like air. Because the soul was material, it had a natural place of rest, and this was within the human body to which it was inextricably connected.[17] The soul (*anima*) was both the force animating the body and the formal cause of the body itself, and therefore could "not exist without a body."[18] The death of the body meant the death of the soul; metempsychosis, metensomatosis, and the transformation of a human being into any other animal, therefore, was simply impossible.

Christianity emerged from and within a Greco-Roman textual world of shape-shifting tales and competing philosophical discourses—particularly those of Plato and Aristotle—on the nature of matter and the human soul. Writing in the late second and early-third centuries CE, the Christian apologist Tertullian was forced to negotiate this textual landscape while preserving Christian tenets such as the human-corporeality of Christ's flesh—and therefore the essential goodness of matter—as well as the immortality of the individual human soul redeemed through His sacrifice.[19] In his treatise *On the Soul*, Tertullian argues, like Aristotle, that the human soul is a single, incorporeal-yet-material substance tied to the flesh and engrained in the being, adding that it may be "invisible to the flesh, but perfectly visible to the spirit."[20] Following Aristotle, he likewise argues that the soul is the formal cause of the body, shaping and animating its form, and is therefore non-transferable.[21] Against Aristotle, however, Tertullian argues that the human soul is in essence a reflection of the Christian god, and is therefore rational, indivisible, immutable, and immortal—premises that bring him into alignment with Platonic philosophy.[22] Because of its rationality and divine origin, Tertullian asserts that the human soul could neither become an irrational animal soul, nor could it be the formal cause of a base animal body. Shape-shifting creatures such as werewolves could not possibly exist and in his estimation, only foolish pagans would believe such things to be true. Written almost two hundred years later than Tertullian's *On the Soul*, Augustine's *City of God* once again addresses the idea of metempsychosis and the physical transformation of human flesh into animal. After recounting several werewolf tales culled from ancient and contemporary sources, Augustine argues that "these things are either false, or so extraordinary as to be with good reason disbelieved."[23] Nevertheless, he continues, God's power is great, and he might very well allow demons to create illusions—either phantasies in the mind, such as when one is dreaming, or by manipulating "the appearance of things created by the true God so as to make them seem to be what they are not." Physical transformation of a human being into a werewolf, according to Augustine, remained impossible; the very real shared illusion of such a transformation, however, was altogether possible through the agency of melancholic demons.

Tertullian's pastiche of the Aristotelian and Platonic soul, at once bound to the flesh as its formal cause yet immortal through divine agency, as well as Augustine's argument regarding demonic phantasy became authoritative structures used by medieval theologians in the rebuttal of human-to-animal transformations. Learned sources such as the ninth-century *Canon Episcopi* cited in Gratian's *Decretals* (1140) affirm that the powers of witches, including the night flight and their ability to change themselves and others into wild beasts are not physical transformations but demonic illusions. To believe that "any creature can be changed to better or to worse or be transformed into another species or similitude, except by the Creator himself," is not only foolish, but heretical.[24] An individual's belief in werewolves and other transgressive creatures marked him as an infidel not only because such beliefs questioned the sovereign power of God and debased creation, but also because they were inherent to persistent pagan narratives. The consistent rejection of human-to-animal metamorphosis by learned textual authorities shaped the depiction of werewolves in twelfth-century sources such as Gerald of Wales' *Topography of Ireland* (1187), which features the oft-recounted tale of the Werewolves of Ossory.[25] In this narrative, a priest sitting by a campfire is approached by a large wolf who asks for his help. Amazed at an animal that has the power of human speech, the priest engages him in dialogue and learns that the wolf and his ailing wife were forced to quit "entirely the human form" by Saint Natalis of Ulster. The wolf then asks the priest to perform the viaticum for his wife, including the administration of the Eucharist. When the priest is unwilling to give the consecrated host to a base animal, the wolf, "using his claw for a hand ... tore off the skin of the she-wolf from the head down to the navel," revealing "the form of an old woman."[26]

As Carolyn Walker Bynum has argued, the wolf and his wife were not truly transformed in the flesh, but instead were wearing the outward appearance or skin of a wolf, beneath which they retained not only their essential human form but also their rational souls.[27] Similar themes resound in the twelfth-century *Bisclavret* of Marie de France, in which a noble knight transforms into a wolf, is betrayed by his wife, and is rescued by the king who recognizes his fundamental humanity despite his lupine form. In observing the wolf's courtly behavior, the king notes that Bisclavret "has the mind of a man," exhibits "understanding and judgment," and is therefore a rational being.[28] Once Bisclavret's wicked wife is brought to justice, he is once again returned to his true form by donning human clothing. Beneath layers of outward identity—wolf skin, human flesh, and vestments—Bisclavret's rational soul, at once human and divine, radiates outward to reveal his true self. In both the Werewolves of Ossory and the *Bisclavret*, the beasts retain their essential humanity; they are rational, Christian, humble, and disciplined. Their appearances are merely accidents, disguises serving a didactic purpose, illuminating what it means to be truly human.

In the academic circles of the thirteenth century, processes of material change and the potential transformation of human flesh once again came under scrutiny as scholars attempted to order the seen and unseen natural worlds through the compound lens of Aristotelian natural philosophy and the received authority of theology. As part of the scholastic project, theologians were particularly keen to investigate, codify, and rationalize phenomena that seemed not to conform to expected categories. For example, reports of healing miracles performed at the shrines of aspirant-saints were carefully scrutinized by papal authorities. Word of mouth and the authority of the local bishop were no longer sufficient to proclaim the miraculous; instead, papal authorities demanded the testimony of eyewitnesses and proof backed by learned medicine verifying that the supplicant had been healed beyond the law of nature.[29] Behind the newly instituted processes of canonization lay not only an increasingly powerful and centralized Church bureaucracy, but also a scholarly assumption that the natural world contained many wonders, most of which could be explained through an ever-growing knowledge of natural philosophy, leaving very few things that were truly miraculous. The paradigmatic example of miraculous transformation was the transubstantiation of the Eucharist, which after 1215 became official doctrine. Aquinas explained the process of transubstantiation in Aristotelian terms, arguing that while the accidents remained those of bread, the power of God, working beyond nature, transformed the substantial cause of the bread into the flesh of Christ.[30] This transformation could not be proven by physical means, but had to be accepted by faith alone. As Tertullian had written of the soul, Christ's body in the bread was "invisible to the flesh," but for the faithful, was "visible in the spirit."

With the Eucharist as the paradigm for the truly miraculous, scholars such as the canonist Gervase of Tilbury collected and expounded upon the marvels of the natural world.[31] In his *Otia Imperialia* (c. 1211), dedicated to Emperor Otto IV, Gervase writes that women can transform into snakes—an association echoed in the *Secrets* of Psuedo-Albertus Magnus—and that men can be transformed into wolves under the influence of the moon.[32] Following the received authority of Augustine, Gervase then argues that although people believe in werewolves, such transformations are in truth the result of demons either playing "an optical trick" or controlling "the reconstitution of elements" in terrifying forms.[33]

Later in his treatise, however, Gervase recounts two werewolf tales, both of which feature corporeal transformations. In the first story, a knight is forsaken by his lord wanders alone through the forest until one night, by the light of the moon, he goes mad, transforms into a wolf, and commences terrorizing the old and eating the very young.[34] The werewolf's human condition is only revealed by the severing of one of his paws, which begins his transformation from wolf to human—a theme that will become a salient feature in future retellings of the werewolf legend. The second story concerns an unapologetic werewolf who removes his clothes and changes into his animal form by the light of the new moon, under which he hunts for his prey with his jaws wide open. In neither of these later tales does Gervase invoke Augustine's authority and the power of demonic phantasy; instead, he lets them stand open-ended, leaving the reader to wonder at the possibility of werewolves and thereby heightening their power to titillate and entertain—a primary function of his collection.

For the scholastic authors William of Auvergne and Thomas Aquinas, who did not write for the delectation of royalty, ambiguity about the transformation of matter was not to be tolerated but probed and explained through Aristotelian philosophy within the bounds of Christian theology. Auvergne, bishop of Paris from 1228 to 1249, was keenly interested in the nature of magic and the role of demons in material transformation; his work *De Universo* detailed the order of all creation, including those entities and phenomena that did not seem to fit into the specific rationality of scholasticism, such as werewolves.[35] In the second section of *De Universo*, he tells the story of a man who was accused of transforming into a wolf and terrorizing his neighbors. Having heard rumors circulating among the people, a local priest reveals that the man is not a werewolf, but instead is possessed by a demon that impresses the image of a wolf upon his imagination and convinces him to hide.[36] While the man is fast asleep, the demon enters into the body of a natural wolf and commits acts of violence, thereby deceiving both the man possessed—who truly believes that he transforms into a wolf—and the villagers alike. In accordance with Augustinian authority, William argues that no physical transformation from man into animal has taken place, except as a convincing artifact of a very real demonic illusion. Aquinas likewise rejects the possibility of human-to-animal transformation in any physical sense. In question 114, Article 4 of the *Summa Theologica*, he argues that "those transformations of bodies which cannot be produced by the power of nature cannot in reality be effected by the operation of demons; for instance, that the human body be changed into the body of a beast." While demons cannot cause material transformation beyond the bounds of natural law, they can nevertheless give illusions the "semblance of reality" either by pressing upon the human imagination from within and manipulating the "corporeal senses," or by forming a physical body from air and using this to "clothe any corporeal thing with any corporeal form." Such demonic phantasies might work upon one man's imagination while offering "the same picture to another man's senses." Therefore, although demonic illusions are not truly miraculous bodily transformations, they nevertheless have their own nascent corporeality both within and beyond the vulnerable human imagination.

According to both William of Auvergne and Aquinas, werewolves might only truly exist as demonic illusions; those most susceptible to demonic manipulation were women and melancholics. Because of their cold humoral compositions, both groups lacked the vital heat crucial to the production of rational *pneuma* and were least able to control the passions of the soul and body.[37] Following Aristotle, Aquinas argued that, because the "human soul is in the form of a body," soul and body are intrinsically connected and therefore exert reciprocal influences upon one another. The "weak temperament" of a woman's body, in part, led her to be "unstable of reason" and "easily led astray" by all manner of phantasy and desire. "On account of their earthly temperament," melancholics were likewise "most vehemently aroused" by carnality and the irrational impulses of their flesh, a condition that left them open to demonic delusions. The belief that melancholics were humorally unstable and therefore open to spiritual corruption and mental delusion was in part reified by learned medical authorities who argued that an overabundance of black bile, particularly the burnt variety (*adust*), produced powerful vapors that rose to the brain and clouded it, inhibiting judgment and producing phantasms that seemed all too real.[38] In commenting on Ishaq Ibn-Imran's *De Melancholia* in his *Compendium Medicinae*, Gilbertus Anglicus noted that those suffering from black bile melancholy "see before their eyes terrible and frightening and black shapes such as monks, black men killing them ... and demons."[39] Beyond hallucinations, melancholia caused insatiable cravings for warm wet substances, such as blood, and induced strange behaviors in the patient, such as sudden fits of rage and rapacity, terror, moroseness, lovesickness, and the desire to wander alone through empty spaces, such as graveyards.[40] Black bile melancholy was associated with rabies, not only because wolves, dogs, and foxes were dominated by black bile, but also because symptoms of this infectious condition, including intense aggression, mimicked those of black bile melancholia.[41] As in the theological tradition, medical texts consistently denied human-to-animal transformation, rationalizing such things as hallucinations, in this case brought on through completely natural biological processes.

Transformation: Witchcraft Treatises and the Satanic Werewolf

Throughout the Middle Ages, scholastic theologians continued to follow Augustine in arguing that werewolves could not exist within the bounds of nature and were therefore illusions caused by demons or the perils of fleshy embodiment. Scholars likewise maintained that the human soul, as a reflection of the divine, made human to animal transformation absolutely impossible. In witchcraft treatises from the late medieval and early modern periods, however, the werewolf began a textual transformation, at first subtle, from mere illusion to terrifying and potentially real creature allied with Satan and codified as evil. The werewolf's textual journey from phantasy to plausibility begins in the fifteenth century. In his *Malleus Maleficarum* (1486), Heinrich Kramer addresses the power of witches to transform men into beasts. At first, he reinforces the orthodox views of Augustine and Aquinas, arguing that "without the help of some Higher Power," witches and demons cannot "work such spells as the mutation of the elements, or the harming of the bodies both of men and beasts."[42] Even when it appears that humans have been transformed through witchcraft, he affirms that these events "are not miracles, which are things done outside the order of the whole of created nature." Instead, Kramer argues, they are illusions brought on by "devils" who can "stir up and excite the inner perceptions and humors ... so that men imagine these things to be true."[43] By entering the body, demons can "affect the inner fancy and darken the understanding" and, by manipulating images in the brain, can cause "such a sudden change and confusion that such objects are necessarily thought to be actual things seen with the eyes."[44] Throughout the initial chapters of the *Malleus*, therefore, Kramer conforms with accepted theological authority, arguing that witches and demons are confined within the bounds of natural law, and that any apparent transformation of matter is merely a phantasy or glamour planted by demons in the mind of the viewer with the permission of God.

At the same time that he gives voice to these orthodox arguments, however, Kramer vehemently argues for the reality of witches and their ability to transform bodies through demonic agency, as well as the need to root them out and physically destroy them in order to purify Christendom.[45] In fact, Kramer argues, to not believe in Satanic witches and their powers was tantamount to heresy.[46] This contradictory approach, which on one hand denies the existence of material change through witchcraft while providing purported evidence of its reality, reveals a centuries-old tension between the *de facto* belief in creatures such as werewolves and the theological imperative to deny them. This official denunciation of werewolves in the face of eyewitness testimony and the belief in their existence will become a salient theme in werewolf tales, one that will be echoed through the textual descendants of the *Malleus Maleficarum* and into modernity.

The bifurcated and contradictory arguments regarding the power of demons and witches established in the *Malleus Maleficarum* opened a textual door, allowing future authors of witchcraft treatises to explore the existence of otherwise impossible creatures, such as werewolves, while preserving the authority of accepted theology.[47] In 1580, the French jurist Jean Bodin published *On the Demonmania of Witches*, a treatise so popular that it was translated into Italian, German, and Latin in twenty-three editions.[48] Throughout his text, Bodin provides evidence from court cases and twice-told tales for the existence of Satanic witches and their ability, in collusion with demons, to wreak havoc in Christian society. Adhering to the structures of earthbound evil first codified by scholastic theologians in the thirteenth century, Bodin constructs witchcraft as an upside-down Satanic system that mocks the rites and rituals of Christianity. According to Bodin, witches made "express agreements" with Satan, signing a pact in blood to serve their evil master; in return, they were given the Devil's mark, "like a paw, or the track of a hare, that had no feeling."[49] Having been "re-baptized in the Devil's name," the witches were made to gather at Sabbaths, often transported by demons "faster than a bowshot"; there they would receive poisons, render an account of their evil deeds to Satan, consume the flesh of infants, and engage in orgiastic sex with demons.[50] In some cases, the product of such copulations were *vechselkind*, changelings who because of their earthbound corruption were "heavier" than other human babies, "but always thin and would dry up three nurses without getting fat."[51] Bodin's inclusion of *vechselkind* contradicts the authority of Aquinas, who argued that demons did not have warm physical bodies and could not therefore produce sperm; if children resulted from demonic copulations, Aquinas asserted that they were fully human, born of sperm stolen from a human man and planted in a wanton womb.[52] Bodin likewise contradicts received authority in arguing that men can be transformed into werewolves through the power of Satan, who operates upon the body while leaving the human soul, including a person's "intelligence" and "understanding," untouched.[53] As evidence he cites the 1537 case of Gilles Garnier, a man who confessed to becoming a werewolf and gleefully devouring children in the local vineyard—a scene rich with Eucharistic interpretations that echoes ritual murder accusations launched at both Jews and witches.[54] In his confession, Garnier admitted that he enjoyed killing children in both his lupine and human forms. His physical transformation, then, merely reflected the degenerate state of his own true self—the wicked wolf within.

In *Demonmania of Witches*, the werewolf is no longer a demonic phantasy existing solely in the minds of susceptible individuals, but a material product of witchcraft serving as evidence for vermin-like multiplication of evil in the sixteenth century. In making the werewolf a "confederate of old witches," Bodin codifies a new creature—the Satanic werewolf—whose biology and ethos conform with the realm of melancholic and inverted evil.[55] For example, Bodin noted that in a case from 1512, two men made a sworn pact with the Devil and routinely sacrificed to him so that they might be transformed into powerful wolves.[56] In some cases, the catalyst to their metamorphoses was the lighting of a blue- or green-flamed candle or the application of an ointment similar to that used by witches before their night flight. Having sprouted fur and fangs, the two would run into the forest and frenetically copulate with female wolves. They would then seek to satiate another hunger by attacking and eating small children or by poisoning good Christian adults with maleficent powder received at the Witches' Sabbath.[57] In Bodin's imagination, werewolves—much like witches and by extension, Jews—make the conscious decision to reject Christ and "worship Satan." As evil non–Christians, Bodin's werewolves are not tragic victims but willing participants in their own transformation into earthbound and melancholic beings possessed by a demonic lust for blood and sex.[58] The ability of these werewolves to conform to ritual expectations and to perform human tasks, such as the application of poisons, suggests that even in lupine form the rational mind—albeit bent toward evil—remains intact.

Bodin does not discuss the impossibility or the sacrilege of a human soul residing in the bestial body of a Satanic "other." Instead, he argues that all maleficence, including the metamorphosis of the werewolf, is performed by "Satan, at the prayer of the witches, by the just permission of God."[59] In his attempt to preserve the sovereignty of the divine while allowing for human-to-animal metamorphosis and all manner of wickedness, Bodin creates a circular argument similar to that of Heinrich Kramer. For if God creates werewolves through Satan, then why must they be destroyed? If witches are praying to Satan and doing God's work, why must they be burned? Bodin also lands in a theological muddle regarding the human soul. If the soul, following Aristotle, provides the substantial form for the body, and if it is a reflection of the divine and therefore perfect in some part, then how can it possibly be reflected in the base flesh of a melancholic beast? Like Kramer before him, Bodin walks away from these discursive complications, in part so that the werewolves prowling in his text and appearing in his judicial sight might be allowed to exist in tooth and fang.

In his assertion that werewolves and witches were inextricably bound to the Satanic and physically transformed into lupine "others," Bodin was responding, at least in part, to the work of Johann Weyer, a sixteenth-century skeptic, physician and philosopher. In his treatise *On the Illusions of the Demons and on Spells and Poisons* (1563), Weyer sets out to "fight with natural reason against the deceptions that proceed from Satan and the mad imagination of the so-called witches."[60] While he does not deny the existence and power of Satanic forces, he does question the reality of Satanic witchcraft and the efficacy of its *maleficum*. Women who believe that they are devoted to the Devil, fly to the Sabbath on their broomsticks, and can transform themselves and others into animals such as cats and wolves are not mistresses of Satan with demonic powers, he maintains, but are instead suffering from a medical condition, rooted in melancholia, which causes hallucinations. In short, "so-called witches" were not witches at all, but suffering from a form of mental illness that required the services of a physician, not a lawyer. Weyer's argument would gain traction among seventeenth century medical men such as Jean de Nynauld.[61] In his own day, however, Weyer and his theories were far from popular, in part because they questioned the textual authority and intellectual structures of the Church, including the existence of an inverted and Satanic evil conspiracy predicated on the philosophy of Aristotle as interpreted through scholasticism.[62] It likewise incensed Bodin and his fellow jurists who were responsible for the trial and execution of those "proven" to be maleficent members of Satan's ever-expanding army. As judges, these men abhorred the idea that witches and werewolves might be innocent victims rather than wicked criminals. If witches and their ilk were deemed mentally ill, they could not be persecuted and would be free to worship Satan and spread their melancholic evil through the Christian social body.[63]

In the seventeenth century, Henry Boguet and Pierre de Lancre wrote witchcraft treatises that, following in the long shadow of Jean Bodin, conflated werewolves with Satanic witchcraft. The second edition of Henry Boguet's *An Examen of Witches* (1602) argues that the werewolf and the witch are one and the same being; witches who attended the Sabbath and who "copulated, danced ... and made their ointment" had the power to transform themselves into werewolves at will.[64] As evidence he cites a case from 1597 in which male and female members of a witch coven confessed to turning themselves into werewolves in order to attack small children. Unlike natural wolves, these werewolves only ate flesh from the sinister left-hand side of their victim's bodies and "never touched the right side."[65] Witches also transformed into werewolves when they wanted to witness the effects of their maleficence, such the destruction of crops by hail storms, from a safe distance.[66] In his treatise *On the Inconstancy of Witches* (1612), Pierre de Lancre likewise argues that witches have the power to transform into wolves at the Sabbath, and that such werewolves are native to the "depths of Hell, where they serve their master, Satan."[67] Several elements of the inverted paradigm of Satanic witchcraft are evident in Lancre's retelling of the case of Jean Grenier, "a young boy, thirteen or fourteen years of age," who was tried as a werewolf in 1603.[68] At trial, Grenier confessed that he had "transformed himself into a wolf ... killed dogs and sucked their blood ... and that boys and girls were much more pleasant and agreeable to eat."[69] He also claimed that one night, deep in the forest, he and his friend met with a large man "dressed in black and mounted on a black horse" who "kissed" them with an extremely cold mouth.[70] Upon their next meeting, the dark man "marked both of them on the buttocks with a pin that he held in his hand, and in fact he had on his left buttock a round mark in the shape of a little shell," and then gave them wine. From this moment on, whenever he desired to run as a werewolf—most often "under the moon at one or two o'clock in the morning"—the Lord of the Forest brought him a red wolf skin and a pot with "some kind of grease."[71] On some occasions, Jean's father Pierre helped him apply the witch's ointment and the wolf skin, suggesting that he, too, was a werewolf in the service of Satan, and he was therefore arrested for "the crime of witchcraft."[72]

While Boguet and Lancre were willing to accept werewolves as manifestations of witchcraft, they both refused to advocate for the physical transformation of human beings into wolves at the expense of theological authority—all of which bound them in a familiar paradox. In one section, Boguet recounts the case of a woman who confessed to being a werewolf in 1588 and was burned as a witch in Ryon, all of which was related to him by a close and reliable friend. "So much of men being changed into the shape of wolves," he writes, as if his colleague's eyewitness testimony and the pronouncement of the judge resolved any lingering doubt as to the reality of werewolves.[73] He then goes on to detail myriad cases of human-to-animal metamorphoses, from the authoritative and ancient texts of Homer and Ovid to contemporary tales of witches transforming into cats. Despite all of this evidence, Boguet states, "[I]t has always been my opinion that Lycanthropy is an illusion, and that the metamorphosis of a man into a beast is impossible." Following his textual forebears, he argues that it is "impossible for the body of a brute beast to contain a reasoning soul," and that the soul cannot be removed from the body, for "Aristotle was far nearer the truth when he said that the soul no more leaves its body than a pilot leaves his ship."[74] Following Augustine and Aquinas, Boguet then claims that werewolves are mere illusions brought on by demons. When a witch claims to transform into a wolf, the Devil merely "confuses the witch's imagination"; when people claim to have seen a werewolf, it is because "the Devil befogs and deceives their sight so that they think they see what is not, for such fascination is commonly used by the Devil and his demons."[75] Boguet reminds his readers that although demons have the power to manipulate the human mind and cause great calamity, human beings do not need demonic influence to commit acts of horrifying violence. Just as wolves stalk and kill humans, so too do human beings, especially "those who have first renounced God and Heaven." As the proverb says, "Man is a wolf to man."[76]

Lancre follows the same convoluted path of argumentation as Boguet, first providing detailed discourse on the physical transformation of werewolves, including evidence from historical and current sources and quoting Aquinas on the power of "good and bad" angels to "transform our bodies." As if to put an end to all doubt, he adds, "[I]t must not be said that this transformation" mentioned by Aquinas "is merely an illusion."[77] Lancre then contradicts himself, arguing, "[T]he Evil Spirit cannot really transform a human being—its essence—into an animal" because of the rational human soul that is attached to human flesh.[78] "It is folly to believe that the Devil transforms men into wolves, either in soul and body, or in body alone. Thus the transformations he performs are merely illusions."[79] In some cases, the Devil preys upon the innocent, causing them to fall asleep while he possesses a wolf to commit horrible acts, thereby leading people to believe that the sleeper has become a werewolf. In other cases, wicked humans sign a pact with the Devil and receive a wolf skin to wear or are given a false body of coagulated air that fits them perfectly. "And when this happens, they do not fail to leave signs and make both the tracks and paw prints of wolves when they walk on the ground, as if they were really wolves or wore a real wolf's skin."[80] And yet, Lancre's description of the young werewolf Grenier, who was convicted of maleficence but sentenced to a monastery rather than death because of his age, mental acuity, and upbringing, leaves room for multiple interpretations. In reading the young man's body, Lancre finds physical proof of his werewolfism: He observes Grenier's "wild-looking eyes ... sunken and black, and completely distraught," as well as his "very long and bright teeth that were wider than normal, protruding somewhat and rotten and half black." His fingernails "were also quite long" and "black from the base to the tip." All of these physical signs, manifested in the boy's very human body, indicated to Lancre that he "was indeed a werewolf, and that he used his hands both for running and for grabbing children and dogs by the throat."[81] No mere demonic phantasy, Grenier's true lupine form was written in his flesh—at least as interpreted through the complex lens of a Catholic jurist charged with judging witchcraft cases in Bordeaux.

In constructing witchcraft treatises, sixteenth- and seventeenth-century authors across Europe were forced to navigate unquestionable textual authorities and contradictory sources while engaging with a growing belief in the increasing power of Satanic evil in the world, one manifestation of which was the werewolf.[82] As in the case of Satanic witchcraft, common beliefs about werewolves were culled from testimony given at trial and incorporated into learned treatises. In attempting to fit these ideas into a scholastic framework, authors codified the werewolf as Satanic and linked it with the world of inverted and melancholic evil. Through this process, the werewolf came to be associated with witches and the rituals of their Sabbath, including the consumption of Christian children, as well as all things black and cold, such as nighttime and the seasons of autumn and winter. Like witches, werewolves ran in familial packs, of which the Greniers were but one example. Just as witches offered their virginal daughters to the Devil, so too did fathers give their sons over to the Lord of the Forest, and in this way werewolves spread like a plague that corrupted the Christian body and fed upon its tender flesh.

Added to this already mixed stew of werewolf associations, early modern witchcraft treatises incorporated narrative fragments from earlier tales: the wicked werewolf who undergoes a willful metamorphosis through the agency of the Devil; the noble and tragic victim of lycanthropy; the severing of a paw or head to reveal the human within the beast's flesh; the tell-tale wound marking an individual in both his werewolf and human forms. Embedded throughout werewolf discourses is the tension between "what everybody knows" to be true and learned authorities who deny the existence of humans who transform bodily into wolves, even when physical evidence appears before their eyes. In the modern world, all of these incongruous elements remain salient features of the melancholic werewolf, a contradictory creature whose characteristics and habits adapt to the needs of the narrative and change shape according to the lens of his spellbound audience.

Modern Metamorphosis: The Demands of the Flesh

Early modern discourses on the werewolf center on the essential unity of the human body and rational soul, a premise rooted in Aristotelian natural philosophy and medieval constructions of the body; the modern werewolf, however, walks in a post–Cartesian world where mind and body are separate entities. The modern search for the werewolf, then, is naturally bifurcated. For example, the twentieth-century psychoanalysts Carl Jung and Sigmund Freud sought the werewolf in the dark recesses of the human mind. Jung argued that the werewolf was an archetype of our own primal selves, the repressed "shadow" that lurked along with the "anima" just beneath the "persona" or mask that we wear as part of civilized society. Through this shadow, "we have a share in the historical collective psyche, we live naturally and unconsciously in a world of werewolves, demons…"[83] For Freud, the werewolf was an expression not of a collective primal archetype, but of individual experiences during the developmental stages of childhood. In his famous case "The Wolf Man," for example, Sergei Pankejeff has terrifying nightmares about wolves; for Freud, these wolves signify infantile neurosis, a bubbling-up of the primordial unconscious mind resulting from Pankejeff's repressed memories of his parents having sex.[84] In *Civilization and Its Discontents*, Freud argues that the wages of civil society require that we repress our animalistic impulses, including murder and sex. Beneath the surface of our humanity, however, lurking in the subconscious mind, we are all monsters, creatures of bloodlust, primal and hungry.

While Jung, Freud, and their intellectual descendants have rationalized the werewolf as a product of the mind, other recent authors have argued that lycanthropy is located in the body. For example, *hypertrichosis* and *porphyria* have both been proposed as medical—and therefore authoritative and rational—reasons for medieval werewolves. This reductive approach has been a favorite of physicians who use retrospective diagnosis to rip ancient and medieval phenomena from their historical contexts and to reshape them in modern terms—an approach that reveals more about our own cultural biases than the world of medieval lycanthropy.[85] Modern post–Cartesian theories have not resolved any of the conflicts inherent in the discursive regime of the werewolf, but added further layers of interpretation to a shape shifter who has been a salient character in Western culture from its earliest foundations.

The depiction of werewolves in Anglo-American horror films reflects the myriad traditions and sometimes conflicting constructions imbedded in its convoluted history. Werewolf films tend to eschew the blatantly Satanic elements common to witchcraft treatises like Jean Bodin's *Demonmania*. Nevertheless, almost all of them use either inverted signifiers, such as black candles and pentagrams, or elements coded as melancholic, such as autumn, the forest, and the moon, to suggest the presence of un-namable evil. Unlike the early-modern witchcraft tradition, the modern werewolf is rarely a creature of absolute *maleficum*, born of a Satanic pact at the behest of the shape shifter itself. Instead, following the tradition of twelfth-century romances such as the *Bisclavret*, the cinematic werewolf is most often a completely innocent victim randomly attacked by external and uncontrollable forces, although some human flaw, such as self-obsession of lovesickness, might serve as a catalyst to his or her tragic fate.[86] The post–Cartesian rupturing of the Aristotelian link between body and soul has freed the body of the werewolf and allowed for the full on-screen metamorphosis—painful, ecstatic, and depicted in pornographic detail—of human into wolf-monster. The prosthetic physicality of the werewolf's transformation is a fundamental element of the werewolf narrative, serving as a form of proof to on-screen characters and disbelieving audiences of the lycanthrope's existence. This focus on the physical (dis)ordering of the body is often coupled with discourses drawn from Freudian psychoanalysis. The werewolf's inner animal, for example, might rupture outward because he is repressed or has experienced some trauma that has facilitated the return of the primal uncanny. Despite the weaving together of these disparate pieces, the relationship between the wolf body and human "thinking stuff" is rarely worked out in horror narratives, leaving us with many of the same existential questions asked by our early-modern intellectual ancestors. As the werewolf stalks the night and slaughters its prey, does its rational human soul remain intact, witnessing the carnage unfolding around it with abject horror or, worse yet, glee? The transformation of the werewolf brings into question not only the relationship between body and soul, but also between humanity and the natural world. Is the werewolf an abhorrent form, or is it our true human self—an animal after all—without the thin veneer of civilization? At the deepest level, our encounter with the werewolf is a meditation, conducted in front of a mirror, on the horrifying experience of otherness, isolation, and longing that results from our own abject embodiment. Even in a pack, we hunt alone. And one dark night, our flesh, like that of the werewolf, will transform into an earthbound and melancholic corpse-monster too terrible to fathom.

The Persistence of Wicked Inversion

Mainstream Anglo-American werewolf films from the twentieth and twenty-first centuries reveal the persistence of medieval and early-modern structures for inverted and melancholic evil, including the signifiers of Satanic evil, elements culled from witchcraft treatises, and the power of cold natural forces such as the moon. Few werewolf films feature overt Satanism, with one troubling exception being *Werewolf of London* (1935), in which Dr. Yogami of the University of Carpathia describes the werewolf as "neither man nor wolf, but a Satanic creature with the worst qualities of both." He then states that "werewolfery" or "lycanthrophobia" is a medical condition temporarily curable with the juice of a moon flower called the Mariphasa. The invocation of Satan here is used to heighten terror, but causes problems. If the were-wolf is inherently Satanic, a condition that involves the human soul, then how can any physical remedy cure him? Other films avoid direct references to Satan, instead using signifiers to suggest the presence of demonic involvement. In *The Undying Monster* (1942), for example, Oliver Hammond describes his encounter with the lycanthropic Hammond monster as "like a blast furnace, but it wasn't hot," a "darkness that went all red, dark red until a splash of fire split it up and put it out." The cold flames here signify the icy depths of hell; the red and black harken back to medieval color theory, which associated these colors with death and melancholic evil. The five-pointed star, or pentagram, is a prominent symbol woven throughout Universal Studios' *The Wolf Man* (1941); it is featured not only on the head of Larry Talbot's silver cane, but also on a talisman given to him by Maleva the Gypsy, who tells him that it is "the sign of the wolf."[87] After his attack by Bela the werewolf,

Larry's wound becomes a star-shaped scar that, like the Devil's mark in witchcraft treatises, heals almost instantly and without pain. The symbol is again echoed in *An American Werewolf in London* (1981), where it appears on the sign of the Slaughtered Lamb pub.

In Hammer's 1961 film *The Curse of the Werewolf*, lycanthropy is linked with demonic possession. The werewolf Leon was born to a mute woman (who had been raped by a beastly man) on Christmas Eve at the ringing of the church bells. The midwife, who becomes his adoptive mother, notes that "an unwanted child born at the same time as Christ is a mockery to the Lord," an echo of inverted Christian rituals prevalent in witchcraft treatises. After a young Leon begins dreaming that he is a wolf "drinking blood" and develops hairy palms, his adoptive father goes to the local priest who tells him that "there are elemental spirits about us at all times ... spirits without bodies, creatures that have never lived."[88] One of these non-human spirits, a demon in the form of a wolf, possessed Leon at the moment of his birth, and now his "soul and the spirit are constantly at war." When his human soul is weak, the wolf-demon wins and he transforms into a werewolf. According to the priest, the exorcism of the wolf is possible through unconditional love; should this not work, the only means to destroy the werewolf is to "burn him alive" in cleansing fire, just like a heretic or witch.[89] Leon is ultimately destroyed by a silver bullet cast from a silver crucifix blessed by the bishop. The silver bullet's power to kill a werewolf is not cited in medieval sources; however, the use of holy Christian rituals and objects, such as the sign of the cross, the crucifix, and the Eucharist, were all believed to be efficacious against demonic evil. In this case, the power of the silver bullet to kill Leon comes not from the silver itself, but from the sanctified object from which it was cast. Like the Eucharist, its true power lies in its otherwise invisible substance rather than its accidents.

Signifiers of evil culled from witchcraft treatises abound in werewolf films, especially when the werewolves in question are women. For example, in Hammer's *Children of the Full Moon* (1980), Sarah, a newlywed, is raped and impregnated by a werewolf. As the fetus grows within her, she is transformed from a sweet and loving wife fond of wearing white to a black-robed vixen who craves raw meat and demands violent sex from her husband. *The Howling* (1981) features a werewolf named Marsha Quist who in her human form is a sexually rapacious "nymphomaniac" who stalks the forest in a low-cut leather dress beneath which she is completely naked.[90] Marsha hunts men in both her human and lupine forms, stalking them simultaneously as food and sexual prey. *Ginger Snaps* (2000) documents the transformation of a misanthropic and edgy teen named Ginger into a slutty gothic vixen who can't control her primal urges. When her sister Beatrice asks what her transformation into a werewolf feels like, she says that she gets an "ache" that seems like a desire for sex but quickly turns into the need to "tear everything into pieces." In short, Ginger feels "wicked." While none of these werewolves are specifically labeled as witches within their respective films, they are each manifestations of irrational, destructive, blood-hungry and rapacious feminine evil as constructed in witchcraft treatises.

Also in alignment with the witchcraft paradigm, maleficent werewolves run in families. In some cases, lycanthropy is a hereditary curse, with each generation tainted by the sins of the previous one. In *The Undying Monster*, for example, the Hammond family is said to be plagued by evil because of an ancestor who "sold his soul to the devil" during the crusades and who "still lives in a secret room in Hammond Hall, issuing forth at intervals to make the sacrifice of a human life in order to prolong his own." *The Curse of the Werewolf*'s Leon becomes a lycanthrope because both his father and mother lived like animals, one kept like a dog in a dungeon and the other wandering feral in the forest. Born at the wrong moment, Leon is cursed in the blood, his fate inescapable, through no fault of his own. *Children of the Full Moon* features an entire family of werewolves, including a brood of "cheeky little pups ... the little horrors." By day, the Ardoy children subsist on mutton broth and wine; by night, they hunt and kill sheep in the vineyard, an image embedded with Eucharistic associations. After feeding, the children are so exhausted that "sometimes the devil himself can't wake them." While the Ardoys enjoy an idyllic family life out in their forest mansion, complete with committed father and doting mother, the werewolf family of *Dog Soldiers* (2002) endures a more complicated existence. "Do you think I like being a member of this fucked-up family?" asks daughter Megan. "Do you think I chose to run with the pack?"

Not all werewolves are hereditary, of course; in keeping with witchcraft treatises, some are created by contact with toxic and "beastly" outsiders who contaminate the good Christian body with evil.[91] In *The Wolf Man*, the Talbot family's ancestral hamlet is polluted with lycanthropy by the witch-like gypsies who arrive every autumn under the full moon.[92] Only when Larry is bitten by Bela does he contract the curse of lycanthropy. Likewise, in *Bad Moon* (1996), Uncle Ted only becomes a werewolf after he is bitten during a research expedition in Nepal—the same tale as Dr. Glendon in *Werewolf of London*. *The Howling* and *Ginger Snaps* feature native werewolves, locally grown monsters who feed on their own communities. Whether through a distant curse or through attack, the engendering of werewolves is a sign that society has been penetrated and polluted with evil—a theme that Heinrich Kramer and Jean Bodin would find terrifyingly familiar.

Werewolf films share another common feature with witchcraft treatises, one rooted in medieval medicine and natural philosophy: the transformative power of the moon. Because physicians held that the microcosmic human body was unbounded and therefore open to the influences of stars and planets, astrology was a core component of medieval medical practice. Following Aristotle, the moon was qualitatively cold and increased in moisture in its fourth phase; observing the full moon's effect on the tides, scholars argued that "the moon is the entire source and cause of motion in liquids," not only those in the ocean, but also within the body, including "the marrow in the bones" and the "brains in the head."[93] Because the brain swelled and blood flowed forcefully into all of the organs during the full moon, some human beings were held to experience a sort of madness known as lunacy. Theologians such as Pseudo-Albertus Magnus and Gerald of Wales argued that this madness was not caused by the moon alone, but by the Devil, "who takes advantage of the moon's seasons to shame the creature to the blasphemy of his creator."[94] Kramer added that demons themselves, being cold in nature, were "deeply affected by certain phases of the moon," most notably the full moon, which was also associated with material corruption.[95] Drawing on the *Centriloquium* of Claudius Ptolemy as well as the works of Albertus Magnus, Pseudo-Albertus Magnus argued that "the moon by its nature increases humidity" to such an extent that "if fresh meat is placed at night in the rays of the moon" in its fourth phase, "worms will be generated there."[96] Associated with lunacy, demonic activity, and earthbound processes of decay, the full moon would become the perfect catalyst for all manner of natural and Satanic transformation.

Wicked Bodies, Sick Minds, Medieval Contradictions

Perhaps the most telling inheritance from medieval discourse is the paradoxical nature of the werewolf's physical transformation. As in medieval and early-modern texts, there is a tense co-existence between belief and disbelief in modern werewolf narratives. For example, in a single scene from *Bad Moon*, a child named Brett explains werewolves to his Uncle Ted, saying, "That's just how it works ... when there's a full moon, he turns into a werewolf. *Everybody knows* that." When Ted asks Brett whether he believes in werewolves, the boy says, "*Everybody knows* there's no such thing as werewolves." In films from *The Wolf Man* to *Ginger Snaps*, both the on-screen characters and the off-screen audience know everything about werewolves and the story about to unfold, from full moons and wolfsbane to silver bullets and the power of fire. We observe the werewolf transform before our very eyes—we demand to see the sprouting of every hair—and yet we are left unconvinced of his metamorphosis, opting instead to deny the werewolf's existence by rationalizing away what we have just witnessed.[97] This process can be seen in *Werewolf of London*, which presents lycanthropy as a medical phenomenon, one that can be explained through modern science rather than "superstitions." Despite having dismissed lycanthropy as either a medical condition rooted in the body or "auto-suggestion and self-hypnosis" rooted in the mind, Dr. Glendon is ultimately confronted with the truth of his own metamorphosis. As his on-camera transformation progresses, both Glendon and the audience are provided with undeniable proof of his lycanthropy and bloodlust. After attacking his wife, he is shot by a policeman who later submits a false report in order to hide the werewolf's inexplicable and impossible existence: "In my report I will say that I shot him by accident while he was trying to protect his wife." Both the on-screen characters and the audience have just witnessed physical proof of the werewolf; despite this, his existence is denied in the official records. Jean Bodin would appreciate this conflicting state of affairs.

The paradoxes between witness and denial, belief and rationalization, superstition and science run throughout *The Undying Monster*. When Robert, a forensic investigator for Scotland Yard, is brought in on the Hammond case, he is told that even though he believes that "from the viewpoint of science, all phenomena have a material basis," he "best be prepared to deal with something perhaps supernatural." In analyzing evidence at the Hammond estate, Robert repeatedly affirms the natural and material over the supernatural, arguing that "even a supernatural being would have to take on material form in order to afflict such injuries," and that "superstitions are often based on fact." Examining a hair sample, Robert postulates that the culprit is a real wolf, even though "there haven't been wolves running around England since the Middle Ages." As Robert places the hair in his spectrometer, it matches the striations of wolf fur, then disappears in the machine's bright light. The inspector reminds Robert that there are "some things in this world that science hasn't found out about."

We then observe the bodily transformation of Oliver Hammond into a bipedal werewolf, complete with fur and fangs, and his subsequent transformation back into his human form. After Oliver's death, his doctor explains to Robert that his patient was suffering from a "dreadful kink in his brain ... which he had inherited from his ancestors." When asked if Oliver knew he was a "victim of lycanthropy," the doctor argues that Oliver thought he was merely suffering from a "nervous affliction." The female assistant Christie asks, "In the Middle Ages they called such men werewolves, didn't they?" The doctor affirms this, saying that lycanthropy was really "a form of mania that caused its victims to imagine, consciously or subconsciously," that they became werewolves. As convoluted as any witchcraft treatise, this film simultaneously provides visual and "scientific" evidence for the physical transformation of Oliver into a werewolf while arguing that he had a "kink in his brain" or some form of "mania." If Oliver was merely deluded into believing he became a werewolf, then how did we witness his transformation? What explains the disappearing wolf hair in the spectroscope? Having revealed the monster, the film is trapped in a circular logic that would have been as familiar in the sixteenth century as it is today.

Most modern werewolf films use arguments based on the inner turmoil and psychological delusion of the werewolf alongside a commitment to the monster's physical transformation. In *The Wolf Man*, for example, "everyone knows about werewolves," but the erudite Sir John Talbot dismisses such beliefs, arguing that lycanthropy is "a disease of the mind in which human beings imagine they are wolf men," "a variety of schizophrenia" that reflects the "good and evil in every man's soul. In this case the evil takes the shape of an animal." He denies that men can turn into wolves, but admits that "almost anything can happen to a man in his own mind."[98]

Spinning this narrative on its head, *The Howling* presumes that werewolves are real, and that psychology (and psychologists) are merely using New Age cognitive therapies to disguise the ugly truth of it all—that the human condition is one of violence and cruelty, and that we are all wild beasts. *The Howling*'s pop-psychologist Dr. Waggner holds to Freud's theory that "repression is the father of neurosis, of self-hatred." Mindlessly repressing our animal impulses results in mental illness and violent behavior; mindful awareness of these impulses, however, can make us more fully human. As part of his research, and in order to help werewolves integrate into society, Waggner has founded a mental health retreat known as the Colony. There, the werewolves are encouraged to talk about their feelings and are conditioned not to kill and eat human beings. The werewolves under his care represent stereotypes from across white America: the homeless man, the deranged hippie youth, the elderly woman, the wicked vixen, the soccer mom, the businessman. All are equally lycanthropic.

After an encounter with a werewolf named Eddie Quist at a porno theater while on assignment, innocent news reporter Karen White is sent to the Colony by Waggner so that she can "remember who we really are" as human beings. She is joined by her husband, a pacifist vegetarian, who after only a few days at the Colony takes up hunting and eating raw meat. Bitten by the nymphomaniac "bitch in heat" Marsha, he rejects the sweet and sexually naïve Karen and joins the pack. While Karen is sequestered at the Colony, her journalist friends back in the city research theories of lycanthropy. At an occult bookstore, The Other Side, the storeowner explains that "your classic werewolf could change shape any time it wants, day or night," and that "silver bullets and fire" are the "only way to get rid of them."[99] When asked whether he believes in these things, the huckster says, "What am I, an idiot? I'm making a buck here. You want books, I got books. I got chicken blood, dog embryos, black candles, wolfsbane, silver bullets," then cynically adds that he takes cash or credit. Culling "facts" from supernatural authorities and werewolf movies, Karen's friends become convinced that she is in a clandestine colony of werewolves; Karen witnesses Eddie Quist's graphic transformation into a drooling werewolf and learns that they are right. The Colony's werewolves are not only real—they are refusing treatment and rebelling against their therapist. "Humans are our prey. No more of this channel our energies crap ... you can't tame what's meant to be wild, Doc. It ain't natural." While the werewolves descend on their therapist in order to devour him, Karen and her colleague escape from the Colony. Infected, she goes on live television and says, "from the day we are born there is a battle we must fight, a struggle between what is kind and peaceful in our natures, and what is cruel and violent ... this is our birthright." She then begins her transformation into a gingery werewolf, hoping to warn the population about the very real werewolves in its midst. Even after she is shot with a silver bullet on-camera, television viewers do not believe her, explaining away what they have just witnessed as "special effects." Their disbelief proves to be the werewolves' greatest asset, allowing them to feed and multiply in society's shadows.[100]

Postmodern Fluidity: The Transformative Power of Otherness

Like the witch and the vampire, the modern werewolf is a flesh canvas on which we inscribe our ever-changing constructs of abject otherness. While the foundational werewolf narrative, including the physical nature of his metamorphosis, remain salient, the meaning of the creature itself is continually rewritten in order to reflect shifting ideals and perceptions, such as those surrounding gender. Male werewolves often provide commentary on the cultural construction of a bifurcated masculinity in which men are supposed to be domesticated as good hetero-normative husbands, sons, and fathers but still primal and powerful.[101] In *WereWolf of London*, Glendon is torn between ego gratification through his botanical research and being a loving husband. After promising his wife that as soon as he completes his experiment he will "try to be, well, more human," he snaps, "I should divorce you and beat you for getting me into this mess." In *The Curse of the Werewolf*, Leon is both a faithful son and a wild beast who lashes out at his father. Uncle Ted, the father figure in *Bad Moon*, loves his sister and her son; ultimately, he destroys her bedroom in his attempt to feed upon the little family. The unemployed monster-uncle who lives in a trailer in the backyard and routinely penetrates his sister's house and bedroom leaves this particular narrative open to a disturbing interpretation of incest. *Silver Bullet* features the ultimate father-werewolf, a lycanthropic priest, the Reverend Lowe, who feeds on his flock.[102] Despite his physical prowess and authoritative power, he is defeated by a mobility-impaired boy named Marty, whose family sees him as a helpless cripple and a burden, and his Uncle Red, who sees the future man within his nephew, teaching him how to swear, play poker, and drive a hot rod wheelchair. Many werewolf films feature the lycanthrope's true foil— the faithful family dog.[103] In *Werewolf of London*, bossy Aunt Ettie's tiny dog represents culturally bound fears of male submission and domestication. In *Bad Moon*, Thor the German Shepherd is the true man of the house, a good husband and father who protects his family against the wild male outsider. *Children of the Full Moon* complicates this narrative. Tom Martin, human to the end, is a self-absorbed lawyer; away weeks at a time, he hardly has time for a wife, never mind a family. The werewolf Mr. Ardoy, however, is a woodsman and always near his "many pups," for whom he provides a large house and all that they need to "nurture their human side."

Cultural constructions of femaleness are likewise reflected in werewolf narratives. Early films often feature headstrong young women such as Lisa Glendon in *WereWolf of London* who stands up to her husband and does as she pleases. In *The Wolf Man*, Gwen remains steadfast against the villagers who accuse her of being a loose woman. Helga in *The Undying Monster* is willing to go out and search for the beast; grabbing her gun, she barks, "I'm sure there is some rational explanation for all of this; but if there is something going on down there, I'd like to get a crack at it. I'm a pretty good shot!"

When the werewolf itself is female, however, the theme of the feisty and independent woman is magnified and complicated through a feminist lens. *The Howling* reveals the persistence of medieval male clerical constructions of woman, with Karen playing the white-clad, demure, and faithful wife— the holy woman—pitted against the black-clad, sex-hungry, and wicked Marsha. Even when Karen ultimately transforms, she becomes something closer to a ginger Pekinese, nothing like the hairy, drooling, and murderous monster manifested by Marsha. In both her human and vulpine forms, Marsha is a creature of sexual liberation and power; untamed, undomesticated, she lives by the laws of nature alone. In one sense, Marsha is a manifestation of female empowerment, a crusader for feminism; coded as evil, Marsha is likewise an object lesson for weary men in the dangers of women's liberation, of female power unbound. This dialectical construction of femaleness haunts *The Company of Wolves* (1984) and *Ginger Snaps*, both of which feature pubescent teens who must confront their own metamorphoses from innocent girls to sexually active women, from little lambs to hungry wolves. *The Company of Wolves*, based on the work of Angela Carter, is a retelling of Little Red Riding Hood woven through with bits of narrative culled from medieval and early modern sources; the severed human hand that reveals the werewolf's identity, the vengeful witch who turns her enemies into werewolves, the boys who meet the dark Lord of the Forest, sign his pact, and receive a wicked ointment all make appearances in the film.[104] Across a fragmented dreamscape replete with reproductive imagery, little Rosaleen must decide whether to stay on the path and become a good wife to a daft village boy, or to explore the forest and find liberation with feral and manly werewolves. Ultimately, Rosaleen takes off her clothes, seduces the werewolf, and runs off with the pack, leaving her family and her innocence behind.

Unlike Rosaleen, the sixteen-year-old Ginger of *Ginger Snaps* is not open to her changing body, nor does she choose to become a werewolf. One night while she and her sister Beatrice are walking across their childhood playground, she starts to bleed. "I've got the curse," she mutters, and is immediately attacked by a werewolf.[105] Infected through fluid exchange, Ginger's body starts to transform; she grows hair out of the slit-like scars on her shoulder, a small tail, and fangs. At first, she is embarrassed by these changes, shouting that "I may have hormones, and they may make me ugly, but they do *not* make me a monster." Not long into her transformation, however, Ginger starts to enjoy her new self. She becomes a vixen, flaunting her body and seeking out sexual contact with boys at school, prompting a cheerleader to tell Beatrice, "Why don't you get your slut sister a leash." A true bitch, however, Ginger will not be chained. In the transgressive body of the werewolf, Ginger takes on the role of the rapacious teenage male. She rapes Jason in his car; when his body begins to show signs of transformation, Beatrice yells at Ginger, "You gave it to him. You had unprotected sex and you infected him"—a thinly veiled reference to STIs or pregnancy. Ginger's only response is "Oops." Jason's transformation is likewise gender transgressive, "way out on the corner of fucked-up and evil"; he gets his period, becomes confused and irrational, and tries to eat small children, just like a late-medieval witch. Ginger's transformation into a rapacious male beast, a "goddamn force of nature" that wants to have sex with her sister—"we'll scratch, swap some juice; we'll be our own pack like before"—is a satire on the options available to women in the gender-constructed world of modern suburbia. As they bury the body of a cheerleader in their old playhouse, Ginger sums up the essential problem: "Look, no one ever thinks girls do shit like this. Girls can only be a slut, bitch, tease, or the virgin next door." At its core, *Ginger Snaps* reveals the wicked persistence of the witch-virgin binary codified centuries ago, and the strain it places on women leading honest lives of meaning and fulfillment beyond its constraints.

Epilogue

For the Love of the Ensouled Human Monster

Everyone knows about werewolves, vampires, and witches, but no one believes in them. And yet, we continue telling their tales. The Old monsters speak to us through the inverted structures of Satanic evil that have become so deeply embedded in Western culture that we are scarcely aware of them. Like distant ghosts, these signifiers whisper messages of evil, danger, imperfection, and alterity. The melancholic monster body also speaks of a pre–Cartesian embodiment that reflects the wholeness of human experience and our fundamental connection to all things. I believe that this provides one reason for their continued popularity alongside post–Cartesian ghosts, zombies, and the transhuman machine-monster. I would also argue that the witch, the vampire, and the werewolf remain such powerful characters in Western popular culture because—despite their seeming "otherness"—they are painfully and beautifully human. Born to human parents, they were once infants, loved and adored, but along the way became lost, either seduced onto the left-hand path and rejected by human society, or rejected as an "other" and cast in the shape of evil.

And yet even in their wretched state, they—like us—might still be redeemed, made whole once again through salvific human love.

Chapter Notes

Introduction

1. On the circuitous logic of the paranormal, see Terrence Hines, *Pseudoscience and the Paranormal* (New York: Prometheus Books, 2003).
2. See Lilli Alanen, *Descartes's Concept of Mind* (Cambridge: Harvard University Press, 2003). See also Dennis Des Chene, *Spirits and Clocks: Machine and Organism in Descartes* (Ithaca: Cornell University Press, 2000).
3. Consider the *Scooby-Doo* cycle: those who enjoyed the show in the seventies passed it on to their children in the nineties. Accordingly, there should be another resurgence of *Scooby-Doo* in five to ten years as grandchildren come of age for such things.
4. On contamination, see Mary Douglass, *Purity and Danger* (New York: Routledge, 1966); on abjection, Julia Kristeva, *The Powers of Horror: An Essay on Abjection* (New York: Columbia University Press, 1982).
5. Timothy K. Beal, *Religion and Its Monsters* (London: Routledge, 2001); Jerome Jeffrey Cohen, *Hybridity, Identity, and Monstrosity in Medieval Britain: On Difficult Middles* (Basingstoke: Palgrave, 2006); Sarah Alison Miller, *Medieval Monstrosity and the Female Body* (London: Routledge, 2010); *Monstrous Middle Ages*, eds. Bettina Bildhauer and Robert Mills (Toronto: University of Toronto Press, 2003). See also, Bettina Bildhauer, *Medieval Blood* (Cardiff: University of Wales Press, 2010).
6. For example, see *The Ashgate Research Companion to Monsters and the Monstrous*, eds. Asa Simon Mittman and Peter Dendle (Burlington, VT: Ashgate, 2013); *Monsters and Their Meanings in Early Modern Culture: Mighty Magic*, ed. Wes Williams (Oxford: Oxford University Press, 2011). *Monstrous Bodies/Political Monstrosities in Early Modern Europe*, eds. Laura Lunger Knoppers and Joan B. Landes (Ithaca: Cornell University Press, 2004).
7. Steven T. Asma, *On Monsters: An Unnatural History of Our Worst Fears* (New York: Oxford University Press, 2011); W. Scott Poole, *Monsters in America* (Waco, TX: Baylor University Press, 2011). David Skal, *The Monster Show: A Cultural History of Horror* (San Francisco: Faber & Faber, 2001).
8. See for example Steven J. Schneider, *Horror Film and Psychoanalysis: Freud's Worst Nightmare* (Cambridge: Cambridge University Press, 2009). See also Barbara Creed's extensive use of Kristeva in *The Monstrous-Feminine: Film, Feminism, Psychoanalysis* (London: Routledge, 1993).
9. All of these psychological approaches are exemplified in *Speaking of Monsters: A Teratological Anthology*, eds. Caroline Joan S. Picart and John Edgar Browing, (Basingstoke: Palgrave, 2012). Emmanuel Levinas, *Alterity and Transcendence*, trans. Michael B. Smith (New York: Columbia University Press, 2000). Alex Neville Sharpe, *Foucault's Monsters and the Law* (London: Routledge 2010). Margarit Shildrick, *Leaky Bodies and Boundaries: Feminism, Postmodernism, and Bioethics* (London: Routledge, 1997). *The Dread of Difference: Gender and the Horror Film*, ed. Barry Keith Grant (Austin: University of Texas Press, 1996); Carol J. Clover, *Men, Women, and Chainsaws: Gender and the Horror Film* (Princeton: Princeton University Press, 1993); Judith Halberstam, *Skin Shows: Gothic Horror and the Technology of Monsters* (Durham, NC: Duke University Press, 1995); Harry M. Benshoff, *Monsters in the Closet: Homosexuality and the Horror Film* (Manchester: Manchester University Press, 1997). Deborah Christie and Sarah Juliet Lauro, *Better Off Dead: The Evolution of the Zombie as Post-Human* (New York: Fordham University Press, 2013).
10. This in place of Aristotle's Prime Mover, who set the cosmos into motion out of love. See Aristotle, *Metaphysics*, 6:7
11. See François Azouvi, "The Plague, Melancholy, and the Devil" *Diogenes* 27 (1979), 112–30.
12. On the *Malleus* and its popularity, see Hans Peter Broedel, *The Malleus Maleficarum and the Construction of Witchcraft Theology and Popular Belief* (Manchester: Manchester University Press, 2003). On inversion, see Stuart Clark,

Thinking With Demons (Oxford: Oxford University Press, 1997).

13. A phenomenon reflected in the Satanic Panic of the late twentieth century. For a history of these discursive structures, see David Frankfurter, *Evil Incarnate: Rumors of Demonic Conspiracy and Ritual Abuse in History* (Princeton, NJ: Princeton University Press, 2006).

14. Thomas Aquinas, *Summa Theologica*, 51:3:6: "Still if some are occasionally begotten from demons, it is not from the seed of such demons, nor from their assumed bodies, but from the seed of men taken for the purpose; as when the demon assumes first the form of a woman, and afterwards of a man; just as they take the seed of other things for other generating purposes, as Augustine says (De Trin. ii.), so that the person born is not the child of a demon, but of a man."

15. See, for example, Lucy Fischer, "Birth Traumas: Parturition and Horror in Rosemary's Baby," *Cinema Journal* 31:3 (1992), 3–18.

16. See Nancy Caciola, *Discerning Spirits: Divine and Demonic Possession in the Middle Ages* (Ithaca: Cornell University Press, 2003).

17. *Thomas Cantimpré: The Collected Saints' Lives*, ed. Barbara Newman, trans. Margot King and Barbara Newman (Turnhout: Brepols, 2008).

18. On the fundamentally physical nature of the feminine, see Elizabeth Robertson, "The Corporeality of Female Sanctity in *The Life of Saint Margaret*," *Images of Sainthood in Medieval Europe*. (Ithaca: Cornell University Press, 1991), 268–287.

19. Nancy Caciola, "Mystics, Demoniacs, and the Physiology of Spirit Possession in Medieval Europe," *Comparative Studies in Society and History*, 42:2 (2000), 268–306.

20. See Helen Rodnite Lemay's edition of Pseudo-Albertus' *De Secretis Mulierum*, a late-thirteenth Latin text purporting to reveal the secrets and foul inner workings of female anatomy. This pseudo-medical text used medical theories drawn from the works of Hippocrates, Galen, Avicenna, and al-Magusi and applied them nonsystematically in order to legitimize theological and popular beliefs about the bodies of women. *Women's Secrets: A Translation of Pseudo Albertus Magnus' De Secretis Mulierum with Commentaries* (Albany, NY: SUNY University Press, 1992).

21. On the hermeneutic Jew, see Jeremy Cohen, *Living Letters of the Law: Ideas of the Jew in Medieval Christianity* (Berkeley: University of California Press, 1999).

22. Miri Rubin, *Gentile Tales: The Narrative Assault on Late Medieval Jews* (New Haven: Yale University Press, 1999). See also Joshua Trachtenberg, *The Devil and the Jews: The Medieval Conception of the Jew and its Relation to Modern Antisemitism* (New York: Jewish Publication Society, 2002).

23. Irven M. Resnick, "Medieval Roots of the Myth of the Jewish Male Menses," *Harvard Theological Review* (2000), 241–63.

24. On revenants, see Nancy Caciola, "Wraiths, Revenants, and Ritual in Medieval Culture," *Past and Present* 152 (1996), 3–45.

25. Leslie A. Sconduto, *Metamorphosis of the Werewolf: A Literary Study from Antiquity through the Renaissance* (Jefferson, NC: McFarland, 2008). Carolyn Walker Bynum. *Metamorphosis and Identity* (Cambridge: Zone Books/MIT Press, 2001).

26. On the circularity of this argument, see Sydney Anglo, "Evident Authority and Authoritative Evidence: The *Malleus Maleficarum*," *The Literature of Witchcraft*, ed. Brian P. Levack (New York: Routledge, 1992), 1–32

27. One notable skeptic was Johann Weyer, who believed that both witchcraft and lycanthropy were medical conditions related to black bile melancholia, not maleficence or Satanic evil. See *Witches, Devils, and Doctors in the Renaissance: Johann Weyer's Praestigiis Daemonum*, ed. George Mora (Binghamton: Medieval and Renaissance Texts and Studies, 1993).

28. Jean Bodin, *On the Demonmania of Witches*, trans. Randy A. Scott (Toronto: Centre for Reformation and Renaissance Studies, 1995). 122–130.

Chapter 1

1. Quoted in Thomas Aquinas, *Scriptum Super Sententiis*, 45:1:3: "Praeterea, Hieronymus ibidem arguit sic: cum Diabolus et Daemones toto vagentur orbe, et celeritate nimia ubique praesentes sint; martyres post effusionem sanguinis ara operientur inclusi, et inde exire non poterunt? Ex quo potest concludi non solum de bonis, sed etiam de malis, quod sua receptacula interdum exeant, cum non habeant majorem damnationem quam Daemones, qui ubique discurrunt."

2. Richard Kieckhefer, "The Specific Rationality of the Middle Ages," *The American Historical Review*, 99:3 (1994), 813–36.

3. See Boethius, *Consolation of Philosophy*, ed. Peter Walsh, trans. P. G. Walsh (Oxford: Oxford University Press, 2008).

4. On Aristotle's natural philosophy in the medieval Liberal Arts curriculum, see Edward Grant, *The Nature of Natural Philosophy* (Washington, D.C.: Catholic University of America Press, 2010), 29–34. For Aristotelianism at Paris and Oxford, see Gordon Leff, *Paris and Oxford Universities in the Thirteenth and Fourteenth Centuries: An Institutional and Intellectual History* (New York: Wiley, 1968). For medieval universities in general, see John Van Engen, *Learning Institutionalized: Teaching in the Medieval University* (Notre Dame: University of Notre Dame Press, 2000).

5. For a view of this process from the fourteenth century, see Steven J. Livesey, *Theology and Science in the Fourteenth Century: Three Questions on the Unity and Subalternation of the Sciences from John of Reading's Commentary on the Sentences* (Leiden: Brill, 1989).

6. On the shift from Platonism to Aristotelian

modes of thinking in hagiography, see Sister Benedicta Ward, *Miracles and the Medieval Mind: Theory, Record, and Event, 1000-1215* (Philadelphia: University of Pennsylvania Press, 1987).

7. On the Condemnations of 1277 and their contribution to medieval science, see Edward Grant, *The Foundations of Modern Science in the Middle Ages* (Cambridge: Cambridge University Press, 1996), 70 ff.

8. See J. P. Anton, *Aristotle's Theory of Contrariety* (New York: Humanities Press, 1957).

9. Stuart Clark, "Inversion, Misrule, and the Meaning of Witchcraft," *Past and Present*, 87:1 (1980), [105] 98–127. Stuart Clark, *Thinking with Demons* (Oxford: Oxford University Press, 1997), 45.

10. Aristotle, *Metaphysics*, 188b:25–30; CF: Aristotle, *Categories*, 11b: 15–20. On white and black as the source of all other colors, see Aristotle *De Sensu*, 3:2: "Another is that the Black and White appear the one through the medium of the other, giving an effect like that sometimes produced by painters overlaying a less vivid upon a more vivid color."

11. Stuart Clark, *Thinking with Demons*, 35.

12. *Thinking with Demons*, 110.

13. *Ibid.*

14. The cosmos and the earth at its core have always been spherical, never flat. See Jeffrey Burton Russell, *Inventing the Flat Earth: Columbus and Modern Historians* (Santa Barbara: Praeger Publishing, 1991).

15. Aristotle, *Metaphysics*, 6:7, states that the Prime Mover set the cosmos in motion out of love. See also Aristotle, *Physics*, 8.

16. For more on the medieval conception of the cosmos, see Ed Grant, *Planets, Stars, and Orbs: Medieval Cosmos, 1200–1687* (New York: Cambridge University Press, 1994). On ether as an element, see Wildberg, Christian. *John Philoponus' Criticism of Aristotle's Theory of Aether.* (Berlin: De Gruyter, 1988), 12.

17. Aristotle, *De Caelo*, 1:3

18. Aristotle, *Metaphysics*, 1:3,7; Aristotle, *On Generation and Corruption*, 1:1 and 2:1. This hierarchy describes each element's place of rest according to its assigned qualities; while the elements theoretically desire to be in their natural places of rest, in actuality they rarely achieve them because of the continual motion and change that predominate in the chaotic sublunary realm.

19. Aristotle, *Meteorology*, 1:2.

20. "These four bodies are fire, air, water, earth. Fire occupies the highest place among them all, earth the lowest, and two elements correspond to these in their relation to one another, air being nearest to fire, water to earth. The whole world surrounding the earth, then, the affections of which are our subject, is made up of these bodies." Aristotle, *Meteorology*, 1:2. See also Aristotle, *Metaphysics*, 1:3,7; *On Generation and Corruption*, 1:1 and 2:1. While each of the elements theoretically had a natural place of rest, in actuality they were in constant motion. All sublunary matter was composed of the four elements in different proportions and degrees; in the inherently corrupt and unstable terrestrial world, these elements were perpetually shifting and mixing, aspiring towards their natural places of rest, and in the process transforming old matter into new, transmuting one substance into another.

21. See Edward Grant, *The Foundations of Modern Science in the Middle Ages* (Cambridge: Cambridge University Press, 1996), 54–70.

22. Alexander of Hales envisioned these extremes in terms of light and opacity. See Colleen McDannell and Bernhard Lang, *Heaven: A History* (New Haven: Yale University Press, 2001), 83.

23. Thomas Aquinas, *Summa Theologica* (*ST*), 1a9:1–2; 1a10:1.

24. Edward Grant, *Planets, Stars, and Orbs: The Medieval Cosmos, 1200–1687* (Cambridge: Cambridge University Press, 1996), 373.

25. John Ruusbroec (1293–1381), quoted in Colleen McDannell and Bernhard Lang, *Heaven: A History* (New Haven: Yale University Press, 2001), 82; Thomas of Strasbourg, "Sentences," in Grant, *Planets, Stars, and Orbs*, 373.

26. *ST*, q57:a1

27. *ST*, q45:a2

28. *ST*, q57: a1.

29. Sharon Elkins, "Gertrude the Great and the Virgin Mary," *Church History*, 66:4 (1997), 720–734; here, 727.

30. Marina Warner, *Alone of All Her Sex: The Myth and the Cult of the Virgin Mary* (New York: Vintage, 1976), 99.

31. Gertrude of Helfta had a more complicated relationship with the Holy Mother, feeling at once obligated to honor her but jealous of her relationship with Christ. See Sharon Elkins, "Gertrude the Great and the Virgin Mary."

32. McDannell, and Lang, *Heaven*, 83.

33. David Keck, *Angels and Angelology in the Middle Ages* (Oxford: Oxford University Press, 1998), 113.

34. On the ordering of angels, see Aquinas, *ST*, Part One, Question 108.

35. *ST*, a57

36. See Thomas Cantimpré, "Life of Christina the Astonishing," in *Thomas Cantimpré: The Collected Saints' Lives*, ed. Margot King and Barbara Newman, (Turnhout: Brepols, 2008), 131: "And see how quick the Angels were to obey the bidding of the Lord!"

37. John Bossy, *Christianity in the West 1400–1700* (Oxford: Oxford University Press, 1985).

38. Peter Dendle, *Satan Unbound: The Devil in Old English Narrative Literature*, (Toronto: University of Toronto Press, 2001), 24.

39. Alexander of Hales, quoted in *Heaven*, 83.

40. Albertus Magnus, *On the Elements*, trans. Irven M. Resnick (Milwaukee: Marquette University Press, 2010), 21.

41. British Library, *The Neville of Hornby Hours*, Egerton MS 2781, f.1v, c.1340.

42. For the significance of the Ptolemaic center of the earth in Dante's *Inferno*, see John Freccero, "The Sign of Satan," *MLN*, 80:1 (1965), 11–26.

43. Jeffrey Burton Russell, *Lucifer*, 167.
44. *Lucifer*, 180.
45. John Freccero, "Sign of Satan," 18: CF: Bartholomew the *On the properties of things : John Trevisa's translation of Bartholomaeus Anglicus De proprietatibus Rerum*, trans. M. C. Seymour (Oxford: Clarendon Press, 1975–1988).
46. "Sign of Satan," 18.
47. For the devil as sultry woman, see Athanasius of Alexandria, *The Life of Antony and the Letter to Marcellinus*, trans. Robert C. Gregg (Mahwah, NJ: Paulist Press, 1980). On the Devil as shape shifter see Gregory the Great, who calls the Devil *"lupus circumiens,"* as well as the chapter on werewolves, below. Satan likewise takes the shape of a decrepit old woman in the Old English *Life of Nicholas*: see Peter Dendle, *Satan Unbound*, 43–44.
48. Jeffrey Burton Russell, *Lucifer: The Devil in the Middle Ages* (Ithaca: Cornell University Press, 1986), 210.
49. R. B. Pynsent, "The Devil's Stench and Living Water: A Study of Demons and Adultery in Czech Vernacular Literature of the Middle Ages and Renaissance," *The Slavonic and East European Review*, 71:4 (1993), 621.
50. See, for example, Giotto's fresco at the Arena Chapel in Padua (1306), or the fresco at San Petronio in Bologna (1410).
51. On the *osculum infame*: "Waldensians and diabolists in Arras kissed the backside of the Devil, who took the form of a goat." Martha Bayless, *Sin and Filth in Medieval Culture: The Devil in the Latrine* London: Routledge, 2011). 85. On the Devil eating feces, see Bayless, 81.
52. Pynsent, "The Devil's Stench," 603. Likewise, pitch and bitumen are combined with sulphur as the odors of hell; the river Phlegeton "stinks of pitch and sulphur, and it is so cruelly cold that it overwhelms all of the fires of hell." Pots of lead, pitch, and sulphur are used to torment the damned. Sulphur was also linked to volcanos which were believed to be the gateways to hell.
53. Pynsent, "The Devil's Stench," 616.
54. On copulation with demons, see Aquinas, *ST*: ""Devils do indeed collect human semen, by means of which they are able to produce bodily effects; but this cannot be done without some local movement , therefore devils can transfer the semen which they have collected and inject it into the bodies of others."
55. *ST*, Part One, Question 114, Article 2: "The demons know what happens outwardly among men; but the inward disposition of man God alone knows ... it is this disposition that makes man more prone to one vice than to another: hence the devil tempts, in order to explore this inward disposition of man, so that he may tempt him to that vice to which he is most prone."
56. Gregory the Great, *Moralia in Job*, 4:27.
57. Jeffrey Burton Russell, *Lucifer: The Devil in the Middle Ages* (Ithaca: Cornell University Press, 1984), 181.
58. Jerome: "The devil and the demons rove all over the earth." Quoted in Dendle, *Satan Unbound*, 10.
59. Aquinas argued that demons were essentially melancholy, unable to do physical penance, unable to rise into the light, forever doomed to the world below the moon. See *ST*, Part One, Question 64, Article 3. See also the *Malleus Maleficarum*, 147: "For in devils there are three things to be considered—their nature, their duty, and their sin; and by nature they belong to the empyrean of heaven, through their sin to the lower hell, but by reason of the duty assigned to them, as we have said, as ministers of punishment to the wicked and trial to the good, their place is in the clouds of the air." According to Aristotle, *Meteorology* 1:3, clouds and winds have their source in the marshy places of the earth.
60. See Brenda Gardenour Walter, "Corrupt Air, Poisonous Places, and the Toxic Breath of Witches in Late-Medieval Medicine and Theology," in *Toxic Airs: Chemical and Environmental Histories of the Atmosphere*. (Pittsburgh: University of Pittsburgh Press, 2014). See also the *Malleus Maleficarum*, Part II, Question 1, 92: "There were also three companions walking along a road, and two of them were struck by lightning. The third was terrified, when he heard voices speaking in the air, 'Let us strike him, too.'"
61. Thomas Aquinas, *De Substantiis Separatis*, Chapter Nineteen, "*De Distinctione Angelicorum Spirituum.*" From *ST*, Part One, Article 64: "Consequently a twofold place of punishment is due to the demons: one, by reason of their sin, and this is hell; and another, in order that they may tempt men, and thus the darksome atmosphere is their due place of punishment."
62. "...ever fertile in fresh deceptions, they change the perceptions and befoul the emotions of men, they confound the watchful, and in dreams disturb the sleeping." *Malleus Maleficarum*, Part I, Question II, 23. "For in these also the devils can stir up and excite the inner perceptions and humours, so that ideas retained in the repositories of their minds are drawn out and made apparent to the faculties of fancy and imagination." *Malleus*, Part I, Question VII, 50.
63. Jean Verdon, *Night in the Middle Ages* (Notre Dame: University of Notre Dame Press, 2002), 51.
64. Caesarius of Hiesterbach, *Dialogues*, II. For another miracle tale involving a demonic hairy worm, see "VitaSancti PetriMartyrisdeOrdineFratrumPredicatorum," ActaSanctorum (*AASS*).
65. Fabian Alejandro Campagne, "Demonology at the Crossroads: The Visions of Ermine de Rheims and the Image of the Devil on the Eve of the Great European Witch Hunt," *Church History*, 80:3 (2011), 471–2.
66. Guibert of Nogent: "Then quite near, in the midst of the darkness of that enormous shadow, I contemplated the demon in its own shape." Verdon, *Night in the Middle Ages*, 51. CF: *Malleus Maleficarum*, "...their power remains confined to the privy parts and the navel." Part I: Question 3, 24.

67. Bayless, *Sin and Filth*, 3. "'For you were created to live in heaven, and now you seek out toilets and go visiting latrines.' After the Brother had said these things, the demon blushed and departed in a confused fashion." Salimbene de Adam, 13th century, quoted in *Sin and Filth* 2.

68. Aquinas: "The intestines will rise again in the body, just like the other members. And they will be full, not, certainly, of shameful superfluities, but of noble humors." In fourth- and fifth-century monastic texts, demons appear as black and foul-smelling women: "A young monk beset by thoughts of sex encountered an Ethiopian woman with a foul smell.... An older monk found an Ethiopian girl he remembered seeing in his youth sitting on his knees; driven mad, he struck her, and a foul odor adhered to his hand." See David Brakke, "Ethiopian Demons," 501. In a medieval source, a demon is described as black sulphurous sow that disembowels a corpse and then disappears, leaving "a great stench behind it" Pynsent, "The Devil's Stench, " 611.

69. Nancy Caciola, *Discerning Spirits*, 197.

70. *ST*, Question 51, Article 3, Reply to Objections 6: "Still if some are occasionally begotten from demons, it is not from the seed of such demons, nor from their assumed bodies, but from the seed of men taken for the purpose; as when the demon assumes first the form of a woman, and afterwards of a man; just as they take the seed of other things for other generating purposes, as Augustine says (De Trin. ii.), so that the person born is not the child of a demon, but of a man."

71. On the multiplicity and unruliness of demons, see Dendle, *Satan Unbound*, 89–90

72. *ST*, Question 114, Article 4.

73. Aquinas, *On the Sentences*, II, d. 7, q. 2, a.1

74. See Miri Rubin, "Europe Remade: Purity and Danger in Late Medieval Europe," *Transactions of the Royal Historical Society*, 6:11 (2001), 101–124.

75. For the background to this controversy, see Roland Bainton's indispensable *Early Christianity* (Princeton, NJ: Van Nostrand Press, 1960).

76. Gregory the Great. *Bibliotheca Nacional de Madrid*, MS 11544: folio 13v.

77. See also Samantha J E Riches, "Encountering the Monstrous: Saints and Dragons in Medieval Thought," *Monstrous Middle Ages*, ed. Bettina Bildhauer (Toronto: University of Toronto Press, 2003), 196–218.

78. On Saint Lifard, *AASS*, June 3; On Saint Marcel of Paris, see Gregory of Tours, *Eight Books of Miracles*. Brewer, *Dictionary of Miracles*, 116.

79. See the "Accusations of Cannibalism" in Minucius Felix, Octavius, R. E. Wallis, trans. in *The Ante-Nicene Fathers* (Buffalo, N. Y.: The Christian Literature Publishing Co., 1887), Vol. 4, 177–178. See also David Frankfurter, *Evil Incarnate: Rumors of Demonic Conspiracy and Ritual Abuse in History* (Princeton, NJ: Princeton University Press, 2006).

80. See *Power and Purity: Cathar Heresy in Medieval Italy* (New York: Oxford University Press, 2001). For a micro-historical perspective, see Emmanuel Le Roy Ladurie, *Montaillou: Promised Land of Error* (New York: G. Brazillier, 1978).

81. Ralph of Coggeshall, "The Witch of Rheims," in *Witchcraft in Europe: 1100–1700*. Alan C Kors and Edward Peters, eds. (Philadelphia: University of Pennsylvania Press, 1972), 47.

82. See Donald Prudlho, *The Martyred Inquisitor: The Life and Cult of Peter of Verona* (Burlington, VT: Ashgate Publishing, 2008).

83. Stephen of Bourbon, *De Superstitione*, accessible at: http://www.fordham.edu/halsall/source/guinefort.asp. See also Suzanne Schiffman's movie adaptation, *Le moine et la sorcière* (1987). See also the recent reissue of a classic text, Jean-Claude Schmidtt, *The Holy Greyhound: Guinefort, Healer of Children since the Thirteenth Century* (Camridge: Cambridge University Press, 2009).

84. Barbara Tuchman, *A Distant Mirror: The Calamitous Fourteenth Century* (New York: Alfred Knopf, 1978).

85. Rosemary Horrox, *The Black Death* (Manchester: Manchester University Press, 1994). For some controversial views, see David Herlihy, *The Black Death and the Transformation of the West* (Cambridge, MA: Harvard University Press, 1997). Recent trends in the history of the Black Death (and leprosy) focus on biomedical and epidemiological approaches. For cutting-edge genomics work on the plague, see http://contagions.wordpress.com/2011/10/16/black-death-genome-fished-out-of-east-smithfield/

86. See Anne Hudson, *The Premature Reformation: Wycliffite Texts and Lollard History* (New York: Oxford University Press, 1988).

87. Joachim de Fiore and Peter of John Olivi both wrote works on the Antichrist and suggested that he may indeed be residing in the Vatican. See Bernard McGinn, *Antichrist: Two Thousand Years of the Human Fascination with Evil* (New York: Columbia University Press, 2000), 149–166.

88. On Peter of John Olivi, see David Burr, "The Persecution of Peter Olivi," *The Transactions of the American Philosophical Society*, 66 (1976). On Joachim de Fiore, see Robert E. Lerner, "Antichrists and Antichrist in Joachim de Fiore," *Speculum*, 60 (1985), 553–70; Bernard McGinn, *The Calabrian Abbot: Joachim of Fiore in the History of Western Thought* (New York: Macmillan, 1985).

89. David Burr, *The Spiritual Franciscans: From Protest to Persecution in the Century after Saint Francis* (Philadelphia: Pennsylvania State University Press, 2001), 1.

90. The contest between Papal and quasi-secular power was an old one, attested to by the troubled relationship between Pope Gregory VII and Emperor Henry IV in the eleventh century. CF: The Walk to Canossa.

91. On the three-headed depiction of the Antichrist, see Bernard McGinn, *Antichrist: Two Thousand Years of the Human Fascination with*

Evil (New York: Columbia University Press, 2000) 148.

92. Michael D. Bailey, *Battling Demons: Witchcraft, Heresy, and Reform in the Later Middle Ages* (Philadelphia: Pennsylvania State Press, 2002), 102.

93. Since Wycliffe was already deceased, his remains were ceremonially exhumed and thrown on the pyre; Jan Hus, however, was burned alive while prelates looked on with satisfaction, wrongly presuming that they had destroyed the sources of the Church's heretical infestation.

94. See Michael D. Bailey and Edward Peters, "A Sabbat of Demonologists: Basel 1430–1441," *The Historian*, 65 (2003), 1375–1395.

95. On the significance of Basel, see Bailey and Peters, "Sabbat of Demonologists," as well as Michael Bailey, *Battling Demons Witchcraft, Heresy, and Reform in the Later* Middle Ages (Philadelphia: Pennsylvania State Press, 2002).

96. "Sabbat of Demonologists," 1379.

97. Johannes Nider, "Formicarius," *The Witchcraft Sourcebook*, ed. Brian P. Levack (New York: Routledge, 2004), 54.

98. On the conflation of regional particularities, see Richard Kieckhefer, "Mythologies of Witchcraft in the Fifteenth Century," *Magic, Ritual, and Witchcraft*, 1:1 (2006), 79–108.

99. See the On the *Malleus Maleficarum*, see Christopher S. Mackay's critical edition published by Cambridge University Press (2006).

100. Discernment between the truly miraculous and demonic deception, therefore, became of increasing concern during this period. *Malleus Maleficarum*, 126; for a broader discussion, see Hans Peter Broedel, *The Malleus Maleficarum and the Construction of Witchcraft Theology and Popular Belief* (Manchester: Manchester University Press, 2003), 50–1.

101. *Malleus* PI: Q4, 30
102. *Malleus*, P1: Q2
103. *Malleus* P1:Q3 21
104. *Malleus Maleficarum*, 101.
105. *Malleus Maleficarum*, 100; Remy 93.
106. Alain Boureau, *Satan the Heretic: The Birth of Demonology in the Medieval West* (Chicago: University of Chicago, 2006).
107. *Malleus Maleficarum*, 96.

108. See Josef Schmidt and Mary Simon, "Holy and Unholy Shit: The Pragmatic Context of Scatological Curses in Early German Reformation Satire," in *Fecal Matters in Early Modern Literature and Art*, eds. Jeff Persels and Russel Ganim (Aldershot: Ashgate Press, 2004), 113–4.

109. *Malleus Maleficarum*, 100, 139, 117 [respectively].

110. On the application of this paradigm to Jews in the medieval world, see Miri Rubin, *Gentile Tales: The Narrative Assault on Late Medieval Jews* (New Haven: Yale University Press, 1999). For a discussion of Satanic paradigms, Jews, and vampirism, see chapter six below.

111. See Michael D. Bailey, "The Medieval Concept of the Witches' Sabbath," *Exemplaria* 8 (1996), 419–39.

112. "She said that she often saw children baptized at the Sabbath; she explained to us that these were the children of witches and no others; they are accustomed to having their children baptized at the Sabbath rather than at church, and they present them to the Devil rather than to God." Pierre de Lancre, *On the Inconstancy of Witches* (1612), 153.

113. On the ritual use of Satan's urine, Lancre, *On the Inconstancy of Witches* (1612), 151.

114. "For she had very often seen both types of children [baptized and unbaptized] served and eaten ... they are cut into quarters at the Sabbath in order to have several parishes partake of them." Lancre, 154.

115. On the black bread, see Lancre, 213: "In 1609, something quite memorable happened in the city of Limoges. It had to do with this little dough made of black millet that the witches give to the little children to eat. It smells worse than anything imaginable, and they use it to confuse their senses and bind them to Satan."

Chapter 2

1. The internet has made twentieth and twenty-first century films, television programs, and other media from around the globe instantly accessible, compressing time, conflating regional particularities, and producing some very complex transnational transmissions of horror. See Brenda Gardenour Walter, "Ghastly Transmissions: The Horror of Connectivity and the Transnational Flow of Fear," in *Transnational Horror Across Visual Media: Fragmented Bodies* (New York: Routledge, 2013).

2. For voyeurism in horror cinema, see Laura Mulvey's now classic "Visual Pleasure and Narrative Cinema," *Screen* 16:3 (1975), 6–18.

3. On black in medieval color theory, see John Freccero, "Sign of Satan," *MLN*, Vol. 80, No. 1, Italian Issue (Jan., 1965), 18

4. Later in the film we discover that Poelzig's basement contains the preserved lifeless bodies of several white-clad women entombed in glass, much like a modern version of Dracula's brides lurking in the castle's basement. In witchcraft treatises, cats were seen as close to the earth and born of corruption, like mice; because of their color, black cats were seen as the most melancholic and corrupt of all.

5. The cold wind and the shifting phases of the moon are indicative of demonic presence, element earth, and transformation. On Karloff's robes, note that they are modified versions of doctoral robes, with velvet stripes along the sleeves, an indication of his dangerous education and intellect. The obelisks are a nod towards eastern occultism, which for many Americans was cast into the same non-Christian "other" category as Satanism, Judaism, and communism.

6. Their insanity is best evidenced in their choice of Bauhaus architecture and modern art—for many in the early twentieth century undisputable signs of un-American evil.

7. On magic high and low, see Kieckhefer, *Magic in the Middle Ages* (Cambridge: Cambridge University Press, 1990) and *European Witch Trials: Their Foundations in Popular and Learned Culture* (Berkeley: University of California Press, 1976). For an overview of the textual tradition, see Claire Fanger, *Conjuring Spirits: Texts and Traditions of Medieval Ritual Magic* (Stroud: Sutton Publishing, 1998).

8. In Wheatley's novel, Simon is a Jew—an element left out of the film version. For the magic contest between Simon Magus and Peter, see "The Apocryphal Acts of Peter and Paul," *The Other Bible* (New York: Harper Collins, 2005), 435. In Pierre de Lancre's *On the Inconstancy of Witches*, Simon Magus is linked directly with Satan (141).

9. Mind control here can be traced to the occult tradition, Victorian mesmerism, and medieval discourse on the power of demons to create phantasies of the mind.

10. On the Renaissance Magus, see Frances Yates' seminal *Giordano Bruno and the Hermetical Tradition* (Chicago: University of Chicago Press, 1964).

11. The "magic circle" motif appears in the thirteenth-century *Dialogus Miraculorum* of Caesarius of Heisterbach. See *Witchcraft in Europe 1100-1700*, ed. Kors and Peters (Philadelphia: University of Pennsylvania Press, 1972).

12. The Christianization of Richelieu's magic may have had more to do with Hammer's fear of censure by the Church. According to Christopher Lee, "After years of urging black-magic themes on Hammer, I had a breakthrough with The Devil Rides Out. Conservative, Hammer had always worried about the Church's reaction to the screening of the Black Mass. But we thought the charge of blasphemy would not stick if we did the thing with due attention to scholarship."

13. According to the specific rationality of medieval scholasticism, Mocata's magic works through demonic agency and the manipulation of the natural world. Richelieu's magic, while labeled "white" and somehow Christian is nevertheless still suspect; he is not working miracles, therefore he is as guilty of demonic magic as Mocata.

14. The "magic contest" is a very old trope, one example of which is the story of Simon Magus and Peter in the *Apocryphal Acts of Peter and Paul*. It is likewise echoed in Tolkien's *Lord of the Rings*, C. S. Lewis' *Chronicles of Narnia*, and Walt Disney's *Sword in the Stone*.

15. The purple robes may echo the purple chasuble worn by the Catholic priest during Requiem masses.

16. As discussed in Chapter One, the trope of the nighttime cannibalistic orgy can be traced back to Ancient Rome and Greece.

17. For an analysis of Freemasonry in the broader context of conspiracy theory, see Michael Barkun, *A Culture of Conspiracy: Apocalyptic Visions in Contemporary America* (Berkeley: University of California Press, 2003), 136.

18. For aliens as organized and threatening others, see Michael Barkun, *A Culture of Conspiracy: Apocalyptic Visions in Contemporary America* (Berkeley: University of California Press, 2003). In this book as well as in his essay, "Myths of the Underworld in Contemporary American Millennialism," *Experiences of Place*, ed. Mary N. MacDonald (Cambridge: Harvard University Press, 2003), Barkun describes conspiracies that place alien organizations under the earth's surface, a nice bit of medieval infernal inversion indeed.

19. On the Lovecraftian ethos, see Timothy H. Evans, "A Last Defense against the Dark: Folklore, Horror, and the Uses of Tradition in the Works of H. P. Lovecraft," *Journal of Folklore Research*, Vol. 42, No. 1 (Jan.—Apr., 2005), 99-135.

20. The idea of a hidden, corrupt, and evil New England is a favorite theme of H. P. Lovecraft. See, for example, "Pickman's Model," which tells of tunnels and caverns beneath Boston that house flesh-hungry changelings.

21. For example: *Friday the Thirteenth* (1980), *Evil Dead* (1981; remake 2013), *Cabin Fever* (2002), *The Corridor* (2010), *Don't Go Into the Woods* (2010), *The Cabin in the Woods* (2011).

22. The ankh is the Egyptian symbol for "Life"—one of the few readily recognizable hieroglyphs in Western popular culture thanks in part Howard Carter's discovery of King Tutankhamen's tomb in 1922 and the sempiternal Tutmania that has followed.

23. On natural magic as demonic, see Richard Kieckhefer, *Magic in the Middle Ages* (Cambridge: Cambridge University Press, 1990).

24. For a first-hand account of some of these changes, see John W. O'Malley, *What Happened at Vatican II* (Cambridge: Harvard University Press, 2008).

25. On the power of garlic to fend of venomous creatures, see Chapter Five, below.

26. For twentieth-century American fears of the "New Age" and the "New World Order," see W. Scott Poole, *Satan in America: The Devil We Know* (New York: Rowman and Littlefield, 2010).

27. Dracula as both an expression of and conflation with Satan will be discussed in detail in Chapter Three below.

28. In paintings of the Black Death, plague arrows are often shot down from the air by black demons; melancholic Jews were likewise accused of poisoning the wells and causing plague. See Rosemary Horrox, *The Black Death* (Manchester: Manchester University Press, 1994), 207-222. On conspiracy theories, see Michael Barkun (above).

29. "She said that she often heard mass said by some priests ... dressed in red and white." Pierre de Lancre's description of the Black Mass, 155.

30. "Let it be known to all the spirits that I am a Capricorn living in the tenth house, the house of our lord Satan ... let all the spirits here know that I am the first born son of Satan ... let it be known, sons and daughters, that Satan was an acid head. Drink from his cup ... pledge yourselves, and together we'll all freak out."

31. For a brief overview of *Blood on Satan's Claw*, see Bartlomiej Paszylk, *The Pleasure and Pain of Cult Horror Films: A Historical Survey* (Jefferson, NC: McFarland Press, 2009), 119–120.

32. For connections to paganism, see Leon Hunt, "Necromancy in the UK: Witchcraft and the Occult in British Horror," in *British Horror Cinema*, eds. Steve Chibnall and Julian Petlay (London: Routledge, 2002), 82–98.

33. We might also compare this with *The Wicker Man* (1973), which tells a tale of the dangers of paganism—or perhaps its joys—depending on who is watching it. Against both *Blood on Satan's Claw* and *The Wicker Man* we might place Kenneth Anger's *Lucifer Rising* (1972), a cult film of the counter culture that extolled the virtues of rock and roll, self-actuation, and personal freedom—simultaneously conflating images and ideas from the hermetic traditions, the New Age movement, and Satanism as a form of anti–Christianity/mainstream culture. See also Alejandro Jodorowsky's *The Holy Mountain* (1973), which makes fun of Christians, Satanists, Alchemists, pagans, and everyone else seeking enlightenment through organized systems.

34. The wholesomeness and purity of the American landscape is the centerpiece of books by nature writers such as Edward Abbey (*Desert Solitaire*) and Aldo Leopold (*Sand County Almanac*).

35. The desert Southwest likewise serves as the base of operations for a border-crossing Satanic cult in *Enter the Devil* (1974). Set in Texas' Big Bend country, a coven wearing monastic robes descends through rocky crevices into a subterranean sacred space where they conduct human sacrifices. The victim is sliced three times in mockery of the trinity, tied to a stone altar, and then stabbed with a blackened cross/stake in the hands, feet, and side in mockery of the stigmata. These are the Disciples of Death, a strange cross between Catholicism and Mexican religion with a Satanic bent. At the core of this film are American Anti-Catholicism and fears about illegal immigration.

36. For an excellent overview of film noir, see Mark Bould, *Film Noir: From Berlin to Sin City: Short Cuts, Volume 27*, (New York: Columbia University Press, 2012).

37. See David Abrahamsen, M.D. *Confessions of Son of Sam* (New York: Columbia University Press, 1985).

38. Ira Levin, *Rosemary's Baby* (New York: Random House, 1967).

39. See also Dario Argento's *Inferno*, which features a New York apartment building that serves as a fetid womb for the ancient witch, Mater Tenebrarum.

40. Which is, of course, a Western and predominantly Christian misconception of syncretic religions such as Santeria and Vodun. See also the conflation of Voodoo and Satanism in *The Devil's Hand* (1962) and Hammer Horror's *Plague of Zombies* (1966).

41. Jeffrey Burton Russell, *Lucifer: The Devil in the Middle Ages* (Ithaca: Cornell University Press, 1984), 72.

42. For a strange film about Satan in space, see *The Dark Side of the Moon* (1990), directed by D J Webster.

43. Bernard McGinn, *Antichrist: Two Thousand Years of the Human Fascination with Evil* (New York: Columbia University Press, 2000), 89–90.

44. See Jerome, *Commentary on Daniel 7:8*, ed. Glorie, 843–44. On Hildegard's Antichrist, see Richard K. Emmerson, "The Representation of Antichrist in Hildegard of Bingen's *Scivias*: Image, Word, Commentary, and Visionary Experience," *Gesta* 41:2 (2002), 95–110.

45. Bernard McGinn, *Anti-Christ: Two Thousand Years of the Human Fascination with Evil* (New York: Columbia University Press, 2000). As depicted in Satanic cinema, the Anti-Christ is almost always male, an expectation that reflects our cultural assumptions about power and masculinity.

46. Thomas Aquinas, *Summa Theologica*, 1:55:53: "Still if some are occasionally begotten from demons, it is not from the seed of such demons, nor from their assumed bodies, but from the seed of men taken for the purpose; as when the demon assumes first the form of a woman, and afterwards of a man; just as they take the seed of other things for other generating purposes, as Augustine says in *De Trinitate*, so that the person born is not the child of a demon, but of a man." CF: *Malleus Maleficarum*, 1:3.

47. For a delightful cinematic vision of the birth of demonic offspring, see the silent film *Häxan* (1922).

48. Scott Poole, *Satan in America: The Devil We Know* (New York: Rowman and Littlefield, 2009).

49. The Bramford, of course, is the Dakota Building in Manhattan's Upper West Side, once home to John Lennon and Yoko Ono.

50. For feminist critique of Rosemary's Baby, see Lucy Fischer, "Birth Traumas: Parturition and Horror in Rosemary's Baby," *Cinema Journal* 31:3 (1992), 3–18.

51. Astaroth is listed in the seventeenth-century grimoire, *Ars Goetica*, as a male demon with the power over serpents and having deadly breath (CF: heretics, serpents, and plague). Astaroth and his star also make an unlikely appearance in the Walt Disney film, *Bedknobs and Broomsticks* (1971), although the demonic element is of course left out.

52. Medieval depictions of Judas Iscariot's death often depict his evil spirit bursting forth from his abdomen rather than passing through his mouth, as with holy people. See Caciola, *Discerning Spirits: Divine and Demonic Possession in the Middle Ages* (Ithaca: Cornell University Press, 2003), 201.

53. Dennis Wheatley, *To The Devil—A Daughter* (London: Hutchinson, 1953).

54. On the ensoulment of fetuses and various opinions on the role of male and female seed in

conception, see Danielle Jacquart and Claude Thomasset, *Sexuality and Medicine in the Middle Ages* (Princeton, NJ: Princeton University Press, 1988) and Joan Cadden, *The Meaning of Sex Difference in the Middle Ages* (Cambridge: Cambridge University Press, 1995)

55. Mary conceived Christ when the logos of God entered her ear through His angelic messenger; Kelly conceives the Antichrist when Satanic slime enters her ears, nose and mouth.

56. Throughout the film, Damien is flanked by black dogs, a reference not only to his canine parentage but also to his demonic nature; in Nicholas Remy's *Demonolatry*, he states that demonic familiars often take the form of black dogs, and notes that the famed Magus, Cornelius Agrippa, himself had demon in "the shape of a black dog with a leather collar studded with nails forming a magic inscription" (70).

57. William Paul, *Laughing Screaming: Modern Hollywood Horror and Comedy*, (New York: Columbia University Press, 1995), 237. The horror of evil children can also be seen in *The Village of the Damned* (1960, 1995), based on the novel *The Midwich Cuckoos* by John Wyndham, *The Children of the Damned* (1963), *The Children of the Corn* (1984), and its legion of descendants. *The Children of the Corn*, set in Gatlin, Nebraska, has Satanic nuances, but no direct evidence of Satanic involvement. Isaac, for example, has a strange altar with pagan elements, crosses made out of corn, and the repeated use of goat horns. There is also a painting of Jesus in which his skin has been painted grey. When the children sign their pact with "he who moves behind the rows," they do so in their own blood, which they collect after carving the star-in-circle motif on their chests; this blood is then consumed by the congregation. Biblical phrases hint that the child-corn cult is Satanic: "And a little child shall lead them"; "And the devil that deceived them was cast into the lake of fire and brimstone." These signifiers, however, seem not to be integral to the plot (the children could simply be brutal and misled without any supernatural interference), but instead used to heighten the fear of the audience who will read deeper meaning into them.

58. Damien is also connected to the late medieval tradition of child witches. See Robert S. Walinski-Kiehl, "The Devil's Children: Child Witch Trials, *New Perspectives on Witchcraft, Magic, and Demonology: Witchcraft in Continental Europe*, ed. Brian P. Levack (New York: Routledge, 2001), 413–31; in the same volume, see Lyndal Roper, "Evil Imaginings and Fantasies: Child-Witches and the End of the Witch Craze," 433–65.

59. Hippocrates, *On the Sacred Disease*: "By these veins we draw in much breath, since they are the spiracles of our bodies inhaling air to themselves and distributing it to the rest of the body, and to the smaller veins, and they and afterwards exhale it. For the breath cannot be stationary, but it passes upward and downward, for if stopped and intercepted, the part where it is stopped becomes powerless." Also see Hippocrates, *On Breaths*.

60. See Brenda Gardenour Walter, "Corrupt Air, Poisonous Places, and the Toxic Breath of Witches in Late-Medieval Medicine and Theology," in *Toxic Airs: Chemical and Environmental Histories of the Atmosphere* (Pittsburgh: University of Pittsburgh Press, 2013).

61. On the malleability of female flesh and its susceptibility to demonic possession, see Nancy Caciola, *Discerning Spirits: Divine and Demonic Possession in the Middle Ages* (Ithaca: Cornell University Press, 2003), 140–148. See also Barbara Newman, "Hildegard of Bingen: Visions and Validation," *Church History* 54:2 (June, 1985), 163–75.

62. Nancy Caciola, *Discerning Spirits*, 198.

63. Caciola, *Discerning Spirits*, 197.

64. Caciola, *Discerning Spirits*, 157. For a disturbing exorcism of the demons in a woman's bowels, see Ken Russell's *The Devils*, in which the inquisitor admonishes his colleague to "Be assured, the fiend is lurking in some hidden recess of her body. This medical examination shall reveal it," just as he tortures her with an enema on a sacred altar. The suggestion, of course, is that the Church is far more Satanic than any coven could ever be.

65. For example, see *Two Lives of St. Cuthbert*, ed. Bertram Colgrave (Cambridge: Cambridge University Press, 1940)

66. On miracles in the medieval cult of saints in general, see Benedicta Ward, *Miracles and the Medieval Mind: Theory, Record, and Event, 1000–1215* (Philadelphia: University of Pennsylvania Press, 1982).

67. For exorcism in the Middle Ages, see Caciola, *Discerning Spirits*, passim; Richard Kieckhefer, *Magic in the Middle Ages*, 76–77 and 166–69; and Andre Goddu, "The Failure of Exorcism in the Middle Ages," in *Possession and Exorcism: Articles on Witchcraft, Magic, and Demonology Volume 9*, ed. Brian P. Levack (New York: Taylor and Francis, 1992), 9–29.

68. Caciola, *Discerning Spirits*, 225.

69. William Peter Blatty, *The Exorcist* (San Francisco: Harper and Row, 1971). For another example of the demonic transformation of seemingly virtuous female flesh, see Sam Raimi's *EvilDead* (1981, 2013).

70. On American culture and the Ouija Board, see Bill Ellis, "The @#$%&! Ouija Board" *Lucifer Ascending: The Occult in Folklore and Popular Culture* (Lexington: University of Kentucky Press, 2004), 174–196.

71. The demon is unearthed by Lankester Merrin, a German priest and exorcist who is working on an archaeological dig in Iraq. The Ouija board element of *The Exorcist* inspired several films about its dangers as an unclean portal to the evil realm, including *Witchboard* (1986), *Witchboard 2: The Devil's Doorway* (1993), and *Witchboard 3: The Possession* (1995).

72. Compare Regan's abilities with this passage from Jean Bodin's *On the Demonmania of Witches* (1580): "the demoniacs spoke various languages that they had never learned. And sometimes the evil spirit speaks as from within

the stomach, when the woman's mouth is closed, sometimes with the tongue stretch half a foot out of the mouth, sometimes through the shameful parts." *On the Demonmania of Witches*, (1580), 109.

73. When Father Karras asks the demonic being where Regan is, it says "She's in here with us." Again, in *The Exorcist III: Legion*, Karras' soul is trapped in the heart, tormented by demons and the human spirit of the Gemini Killer.

74. In the twentieth century, members of the Pentecostal movement argued that demons might readily take the shape of psychological or behavioral issues such as depression or drug addiction. See W. Scott Poole, *Satan in America: The Devil We Know* (New York: Rowman and Littlefield, 2010).

75. The film suggests that Karras is liberated from demonic possession by this selfless act and his subsequent death. In Blatty's second novel, *Legion* (1983) and its 1990 film adaptation, however, we learn that Pazuzu was so angry at being removed from Regan that he forced the deranged soul of a serial murderer known as the Gemini Killer into Karras' body to torment him. While it makes for a good story, there is not medieval precedent for the transfer of human spirits between bodies. Only the soul, which is imprinted with the divine, survives death. The pneuma, or human spirit, perishes with the flesh.

76. Scholarship surrounding *The Exorcist* is abundant. See Mark Kermode, *The Exorcist* (London: British Film Institute, 1997); Alexandra Heller-Nicholas, "The Power of Christ Compels You: Moral Spectacle and The Exorcist Universe," *Roman Catholicism in Fantastic Film: Essays on Belief, Spectacle, Ritual, and Imagery* (Jefferson, NC: McFarland, 2011), 65–80. See also, James Clifton, "The Face of a Fiend: Convulsion, Inversion, and the Horror of the Disempowered Body," *Oxford Art Journal: Early Modern Horror,* 34:3 (2011), 373–92.

77. For a discussion of the "para-para-cinematic" exploitation films based on the exorcist, see Alexandra Heller-Nicholas, "The Power of Christ Compels You: Moral Spectacle and *The Exorcist* universe," in *Roman Catholicism in Fantastic Film* (Jefferson, NC: McFarland, 2011), 65–80.

78. An interesting take on this theme is *The Possession of David O'Reilly* (2010), which tells the tale of a male being tormented by invisible spirits, purportedly demons, but never actually possessed. The creatures "get into his head," so to speak, but definitely not into his body.

79. See Brenda Gardenour Walter, "*Phantasmic Science*: Medieval Theology, Victorian Spiritualism, and the Specific Rationality of Twenty-First Century Ghost Hunting," *Jefferson Journal of Science and Culture* (2013).

Chapter 3

1. Dimiri Gutas, *Greek Thought, Arab Culture: The Greco-Arabic Translation Movement in Baghdad and Early Abbasid Society* (London: Routledge, 1998).

2. For a comprehensive overview, see Peter E. Pormann and Emilie Savage-Smith, *Medieval Islamic Medicine* (Washington, D.C.: Georgetown University Press, 2007).

3. See the *Studies in Ancient Medicine* collection, *Constantine the African and Ali Ibn al Abbas al Magusi: The Pantegni and Related Texts*, eds. Charles Burnett and Danielle Jacquart (Leiden: Brill, 1994).

4. On translation teams, see Thomas Glick, "My Master the Jew: Observations on Interfaith Scholarly Interaction in the Middle Ages," *Jews, Muslims and Christians In and Around the Crown of Aragon*, ed. Harvey J. Hames (Leiden: Brill, 2004), 157–82. Also, Charles Burnett, "Translation from Arabic into Latin in the Middle Ages in *Übersetzung—Translation—Traduction*, ed. H. Kittel et al. (Berlin: De Gruyter, 2007), 1231–37.

5. Cornelius O' Boyle, *The Art of Medicine: Medical Teaching at the University of Paris 1250–1400* (Leiden: Brill, 1998). Medicine and the Arts were taught simultaneously at Bologna. See *Medieval Medicine*, edited by Faith Wallis (Toronto: University of Toronto Press, 2010), 159.

6. Jacques Verger, "The First French Universities and the Institutionalization of Learning: Faculties, Curricula, Degrees," *Learning Institutionalized: Teaching in the Medieval University*, ed. John Van Engen (Notre Dame: University of Notre Dame Press, 2000).

7. Thomas Cantimpré, *De Anathomia Humanii Corporis*, Palatina Manuscripts of the Twelfth through Fifteenth Centuries, entry number 1066, CD-ROM, 2001; Thomas Cantimpré, *Liber de Natura Rerum*, Codices Illuminati Medi Aevi, Number 55, Munich, 2001. CF: "*Tacuinum Sanitatis,*" *Medieval Medicine: A Reader*, ed. Faith Wallis.

8. See Faith Wallis, *Medieval Medicine*, 17–25.

9. On temperaments, or complexion theory, see Nancy Siraisi, *Medieval and Early Renaissance Medicine: An Introduction to Knowledge and Practice* (Chicago: University of Chicago, 1990).

10. See Luis García Ballester and John Arrizabalaga (eds.), *Galen and Galenism: Theory and Medical Practice from Antiquity to the European Renaissance.* (Burlington, VT: Ashgate Press, 2002). See also Owsei Temkin, *Galen and Galenism: Rise and Decline of a Medical Philosophy* (Ithaca, NY: Cornell University Press, 1973) and the extensive works on Galen by Vivian Nutton.

11. These digestive organs include the stomach, the liver where food is processed into blood, and the rest of the organs that receive the blood and process it into nutriments. For Maimonides on this ancient, three-fold process of digestion, see Gerrit Bos, "Maimonides on the Preservation of Health," *Journal of the Royal Asiatic Society* 4(1994), 218 [213–235].

12. See Volker Langholf, *Medical Theories in Hippocrates: Early Texts and the Epidemics*. (Berlin: De Gruyter, 1990), 79–84.

13. Hippocrates, *Airs, Waters, Places,* Books 3–6; *Epidemics,* Books 1 and 3; *On the Sacred Disease, passim:* "Therefore, they are attacked during changes of the winds, and especially south winds, then also with north winds, and afterwards also with the others. These are the strongest winds, and the most opposed to one another, both as to direction and power. For, the north wind condenses the air, and separates from it whatever is muddy and nebulous, and renders it clearer and brighter, and so in like manner also, all the winds which arise from the sea and other waters; for they extract the humidity and nebulosity from all objects, and from men themselves, and therefore it (the north wind) is the most wholesome of the winds. But the effects of the south are the very reverse."

14. Hippocrates, *Airs, Waters, Places,* Book 3

15. On medical astrology in medieval medicine, see Nancy Siraisi, *Medieval and Early Renaissance Medicine,* 134–5. See also, French, Roger. "Foretelling the Future: Arabic Astrology and English Medicine in the Late Twelfth Century," *Isis* 87:3 (1996), 453–480.

16. Arnaldi de Villanova, *Opera Medica Omnia—de Esu Carnium, Vol. XI,* ed. Dianne M. Bazell (Barcelona: University of Barcelona Press, 1999), 163.

17. Villanova, 164.

18. Villanova, 167.

19. On the virago, see Lesley Dean-Jones, *Women's Bodies in Classical Greek Science* (Oxford, Clarendon, 1996).

20. Galen, *On Diseases and Symptoms,* trans. Ian Johnston (Cambridge: Cambridge University Press, 2011), 233.

21. Following Aristotle, "a person awakes when digestion is completed." *De Somno et Vigilia,* Part 3.

22. Arnau de Villanova (1301), *Repetitio super canonem Vita brevis* (excerpt on the diagnostic process, trans. M. R. McVaugh).

23. *Ibid.*

24. On uroscopy as prognosis, see Faith Wallis, "Signs and Senses: Diagnosis and Prognosis in Early Medieval Pulse and Urine Tests," *Social History of Medicine* 13:2 (2000), 265–27.

25. John Beare, *Greek Theories of Elementary Cognition from Alcmaeon to Aristotle* (Oxford: Clarendon Press, 1906), 272.

26. Galen, *On the Errors and Passions of the Soul,* trans. Paul W. Harkins (Columbus: Ohio State University Press, 1963).

27. R. J. Hankinson, "Galen's Anatomy of the Soul," *Phronesis* 36:2 (1991), 203 [197–233].

28. "Among the non-naturals he should attend to the patient's habits … habits cover all the non-naturals, so through habit is considered the air he breathes and his normal exercise or rest and his meals and sleep and waking and emotions and excretions." Arnau de Villanova (1301)

29. When a patient is prescribed a change in dietary regimen, the changes are not immediate, and there is room to question the efficacy of the treatment plan; when hellebore is used, the efficacy of the treatment cannot be denied, since the effects are very physical and immediate.

30. Linda E. Voigts and Michael R. McVaugh, "A Latin Technical Phlebotomy and Its Middle English Translation," *Transactions of the American Philosophical Society,* 74:2 (1984), 5–6 [1–69].

31. For an example, see Huntington HM64, 8v-10v, *Ad minuendum sanguinem,* digitized online at: http://dpg.lib.berkeley.edu/webdb/dsheh/heh_brf?Description=&CallNumber=HM+64.

32. In medieval medicine, the boundaries between foods and drugs were fluid; red wine and honey, for example, were at once foodstuffs and *materia medica*. Simple medicines such as those listed in the thirteenth-century Latin translation of Ibn-Serapion the Younger's herbal manual, *Liber de Simplici Medicina* were non-compounded, their inherent qualities strong enough to promote humoral rebalancing. More complex medical conditions often required composite medicines, recipes for which might be found in the *Viaticum,* the *Qanun,* and the *Pantegni*. Composed of two or more simples and compounded into pills, syrups, electuaries, and oils, these powerful drugs were more not only more complicated in their formulations, but also in their pharmacokinetics, or the ways in which they interacted with the body.

33. This is the same principle behind homeopathic medicine, which was established in 1796 by Samuel Hahnemann and is still practiced as one component of holistic healing today. For a modern perspective on the homeopathic debate and its relationship to modern science, see Nina Degele, "On the Margins of Everything: Doing, Performing, and Staging Science in Homeopathy," *Science, Technology, and Human Values* 30:1 (2005), 111–136.

34. Christiane Nockels Fabbri, "Treating Medieval Plague: The Wonderful Virtues of Theriac," *Early Science and Medicine,* 12:3 (2007), 252 [247–283]. The magical properties of theriac were enhanced by the expensive and rare nature of its ingredients. On the mysterious efficacy of the otherwise "unattainable," see Marcus Milwright, "The Balsam of Ma ariyya: An Exploration of a Medieval Panacea," *Bulletin of the School of Oriental and African Studies* 66:2 (2003), 193–209.

35. Nockels Fabbri, "Treating Medieval Plague," 254.

36. The human soul prevented transformation between species, however. See Chapter Six below.

37. On the use of medical arguments in theological discourse, see Joseph Ziegler, "*Ut Dicunt Medici*: Medical Knowledge and Theological Debates in the Second Half of the Thirteenth Century" *Bulletin of the History of Medicine* 73:2 (1999).

38. Robert E Lewis, *De Misera condicionis humane,* Pope Innocent III, 1978, 204–06.

39. Quoted in Martha Bayless, *Sin and Filth in Medieval Culture: The Devil in the Latrine* (New York: Routledge, 2011), 119.

40. For Aquinas, "Evil was thus a necessary consequence of good, given that all sublunary

phenomena were susceptible to corruption." Stuart Clark, *Thinking With Demons*, 45. All bodies were corruptible, all bodies were created from the dust of the earth, but female bodies were particularly malleable and therefore dangerous.

41. Aristotle on the hot and cold binary: "The heat or cold is the direct cause of growth or decay.... Heat causes growth, and fits the foodstuff for alimentation; it attracts [into the organic system] that which is light [viz. the sweet], while the salt and bitter it rejects because of their heaviness. In fact, whatever effects external heat produces in external bodies, the same are produced by their internal heat in animal and vegetable organisms." (*De Sensu*, Section 1, Part 4, Section C)

42. On Aristotle and the male-female dichotomy see the *Politics*, 1:5: "Again, the male is by nature superior, and the female inferior; and the one rules, and the other is ruled; this principle, of necessity, extends to all mankind." On the biological superiority of men and the concomitant weakness of women, see Aristotle, *On the Generation of Animals*, passim. See also Lesley Dean-Jones, *Women's Bodies in Classical Greek Science* (Oxford: Oxford University Press, 1996).

43. Augustine, *Confessions* (New York: Oxford University Press, 2009).

44. This following Galen, not Aristotle, who argued that the rational faculties resided in the heart.

45. See James Bono, "Medical Spirits and the Medieval Language of Life" *Traditio*, 40, (1984), 115–6 [91–130]. See also Alcuin Blamires, "Paradox in the Medieval Gender Doctrine of Head and Body," *Medieval Theology and the Natural Body*, eds. Peter Biller and A. J. Minnis (York: York Medieval Press, 1997) 12–20.

46. Of note, angelic beings always assume a male form, yet another reflection of perfection. See Dyan Elliott "The Physiology of Rapture and Female Spirituality," *Medieval Theology and the Natural Body*, 157.

47. On this contrariety, see Stuart Clark, *Thinking with Demons*, passim.

48. Nancy Caciola, *Discerning Spirits*: women's bodies are "pierced with more holes, and are generally more porous, than men" whose bodies were "sealed and closed off in all its parts," 290.

49. See Dyan Elliott, "The Physiology of Rapture and Female Spirituality," 141–74.

50. Aquinas, *Summa Theologica*, "Whether to Tempt is Proper to the Devil," reply to objection two: "The demons know what happens outwardly among men; but the inward disposition of man God alone knows.... It is this disposition that makes man more prone to one vice than to another; hence the devil tempts in order to explore this inward disposition of man, s that he may tempt him to that vice to which he is most prone."

51. For a literal transformation of the heart-through prayer, see Katharine Park, *Secrets of Women: Gender, Generation, and the Origins of Human Dissection* (Cambridge: Zone Books/MIT Press, 2010).

52. C. H. Lawrence, *Medieval Monasticism: Forms of Religious Life in Western Europe in the Middle Ages* (London, 1984).

53. B. L. Venarde, *Women's Monasticism in Medieval Society: Nunneries in France and England (890–1215)* (Ithaca: Cornell University Press, 1997 See also Jo Ann Kay McNamara, *Sisters in Arms: Catholic Nuns Through Two Millennia* (Cambridge: Harvard University Press, 1998).

54. Fourth Lateran Council, Canon 21, "Omnis utriusque sexus."

55. See Carolyn Walker Bynum's now classic, *Holy Feast, Holy Fast: The Religious Significance of Food to Medieval Women* (Berkeley: University of California Press, 1988).

56. See Amy Hollywood, "Inside Out: Beatrice of Nazareth and Her Hagiographer," *Gendered Voices: Medieval Saints and Their Interpreters*, ed. Catherine M. Mooney (Philadelphia: University of Pennsylvania Press, 1999), 78–98.

57. On the fundamentally physical nature of the feminine, see Elizabeth Robertson, "The Corporeality of Female Sanctity in *The Life of Saint Margaret*," *Images of Sainthood in Medieval Europe*. (Ithaca: Cornell University Press, 1991), 268–287.

58. Beguines were women who took personal vows of chastity, poverty, and obedience, but were not committed to lifetime service in any given order. See Walter Simmons, *Cities of Ladies: Beguine Communities in the Medieval Low Countries: 1200–1565* (Philadelphia: University of Pennsylvania Press, 2003).

59. See also Anneke B.. Mulder-Bakker, *Marie d'Oignies: Mother of Salvation* (Turnhout: Brepols, 2006); CF: Elizabeth Petroff, "Transforming the World: The Serpent Dragon and the Virgin Saint," *Body and Soul: Essays on Medieval Women and Mysticism*, ed. E.A Petroff (Oxford: Oxford University Press, 1994), 101: "...before He dwelt in you, you were merely earth..."

60. "Her soul chose suspension, because it often flew higher for whole days at a time and she gazed on the sun of justice like an eagle, not cast back down below by the rays of the sun. All the humors of her senses were dried out by these rays and, purged from the cloud of all corporeal images and from every fantasy and imagining, she received in her soul simple and divine forms as if in a mirror." Jacques de Vitry, "Life of Marie d' Oignies," in *Two Lives of Marie d'Oignies*, trans. Margot King, eds. Margot King and Miriam Marsolais (Toronto: Peregrina Publishing, 1998), 124.

61. Jacques de Vitry, "Life of Marie d'Oignies," 54.

62. Vitry, 65.

63. Vitry, 134, 64. "The holy bread strengthened her heart; the holy wine inebriated her mind, filling it with rejoicing; the holy Body made her fat and the life-giving blood washed and purified her." 135

64. *Ibid.* 79.

65. *Ibid.* 65, 118, 98.

66. "Twice it happened to her while she was ill that as she was receiving the body of Christ, her face shone as if with rays of light." Vitry, 105;

"Her face did not appear pallid or blue after death, as usual," but was "bright and clear." Vitry, 153; On Marie's ability to repel and command demons, 72-73.

67. *Thomas Cantimpré: The Collected Saints' Lives*, ed. Barbara Newman, trans. Margot King and Barbara Newman (Turnhout: Brepols, 2008), 3.

68. Christ "gave her the grace of an inward sweetness and very often visited her with heavenly secrets." Cantimpré, "Life of Christina the Astonishing," in *The Collected Saints' Lives*, 129.

69. Cantimpré, 130.
70. Cantimpré, 132.
71. *Ibid.*, 136.
72. *Ibid.*, 133. For another thirteenth-century female saint whose body was on fire with the divine, see Amy Hollywood, "Inside Out: Beatrice of Nazareth and Her Hagiographer," 89: "Her heart, deprived of strength by this invasion gave off a sound like a shattering vessel ... also the blood diffused through her bodily members boiled over through her open veins.... Holy longing and love blazed up as a fire in all of her bodily members, making her perceptibly (*sensabiliter*) hot in a wondrous way."

73. Cantimpré, 136.
74. "Life of Lutgard of Aywiéres," 224.
75. Cantimpré, 231, 228, on driving out demons 248.
76. *Ibid.*, 255-56. On the inability of the weak female heart to contain the Love of Christ, see Nancy Caciola, *Discerning Spirits: Divine and Demonic Possession in the Middle Ages* (Ithaca: Cornell University Press, 2003), 212.
77. Cantimpré, 256.
78. See Alcuin Blamires, "Paradox in the Medieval Gender Doctrine of Head and Body," *Medieval Theology and the Natural Body*, eds. Peter Biller and Alastair Minnis (London: Boydell and Brewer, 1997), 13-29.
79. Cantimpré, 248.
80. John Coakley, "Friars as Confidants of Holy women in Medieval Dominican Hagiography *The Life of Saint Margaret*," *Images of Sainthood in Medieval Europe*. (Ithaca: Cornell University Press, 1991), 229.
81. Coakley, "Friars as Confidants," 231.
82. *Ibid.* On the authority of mystical woman, see Barbara Newman, "Hildegard of Bingen, Visions and Validation," *Church History* 54:2, 1985.
83. Jacques de Vitry, *Sermones ad Status*, in *The Faces of Women in the Sermons of Jacques de Vitry*, trans. Carolyn Muessig, (Toronto: Peregrina Publishing, 1999), 92. See also Albert the Great, *Quaestiones super de animalibus*: "A woman is nothing but a devil fashioned into a human appearance.... For a woman is a flawed male and, in comparison to the male, has the nature of defect and privation, and this is why naturally she mistrusts herself. And this is why whatever she cannot acquire on her own she strives to acquire through mendacity and diabolical deceptions ... one must be as mistrustful of every woman as of a venomous serpent and a horned devil." Quoted in Irven M. Resnick, *Marks of Distinction: Christian Perceptions of Jews in the High Middle Ages* (Washington, D.C.: Catholic University of America Press, 2012), 26.

84. Jacques de Vitry, *Sermones Feriales et Communes 18.4* in *The Faces of Women in the Sermons of Jacques de Vitry*, trans. Carolyn Muessig, (Toronto: Peregrina Publishing, 1999), 25.

85. Jacques de Vitry, *Sermones de Sanctis 3.4*, 66.

86. See Sarah Alison Miller, *Medieval Monstrosity and the Female Body* (New York: Routledge, 2010), 53-90.

87. *Isidore of Seville: The Medical Writings*, 48. See also Rabanus Maurus *De Universo* 6:1 (*PL* 111: 174 B) "From the mere contact with menstrual blood crops will not germinate, new wine sours, plants die, trees lose their fruit. It causes iron to rust and tarnishes bronze. If dogs lap it up they become rabid." See also Sharon Faye Koren, "The Menstruant as 'Other' in Medieval Judaism and Christianity," NASHIM (2009), 41-42. For medical perspectives on women's bodies, see Monica Green, *The Trotula: A Medieval Compendium of Women's Medicine* (Philadelphia: University of Pennsylvania Press, 2002).

88. Michael Scotus, "De Menstruis Mulierum," *Tractatis de Secretis Naturae*, 27: "Quoniam mulieres non habent in se tantum calorem innatum: quae malos humores in eis abundantes..."

89. Jacques de Vitry, *Sermones Feriales et Communes 25.2*, 30-31.

90. Helen Rodnite Lemay, *A Translation of Pseudo Albertus Magnus' De Secretis Mulierum with Commentaries* (Albany, NY: SUNY University Press, 1992), 88-89: "Because the penis is a porous and thin member which quickly absorbs this matter; and because all veins come together there, it is quickly dispersed through the body." CF: 131.

91. *De Secretis*, 131.
92. "Do not go near a menstruating woman, because from this foulness the air is corrupted, and the insides of a man are brought to disorder."
93. *De Secretis*, 128.
94. See Mark A. Smith's critical translation, *Alhacen's Theory of Visual Perception* (Philadelphia: Transactions of the American Philosophical Society, 2001).
95. *De Secretis*, 129: "This is caused in menstruating women by the flow itself, for the humors first infect the eyes, then the eyes infect they air, which infects the child."
96. *De Secretis*, 131.
97. *Ibid.*, 96.
98. *Ibid.*, 131.
99. *Ibid.*, 131.
100. Caciola, *Discerning Spirits*, 198.
101. *De Secretis*, 127: "The more women have sexual intercourse, the stronger they become, because they are made hot by the motion that the man makes during coitus. Further, male sperm is hot because it is of the same nature as air and

when it is received by the woman it warms her entire body, so women are strengthened by this heat."

102. Thomas Aquinas, *Quodlibeta*, Q2:A8. CF: *Malleus Maleficarum*, 124–25: "All angels, good and bad, by their natural power, which is superior to all bodily power, are able to transmute our bodies ... although to enter the soul is possible only to God who created it, yet devils can, with God's permission, enter our bodies."

103. Caciola, *Discerning Spirits*, 218.

104. For a young boy who became possessed by staring into the eyes of a dead cat, see Caciola, 42.

105. Caciola, *Discerning Spirits*, 47.

106. See Martha Bayless, *Sin and Filth in Medieval Culture: The Devil in the Latrine* London: Routledge, 2011).

107. Jean Bodin recounts the possession of several Italian women who had recently converted from Judaism to Christianity in 1554: "The Jews sent them [the devils] into the bodies of these women ... the demoniacs spoke various languages that they had never learned. And sometimes the evil spirit speaks as from within the stomach, when the woman's mouth is closed, sometimes with the tongue stretch half a foot out of the mouth, sometimes through the shameful parts." *On the Demonmania of Witches, On the Demonmania of Witches* (1580), trans. Randy A. Scott (Toronto: Centre for Reformation and Renaissance Studies, 1995), 109.

108. Caciola, *Discerning Spirits*, 41–47.

109. See Gordon Leff, "The Fourteenth Century and the Decline of Scholasticism," in *Heresy, Philosophy, and Religion in the Medieval West* (Burlington, VT: Ashgate Press, 2002).

110. For general patterns, see Donald Weinstein and Rudolph M. Bell, *Saints and Society: The Two Worlds of Western Christendom, 1000–1700* (Chicago: University of Chicago Press, 1986); see also Andre Vauchéz, *Sainthood in the Later Middle Ages* (Cambridge: Cambridge University Press, 1997); Michael Goodich, "The Contours of Female Piety in Later Medieval Hagiography," *Church History* 50:1 (1981), 20–32.

111. "Demoniacs, as well as mystics, were reported to levitate, bloat, prophesy, speak in tongues, enter immobile trance states, acquire unusual bodily marks, perform miracles, and so forth. We can, then, legitimately speak of two kinds of spirit possession existing in the Middle Ages-one malign and one benign-that were outwardly indistinguishable from one another." Nancy Caciola, "Mystics, Demoniacs, and the Physiology of Spirit Possession in Medieval Europe," *Comparative Studies in Society and History*, 42:2 (2000), 268–306 [here, 272].

112. On this transition, see Rudolph M. Bell, *Holy Anorexia* (Chicago: University of Chicago, 1987), 150–1.

113. Dyan Elliott, *The Bride of Christ Goes to Hell* (Philadelphia: University of Pennsylvania Press, 2012).

114. "Women are naturally more impressionable, and more ready to receive the influence of a disembodied sprit; and that when they use this quality well they are very good, but when they use it ill they are very evil.... Since they are feebler both in mind and body, it is not surprising that they should come more under the spell of witchcraft" *Malleus*, 44.

115. See Hans Peter Broedel, *The Malleus Maleficarum and the Construction of Witchcraft Theology and Popular Belief* (Manchester: Manchester University Press, 2003). On Kramer as hagiographer, see Tamar Herzig, "Witches, Saints, and Heretics: Heinrich Kramer's Ties with Italian Women Mystics," *Magic, Ritual, and Witchcraft* (2006), 25–51.

116. See Dyan Elliott, *The Bride of Christ Goes to Hell* (Philadelphia: University of Pennsylvania Press, 2012).

117. *Malleus*, 21.

118. "As late as 1631 ... Gaspar Navarro published his *Tribunal de la Supersticion Ladina*, in which he explicitly accepted the reality of diabolical pacts, *maleficia*, and the witches' Sabbath and called for the exemplary punishment of witches. The work frequently quoted from the famous *Malleus Maleficarum* in support of its arguments..." Stephen Haliczer, "The Jew as Witch: Displaced Aggression and the Myth of the Santo Niño de La Guardia" in *New Perspectives on Witchcraft, Magic, and Demonology: Witchcraft in Continental Europe*, ed. Brian P. Levack (New York: Routledge, 2001), [265] 264–274.

119. Despite the efforts of men like Paracelsus and John Harvey, the successful questioning and rejection of medieval medical authority in Western medicine would not be complete until the nineteenth century and the advent of germ theory. Variants on basic humoral/balance theory remain vital components of healing practices in various traditions around the world, from Traditional Chinese Medicine and Ayurveda to the hot-cold systems of Latin America and the Caribbean.

120. *Malleus*, 146.

121. *Malleus*, 18. The evil-eye remained a salient feature of witchcraft treatises, even those that were skeptical of its mechanisms of action; Henry Boguet's *Examen of Witches* (1602), for example, argues that if witches' eyes are poisonous, their power to cause harm comes directly from the Devil, "For in such cases it is Satan who secretly causes death or casts the evil spell" (80).

122. See discussion of the *De Secretis Mulierum* above; n. 96. For discourse on the history of the evil eye, see Leonard W. Moss and Stephen C. Cappannari, "Mal'occhio Ayin ha ra, Oculus fascinus, Judenblick: The Evil Eye Hovers Above," *The Evil Eye*, ed. Clarence Maloney (New York: Columbia University Press, 1976) 1–15.

123. The *Malleus* follows Saint Bernard in arguing that the voice of women was "like a burning wind, and their voice a hissing of serpents," a reference to the serpentine seduction of women and their propensity to lie, much like the Devil himself. Noxious fumes might also escape

through their ears. See Nancy Caciola, *Discerning Spirits*, 188.
124. *Malleus*, 137.
125. *Ibid.*
126. Hippocrates, *Airs, Waters, Places*, Book 3.
127. Nicholas Remy, *Demonolatry*, trans. Montague Summers (New York: Dover, 2008), 116.
128. Francesca Maria Guazzo, *Compendium Maleficarum*, trans. Montague Summers (New York: Dover, 1988), 39.
129. Freccero, "Sign of Satan," *MLN*, Vol. 80, No. 1, Italian Issue (Jan., 1965), 18
130. Remy, *Demonolatry*, 3.
131. Bodin, *On the Demonmania of Witches*, 116-7.
132. Remy, *Demonolatry*, 104; the sulfuric-flamed candle is a signifier for hellish evil because of its foul smell, which is linked to the bowels of the earth as well as the bowels of the body.
133. Remy, *Demonolatry*, 6; Guazzo, 91; *Matthew*: 5. See also Guazzo, 100: "At once there appeared a demon in the form of a cat, who told her to pound a slug's head to powder and sprinkle it over Barbara's clothes ... she therefore blew the powder over her and the cattle that were with her and they all at once died."
134. "But it must be known that before they go to the Sabbath, they anoint themselves upon some part of their bodies with an unguent made of various foul and filthy ingredients, but chiefly from murdered children." Guazzo, 34. On ointments, "most are made from the fat of small children killed by the female witches on account of Satan." Pierre de Lancre, *On the Inconstancy of Witches*, , trans. Joseph O'Connor et al. (Tempe: ACMRS Publications, 2006), 139.
135. On poisons, see Frederick W. Gibbs, "Specific Form and Poisonous Properties: Understanding Poison in the Fifteenth Century." *Preternature: Critical and Historical Studies on the Preternatural* 2:1 (2013), 19-46; for an example of a poison maiden, see Nathanial Hawthorne's *Rappaccini's Daughter*.
136. "And as touching air and water, what may be more easily corrupted than those elements shall neither be wholesome nor profitable to any, rather pestiferous and hurtful.... And look by what means the water may be corrupted, by the same also may be the air, because that filthy savour is dispersed and spread abroad through them both." (Note that these are environmental air and water, not pure elementals.) Quoted in *The Witchcraft Sourcebook*, ed. Brain P. Levack (New York: Routledge, 2004), 74-5. See also Oliver Fatio, "Lambert Daneau: 1530-1595" *The Literature of Witchcraft: Articles on Witchcraft, Magic, and Demonology*, ed. Brian P. Levack (New York: Routledge, 1992), 69-83.
137. *Ibid.*
138. Boguet, 72.
139. All melancholic monsters will become disease vectors: vampires of the plague and werewolves of lycanthropy; this can be traced back to the infectious nature of heresy. CF: Jean Bodin, *Demonmania*, witches as a "vermin" that has "always multiplied," 113. See also Lucinda Cole, "Of Mice and Moisture: Rats, Witches, Miasma, and Early Modern Theories of Contagion," *The Journal of Early Modern Cultural Studies* 10:2, (2010), 65-84.
140. *Malleus*, 66.
141. The witch Walpurgis (!) taught other women to maintain inhuman silence by "cooking their first-born sons in an oven." *Malleus*, 102.
142. The worst class of witches "are in the habit of eating and devouring the children of their own species.... But these are only the children who have not been re-born by baptism at the font, for they cannot devour those who have been baptized, nor any without God's permission." *Malleus*, 99; "Then we secretly take them from their graves, and cook them in a cauldron, until the whole flesh comes away from the bones to make a soup which may be easily drunk." *Malleus*, 101.
143. Remy, 115.
144. Of the more solid matter we make an unguent which is of virtue to help us in our arts and pleasures and our transportations. And with the liquid we fill a flask or skin, whoever drinks from which, with the addition of a few other ceremonies, immediately acquires much knowledge and becomes a leader in our sect." *Malleus*, 101.
145. Article on midwives and witches; "She had opened a secret pot and found the heads of a great many children..." *Malleus* 100
146. Bodin, 210-11
147. Marsilio Ficino would remark that witches "suck the blood of infants and children and become rejuvenated from it." Quoted in Charlotte Wells, Leeches on the Body Politic: Xenophobia and Witchcraft in Early Modern French Political Thought" *French Historical Studies*, 22:3 (1999), 355.
148. On the ritual baptism of the witches' offspring, see de Lancre, 153: "they are accustomed to having their children baptized at the Sabbath rather than at church, and they present them to the Devil rather than God."
149. *Malleus* 153
150. Also because of their fundamentally carnal nature, for a woman is "more carnal than a man, as is clear from her many carnal abominations." Malleus 44.
151. *Malleus* P1: Q3 (24) CF: Remy, "the rabble of witches is chiefly composed of that sex, which, owing to its feebleness of understanding, is least able to resist and withstand the wiles of the Devil" (90).
152. "All witchcraft comes from carnal lust, which is in women insatiable ... the mouth of the womb (never satisfied) ... for the sake of fulfilling their lusts they consort with even the devils." *Malleus* 47; On the dog, see Boguet, 32.
153. *Malleus*, 47
154. *Malleus* 97
155. *Malleus* 99, 109. Demons were often visible to witches during sex but invisible to others;

in one case, a man went into the woods and saw naked women with their legs in the air and a "very black vapour, of about the stature of a man" which rose up after orgasm.

156. Authors of witchcraft treatises repeatedly confirmed medieval arguments against demonic reproduction, save by the transferal of human semen. While theologically impossible (demons are too cold to give life, do not have truly physical bodies, and therefore cannot produce their own semen or reproduce their own kind), witchcraft treatises often contain references to monstrous births, which are stifled by complicit midwives, or even the birth of changelings, both of which speak to the folkloric roots of the witchcraft paradigm. On changelings, or Vechselkind, see Bodin, 132: these mysterious infants are "heavier than others, but always thin."

157. *Malleus*, 113. "But the reason that devils turn themselves into Incubi or Succubi is not for the cause of pleasure, since a spirit has not flesh and blood; but chiefly it is with this intention, that through the vice of luxury they may work a twofold harm against men, that is, in body and in soul, that so men may be more given to all vices. And there is no doubt that they know under which stars the semen is most vigorous, and that men so conceived will be always perverted by witchcraft." *Malleus*, 25. On unpleasant coitus, not only is demonic seed frigid and horrifying, but the demonic member is enormous: "All female witches maintain that the so-called genital organs of their Demons are so huge and so excessively rigid that they cannot be admitted without the greatest pain." Remy, 13–14 The devil's penis was particularly disgusting, for it was "covered with scales that are like a poison; they tighten up as the Devil enters her and they lift up and pinch her as his organ is withdrawn." It is "about as long a half of an alder bush, of modest size, red, dark and twisted, very stiff and pointy at the tip." de Lancre, 239.

158. See Dyan Elliott, "The Physiology of Rapture," 141

159. *Malleus* 26; CF: Aquinas, "For the Devil tempts us according to the vice to which we are most prone."

160. *Malleus* 91

161. "The hag turned angrily upon me and said, "Curse you! Why did you cross yourself?" *Malleus*, 97.

162. *Malleus* 46
163. *Malleus*, 55.
164. *Malleus*, 98
165. *Malleus*, 58.

166. *Malleus*, 121. For more on the nest of penises motif and its potential significance, see Moira Smith, "The Flying Phallus and the Laughing Inquisitor: Penis Theft in the Malleus Maleficarum," *Journal of Folklore Research* 39:1 (2002), 85–117.

167. See Catherine Rider, *Magic and Impotence in the Middle Ages* (New York: Oxford, 2006).

168. Witches become cold and rigid during their night flight and "witches contract and can retain for some time this sort of frigidity from their contact with Demons" Remy, 11.

169. For one such hag, see Guazzo, 48–9.

170. For the leaky nature of the transgressive body, see Margrit Shildrick, *Leaky Bodies and Boundaries: Feminism, Postmodernism, and Bioethics* (London: Routledge, 1997).

171. Boguet, 64.

172. On toads and their strange relationship with witches, see Lancre, 153.

Chapter 4

1. Shakespeare, *Macbeth*, 4:1, 14–15.

2. See *Thomas of Cantimpré: The Collected Saints' Lives*, ed. Barbara Newman and Margot King (Turnhout: Brepols, 2008).

3. See Nancy Caciola, *Discerning Spirits: Divine and Demonic Possession in the Middle Ages* (Ithaca: Cornell University Press, 2006).

4. Laura Mulvey, "Visual Pleasure and Narrative Cinema," *Screen* 16:3 (1975) 6–18.

5. For a mother, daughter, demon ménage-a-trois, see Nicolas Remy, *Demonolatry*, 93.

6. For a broad discussion of Catholicism and Horror, see *Roman Catholicism and the Horror Film: Essays on Belief, Spectacle, Ritual, and Imagery*, ed. Regina Hansen (Jefferson, NC: McFarland Press, 2011).

7. For Foucault on deep structures and the architecture of power, see *The Archaeology of Knowledge* (New York: Vintage, 1982); for "othering," see *The Birth of the Clinic: An Archaeology of Medical Perception* (New York: Vintage, 1994).

8. Carol Clover, *Men, Women, and Chainsaws: Gender in the Modern Horror Film* (Princeton, NJ: Princeton University Press, 2011). Barbara Creed, *Phallic Panic: Film, Horror, and the Primal Uncanny* (Melbourne: Melbourne University Press, 2005).

9. Julia Kristeva, *The Powers of Horror: An Essay on Abjection* (New York: Columbia University Press, 1982).

10. On viewer as voyeur and perpetrator, see Laura Mulvey, "Scopophilia"; on penetration by the male gaze, see Brenda Gardenour Walter, "Thrust and Probe: The Physician's Phallic Blade" in *Sensational Pleasures in Cinema, Literature, and Visual Culture: The Phallic Eye*, eds. Gilad Padva and Nurit Buchweitz (London: Palgrave MacMillan, 2014).

11. Frank L. Baum, *The Wonderful Wizard of Oz* (Chicago: George M. Hill Co., 1900).

12. See Chapter Five on Vampires, below.

13. Frank L. Baum, *The Wonderful Wizard of Oz*, Chapter 12, "The Search for the Wicked Witch.

14. See Deborah Harkness, *John Dee's Conversations with Angels: Cabala, Alchemy, and the End of Nature* (Cambridge: Cambridge University Press, 2006).

15. In medieval sources, the direction of West was associated with the season of autumn

and melancholia. See Resnick, *Marks of Distinction*, 21.

16. Valerie Solanas, *SCUM Manifesto* (London: Verso Press, 2004).

17. The fear that the middle class family fortress might be penetrated by outside forces is a salient theme in horror films founded on techno-fear. See Brenda Gardenour Walter, "Ghastly Transmissions: The Horror of Connectivity and the Transnational Flow of Fear," in *Horror across Visual Media: Fragmented Bodies*, ed. Dana Och (London: Routledge, Taylor and Francis, 2013).

18. As a genre, the Nunsploitation film preexisted *The Exorcist*, for example, Ken Russell's masterful *The Devils* (1971); for possession-exploitation before the *Exorcist*, see *Mark of the Devil* (1970). After *The Exorcist*, demon possession became a central theme in the Nunsploitation genre. See also Maureen A. Sabine, *Veiled Desires: Intimate Portrayals of Nuns in Postwar Anglo-American Film* (New York: Fordham University Press, 2013).

19. For the link between witches, cold air, tempests, and clouds, see Brenda Gardenour Walter, "Corrupt Air, Poisonous Places, and the Toxic Breath of Witches in Late-Medieval Medicine and Theology" in *Toxic Airs: Body, Place, Planet in Historical Perspective*, eds. Jim Fleming and Ann Johnson (Pittsburgh: University of Pittsburgh Press, 2013).

20. "For in these also the devils can stir up and excite the inner perceptions and humors, so that ideas retained in the repositories of their minds are drawn out and made apparent to the faculties of fancy and imagination." *Malleus*, 50.

21. Bianca likewise has a Tibetan servant, named Ahmet, who once belonged to "an ancient cult of worshippers who believed that sacrifice brought immortality." This speaks not only to the conflation of "non-Christian" religions into a unified evil "other," but also to Western "Orientalism."

22. This rhetorical device extends back to the Roman accusations of cannibalism. See David Frankfurter, *Evil Incarnate: Rumors of Demonic Conspiracy and Satanic Abuse in History* (Princeton: Princeton University Press, 2006).

23. The film's tagline reads STILL ALIVE! THE ANICENT CULT OF VOODOO AS IT IS PRACTICED TODAY!

24. For the use of wax effigies in European witchcraft, see the *Malleus Maleficarum*, 127; 135.

25. See also Carol L. Fry, *Cinema of the Occult: New Age, Satanism, Wicca, and Spiritualism in Film* (Cranbury, NJ: Rosemont Publishing, 2008), 245–51.

26. W. Scott Poole, *Satan in America: The Devil We Know* (New York: Rowman and Littlefield, 2010).

27. For more on the role of electric impulses in paranormal research, see R. J. Noakes, "Cromwell Varley FRS, Electrical Discharge, and Victorian Spiritualism," *Notes and Records of the Royal Society* 61:1 (January, 2007), 5–21, and Sheri Weinstein, "Technologies of Vision: Spiritualism and Science in Nineteenth-Century America," *Spectral America: Phantoms and the National Imaginary*, ed. J. A. Weinstock (Madison: University of Wisconsin Press, 2004), 124–140.

28. Candlemas appears as a date for the Witch's Sabbath in part because of its association with the Pagan holiday of Imbolc. CF: *City of the Dead* (1960); *Black Sunday* (1960), *Malleus Maleficarum*, 102.

29. Daughters were believed to be brought into witchcraft by their mothers and other relatives. For a mother who gave her daughter to the Devil sexually and the participated in a ménage-à-trois, see, see Remy, *Demonolatry*, 93. See also Jean Bodin: "As for the sexual activity she [Jeanette d'Abadie] said that she saw everyone mix together incestuously and against all laws of nature ... admitting to having been deflowered by Satan and of having been known countless times by one of her relatives and by others who dared to ask her to have sex with them." *On the Demonmania of Witches* (154). See also Pierre de Lancre, who states that witches "are accustomed to having their children baptized at the Sabbath rather than at church, and they present them to the Devil rather than God." *On the Inconstancy of Witches*, 153.

30. On the character of the evil doctor in horror cinema, see Brenda Gardenour Walter, "Thrust and Probe: The Physician's Phallic Blade."

31. The name is a reference to Dame Alice Kyteler, the first woman condemned as a witch in Ireland (early fourteenth century). See Anne Neary, "The Origins and Character of the Kilkenny Witchcraft Case of 1324," *Proceedings of the Royal Irish Academy* (1983), 333–350.

32. In this scene, she is crowded in by a pack of ravenous and grasping Satanic elders—a clear quotation from *Rosemary's Baby* (1968).

33. Of note, the Ankh also appears as a Satanic symbol in both *The Brotherhood of Satan* and *The Witchmaker*.

34. Grimoires in general, and the Clavicle of Solomon in particular, are recurring motifs in supernatural horror, from Hammer Horror's *The Devil Rides Out* to Sam Raimi's *Evil Dead* (1981, 2013).

35. Thus, Lilith's womb, like her biblical and Midrashic counterpart, produces only melancholic and earth bound demons.

36. For midwives in the *Malleus Maleficarum*, see Hans Peter Broedel, *The Malleus Maleficarum and the Construction of Witchcraft: Theology and Popular Belief*. (Manchester University Press, Manchester, 2003).

37. Cato's cult, like so many others we have seen, conforms to medieval paradigms in its use of the color black, the subterranean chamber, orgiastic sex, human sacrifice, the consumption of blood, the use of doll-like effigies to cause physical changes in others, the wearing of monastic robes, the use of the goat motif and the pentagram, and the swearing of a pact to "The Prince of Darkness."

38. See Moira Smith, "The Flying Phallus and the Laughing Inquisitor: Penis Theft in the *Malleus Maleficarum*," *Journal of Folklore Research* 39:1 (2002), 85–117.

39. The construction of indigenous men as foolish and irrational reflects the unfortunate persistence of nineteenth-century racial theories that non-whites are non-perfect, non-rational, and non-evolved. See Christine Bolt, *Victorian Attitudes Toward Race* (London: Routledge, 2013); Robert J. C. Young, *Colonial Desire: Hybridity in Theory, Culture, and Race* (London: Routledge, 2005).

40. These are perhaps meant to represent Hands of Glory, which date in writing back to the Nicolas Remy's *Demonolatry* (1595) and the *Compendium Maleficarum* of Francesco Maria Guazzo (1608). The Hand of Glory was a candle made from the left hand of a man executed for murder; when lit, it reputedly opened every door and disabled those who saw it from any movement. See *The Wicker Man* (1973).

41. For the long history of the problematic elite magic vs. common witchcraft binary, see Richard Kieckhefer, *Magic in the Middle Ages*, (Cambridge: Cambridge University Press, 1990).

42. This seems, once again, to be a reference to Voodoo as it exists in the Anglo-American imagination.

43. Like Margaret Murray's *The Witch Cult in Western Europe* (Oxford: Clarendon Press, 1921), *Cry of the Banshee* suggests that witches were simply innocent pagans, earth children who only became evil through the agency of Christian authority.

44. This penetration by flying witch-women is not only a reference to the *Malleus Maleficarum* and the late-medieval witchcraft tradition, but also suggests that witches can cause plague on their night rides; from a post-modernist perspective, it also suggests that they can violently penetrate men against their will, which suggests Kristevan abjection and *jouissance*.

45. "We went to Scotland to research about witches, to put something in it that was maybe different. We met actual witches, you know ... Chris' idea was to make good witches and bad witches, which they are, and they're all related to the old religion, the religion of the druids who came before Christianity." Gordon Hessler interview posted at https://www.youtube.com/watch?v=LiHsmPeAIgY.

46. The name of the coven is a reflection, perhaps, of the aggressive invasion of the once-Catholic Philippines by protestant denominations from the mid-twentieth century forward.

47. George Romero has commented that this is one of his favorite films and would be the one he would most like to remake. http://www.youtube.com/watch?v=0M1OXDWVBlE

48. The use of Autumn in the film is a reference to the chilling season of Halloween and the coming of deathly winter as well as a metaphor for middle age—the autumn of life soon to be replaced by the younger generation in Spring.

49. The scene is a series of cross cuts between Joan, who is touching herself, and a statue of a bull, his horns reminiscent of early fertility cults, ancient pagan practices, and the orgiastic devil of Satanic worship.

50. See Valerie Solanas' *SCUM Manifesto*.

51. For conspiracy theories surrounding the Freemasons, see Michael Barkun, *A Culture of Conspiracy: Apocalyptic Visions in Contemporary America* (Berkeley: University of California Press, 2003). (CF: Matthew Barney, *Cremaster 3*, 2002).

52. On penis theft and endangerment, see Moira Smith, "The Flying Phallus and the Laughing Inquisitor." See also Catherine Rider, *Magic and Impotence in the Middle Ages* (New York: Oxford, 2006).

53. On the idea of cryptonomy, see David Punter, "Spectral Criticism" in *Introducing Criticism at the 21st Century*, Julian Woffreys, ed. (Edinburgh: Edinburgh University Press, 2002).

54. In additions to Freud's *Unheimliche* see Julia Kristeva, *Powers of Horror: An Essay on Abjection* (New York: Columbia University Press, 1982); see also the work of Jacques Lacan on the uncanny, including his *Seminar VI* accessible on line at: http://lacan.com/seminars2.htm

55. This scene combines the image of the murderous midwife-witch, the male fear of emasculation and the myth of the *vagina dentata* with a fear of nascent technology—that of the microwave. On *vagina dentata*, see Sheena J. Vachhani, "Vagina Dentata and the Demonological Body: Explorations of the Feminine Demon in Organization," *Bits of Organization* (Copenhagen: Copenhagen Business School Press, 2009), 163–183; see also Jill Raitt, "The Vagina Dentata and the Immaculatus Uterus Dvini Fontis," *Journal of the American Academy of Religion* 48:3 (1980), 415–31.

56. Another film in which the witch past returns to haunt the present is *Witchery* (1988) which tells the tale of a haunted hotel on an island in Boston Harbor. Once again, male Puritan fathers have failed to destroy feminine evil; while the witch's body is slain, her evil spirit continues to stalk the earth to which it is bound forever. In this film, the witch appears as the ghost of a movie star who moved to the island so that no one would see her grow old; she often manifests as an old woman with grey hair, pallid skin, and red lipstick who wears a black dress, lace gloves, and a diamond pin that flashes a "witch light." Several people become trapped in the old hotel, unable to leave the island because of yet another witchy tempest. Through a haze of infant sacrifice, rape, and demonic insemination, the witch is ultimately born again. It's hard to keep an evil witch down.

57. *Roger Corman: Interviews*, ed. Constantine Nasr (Jackson: University of Mississippi Press, 2011), 21.

58. Likewise her husband writes in his diary, "I cannot look into her eyes without feeling that I am falling into an abyss."

59. For a much earlier film with similar themes, including sexploitation, see *The Naked Witch* (1964).
60. For a discussion of the ambivalent meanings of witchcraft here, see Julie D. O'Reilly, *Bewitched Again" Supernaturally Powerful Women on Television, 1996-2011* (Jefferson, NC: McFarland, 2013).

Chapter 5

1. See Paul Barber, *Vampires, Burial, and Death: Folklore and Reality* (New Have: Yale University Press, 1988); also, G. David Keyworth, "Was the Vampire of the Eighteenth Century a Unique Type of Undead Corpse?" *Folklore*, 117:3 (2006), 241-60.
2. On alterity, see Emmanuel Levinas, *Alterity and Transcendence*, trans. Michael B. Smith (New York: Columbia University Press, 2000).
3. On the didactic purposes of the hermeneutic Jew, see Jeremy Cohen, *Living Letters of the Law: Ideas of the Jew in Medieval Christianity* (Berkeley: University of California Press, 1999).
4. Irven M. Resnick, "Medieval Roots of the Myth of the Jewish Male Menses," *Harvard Theological Review* (2000), 241-63.
5. On ritual murder accusations, see Miri Rubin, *Gentile Tales: The Narrative Assault on Late Medieval Jews* (Philadelphia: University of Pennsylvania Press, 1999).
6. Irven M. Resnick, *Marks of Distinction: Christian Perceptions of Jews in the High Middle Ages* (Washington, D.C.: Catholic University of America Press, 2012).
7. See Margrit Shildrick, *Leaky Bodies and Boundaries: Feminism, Postmodernism, and Bioethics* (London: Routledge, 1997). See also Sarah Alison Miller, *Medieval Monstrosity and the Female Body* (New York: Routledge, 2010).
8. On revenants, see Nancy Caciola, "Wraiths, Revenants, and Ritual in Medieval Culture," *Past and Present* 152 (1996), 3-45.
9. See Willis Martin, "'The Invisible Giant,' Dracula, and Disease." *Studies in the Novel* 39.3(2007), 301-25.
10. Mary Douglas, *Purity and Danger* (New York: Routledge, 1966).
11. For example, Talia Schaffer, "A Wilde Desire Took Me: The Homoerotic History of Dracula." *ELH* 61:2 1994), 381-425.
12. Luke Demaitre, *Leprosy in Pre-Modern Medicine* (Baltimore: Johns Hopkins Press, 2007).
13. Avicenna, "On Melancholy," *Qanun*. "... lean persons with a darker complexion, much hair an large veins are more apt to produce this type of humor (atrabile)." Galen quoted in Jennifer Radden, *The Nature of Melancholy: From Aristotle to Kristeva* (Oxford: Oxford University Press, 2002). *Lepra* is not to be confused with the modern diagnosis of Hansen's Disease; while there may be overlap, the conditions that fell within the category of *lepra* had multiple meanings unique to the medieval milieu.
14. François Azouvi, "The Plague, Melancholy, and the Devil" *Diogenes* 27 (1979), 117.
15. See Arnaldi de Villanova, *Opera Medica Omnia—de Esu Carnium, Vol. XI*, ed. Dianne M. Bazell (Barcelona: University of Barcelona Press, 1999).
16. "Also heavy and dark wine is very much included to produce an atrabilious humor .." Galen in Radden, *The Nature of Melancholy*, 65.
17. Radden, 67.
18. In the *Qanun*, Avicenna suggests that these individuals were particularly susceptible to "demonic influences and similar manias." See Radden, 78.
19. Azouvi, 114.
20. For these relationships, see Ed Grant, *The Nature of Natural Philosophy* (Washington, D.C.: Catholic University of America Press, 2010).
21. See Azouvi; see also Lucinda Cole, "Of Mice and Moisture: Rats, Witches, Miasma, and Early Modern Theories of Contagion," *The Journal for Early Modern Cultural Studies* 10:2 (2010).
22. On universals, see John Marenbon, *Later Medieval Philosophy1150-1350* (London: Routledge, 2002).
23. "The satanic hovers low and abuses the mind." Pierre de Lancre, *On the Inconstancy of Witches*, 281. This drawn from Aquinas and Auvergne.
24. Boureau, Alain. *Satan the Heretic: The Birth of Demonology in the Medieval West* (Chicago: University of Chicago, 2006).
25. .For an overview, see R. I. Moore, *The Formation of a Persecuting Society, Second Edition* (Oxford: Blackwell, 2007) and David Nirenberg, *Communities of Violence: Persecution of Minorities in the Middle Ages* (Princeton: Princeton University Press, 1998).
26. Donald Prudlho, *The Martyred Inquisitor: The Life and Cult of Peter of Verona* (Burlington: Ashgate Publishing, 2008).
27. For the Christian trope of the Jewish child who converts through Mary's love, "a maternal bosom only the perverse would reject or deny," see Miri Rubin, *Gentile Tales*, 8, 28.
28. Robert Chazan, *European Jewry and the First Crusade* (Berkeley: University of California Press, 1987).
29. Israel Yuval, "Vengeance and Damnation, Blood and Defamation: From Jewish Martyrdom to Blood Libel Accusations," *Zion* 58 (1993), 33-90.
30. Fourth Lateran Council, Canons 67-70. On regional variations for the Jewish code, see Benjamin Ravid, "From Yellow to Red: On the Distinguishing Head-Covering of the Jews of Venice," *Jewish History* 6 (1992), 179-210.
31. Fourth Lateran Council, Canon 1.
32. See Joseph Goering, "The Invention of Transubstantiation," *Traditio* 46 (1991), 147-170.
33. See Marilyn McCord Adams, *Some Later-Medieval Theories of the Eucharist: Thomas Aquinas, Gilles of Rome, Duns Scotus, and William Ockham* (New York: Oxford, 2012).
34. Aquinas, *Summa Theologica* (*ST*), 3:75:1:1.

35. See Walter Simmons, *Cities of Ladies: Beguine Communities in the Medieval Low Countries: 1200–1565* (Philadelphia: University of Pennsylvania Press, 2003).
36. Miri Rubin, *Corpus Christi: The Eucharist in Late Medieval Culture* (Cambridge: Cambridge University Press, 1992).
37. Nancy Caciola, *Discerning Sprits*, 198.
38. See Walter Simons, *Cities of Ladies*, 69; On dolls, see Kathleen Ashley, "Cultures of Devotion," in *The Oxford Handbook of Women and Gender in Medieval Europe*, eds. Judith M. Bennett and Ruth Mazo Karras (Oxford: Oxford University Press, 2013), 516–17.
39. Rubin, *Gentile Tales*, 34.
40. Jeremey Cohen, "The Jews as the Killers of Christ in the Latin Tradition, from Augustine to the Friars," *Traditio* 39 (1983), 1–27. CF: Aquinas, *ST*, 1: 114, 5: "Yet afterwards, the demon assailed Him by instigating the Jews to kill Him." On the attack on Christian motherhood, see Denise L Despres, "Immaculate Flesh and the Social Body: Mary and the Jews," *Jewish History* 12 (1998), 47–69.
41. Rubin, *Gentile Tales*, 41.
42. See Eveline Brugger, "Between a Rock and a Hard Place: Rulers, Cities, and "Their" Jews in Austria during the Persecutions of the Fourteenth Century," *Jews in Medieval Christendom: Slay them Not*, eds. Kristine T. Utterback and Merrall L. Price (Leiden: Brill, 2013) 189–200.
43. See Geraldine Heng, "England's Dead Boys: Telling Tales of Christian-Jewish Relations Before andAfter the First European Expulsion of the Jews," *MLN* 127: 5 (2012), 54–85.
44. The tale of William of Norwich is recorded by Thomas of Monmouth in 1173; the Latin can be found in the *Acta Sanctorum, March III*, while a translation is available in A. Jessop and M. R. James, *The Life and Miracles of St. William of Norwich by Thomas of Monmouth* (Cambridge: Cambridge University Press, 1896). See also John M. McCulloh, "Jewish Ritual Murder: William of Norwich, Thomas of Monmouth, and the Early Dissemination of the Myth," *Speculum* 72 (1997), 698–740.
45. Jessop and James, *Life and Miracles*, 21.
46. While subjecting the child to the passion of Christ, the Jews were "gnashing their teeth and calling him Jesus, the false prophet." Matthew of Paris as quoted in Gillian Bennett, *Bodies: Sex, Violence, Disease, and Death in Contemporary Legend* (Jackson: University of Mississippi Press, 2005) 263–4.
47. Ibid.
48. See Denise Despres, "Cultic Anti-Judaism and Chaucer's *Litel Clergeon*," *Modern Philology* 91:4 (1994), 413–27, as well as "Mary of the Eucharist: Cultic Anti-Judaism in Fourteenth-Century English Devotional Manuscripts," *From Witness to Witchcraft: Jews and Judaism in Medieval Christian Thought*, ed. Jeremy Cohen (Wiesbaden: Harrassowitz Press, 1996), 375–401.
49. Joseph Ziegler, "Physiognomy, Science, and Proto-Racism 1200–1500," in *The Origins of Racism in the West*, ed. M. Eliav-Feldon and B. Isaac and J. Ziegler (Cambridge: Cambridge University Press, 2009), 181–99.
50. Canon 68: "Therefore, that they may not, under pretext of error of this sort, excuse themselves in the future for the excesses of such prohibited intercourse, we decree that such Jews and Saracens of both sexes in every Christian province and at all times shall be marked off in the eyes of the public from other peoples through the character of their dress."
51. Resnick, *Marks of Distinction*, 268; images of Psalter from M. Lindsay Kaplan, "Jessica's Mother: Medieval Constructions of Jewish Race and Gender in *The Merchant of Venice*," *Shakespeare Quarterly* 58 (2007), 1–30.
52. For the construction of Jews as irrational animals, see Irven M. Resnick, "Odo of Tournai and the Dehumanization of Medieval Jews: A Reexamination," *Jewish Quarterly Review* 98 (2008), 471–84.
53. Resnick, *Marks of Distinction*, 295.
54. For more on Jews as inverted Christians and demons, see Miri Rubin, *Gentile Tales*, 25.
55. "…for the most part they are melancholics. [They are melancholics] because the melancholic shuns dwelling and assembling with others and likes cut off or solitary places. However, Jews naturally withdraw themselves from society and from being connected with others, as is patent, therefore they are melancholics. Item, they are pallid; therefore they are of melancholic complexion." Peter Biller, "Views of Jews from Paris around 1300." pp. 192–93.
56. Irven Resnick, "Medieval Roots of the Myth of the Jewish Male Menses," *Harvard Theological Review* (2000), 241–63; see also David S. Katz, "Shylock's Gender: Jewish Male Menstruation in Early Modern England," *Review of English Studies* 50 (1999), 440–462.
57. On Caesarius of Heisterbach, see Willis Johnson, "The Myth of the Jewish Male Menses," *Journal of Medieval History* 24:3 (1998), 273–95. On the view that Jewish male menstruation was a punishment for the murder of Christ, see Hugh of St. Cher in Resnick, "Medieval Roots," 251. On the Christian association of Jews with excrement, see Merrall L. Price, "Medieval Antisemitism and Excremental Libel," *Jews in Medieval Christendom: Slay them Not*, ed. Kristine T. Utterback and Merrall L. Price (Leiden: Brill, 2013), 177–88.
58. Resnick, *Marks of Distinction*, 186.
59. Resnick, *Marks of Distinction*, 187.
60. Miri, *Gentile Tales*, 12.
61. For more on this, see Anna Sapir Abulafia, "Bodies in the Jewish-Christian Debate," *Framing Medieval Bodies*, ed. Sarah Kay and Miri Rubin (Manchester: Manchester University Press,1994), 123–37.
62. Resnick, *Marks of Distinction*, 181.
63. Conversion to Christianity and the resultant rebirth of the soul, however, could rejuvenate the body; warmed by Christ, the melancholic body would once again be in balance, logical, and buoyant in nature.

64. Resnick, "Medieval Myth," 253.

65. Jews are aligned with melancholic Saturn in the fifteenth century, a time when Saturn was often depicted as a Jew eating his own children. See Eric Zafran, "Saturn and the Jews," *Journal of the Warburg and Courtauld Institutes* 42 (1979), 16–27.

66. Resnick 198–9; 203

67. Christian authors argued that Jews gave off a foul odor because of melancholia, Saturnine influences, and their usurious practices which were an affront to God. See Miri Rubin, "Europe Remade," 118. See also Resnick *Marks of Distinction*, on the burning of Jews in Prague in 1389: "The city was thus purged of the Jews, and cleansed of their usurious odor," 314.

68. Albert the Great: "When the spleen is weak in drawing in melancholy from the liver, melancholic illnesses befall the body, illnesses such as black morphew, cancer, varicose veins, elephantia, leprosy, and the like." Trans. Resnick, 176, 314.

69. For primary sources detailing the effects of the Plague, see Rosemary Horrox, *The Black Death* (Manchester: Manchester University Press, 1994).

70. Colin Jones, "Plague and its Metaphor in Early Modern France," *Representations* 53 (1996), 97–99.

71. Horrox, *The Black Death*, 210 ff.

72. "The Cremation of Strasbourg Jewry St. Valentine's Day, February 14, 1349," in Jacob Marcus, *The Jew in the Medieval World: A Sourcebook, 315–1791* (New York: JPS, 1938), 43–48.

73. See Wolfgang Seiferth, *Synagogue and Church in the Middle Ages: Two Symbols in Art and Literature* (Ungar, 1970); see also Stuart Clark, *Thinking with Demons: The Idea of Witchcraft in Early Modern Europe* (New York: Oxford University Press, 1999).

74. See Charles Zika, *Exorcizing Our Demons: Magic, Witchcraft, and Visual Culture in Early Modern Europe* (Leiden: Brill, 2010).

75. Charlotte Wells, "Leeches on the Body Politic: Xenophobia and Witchcraft in Early Modern French Political Thought," *French Historical Studies* 22 (1999), 351–377.

76. Stuart Clark, "Inversion, Misrule, and the Meaning of Witchcraft," *Past and Present* 87:1 (1980), [105] 98–127.

77. During this period, a group of Jesuit scholars known as Bollandists were charged by Papal authority with the collection and critical analysis of the lives and miracles of the saints, the *Acta Sanctorum quotquot toto urbuntur*. The glorification of the saints was a core element of the Jesuit mission and the post–Reformation Church. For more on persistence of the ritual murder paradigm, see R. Po-Chia Hsia, *The Myth of Ritual Murder: Jews and Magic in Reformation Germany* (New Haven: Yale University Press, 1988) and *Trent 1475: Stories of a Ritual Murder Trial* (New Haven: Yale University Press, 1992).

78. Resnick, "Medieval Roots," 262.

79. For the persistence of this paradigm, see Robert Chazan, *Medieval Stereotypes and Modern Anti-Semitism* (Berkeley: University of California Press, 1997); see also Joshua Trachtenberg, *The Devil and the Jews: The Medieval Conception of the Jew and its Relation to Modern Antisemitism* (New York: Jewish Publication Society, 2002).

80. *Visum et Repertum* serves as the core text of Paul Barber's *Vampires, Burial and Death: Folklore and Reality* (New Haven: Yale University Press, 1988). Barber argues that close observation of corpses could lead to a conclusion of vampirism due to an unfamiliarity with forensic pathology. See also Paul Barber, "Forensic Pathology and the European Vampire," *Journal of Folklore Research* 24 (1987), 1–32.

81. Arnold Ages, "Calmet and the Rabbis," *The Jewish Quarterly Review* 55 (1965) 340–349.

82. G. David Keyworth, "Was the Vampire of the Eighteenth Century a Unique Type of Undead Corpse?" *Folklore* 117 (2006), 241–260; see also Erik Butler, *Metamorphoses of the Vampire in Literature and Film: Cultural Transformations in Europe, 1732–1933* (Rochester, NY: Camden House Publishing, 2010).

83. Michael Bailey links popular interest in vampirism to official efforts to quell witchcraft superstitions during this same period. See *Magic and Superstition in Europe: A Concise History from Antiquity to the Present* (London: Rowman and Littlefield, 2006), 174.

84. Nancy Caciola, "Wraiths, Revenants, and Ritual in Medieval Culture," *Past and Present* 152 (1996), 32.

85. All of this poses an interesting problem for the history of embalming. In popular perception, the only safe corpse was a completely decomposed corpse. Embalming, is meant to retard this process as long as possible. While embalming was reserved for the very wealthy in the eighteenth century, by the nineteenth century many members of the middle class were embalmed through the new chemical processes devised and perfected by Gannal. Embalming, then, may have contributed in interesting ways to the development of the vampire myth. For the role of the undertaker in Bram Stoker's *Dracula*, see Jani Scandura, "Deadly Professions: Dracula, Undertakers, and the Embalmed Corpse," *Victorian Studies* 40 (1996), 1–30.

86. See Jean-Claude Schmitt's magisterial *Ghosts in the Middle Ages: The Living and the Dead in Medieval Society* (Chicago: University of Chicago Press, 1998).

87. Only God, it seems, could animate a headless corpse, as in the *vita* of Saint Denis as recorded in Gregory Tour's *Glory of the Martyrs*. See translation by Raymond Van Dam (Liverpool: Liverpool University Press, 1988).

88. Caciola, "Wraiths and Revenants," 29. For a general overview of funerary customs in the medieval world, see Philip Aries, *Hour of Our Death* (New York: Vintage, 1982).

89. On the symptoms, see Barber, ""Forensic Pathology," 4–5.

90. On double coding, see Charles Jencks,

What is Post-Modernism? (New York: St. Martin's Press, 1987).

91. Franco Moretti, "The Dialectic of Fear," *New Left Review* (1982), 67–85; Nina Auerbach, *Our Vampires Ourselves* (Chicago: Chicago University Press, 1995).

92. Erik Butler, *Metamorphoses of the Vampire in Literature and Film: Cultural Transformations in Europe, 1732–1933* (Rochester, NY: Camden House Publishing, 2010).

93. James B. Twitchell, *Dreadful Pleasures: An Anatomy of Modern Horror* (New York: Oxford University Press, 1985); Cynthia A. Freeland, *The Naked and the Undead: Evil and the Appeal of Horror* (Boulder: Westview Press, 2002).

94. *Draculas, Vampires, and Other Undead Forms: Essays on Gender, Race, and Culture*, ed. John Edgar Browning and Caroline Joan Kay Picart (New York: Scarecrow Press, 2009).

95. Tabish Khair, *The Gothic, Post-Colonialism, and Otherness: Ghosts from Elsewhere* (London: Palgrave MacMillan, 2009).

96. *Blood Read: The Vampire as Metaphor in Contemporary Culture*, ed. Joan Gordon and Veronica Hollinger (Philadelphia: University of Pennsylvania Press, 1997).

97. John Polidori, *The Vampyre and Other Tales of the Macabre* (Oxford: Oxford University Press,, 2008); Sheridan Le Fanu, *Carmilla*, ed. Kate Costello-Sullivan (Syracuse: Syracuse University Press, 2013); Bram Stoker, *Dracula* (New York: Oxford University Press, 2011).

98. On the plague-like proliferation of remakes in modern horror, see Stephanie Boluk and Wylie Lenz, "Infection, Media, and Capitalism: From Early Modern Plagues to Postmodern Zombies," *Journal for Early Modern Cultural Studies* 10 (2010), 126–47.

99. See Brenda Gardenour Walter, "The Biology of Blood-Lust: Medieval Physiognomy, Physiology, and the Vampire Jew in Twentieth Century Cinema," *Film and History* 41:2, 2011.

100. On thirteenth century academics and the Aristotelian qualities of the moon in its different phases, see Helen Rodnite Lemay, 28; Luke Demaitre, *Doctor Bernard of Gordon*, 134. The textual sources for the Wandering Jew legend date from the thirteenth century; Roger Wendover and Matthew Paris both recall the story of the Jew who chastised Christ while He hung upon the Cross and whose punishment was to wander the earth until Christ's return. Also see George K. Andersen, *The Legend of the Wandering Jew* (Providence: Brown University Press, 1965).

101. Without primal male heat, Nosferatu is unable to properly digest his blood-food, and therefore he is hairless, save for the enormous eyebrows that pervert his face. Contrasted with the young Christian, Hutter, who is at first strong and swift—and who needs to shave—Nosferatu moves slowly through the frames, thin and frail, like an elderly woman.

102. Resnick, *Marks*, 244.

103. The Jew's ear as an odiferous and poisonous opening is echoed much later in a children's book, *Der Giftpilz*, written by Julius Streicher and published by the Nazi propagandist paper, *Der Stürmer*. On the cover is an image of a toadstool with an enormous hooked nose and protruding ears on a drawn, pale face. In this collection of wicked tales, children are told to watch closely for Jews, with "Those sinister Jewish noses!" and "Those dirty, standing-out ears!" Julius Streicher, *Der Giftpilz*, reprinted most recently by Preuss Press, 2006.

104. For a postmodern retelling of the vampire as infectious pollutant of the blood, see Guy Maddin's *Dracula: Pages from a Virgin's Diary* (2002).

105. See Sander Gilman, *The Jew's Body* (New York: Routledge, 1991).

106. "In Herzog's film, it is not just Lucy's body and blood that arouse the count's desire ... even more it is her love, a strong and vitalizing energy, an emotion of force and fearlessness." K. Casper in "Romantic Inversions in Herzog's Nosferatu, " *The German Quarterly*, 64:1(1991), 22.

107. Mary Frances Wack, "The *Liber de heros morbo of Johannes Afflacius and Its Implications for Medieval Love Conventions*," in Speculum 62, 1987, 328.

108. A similar theme is evident in modern zombie narratives, including World War Z and The Walking Dead. See Teresa A. Goddu, "Vampire Gothic," *American Literary History* 11 (1999), 125–41.

109. Once again, the vampire is crafted as an inversion of the Eucharist; his unholy flesh and blood do not offer an eternal life of redemption and ascension in Christ, but an eternal death of carnal and earthly damnation.

110. Arthur Lenning, *The Immortal Count: The Life and Films of Bela Lugosi* (Lexington: University of Kentucky Press, 2003).

111. As well as armadillos and Jerusalem crickets, thanks to on-set filming in southern California.

112. In James of Scotland's *Daemonologie* (1597), he claims that witches manipulated demonic forces, raised a tempest, and nearly sunk his ship.

113. Gibson, Matthew. *Dracula and the Eastern Question: British and French Vampire Narratives of the Nineteenth-century Near East*. (Basingstoke: Palgrave Macmillan, 2006). For the roots of the rustic peasant stereotype, see Paul Freedman, *Images of the Medieval Peasant* (Stanford: Stanford University Press, 1999).

114. The dangers of male transgression into the world of the irrational are writ large in Carl Th. Dreyer's *Vampyr* (1932).

115. For an overview, see Denis Meikle, *A History of Horrors: The Rise and Fall of the House of Hammer* (New York: Scarecrow Press, 2009).

116. The beautiful woman who turns out to be a corpse is a recurring theme in horror, appearing in myriad films including, of course, Stanley Kubrick's *The Shining* (1980).

117. See Scott W. Poole, *Satan in America: The Devil We Know* (New York: Rowman and Littlefield, 2010).

118. For an overview of the undying narrative, see Stacey Abbott, *Celluloid Vampires: Life After Death in the Modern World* (Austin: University of Texas Press, 2009). See also David J. Skal, *Hollywood Gothic: The Tangled Web of Dracula from Novel to Stage to Screen* (New York: MacMillan, 2004).
119. Lindsay Hallam, "A Beautiful Life of Evil and Hate: The Vampire-Witch in Mario Bava's *Black Sunday*," *Dracula's Daughters: The Female Vampire on Film*, eds. Douglas Brode and Leah Deyneka (New York: Scarecrow Press, 2014), 69–82.
120. See Kors and Peters, *Witchcraft in Europe*, 77–8.
121. Tony Thorne, *Countess Dracula: The Life and Times of Elisabeth Bathory The Blood Countess* (London: Bloomsbury, 1998).
122. A similar theme can be seen in *I Vampiri* (1956), in which a wealthy Italian woman, Giselle du Grandan, dominates men in her quest for blood and beauty. Janet S. Robinson, "Your Tale Merely Confirms That Women are Mad and Vain: The Uncanny Rendering of Countess Elizabeth Bathory's Life as Vampire Legend," *Dracula's Daughters*, 139–58.
123. Andrea Weiss, "The Lesbian Vampire Film: A Subgenre of Horror," *Dracula's Daughters*, 21–36.
124. Cathal Tohill and Pete Tombs, *Immoral Tales: European sex and Horror Movies, 1956–1984* (New York: Saint Martin's Griffin, 1995).
125. For such a matriarch see Ellen Rimbauer in Stephen King's *Rose Red* (2002).
126. "Deadlier than Dracula: *Blacula* and the Horror Genre" in Novotny Lawrence, *Blaxploitation Films of the 1970s: Blackness and Genre* (London: Routledge, 2008). See also,
127. Giselle Liza Anatol, "Narratives of Race and Gender: Black Vampires in U.S. Film," *Dracula's Daughters*, 195–218. See also Jane Caputi and Lauri Sagle, "Femme Noire: Dangerous Women of Color in Popular Film and Television," *Race, Gender, and Class* 11:2 (2004), 90–111.
128. The humanity of the vampire is likewise reflected in the film series based on *Twilight*, a paranormal romance, but for Christian Conservative ends.

Chapter 6

1. Leslie A. Sconduto, *Metamorphosis of the Werewolf: A Literary Study from Antiquity through the Renaissance* (Jefferson, NC: McFarland, 2008), 15.
2. Carolyn Walker Bynum, " Metamorphosis, Or Gerald the Werewolf," *Speculum* 73:4 (1998), 987–1013.
3. For more on this legacy, see Danielle Jacquart, "Medical Scholasticism," in *Western Medical Thought from Antiquity to the Middle Ages*, ed. Mirko D. Grmek, (Cambridge, MA: Harvard University Press, 1998), 197–240.
4. François Azouvi, "The Plague, Melancholy, and the Devil" *Diogenes* 27 (1979), 112–30.

5. Werewolves are not formally featured in English sources, perhaps because wolves had been hunted to extinction by the fourteenth century.
6. If not, why did authors argue against them so? For belief in werewolves beyond the learned sphere, see Carlo Ginzburg, *The Night Battles: Witchcraft and Agrarian Cults in the Sixteenth and Seventeenth Centuries* (Baltimore: Johns Hopkins University Press, 2013—with new preface). For these same Livonian werewolves in learned culture, see Stefan Donecker, "The Werewolves of Livonia: Lycanthropy and Shape-Changing in Scholarly Texts, 1550–1720," *Preternature* 1:2 (2012), 289–322.
7. This approach, in particular, has received disapprobation. See Willem de Blécourt, "Monstrous Theories: werewolves and the Abuse of History," *Preternature* 2:2 (2013), 188–212.
8. Zygmunt Bauman, *Liquid Modernity* (Cambridge: Polity, 2000).
9. Homer, *Odyssey*, trans. Walter Shewring, (Oxford: Oxford University Press, 2008).
10. Book I, lines 199–243. Ovid, *Metamorphoses*, trans. A. D. Melville, (Oxford: Oxford University Press, 2009). The Acadian werewolves would make a future appearance in Pliny the Elder's *Natural History*, 8:34:80.
11. A century and a half later, Apuleius (d. 180) would write his own *Metamorphoses*, renamed by Augustine as the *Golden Ass*, in which a fool joins the cult of Isis only to be transformed into a mule—once again, a reflection of his true self.
12. Petronius, *Satyricon*, trans. P. G. Walsh (Oxford: Oxford University Press, 2009). The scene is regrettably omitted from Fellini's 1969 film, *Fellini's Satyricon*.
13. Petronius, *Satyricon*, Chapter 9, 41–42.
14. Porphyry, *Life of Pythagoras*, trans. Kevin Guthrie (1920) aphorism 19; 45. Accessible at: http://www.tertullian.org/fathers/porphyry_life_of_pythagoras_02_text.htm
15. See the "Allegory of the Cave" in Plato's *Republic*, Book VII.
16. Herbert S. Long, "Plato's Doctrine of Metempsychosis and its Source," *The Classical Weekly* 41:10 (1948), 149–55.
17. "For it is not a body, but something which belongs to a body, and for this reason exists in a body, and in a body of such-and-such a kind." Like all matter, the soul was subject to natural law and physics; *Physics*
18. Aristotle, *De Anima* Book II, Part II; see trans. D. W. Hamlyn (Oxford: Clarendon Press, 1.993), 14.
19. This against the dualists who argued that matter was evil. For Tertullian, Christ was fully human, " For in putting on our flesh, He made it His own; in making it His own, He made it sinless," and fully divine. Ante-Nicene Fathers, Volume 3, Tertullian, Part II, Chapter 16.
20. Tertullian, *De Anima*, Chapter Seven: "The Soul's Corporeality Demonstrated Out of the Gospels"; Chapter Ten, "The Simple Nature of the Soul." Tertullian, *De Anima*, Chapter 8.

21. "The soul indeed which in the beginning was associated with Adam's body, which grew with its growth and was molded after its form, proved to be the germ both of the entire substance and that part of creation."
22. Echoed in Saint Ambrose (d. 397) "It is the soul, of course, and not the body, which is according to the likeness and image of God." CF: Sconduto, 17.
23. Augustine, *City of God*, 18:18, "What we should believe concerning the transformations which seem to happen to men through the art of demons."
24. *Witchcraft in Europe, 1100–1700*, eds. Alan C. Kors and Edward Peters (Philadelphia: University Pennsylvania Press, 1972), 28–31.
25. Geraldus Cambrensis, *The Topography of Ireland*, trans. Thomas Forester, ed. Thomas Wright (Cambridge, ON: In Parentheses Publications, 2000), 44–5. See also Robert Bartlett, *Gerald of Wales, 1146–1223* (Oxford: Clarendon Press, 1982).
26. Echoes of Aquinas, for the spirit of the Eucharist goes to the heart, the seat of the rational soul. An animal cannot take the Eucharist, for where would God go?
27. Carolyn Walker Bynum, *Metamorphosis and Identity* (New York: Zone Books, 2001).
28. *The Lais of Marie de France*, trans. Glyn S. Burgess and Keith Busby, (London: Penguin, 1986), 68–72.
29. See Michael Goodich, "The Politics of Canonization in the Thirteenth Century: Lay and Mendicant Saints," *Church History* 44:3 (1975), 294–307 and Andre Vauchéz, *Sainthood in the Later Middle Ages* (Cambridge: Cambridge University Press, 1997). For the role of medicine, see Joseph Ziegler, 'Practitioners and Saints: Medical Men in Canonization Processes in the Thirteenth to Fifteenth Centuries', *Social History of Medicine*, 12 (1999), 191–225.
30. Aquinas, *ST*, 3:75:1:1.
31. Other authors in the encyclopedic tradition include the Dominican Vincent of Beauvais (*Speculum Historiale, Naturale, and Doctrinale*, c. 1260) and Bartholomew the Anglican (*De Proprietatibus Rerum*, 13th century).
32. See Gervase of Tilbury, *Otia Imperialia: Recreation for an Emperor*, edited and translated by S. E. Banks and J. W. Binns (Oxford: Oxford University Press, 2002).
33. "…quod tamen nescio an delusion oculorum spectatium assignem, aut quia daemones discurrunt per mundum, et subit semina rerum, de quibus hic agitur, referent, ut ait Augustinus de virgis, quas Magi verterunt in dracones." *Otia Imperialia*, XV "De oculis apertis post peccatum," 4.
34. "…una nocte nimio timore turbantus, cum mentis alienatione in lupum versus, tantam patriae cladem intulit, quod multorum colonorum mansiones fecit esse desertas. Infantes in forma lupina devoravit."
35. See Thomas B. DeMayo, *The Demonology of William of Auvergne: By Fire and Sword* (New York: Edwin Mellen, 2008) and review by Michael D. Bailey in *Magic, Ritual, and Witchcraft* 4:2 (2009), 226–28.
36. "*Vides igitur in hoc exemplo, qualiter imago lupi, quam in organo imaginationis spiritus ille malignus impresserat, hominem illum a se ipso abstraxerat, & in ipsum lupum sic traxerat, ut nihil de substantia sua…*"
37. See Dyan Elliott, *Proving Woman: Female Spirituality and Inquisitional Culture in the Later Middle Ages* (Princeton: Princeton University Press, 2004) 205–9.
38. Azouvi, "Melancholy," 125.
39. See Catherine Rider, "Demons and Mental Disorder in Late Medieval Medicine," *Mental (Dis)Order in Later Medieval Europe*, ed. Sari Katajala-Peltomaa and Susanna Niiranen, (Leiden: Brill, 2014), 47–69.
40. See discussion of melancholia and the *qutrub* in Ihsan al-Issa's, *Al Junun: Mental Illness in the Islamic World* (International Universities Press, 2000), 45–6.
41. See Behnam Dalfardi, Mohammad Hosein Esnaahsary, Hassan Yarmohammadi, "Rabies in Medieval Persian Literature—the Canon of Avicenna (980–1037)," *Infectious Diseases of Poverty* 3:7, (2014).
42. *Malleus Maleficarum*, 38.
43. *Malleus*, 50.
44. *Malleus*, 52; 125.
45. On the circularity of these arguments, see Sydney Anglo, "Evident Authority and Authoritative Evidence: The *Malleus Maleficarum*," *The Literature of Witchcraft*, ed. Brian P. Levack (New York: Routledge, 1992), 1–32.
46. *Malleus*, 1.
47. For a broader context, see Robin Briggs, "Dangerous Spirits: Shapeshifting, Apparitions, and Fantasy in Lorraine Witchcraft Trials," and Nicole Jacques-Lefèvre, "Images of the Werewolf in Demonological Works," both in *Werewolves, Witches, and Wandering Spirits*, ed. Kathryn A. Edwards (Kirksville, MO: Truman State University Press, 2002).
48. Jean Bodin, *On the Demonmania of Witches*, introduction by Jonathan L. Pearl (Toronto: Renaissance and Reformation Texts in Translation, 1995).
49. Bodin, *Demonmania of* Witches, 109; 113.
50. Bodin, 114–120.
51. Bodin, 132.
52. *ST*, 1: 51:3:RO6: "Still if some are occasionally begotten from demons, it is not from the seed of such demons, nor from their assumed bodies, but from the seed of men taken for the purpose; as when the demon assumes first the form of a woman, and afterwards of a man; just as they take the seed of other things for other generating purposes, as Augustine says (De Trin. ii.), so that the person born is not the child of a demon, but of a man."
53. Sconduto, 135.
54. In consuming the innocent flesh of Christian and drinking their blood among the grapes used to make wine, the werewolf was engaging in a mockery of the Eucharist.

55. Sconduto, 140.
56. Sconduto, 137.
57. Sconduto, 137–8.
58. Sconduto, 138.
59. Bodin, 139. This of course suggests that werewolves are real and exist as a sort of wicked "miracle."
60. *Witches, Devils, and Doctors in the Renaissance: Johann Weyer's Praestigiis Daemonum*, ed. George Mora (Binghamton: Medieval and Renaissance Texts and Studies, 1993).
61. See the critical edition of Jean de Nynauld's, *De la Lycanthropie, Transformation, et Extase des Sorciers*," edited by Nicole Jacques-Chaquin and Maxime Préaud (Paris: Éditions Frénésie, 1990).
62. Bodin was not alone in his refutation of Weyer. See also Lancre, *Inconstancy of Witches*, 297–8. For more on Weyer's context, see Nadine Metzger, "Battling Demons with Medical Authority: Werewolves, Physicians, and Rationalization," *History of Psychiatry* 24 (2013), 341–55. Weyer's legacy would be echoed in the works of seventeenth-century medical men such as Robert Burton and Jacques Ferrand, who argued that werewolves did not physically transform into wolves, nor were they illusions brought on by demons. Instead, werewolves were really patients suffering from a mental illness called lycanthropy. The condition might be treated with dietary and physical regimen that would rebalance the lycanthrope's humors.
63. For the literary war between Weyer and Bodin, see Sam Migliore, "The Doctor, The Lawyer, and The Melancholy Witch," *Anthropologica* 25:2 (1983), 163–92.
64. Boguet, 138; on the ability of witches to command wolves, see Nicholas Remy, *Demonolatry*, 71. See also Oona's ability to command her Sidhe in *Cry of the Banshee* (1970).
65. Boguet, 137
66. Boguet, 139
67. Lancre, 256
68. Lancre, 269
69. Lancre, 270
70. Perhaps an inversion of the Song of Solomon 1:2, "Oh that He would kiss me with the kisses of his mouth," or an inversion of the Kiss of Peace from the Mass.
71. Lancre, 272; on Satan as wolf and Lord of the Forest, see Gregory the Great, who calls the Devil a shape shifter, "*lupus circumiens*."
72. Lancre, 273
73. Boguet, 141
74. Boguet, 144
75. Boguet, 146–7
76. Boguet, 154
77. Lancre, 257
78. Lancre, 257; 261: "To tear the rational soul from the body of a person and change this body into a wolf ... is impossible, since this body was created in the image of God."
79. Lancre, 337
80. Lancre, 337
81. Lancre, 330

82. This pertains whether they were French, German, Swiss, or English, Catholic or Protestant—all inherited a shared scholastic tradition.
83. Carl Jung, *Two Essays on Analytical Philosophy* (London: Routledge, 1953), 93.
84. Sigmund Freud, *The Wolf Man and Other Cases* (New York: Penguin, 2003); see also Whitney Davis, "Sigmund Freud's Drawing of the Dream of the Wolves," *Oxford Art Journal* 15 (1992), 70–87.
85. Willem de Blécourt, "Monstrous Theories: Werewolves and the Abuse of History," *Preternature* 2:2 (2013), 188–212.
86. See Chantal Bourgault de Coudray, "The Cycle of the Werewolf: Romantic Ecologies of Selfhood in Popular Fantasy," *Australian Feminist Studies* 18 (2003), 57–72.
87. The wolf-headed cane also appears in a more vicious form in Stephen King's *Storm of the Century* (1999).
88. The priest adds, "Some say it is to prevent the invasion of these roaming spirits into the highest creation of God's sculpturing hands, that the body of man, before whom all beasts must kneel [that a] man's body stiffens into rigor mortis at the moment of its death [so that the] spirit finds only a dry shell."
89. In *Children of the Full Moon*, the Ardoy children are likewise terrified of fire.
90. An echo here, perhaps, of the wearing of wolf skins as a sign of transformation in medieval literature.
91. *Werewolf of London*, "Who would bring such a beastly plant into Christendom?"
92. As the priest says to the gypsy, Maria, "Fighting against [your] superstition is harder than fighting against Satan himself," indicating that both non–Christian systems are in alignment and therefore evil. Also of note, the Ardoys in *Children of the Full Moon* are of "Hungarian extraction." They, too, are from away.
93. Gerald of Wales, 34. On the humidity of the moon from a medical perspective, see Luke Demaitre, *Doctor Bernard of Gordon*, 134. On the power of the moon over the juices of plants, see the discussion of the Mariphasa in *Werewolf of London*.
94. Gerald of Wales, 34.
95. Malleus, 40; CF: *Curse of the Werewolf*, "... the cycle of the full moon when the spirits of evil are the strongest..."
96. Lemay, *Secrets*, 88.
97. "Knowledge comes into particular crisis when visual media such as film, television, and computer graphics become so sophisticated that we can no longer privilege vision as the vehicle for truth." Susan Hegeman, "Haunted by Mass Culture," *American Literary History* 12, (2000), 307 [298–317].
98. Despite mounting evidence, Lord Talbot refuses to accept that his son is a werewolf until he himself is attacked by the beast and then witnesses its return to human form at the behest of the gypsy Maria. Once again, the werewolf has been proven as physical fact, not mere mental

delusion; however, the official record will state that Larry Talbot died while trying to defend Gwen, honorable to the end.

99. The werewolf's ability to change at any time of the month was necessary for the plot to progress; as in the medieval world, the werewolf changes shape according to the needs of the narrative.

100. All of which smacks of therapeutic discourse: "Admitting you have a problem is the first step to recovery."

101. See Andrew Smith, *Victorian Demons: Medicine, Masculinity, and the Gothic at the Fin-de-siècle* (Manchester: Manchester University Press, 2004).

102. The Reverend Lowe makes the chilling statement that he "would never willingly hurt a child" as he is about to attack Marty on a dark bridge, implying pedophilia.

103. In medieval iconography, the dog at the hearth represents domestication and fidelity.

104. Angela Carter, *The Bloody Chamber: And Other Stories* (New York: Penguin, 1990).

105. For links between the cycle of the werewolf and the menstrual cycle, see April Miller, "The Hair that Wasn't There Before: Demystifying Monstrosity and Menstruation in "Ginger Snaps" and "Ginger Snaps Unleashed, *Western Folklore* 64 (2005), 281–303.

Bibliography

Abbey, Edward. *Desert Solitaire: A Season in the Wilderness* (New York: Ballantine, 1985).

Abrahamsen, David, M.D. *Confessions of Son of Sam* (New York: Columbia University Press, 1985).

Abbott, Stacey. *Celluloid Vampires: Life After Death in the Modern World* (Austin: University of Texas Press, 2009).

Abulafia, Anna Sapir. "Bodies in the Jewish-Christian Debate," *Framing Medieval Bodies*, ed. Sarah Kay and Miri Rubin (Manchester: Manchester University Press, 1994), 123–37.

"Accusations of Cannibalism" in Minucius Felix, Octavius, R. E. Wallis, trans. in *The Ante-Nicene Fathers* (Buffalo, NY: The Christian Literature Publishing Co., 1887), Vol. 4, 177–178.

Ages, Arnold. "Calmet and the Rabbis," *The Jewish Quarterly Review* 55 (1965) 340–349.

Alanen, Lilli. *Descartes's Concept of Mind* (Cambridge: Harvard University Press, 2003).

Albertus Magnus, *On the Causes of the Properties of Elements*, trans. Irven M. Resnick (Milwaukee: Marquette University Press, 2010).

Al-Issa, Ihsan. *Al Junun: Mental Illness in the Islamic World* (International Universities Press, 2000), 45–6.

Allen, Prudence. *The Concept of Woman: The Aristotelian Revolution 750 BC to AD 1250* (Grand Rapids: Eerdman, 1997).

Anatol, Giselle Liza. "Narratives of Race and Gender: Black Vampires in U.S. Film" *Dracula's Daughters: The Female Vampire on Film*, eds. Douglas Brode and Leah Deyneka (New York: Scarecrow Press, 2014) 195–218.

Andersen, George K. *The Legend of the Wandering Jew* (Providence: Brown University Press, 1965).

Anglo, Sydney. "Evident Authority and Authoritative Evidence: The *Malleus Maleficarum*," *The Literature of Witchcraft*, ed. Brian P. Levack (New York: Routledge, 1992), 1–32.

Anton, J. P. *Aristotle's Theory of Contrariety* (New York: Humanities Press, 1957).

Aries, Philippe. *Hour of Our Death* (New York: Vintage, 1982).

Aristotle, *Metaphysics*, trans. W. D. Ross. (Oxford: Clarendon Press, 1924).

Aristotle, *Categories*, trans. H. P. Cooke and Hugh Tredennick (Cambridge: Loeb Classical Library 325, 1938).

Aristotle *De Sensu and De Memoria: Text and Translation with Introduction and Commentary* (Cambridge: Cambridge University Press, 2014).

Aristotle, *Parva Naturalia*, trans. W. S. Hett (Cambridge: Loeb Classical Library 228, 1957).

Aristotle, *De Caelo*, trans. William Keith Chambers Guthrie (Cambridge: Loeb Classical Library 338, 1939).

Aristotle, *On Generation and Corruption*. Trans H. H. Joachim. (Oxford: Clarendon Press, 1922).

Aristotle, *Meteorology*, trans. E. W. Webster (Oxford: Oxford University Press, 1963).

Aristotle, *The Physics, Books I-IV*, trans. P.H. Wicksteed and F.M.Cornford (Cambridge: Loeb Classical Library 228, 1957).

Aristotle, *De Anima*, trans. D. W. Hamlyn (Oxford: Clarendon Press, 1993).

Arnaldi de Villanova, *Opera Medica Omnia—de Esu Carnium, Vol. XI*, ed. Dianne M. Bazell (Barcelona: University of Barcelona Press, 1999).

Ashley, Kathleen. "Cultures of Devotion," in *The Oxford Handbook of Women and Gender in Medieval Europe*, eds. Judith M. Bennett and Ruth Mazo Karras (Oxford: Oxford University Press, 2013), 516–17.

Asma, Steven T. *On Monsters: An Unnatural History of Our Worst Fears* (New York: Oxford University Press, 2011).

Athanasius of Alexandria, *The Life of Antony and the Letter to Marcellinus*, trans. Robert C. Gregg (Mahwah, NJ: Paulist Press, 1980).

Auerbach, Nina. *Our Vampires Ourselves* (Chicago: Chicago University Press, 1995).

Augustine of Hippo, *Confessions*, trans. Henry Chadwick (Oxford: Oxford University Press, 1998).

Azouvi, François. "The Plague, Melancholy, and the Devil" *Diogenes* 27 (1979), 112–30.

Bailey, Michael D. "The Medieval Concept of the Witches' Sabbath," *Exemplaria* 8 (1996), 419–39.

Bailey, Michael D. *Battling Demons: Witchcraft, Heresy, and Reform in the Later Middle Ages* (Philadelphia: Pennsylvania State Press, 2002).

Bailey, Michael S. "The Feminization of Magic and the Emerging Idea of the Female Witch in the Late Middle Ages," *Essays in Medieval Studies* 19 (2002), 120–34.

Bailey, Michael, ed. *Magic and Superstition in Europe: A Concise History from Antiquity to the Present* (London: Rowman & Littlefield, 2006).

Bailey, Michael D. and Edward Peters, "A Sabbat of Demonologists: Basel 1430–1441," *The Historian*, 65:6, 1375–95.

Bainton, Roland. *Early Christianity* (Princeton, NJ: Van Nostrand Press, 1960).

Barber, Paul. *Vampires, Burial, and Death: Folklore and Reality* (New Have: Yale University Press, 1988)

Barber, Paul. "Forensic Pathology and the European Vampire," *Journal of Folklore Research* 24 (1987), 1–32.

Barkun, Michael. *A Culture of Conspiracy: Apocalyptic Visions in Contemporary America* (Berkeley: University of California Press, 2003).

Barkun, Michael. "Myths of the Underworld in Contemporary American Millennialism," *Experiences of Place*, ed. Mary N. MacDonald (Cambridge: Harvard University Press, 2003

Bartholomew the Englishman, *On the properties of things : John Trevisa's translation of Bartholomaeus Anglicus De proprietatibus Rerum*, trans. M. C. Seymour (Oxford: Clarendon Press, 1975–1988).

Bartlett, Robert. *Gerald of Wales, 1146–1223* (Oxford: Clarendon Press, 1982).

Baum, Frank L. *The Wonderful Wizard of Oz* (Chicago: George M. Hill Co., 1900).

Bauman, Zygmunt. *Liquid Modernity* (Cambridge: Polity, 2000).

Bayless, Martha. *Sin and Filth in Medieval Culture: The Devil in the Latrine* (London: Routledge, 2011).

Beal, Timothy K. *Religion and Its Monsters* (London: Routledge, 2001).

Beare, John I. *Greek Theories of Elementary Cognition from Alcmaeon to Aristotle* (Oxford: Clarendon Press, 1906).

Bell, Rudolph M. *Holy Anorexia* (Chicago: University of Chicago, 1987).

Bennett, Gillian. *Bodies: Sex, Violence, Disease, and Death in Contemporary Legend* (Jackson: University of Mississippi Press, 2005).

Bennett, Gillian. "Towards a Reevaluation of the Legend of "Saint" William of Norwich and its Place in the Blood Libel Legend," *Folklore* 116 (2005), 19–39.

Benshoff, Harry M. *Monsters in the Closet: Homosexuality and the Horror Film* (Manchester: Manchester University Press, 1997).

Bildhauer, Bettina. *Medieval Blood* (Cardiff: University of Wales Press, 2010).

Bildhauer, Bettina and Robert Mills, *Monstrous Middle Ages* (Toronto: University of Toronto Press, 2003).

Blamires, Alcuin. "Paradox in the Medieval Gender Doctrine of Head and Body," *Medieval Theology and the Natural Body*, eds. Peter Biller and Alastair Minnis (London: Boydell and Brewer, 1997), 13–29.

Blatty, William Peter. *The Exorcist* (San Francisco: Harper and Row, 1971).

Blatty, William Peter. *Legion* (New York: Simon & Schuster, 1983).

Bodin, Jean. *On the Demonmania of Witches*, trans. Randy A. Scott (Toronto: Centre for Reformation and Renaissance Studies, 1995).

Boguet, Henry. *An Examine of Witches*, trans. Montague Summers (New York: Dover, 2009).

Bolt, Christine. *Victorian Attitudes Toward Race* (London: Routledge, 2013)

Boluk, Stephanie and Wylie Lenz, "Infection, Media, and Capitalism: From Early Modern Plagues to Postmodern Zombies," *Journal for Early Modern Cultural Studies* 10 (2010), 126–47.

Bono, James. "Medical Spirits and the Medieval Language of Life" *Traditio*, Vol. 40, (1984), 91–30.

Bos, Gerrit. "Maimonides on the Preservation of Health," *Journal of the Royal Asiatic Society* 4:2 (1994), 213–35.

Bould, Mark. *Film Noir: From Berlin to Sin City: Short Cuts, Volume 27*, (New York: Columbia University Press, 2012).

Brakke, David. "Ethiopian Demons: Male Sexuality, The Black-Skinned Other, and the Monastic Self," *Journal of the History of Sexuality* 10 (2001), 501–535.

Briggs, Robin. "Dangerous Spirits: Shapeshifting, Apparitions, and Fantasy in Lorraine Witchcraft Trials," *Werewolves, Witches, and Wandering Spirits*, ed. Kathryn A. Edwards (Kirksville, MO: Truman State University Press, 2002).

Broedel, Hans Peter. *The Malleus Maleficarum and the Construction of Witchcraft Theology and Popular Belief* (Manchester: Manchester University Press, 2003).

Boureau, Alain. *Satan the Heretic: The Birth of Demonology in the Medieval West* (Chicago: University of Chicago, 2006).

British Library, *The Neville of Hornby Hours*, Egerton MS 2781, f.1v, c.1340.

Browning, John Edgar and Caroline Joan Kay Picart. *Draculas, Vampires, and Other Undead Forms: Essays on Gender, Race, and Culture* (New York: Scarecrow Press, 2009).

Brugger, Eveline. "Between a Rock and a Hard Place: Rulers, Cities, and "Their" Jews in Austria during the Persecutions of the Fourteenth Century," *Jews in Medieval Christendom: Slay them Not*, ed. Kristine T. Utterback and Merrall L. Price (Leiden: Brill, 2013) 189–200.

Burnett, Charles. "Translation from Arabic into Latin in the Middle Ages in *Übersetzung—Translation—Traduction*, ed.H. Kittel et al. (Berlin-New York: de Gruyter, 2007), 1231–37.

Burr, David. "The Persecution of Peter Olivi," *The Transactions of the American Philosophical Society*, 66 (1976).

Burr, David. *The Spiritual Franciscans: From Protest to Persecution in the Century after Saint Francis* (Philadelphia: Pennsylvania State University Press, 2001).

Burton, Robert. *The Anatomy of Melancholy* (New York: Vintage, 1977).

Butler, Erik. *Metamorphoses of the Vampire in Literature and Film: Cultural Transformations in Europe, 1732–1933* (Rochester, NY: Camden House, 2010).

Bynum, Caroline Walker. *Holy Feast, Holy Fast: The Religious Significance of Food to Medieval Women* (Berkeley: University of California Press, 1988).

Bynum, Carolyn Walker. " Metamorphosis, Or Gerald the Werewolf," *Speculum* 73:4 (1998), 987–1013.

Bynum, Carolyn Walker. *Metamorphosis and Identity* (Cambridge: Zone/MIT Press, 2001).

Caciola, Nancy. *Discerning Spirits: Divine and Demonic Possession in the Middle Ages* (Ithaca: Cornell University Press, 2003).

Caciola, Nancy. "Mystics, Demoniacs, and the Physiology of Spirit Possession in Medieval Europe," *Comparative Studies in Society and History*, 42:2 (2000), 268–306.

Caciola, Nancy. "Wraiths, Revenants, and Ritual in Medieval Culture," *Past and Present* 152 (1996), 3–45.

Cadden, Joan. *The Meaning of Sex Difference in the Middle Ages* (Cambridge: Cambridge University Press, 1995).

Caesarius of Heisterbach, "Dialogus Miraculorum," *Witchcraft in Europe 1100–1700*, ed. Kors and Peters (Philadelphia: University of Pennsylvania Press, 1972).

Cain, Jimmie E. *Bram Stoker and Russophobia: Evidence of the British Fear of Russia in Dracula and the Lady of the Shroud* (Jefferson, NC: McFarland Press, 2006).

Campagne, Fabian Alejandro. "Demonology at the Crossroads: The Visions of Ermine de Rheims and the Image of the Devil on the Eve of the Great European Witch Hunt," *Church History* 80:3 (2011).

Cantimpré, Thomas. *De Anathomia Humanii Corporis*, Palatina Manuscripts of the Twelfth through Fifteenth Centuries, entry number 1066, CD-ROM, 2001.

Cantimpré, Thomas. *Liber de Natura Rerum*, Codices Illuminati Medi Aevi, Number 55, Munich, 2001.

Cantimpré, Thomas. "Life of Christina the Astonishing," in *Thomas Cantimpré: The Collected Saints' Lives*, ed. Margot King and Barbara Newman, (Turnhout: Brepols, 2008).

Caputi, Jane and Lauri Sagle, "Femme Noire: Dangerous Women of Color in Popular Film and Television," *Race, Gender, and Class* 11:2 (2004), 90–111.

Carter, Angela. *The Bloody Chamber: And Other Stories* (New York: Penguin, 1990).

Casper, K. in "Romantic Inversions in Herzog's Nosferatu, " *The German Quarterly*, 64:1 (1991).

Chazan, Robert. *European Jewry and the First Crusade* (Berkeley: University of California Press, 1987).

Chazan, Robert. *Medieval Stereotypes and Modern Anti-Semitism* (Berkeley: University of California Press, 1997).

Christie, Deborah and Sarah Juliet Lauro, *Better Off Dead: The Evolution of the Zombie as Post-Human* (New York: Fordham University Press, 2013).

Clark, Stuart. "Inversion, Misrule, and the Meaning of Witchcraft," *Past and Present* 87:1 (1980), 98–127.

Clark, Stuart. *Thinking with Demons* (Oxford: Oxford University Press, 1997).

Clifton, James. "The Face of a Fiend: Convulsion, Inversion, and the Horror of the Disempowered Body," *Oxford Art Journal: Early Modern Horror*, 34:3 (2011), 373–92.

Clover, Carol. *Men, Women, and Chainsaws: Gender in the Modern Horror Film* (Princeton, NJ: Princeton University Press, 2011).

Coakley, John. "Friars as Confidants of Holy women in Medieval Dominican Hagiography *The Life of Saint Margaret*," *Images of Sainthood in Medieval Europe*. (Ithaca: Cornell University Press, 1991).

Cohen, Jeffrey Jerome. *Hybridity, Identity, and Monstrosity in Medieval Britain: On Difficult Middles* (Basingstoke: Palgrave, 2006).

Cohen, Jeremy. *Living Letters of the Law: Ideas of the Jew in Medieval Christianity* (Berkeley: University of California Press, 1999).

Cohen, Jeremy. "The Jews as the Killers of Christ in the Latin Tradition, from Augustine and the Friars," *Traditio* 39 (1983), 1–27.

Cole, Lucinda. "Of Mice and Moisture: Rats, Witches, Miasma, and Early Modern Theories of Contagion," *The Journal of Early Modern Cultural Studies* 10:2, (2010), 65–84.

Constantine the African and Ali Ibn al Abbas al Magusi: The Pantegni and Related Texts, eds. Charles Burnett and Danielle Jacquart (Leiden: Brill, 1994).

Corman, Roger. *How I Made a Hundred Movies in Hollywood and Never Lost a Dime* (New York: Random House, 1990).

Creed, Barbara. *Phallic Panic: Film, Horror, and the Primal Uncanny* (Melbourne: Melbourne University Press, 2005).

Creed, Barbara. The Monstrous-Feminine: Film, Feminism, Psychoanalysis (London: Routledge, 1993).

Cuffel, Alexandra. *Gendering Disgust in Medieval Religious Polemic* (Notre Dame: University of Notre Dame Press, 2007).

Dalfardi, Benham, Mohammad Hosein Esnaahsary, Hassan Yarmohammadi, "Rabies in Medieval Persian Literature—the Canon of Avicenna (980–1037)," *Infectious Diseases of Poverty* 3:7, (2014).

Davis, Whitney. "Sigmund Freud's Drawing of the Dream of the Wolves," *Oxford Art Journal* 15 (1992), 70–87.

Dean-Jones, Lesley. *Bodies in Classical Greek Science* (Oxford, Clarendon, 1996).

De Blécourt, Willem. "Monstrous Theories: Werewolves and the Abuse of History," *Preternature* 2:2 (2013), 188–212.

Degele, Nina. "On the Margins of Everything: Doing, Performing, and Staging Science in Homeopathy," *Science, Technology, and Human Values* 30:1 (2005), 111–136.

Demaitre, Luke. *Leprosy in Pre-Modern Medicine* (Baltimore: Johns Hopkins Press, 2007).

De Mayo, Thomas B. *The Demonology of William of Auvergne: By Fire and Sword* (Lewiston: Edwin Mellen, 2007).

Dendle, Peter. *Satan Unbound: The Devil in Old English Narrative Literature*, (Toronto: University of Toronto Press, 2001).

Des Chene, Dennis. *Spirits and Clocks: Machine and Organism in Descartes* (Ithaca: Cornell University Press, 2000).

Despres, Denise L. "Immaculate Flesh and the Social Body: Mary and the Jews," *Jewish History* 12 (1998), 47–69.

Despres, Denise. "Cultic Anti-Judaism and Chaucer's *Litel Clergeon*," *Modern Philology* 91:4 (1994), 413–27.

Despres, Denise. "Mary of the Eucharist: Cultic Anti-Judaism in Fourteenth-Century English Devotional Manuscripts," *From Witness to Witchcraft: Jews and Judaism in Medieval Christian Thought*, ed. Jeremy Cohen (Wiesbaden: Harrassowitz Press, 1996), 375–401.

Donecker, Stefan. "The Werewolves of Livonia: Lycanthropy and Shape-Changing in Scholarly Texts, 1550–1720," *Preternature* 1:2 (2012), 289–322.

Douglas, Mary. *Purity and Danger* (New York: Routledge, 1966).

Du Coudray, Chantal Bourgault. "The Cycle of the Werewolf: Romantic Ecologies of Selfhood in Popular Fantasy," *Australian Feminist Studies* 18 (2003), 57–72.

Elkins, Sharon. "Gertrude the Great and the Virgin Mary," *Church History*, 66:4 (1997), 720–734.

Ellis, Bill. "The @#$%&! Ouija Board" *Lucifer Ascending: The Occult in Folklore and Popular Culture* (Lexington: University of Kentucky Press, 2004), 174–196.

Elliott, Dyan. "The Physiology of Rapture and Female Spirituality" in *Medieval Theology and the Natural Body*, eds. Peter Biller and A. J. Minnis (York: York Medieval Press, 1997), 141–74.

Elliott, Dyan. *The Bride of Christ Goes to Hell* (Philadelphia: University of Pennsylvania Press, 2012).

Elliott, Dyan. *Proving Woman: Female Spirituality and Inquisitional Culture in the Later Middle Ages* (Princeton: Princeton University Press, 2004).

Emmerson, Richard K. "The Representation of Antichrist in Hildegard of Bingen's *Scivias*: Image, Word, Commentary, and Visionary Experience," *Gesta* 41:2 (2002), 95–110.

Evans, Timothy H. "A Last Defense against the Dark: Folklore, Horror, and the Uses of Tradition in the Works of H. P. Lovecraft," *Journal of Folklore Research*, 42:1 (2005), 99–135.

Fabbri, Christiane Nockels. "Treating Medieval Plague: The Wonderful Virtues of Theriac," *Early Science and Medicine*, Vol. 12, No. 3 (2007), 247–283.

Fanger, Claire. *Conjuring Spirits: Texts and Traditions of Medieval Ritual Magic* (Stroud: Sutton, 1998).

Fatio, Oliver. "Lambert Daneau: 1530–1595" *The Literature of Witchcraft: Articles on Witchcraft, Magic, and Demonology*, ed. Brian P. Levack (New York: Routledge, 1992), 69–83.

Feinstein, Sandy. "Dracula, Chloral: Chemistry Matters," *Victorian Review* 35 (2009), 96–115.

Ferrand, Jaques. *A Treatise on Lovesickness*, trans. Donald A. Beecher and Massimo Ciavolella (Syracuse: Syracuse University Press, 1990).

Fischer, Lucy. "Birth Traumas: Parturition and Horror in Rosemary's Baby," *Cinema Journal* 31:3 (1992), 3–18.

Foucault, Michel *The Archaeology of Knowledge* (New York: Vintage, 1982).

Foucault, Michel. *The Birth of the Clinic: An Archaeology of Medical Perception* (New York: Vintage, 1994).

Frankfurter, David. *Evil Incarnate: Rumors of*

Demonic Conspiracy and Ritual Abuse in History (Princeton, NJ: Princeton University Press, 2006).

Freccero, John. "The Sign of Satan," *MLN*, Vol. 80, No. 1, *The Italian Issue* (1965), 11–26.

Freedman, Paul. *Images of the Medieval Peasant* (Stanford: Stanford University Press, 1999).

Freeland, Cynthia A. *The Naked and the Undead: Evil and the Appeal of Horror* (Boulder: Westview Press, 2002).

French, Roger. "Foretelling the Future: Arabic Astrology and English Medicine in the Late Twelfth Century," *Isis*, Vol. 87, No. 3. (Sep., 1996), pp. 453–480.

Freud, Sigmund. *The Wolf Man and Other Cases* (New York: Penguin, 2003).

Fry, Carol L. *Cinema of the Occult: New Age, Satanism, Wicca, and Spiritualism in Film* (Cranbury, NJ: Rosemont, 2008).

Galen, *On Diseases and Symptoms*, trans. Ian Johnston (Cambridge: Cambridge University Press, 2011).

Galen, *On the Errors and Passions of the Soul*, trans. Paul W. Harkins (Columbus: Ohio State University Press, 1963).

García Ballester, Luis and John Arrizabalaga (eds.), *Galen and Galenism: Theory and Medical Practice from Antiquity to the European Renaissance*. (Burlington, VT: Ashgate Press, 2002).

Geraldus Cambrensis, *The Topography of Ireland*, trans. Thomas Forester, ed. Thomas Wright (Cambridge, ON: In Parentheses Publications, 2000).

Gervase of Tilbury, *Otia Imperialia: Recreation for an Emperor*, edited and translated by S. E. Banks and J. W. Binns (Oxford: Oxford University Press, 2002).

Gibbs, Frederick W. "Specific Form and Poisonous Properties: Understanding Poison in the Fifteenth Century." *Preternature: Critical and Historical Studies on the Preternatural* 2:1 (2013), 19–46.

Gibson, Matthew. *Dracula and the Eastern Question: British and French Vampire Narratives of the Nineteenth-century Near Eas.* (Basingstoke: Palgrave Macmillan, 2006).

Gilman, Sander. *The Jew's Body* (New York: Routledge, 1991).

Ginzburg, Carlo. *The Night Battles: Witchcraft and Agrarian Cults in the Sixteenth and Seventeenth Centuries* (Baltimore: Johns Hopkins University Press, 2013—with new preface).

Glick, Thomas. "My Master the Jew: Observations on Interfaith Scholarly Interaction in the Middle Ages," *Jews, Muslims and Christians In and Around the Crown of Aragon*, ed. Harvey J. Hames (Leiden: Brill, 2004), 157–82.

Goddu, Andre. "The Failure of Exorcism in the Middle Ages," in *Possession and Exorcism: Articles on Witchcraft, Magic, and Demonology Volume 9*, ed. Brian P. Levack (New York: Taylor and Francis, 1992), 9–29.

Goddu, Teresa. A. "Vampire Gothic," *American Literary History* 11 (1999), 125–41.

Goering, Joseph. "The Invention of Transubstantiation," *Traditio* 46 (1991), 147–170.

Goodich, Michael. "The Contours of Female Piety in Later Medieval Hagiography" *Church History* 50:1 (1981), 20–32.

Goodich, Michael. "The Politics of Canonization in the Thirteenth Century: Lay and Mendicant Saints," *Church History* 44:3 (1975), 294–307.

Gordon, Joan and Veronica Hollinger, *Blood Read: The Vampire as Metaphor in Contemporary Culture* (Philadelphia: University of Pennsylvania Press, 1997).

Grant, Barry Keith, *The Dread of Difference: Gender and the Horror Film*, (Austin: University of Texas Press, 1996).

Grant, Edward. *Planets, Stars, and Orbs: Medieval Cosmos, 1200–1687* (New York: Cambridge University Press, 1996).

Grant, Edward. *The Foundations of Modern Science in the Middle Ages* (Cambridge: Cambridge University Press, 1996).

Grant, Edward. *The Nature of Natural Philosophy* (Washington, D.C.: Catholic University of America Press, 2010).

Green, Monica. *The Trotula: A Medieval Compendium of Women's Medicine* (Philadelphia: University of Pennsylvania Press, 2002).

Gregg, Joan Young. *Devils, Women, and Jews* (Albany: SUNY Press, 1997).

Gregory the Great, *"Moralia sive Exposition in Job" Patrologia Latina* 75, ed. Migne (PLD)

Gregory the Great. *Bibliotheca Nacional de Madrid*, MS 11544: folio 13v.

Gregory the Great, *Glory of the Martyrs*, trans. Raymond Van Dam (Liverpool: Liverpool University Press, 1988).

Guazzo, Francesca Maria. *Compendium Maleficarum*, trans. Montague Summers (New York: Dover, 1988).

Gutas, Dmitri. *Greek Thought, Arab Culture: The Greco-Arabic Translation Movement in Baghdad and Early Abbasid Society* (London: Routledge, 1998).

Halberstam, Judith. *Skin Shows: Gothic Horror and the Technology of Monsters* (Durham, NC: Duke University Press, 1995).

Haliczer, Stephen. "The Jew as Witch: Displaced Aggression and the Myth of the Santo Niño de La Guardia" in *New Perspectives on Witchcraft, Magic, and Demonology: Witchcraft in Continental Europe*, ed. Brian P. Levack (New York: Routledge, 2001), 264–274

Hallam, Lindsay. "A Beautiful Life of Evil and Hate: The Vampire-Witch in Mario Bava's

Black Sunday," *Dracula's Daughters: The Female Vampire on Film*, eds. Douglas Brode and Leah Deyneka (New York: Scarecrow Press, 2014), 69–82.

Hankinson, R. J., "Galen's Anatomy of the Soul," *Phronesis* 36:2 (1991), 203 [197–233]

Hansen, Regina, ed. *Roman Catholicism and the Horror Film: Essays on Belief, Spectacle, Ritual, and Imagery* (Jefferson, NC: McFarland Press, 2011).

Harkness, Deborah. *John Dee's Conversations with Angels: Cabala, Alchemy, and the End of Nature* (Cambridge: Cambridge University Press, 2006).

Hawthorne, Nathaniel, "Rappaccini's Daughter," *Mosses from an Old Manse* (New York: Modern Library Classics, 2003).

Hegeman, Susan. "Haunted by Mass Culture," *American Literary History* 12 (2000), 307 [298–317].

Heller-Nicholas, Alexandra. "The Power of Christ Compels You: Moral Spectacle and The Exorcist Universe," *Roman Catholicism in Fantastic Film: Essays on Belief, Spectacle, Ritual, and Imagery* (Jefferson, NC: McFarland, 2011), 65–80.

Heng, Geraldine. "England's Dead Boys: Telling Tales of Christian-Jewish Relations Before and After the First European Expulsion of the Jews," *MLN* 127: 5 (2012), 54–85.

Herlihy, David. *The Black Death and the Transformation of the West* (Cambridge, MA: Harvard University Press, 1997).

Hiemer, Ernst. *Der Giftpilz* (Nuremberg: Stürmerverlag, 1938).

Hines, Terrence. *Pseudoscience and the Paranormal* (New York: Prometheus, 2003).

Hippocrates, "Airs, Waters, and Places" and "Epidemics" *Hippocrates, Volume I: Ancient Medicine*. Trans. W. H. S. Jones. Cambridge: Loeb Classical Library, 1923.

Hippocrates, "On the Sacred Disease" and "On Breaths," *Hippocrates Vol. II: Prognostic*, trans. W. H. S. Jones (Cambridge, Loeb Classical Library, 148, 1923).

Hollywood, Amy. "Inside Out: Beatrice of Nazareth and Her Hagiographer," *Gendered Voices: Medieval Saints and Their Interpreters*, ed. Catherine M. Mooney (Philadelphia: University of Pennsylvania Press, 1999), 78–98.

Homer, *Odyssey*, trans. Walter Shewring, (Oxford: Oxford University Press, 2008).

Horrox, Rosemary. *The Black Death* (Manchester: Manchester University Press, 1994).

Hudson, Anne. *The Premature Reformation: Wycliffite Texts and Lollard History* (New York: Oxford University Press, 1988).

Hunt, Leon. "Necromancy in the UK: Witchcraft and the Occult in British Horror," in *British Horror Cinema*, eds. Steve Chibnall and Julian Petlay (London: Routledge, 2002), 82–98.

Isidore of Seville. "The Medical Writings," trans. William D. Sharpe. *Transactions of the American Philosophical Society* 54, pt. 2 (1967)

Jacquart, Danielle and Claude Thomasset, *Sexuality and Medicine in the Middle Ages* (Princeton, NJ: Princeton University Press, 1988).

Jacquart, Danielle. "Medical Scholasticism," in *Western Medical Thought from Antiquity to the Middle Ages*, ed. Mirko D. Grmek, (Cambridge, MA: Harvard University Press, 1998), 197–240.

Jacques de Vitry, "Life of Marie d'Oignies," in *Two Lives of Marie d'Oignies*, trans. Margot King, eds. Margot King and Miriam Marsolais (Toronto: Peregrina, 1998)

Jacques de Vitry, *The Faces of Women in the Sermons of Jacques de Vitry*, trans. Carolyn Muessig, (Toronto: Peregrina, 1999).

Jacques-Lefèvre, Nicole. "Images of the Werewolf in Demonological Works," *Werewolves, Witches, and Wandering Spirits*, ed. Kathryn A. Edwards (Kirksville, MO: Truman State University Press, 2002).

Jencks, Charles. *What is Post-Modernism?* (New York: St. Martin's Press, 1987).

Jessop, A and M. R. James, *The Life and Miracles of St. William of Norwich by Thomas of Monmouth* (Cambridge: Cambridge University Press, 1896).

Johnson, Willis. "The Myth of the Jewish Male Menses," *Journal of Medieval History* 24:3 (1998), 273–95.

Jones, Colin. "Plague and its Metaphor in Early Modern France," *Representations* 53 (1996), 97–127.

Jung, Carl. *Two Essays on Analytical Philosophy* (London: Routledge, 1953).

Kaplan, M. Lindsay. "Jessica's Mother: Medieval Constructions of Jewish Race and Gender in *The Merchant of Venice*," *Shakespeare Quarterly* 58 (2007), 1–30.

Katz, David S. "Shylock's Gender: Jewish Male Menstruation in Early Modern England," *Review of English Studies* 50 (1999), 440–462.

Keck, David. *Angels and Angelology in the Middle Ages* (Oxford: Oxford University Press, 1998).

Kermode, Mark. *The Exorcist* (London: British Film Institute, 1997).

Keyworth, G. David. "Was the Vampire of the Eighteenth Century a Unique Type of Undead Corpse?" *Folklore*, 117:3 (2006), 241–60.

Khair, Tabish. *The Gothic, Post-Colonialism, and Otherness: Ghosts from Elsewhere* (London: Palgrave MacMillan, 2009).

Kieckhefer, Richard. "Mythologies of Witchcraft in the Fifteenth Century," *Magic, Ritual, and Witchcraft* 1:1 (2006), 79–108.

Kieckhefer, Richard. "The specific rationality of

medieval magic," *American Historical Review*, 99 (1994), 813–36.

Kieckhefer, Richard. *Magic in the Middle Ages* (Cambridge: Cambridge University Press, 1990).

Kieckhefer, Richard. *European Witch Trials: Their Foundations in Popular and Learned Culture* (Berkeley: University of California Press, 1976).

Kieval, Hillel J. "Representation and Knowledge in Medieval and Modern Accounts of Jewish Ritual Murder," *Jewish Social Studies* (1994), 52–72.

Klaniczay, Gábor. "A Cultural History of Witchcraft," *Magic, Ritual, and Witchcraft* 5:2 (2010), 188–212.

Knoppers, Laura Lunger and Joan B. Landes, *Monstrous Bodies/Political Monstrosities in Early Modern Europe* (Ithaca: Cornell University Press, 2004).

Koren, Sharon Faye. "The Menstruant as 'Other' in Medieval Judaism and Christianity," NASHIM (2009), 41–42.

Kristeva, Julia. *The Powers of Horror: An Essay on Abjection* (New York: Columbia University Press, 1982).

Lacan, Jacques. Seminar VI accessible on line at: http://lacan.com/seminars2.htm

Lancre, Pierre de. *On the Inconstancy of Witches*, trans. Joseph O'Connor et al. (Tempe: ACMRS Publications, 2006).

Langholf, Volker. *Medical Theories in Hippocrates: Early Texts and the Epidemics*. Berlin: Walter de Gruyter, 1990.

Lansing, Carol. *Power and Purity: Cathar Heresy in Medieval Italy* (New York: Oxford University Press, 2001).

Lawrence, C. H. *Medieval Monasticism: Forms of Religious Life in Western Europe in the Middle Ages* (London, 1984).

Lawrence, Novotny. *Blaxploitation Films of the 1970s: Blackness and Genre* (London: Routledge, 2008).

Le Fanu, Sheridan. *Carmilla*, ed. Kate Costello-Sullivan (Syracuse: Syracuse University Press, 2013).

Leff, Gordon. *Paris and Oxford Universities in the Thirteenth and Fourteenth Centuries: An Institutional and Intellectual History* (New York: Wiley, 1968).

Leff, Gordon. "The Fourteenth Century and the Decline of Scholasticism," in *Heresy, Philosophy, and Religion in the Medieval West* (Burlington, VT: Ashgate Press, 2002).

Lemay, Helen Rodnite. *Women's Secrets: A Translation of Pseudo Albertus Magnus' De Secretis Mulierum with Commentaries* (Albany, NY: SUNY University Press, 1992).

Lenning, Arthur. *The Immortal Count: The Life and Films of Bela Lugosi* (Lexington: University of Kentucky Press, 2003).

Leopold, Aldo. *Sand County Almanac* (New York: Ballantine, 1986).

Lerner, Robert E. "Antichrists and Antichrist in Joachim de Fiore," *Speculum*, 60 (1985), 553–70.

Le Roy Ladurie, Emmanuelle. *Montaillou: Promised Land of Error* (New York: G. Brazillier, 1978).

Levack, Brian P., ed. *The Witchcraft Sourcebook* (New York: Routledge, 2004).

Levin, Ira. *Rosemary's Baby* (New York: Random House, 1967).

Levinas, Emmanuel. *Alterity and Transcendence*, trans. Michael B. Smith (New York: Columbia University Press, 2000).

Lewis, Robert E. *De Misera condicionis humane*, Pope Innocent III, 1978 Livesey, Steven J. *Theology and Science in the Fourteenth Century: Three Questions on the Unity and Subalternation of the Sciences from John of Reading's Commentary on the Sentences* (Leiden: Brill, 1989).

Long, Herbert S. "Plato's Doctrine of Metempsychosis and its Source," *The Classical Weekly* 41:10 (1948), 149–55.

Lovecraft, H. P. "Pickman's Model," *Weird Tales* (1927).

Mackay, Christopher S. *Malleus Maleficarum* (Cambridge: Cambridge University Press, 2006).

Magistrale, Tony. *Abject Terrors: Surveying the Modern and Postmodern Horror Film* (New York: Peter Lang Academic Publishers, 2005).

Marcus, Jacob, ed. *The Jew in the Medieval World: A Sourcebook, 315-1791* (New York: JPS, 1938).

Marenbon, John. *Later Medieval Philosophy1150-1350* (London: Routledge, 2002).

Marie de France, *The Lais of Marie De France*, trans. Glyn S. Burgess and Keith Busby, (London: Penguin, 1986), 68–72.

Martin, Willis. "'The Invisible Giant,' Dracula, and Disease." *Studies in the Novel* 39.3(2007), 301–25.

McCord Adams, Marylin. *Some Later-Medieval Theories of the Eucharist: Thomas Aquinas, Gilles of Rome, Duns Scotus, and William Ockham* (New York: Oxford, 2012).

McCulloh, John M. "Jewish Ritual Murder: William of Norwich, Thomas of Monmouth, and the Early Dissemination of the Myth," *Speculum* 72 (1997), 698–740.

McDannell, Colleen and Bernhard Lang, *Heaven: A History* (New Haven: Yale University Press, 2001).

McGinn, Bernard. *Antichrist: Two Thousand Years of the Human Fascination with Evil* (New York: Columbia University Press, 2000).

McGinn, Bernard. *The Calabrian Abbot: Joachim of Fiore in the History of Western Thought* (New York: Macmillan, 1985).

McNamara, Amy Kay. *Sisters in Arms: Catholic Nuns Through Two Millennia* (Cambridge: Harvard University Press, 1998).

Meikle, Denis. *A History of Horrors: The Rise and Fall of the House of Hammer* (New York: Scarecrow Press, 2009).

Metzger, Nadine. "Battling Demons with Medical Authority: Werewolves, Physicians, and Rationalization," *History of Psychiatry* 24 (2013), 341–55.

Migliore, Sam. "The Doctor, The Lawyer, and The Melancholy Witch," *Anthropologica* 25:2 (1983), 163–92.

Miller, April. "The Hair that Wasn't There Before: Demystifying Monstrosity and Menstruation in "Ginger Snaps" and "Ginger Snaps Unleashed, *Western Folkore* 64 (2005), 281–303.

Miller, Sarah Alison. *Medieval Monstrosity and the Female Body* (New York: Routledge, 2010).

Milwright, Marcus. "The Balsam of Ma ariyya: An Exploration of a Medieval Panacea," *Bulletin of the School of Oriental and African Studies*, Vol. 66, No. 2 (2003), 193–209.

Mittman, Asa Simon and Peter Dendle, *The Ashgate Research Companion to Monsters and the Monstrous* (Burlington, VT: Ashgate, 2013).

Moore, R. I. *The Formation of a Persecuting Society, Second Edition* (Oxford: Blackwell, 2007).

Moretti, Franco. "The Dialectic of Fear," *New Left Review* (1982), 67–85.

Moss, Leonard W. and Stephen C. Cappannari, "Mal'occhio Ayin ha ra, Oculus fascinus, Judenblick: The Evil Eye Hovers Above," *The Evil Eye*, ed. Clarence Maloney (New York: Columbia University Press, 1976) 1–15.

Mulder-Bakker, Anneke B. *Marie d'Oignies: Mother of Salvation* (Turnhout: Brepols, 2006).

Mulvey, Laura. "Visual Pleasure and Narrative Cinema," *Screen* 16:3 (1975) 6–18.

Murray, Margaret. *The Witch Cult in Western Europe* (Oxford: Clarendon Press, 1921).

Neary, Anne. "The Origins and Character of the Kilkenny Witchcraft Case of 1324," *Proceedings of the Royal Irish Academy* (1983), 333–350.

Newman, Barbara. "Hildegard of Bingen: Visions and Validation," *Church History* 54:2 (June, 1985), 163–75.

Newman, Barbara. "Possessed by the Spirit: Devout Women, Demoniacs, and the Apostolic Life in the Thirteenth Century," *Speculum* 73:3 (1998), 733–70.

Nirenberg, David. *Communities of Violence: Persecution of Minorities in the Middle Ages* (Princeton: Princeton University Press, 1998).

Noakes, R.J. "Cromwell Varley FRS, Electrical Discharge, and Victorian Spiritualism," *Notes and Records of the Royal Society* 61:1 (2007), 5–21.

Nockels Fabbri, Christiane, "Treating Medieval Plague: The Wonderful Virtues of Theriac," *Early Science and Medicine*, Vol. 12, No. 3 (2007), 247–283.

Nynauld, Jean de. *De la Lycanthropie, Transformation, et Extase des Sorciers*," ed. Nicole Jacques-Chaquin and Maxime Préaud (Paris: Editions Frénésie, 1990).

O'Boyle, Cornelius. *The Art of Medicine: Medical Teaching at the University of Paris 1250–1400* (Leiden: Brill, 1998).

O'Malley, John W. *What Happened at Vatican II* (Cambridge: Harvard University Press, 2008).

O'Reilly, Julie D. *Bewitched Again" Supernaturally Powerful Women on Television, 1996–2011* (Jefferson: McFarland, 2013).

Ottosson, Per-Gunnar, Scholastic medicine and philosophy: a study of commentaries on Galen's Tegni, 1300–1450 (Bloomington: Indiana University Press, 1984).

Ovid, *Metamorphoses*, trans. A. D. Melville, (Oxford: Oxford University Press, 2009).

Owens, Yvonne. "The Saturnine History of Jews and Witches," *Preternature: Critical and Historical Studies on the Preternatural* 3 (2014), 56–84.

Park, Katharine. *Secrets of Women: Gender, Generation, and the Origins of Human Dissection* (Cambridge: Zone Books/MIT Press, 2010).

Paszylk, Bartlomiej. *The Pleasure and Pain of Cult Horror Films: A Historical Survey* (Jefferson, NC: McFarland Press, 2009).

Paul, William. *Laughing Screaming: Modern Hollywood Horror and Comedy*, (New York: Columbia University Press, 1995).

Petroff, Elizabeth. "Transforming the World: The Serpent Dragon and the Virgin Saint," *Body and Soul: Essays on Medieval Women and Mysticism*, ed. E.A Petroff (Oxford: Oxford University Press, 1994)

Petronius, *Satyricon*, trans. P. G. Walsh (Oxford: Oxford University Press, 2009).

Picart, Caroline Joan S. and John Edgar Browning, *Speaking of Monsters: A Teratological Anthology* (Basingstoke: Palgrave, 2012).

Po-Chia Hsia, R. *The Myth of Ritual Murder: Jews and Magic in Reformation Germany* (New Haven: Yale University Press, 1988).

R. Po-Chia Hsia, *Trent 1475: Stories of a Ritual Murder Trial* (New Haven: Yale University Press, 1992).

Polidori, John. *The Vampyre and Other Tales of the Macabre* (Oxford: Oxford University Press, 2008).

Poole, W. Scott. *Satan in America: The Devil We Know* (New York: Rowman & Littlefield, 2010).

Poole, W. Scott. *Monsters in America* (Waco, TX: Baylor University Press, 2011).

Pormann, Peter E. and Emilie Savage-Smith, *Medieval Islamic Medicine* (Washington, D.C.: Georgetown University Press, 2007).

Porphyry, *Life of Pythagoras*, trans. Kevin Guthrie (1920) aphorism 19; 45. Accessible at: http://www.tertullian.org/fathers/porphyry_life_of_pythagoras_02_text.htm

Price, Merrall L. "Medieval Antisemitism and Excremental Libel," *Jews in Medieval Christendom: Slay them Not*, ed. Kristine T. Utterback and Merrall L. Price (Leiden: Brill, 2013), 177–88.

Prudlho, Donald. *The Martyred Inquisitor: The Life and Cult of Peter of Verona* (Burlington, VT: Ashgate, 2008).

Punter, David. "Spectral Criticism" in *Introducing Criticism at the 21st Century*, Julian Woffreys, ed. (Edinburgh: Edinburgh University Press, 2002).

Pynsent, R B. "The Devil's Stench and Living Water: A Study of Demons and Adultery in Czech Vernacular Literature of the Middle Ages and Renaissance," *The Slavonic and East European Review*, Vol. 71, No. 4 (Oct., 1993), 601–30.

Radden, Jennifer. *The Nature of Melancholy: From Aristotle to Kristeva* (Oxford: Oxford University Press, 2002).

Raitt, Jill. "The Vagina Dentata and the Immaculatus Uterus Dvini Fontis," *Journal of the American Academy of Religion* 48:3 (1980), 415–31.

Ralph of Coggeshall, "The Witch of Rheims," in *Witchcraft in Europe: 1100–1700*. Alan C Kors and Edward Peters, eds. (Philadelphia: University of Pennsylvania Press, 1972).

Ravid, Benjamin. "From Yellow to Red: On the Distinguishing Head-Covering of the Jews of Venice," *Jewish History* 6 (1992), 179–210.

Remy, Nicholas. *Demonolatry*, trans. Montague Summers (New York: Dover, 2008).

Resnick, Irven M. *Marks of Distinction: Christian Perceptions of Jews in the High Middle Ages* (Washington, D.C.: Catholic University of America Press, 2012).

Resnick, Irven M. "Medieval Roots of the Myth of the Jewish Male Menses," *Harvard Theological Review* (2000), 241–63.

Resnick, Irven M. "Odo of Tournai and the Dehumanization of Medieval Jews: A Reexamination," *Jewish Quarterly Review* 98 (2008), 471–84.

Riches, Samantha J E. "Encountering the Monstrous: Saints and Dragons in Medieval Thought," *Monstrous Middle Ages*, ed. Bettina Bildhauer and Robert Mills (Toronto: University of Toronto Press, 2003), 196–218.

Rider, Catherine. *Magic and Impotence in the Middle Ages* (New York: Oxford, 2006).

Rider, Catherine. "Demons and Mental Disorder in Late Medieval Medicine," *Mental (Dis)Order in Later Medieval Europe*, ed. Sari Katajala-Peltomaa and Susanna Niiranen, (Leiden: Brill, 2014), 47–69.

Robertson, Elizabeth. "The Corporeality of Female Sanctity in The Life of Saint Margaret," *Images of Sainthood in Medieval Europe*. (Ithaca: Cornell University Press, 1991).

Robinson, Janet S. "Your Tale Merely Confirms That Women are Mad and Vain: The Uncanny Rendering of Countess Elizabeth Bathory's Life as Vampire Legend," *Dracula's Daughters: The Female Vampire on Film*, eds. Douglas Brode and Leah Deyneka (New York: Scarecrow Press, 2014), 139–58.

Roger Corman: Interviews, ed. Constantine Nasr (Jackson: University of Mississippi Press, 2011), 21.

Roper, Lyndal. "Evil Imaginings and Fantasies: Child-Witches and the End of the Witch Craze," *New Perspectives on Witchcraft, Magic, and Demonology: Witchcraft in Continental Europe*, ed. Brian P. Levack (New York: Routledge, 2001), 433–65.

Ross, Ellen M. *The Grief of God: Images of the Suffering Jesus in Late Medieval England* (New York: Oxford University Press, 1997).

Rubin, Miri. *Gentile Tales: The Narrative Assault on Late Medieval Jews* (New Haven: Yale University Press, 1999).

Rubin, Mary. "Europe Remade: Purity and Danger in Late Medieval Europe," *Transactions of the Royal Historical Society* 6:11 (2001), 101–124.

Rubin, Miri. *Corpus Christi: The Eucharist in Late Medieval Culture* (Cambridge: Cambridge University Press, 1992).

Russell, Jeffrey Burton. *Lucifer: The Devil in the Middle Ages* (Ithaca: Cornell University Press, 1984).

Russell, Jeffrey Burton. *Inventing the Flat Earth: Columbus and Modern Historians* (Santa Barbara: Praeger, 1991).

Russell, Jeffrey Burton and Mark W. Wyndham, "Witchcraft and the Demonization of Heresy" *Medievalia* 2 (1976), 1–21.

Sabine, Maureen A. *Veiled Desires: Intimate Portrayals of Nuns in Postwar Anglo-American Film* (New York: Fordham University Press, 2013).

Santana, Carlos. "Black Magic Woman." *Abraxas* (1970). Orig. by Peter Green (1968).

Scandura, Jani. "Deadly Professions: Dracula, Undertakers, and the Embalmed Corpse," *Victorian Studies* 40 (1996), 1–30.

Schaffer, Talia. "A Wilde Desire Took Me: The Homoerotic History of Dracula." *ELH* 61:2 1994), 381–425.

Schmidt, Josef and Mary Simon, "Holy and Unholy Shit: The Pragmatic Context of Scatological Curses in Early German Reformation Satire," in *Fecal Matters in Early Modern Literature and Art*, eds. Jeff Persels and Russel Ganim (Aldershot: Ashgate Press, 2004).

Schmitt, Jean-Claude. *The Holy Greyhound: Guinefort, Healer of Children since the Thirteenth Century* (Cambridge: Cambridge University Press, 2009).

Schmitt, Jean-Claude. *Ghosts in the Middle Ages: The Living and the Dead in Medieval Society* (Chicago: University of Chicago Press, 1998).

Schneider, Steven Jay. *Horror Film and Psychoanalysis: Freud's Worst Nightmare* (Cambridge: Cambridge University Press, 2009).

Sconduto, Leslie A. *Metamorphosis of the Werewolf: A Literary Study from Antiquity through the Renaissance* (Jefferson, NC: McFarland, 2008).

Seiferth, Wolfgang. *Synagogue and Church in the Middle Ages: Two Symbols in Art and Literature* (Ungar, 1970).

Shakespeare, William. *Macbeth*. (New York: Oxford University Press, 2008).

Sharpe, Alex Neville. *Foucault's Monsters and the Law* (London: Routledge 2010).

Shildrick, Margrit. *Leaky Bodies and Boundaries: Feminism, Postmodernism, and Bioethics* (London: Routledge, 1997).

Simmons, Walter. *Cities of Ladies: Beguine Communities in the Medieval Low Countries; 1200-1565* (Philadelphia: University of Pennsylvania Press, 2003).

Siraisi, Nancy. *Medieval and Early Renaissance Medicine: An Introduction to Knowledge and Practice* (Chicago: University of Chicago, 1990).

Skal, David. *The Monster Show: A Cultural History of Horror* (San Francisco: Faber & Faber, 2001).

Smith, Andrew. *Victorian Demons: Medicine, Masculinity, and the Gothic at the Fin-de-siècle* (Manchester: Manchester University Press, 2004).

Smith, Moire. "The Flying Phallus and the Laughing Inquisitor: Penis Theft in the Malleus Maleficarum," *Journal of Folklore Research* 39:1 (2002), 85–117.

Solanas, Valerie. *SCUM Manifesto* (London: Verso Press, 2004).

Stacey, Robert C. "From Ritual Crucifixion to Host Desecration: Jews and the Body of Christ," *Jewish History* 12 (1998), 11–28.

Stephen of Bourbon, *De Superstitione*, accessible at: http://www.fordham.edu/halsall/source/guinefort.asp.

Stoker, Bram. *Dracula* (New York: Oxford University Press, 2011).

Temkin, Owsei. *Galen and Galenism: Rise and Decline of a Medical Philosophy* (Ithaca, NY: Cornell University Press, 1973).

Tertullian, *Ante-Nicene Fathers*, Volume 3: Latin Christianity, ed. A. Cleveland Coxe (1885).

The Other Bible, ed. Willis Barnstone (New York: Harper Collins, 2005).

The Witchcraft Sourcebook, ed. Brain P. Levack (New York: Routledge, 2004).

Thomas Aquinas, *Summa Theologica*, searchable at: http://www.ccel.org/ccel/aquinas/summa.html

Thomas Aquinas, *On the Sentences*, ed. M. F. Moos (Paris: Lethielleux, 1956).

Thomas Aquinas, *De Substantiis Separatis* (Turnhout: Brepols, 2013).

Thomas Cantimpré: The Collected Saints' Lives, ed. Barbara Newman, trans. Margot King and Barbara Newman (Turnhout: Brepols, 2008).

Thorne, Tony. *Countess Dracula: The Life and Times of Elisabeth Bathory The Blood Countess* (London: Bloomsbury, 1998).

Tohill, Cathal and Pete Tombs, *Immoral Tales: European sex and Horror Movies, 1956–1984* (New York: Saint Martin's Griffin, 1995).

Trachtenberg, Joshua. *The Devil and the Jews: The Medieval Conception of the Jew and its Relation to Modern Antisemitism* (New York: Jewish Publication Society, 2002).

Tuchman, Barbara. *A Distant Mirror: The Calamitous Fourteenth Century* (New York: Alfred Knopf, 1978).

Twitchell, James. B. *Dreadful Pleasures: An Anatomy of Modern Horror* (New York: Oxford University Press, 1985).

Two Lives of St. Cuthbert, ed. Bertram Colgrave (Cambridge: Cambridge University Press, 1940).

Vachhani, Sheena J. "Vagina Dentata and the Demonological Body: Explorations of the Feminine Demon in Organization," *Bits of Organization* (Copenhagen: Copenhagen Business School Press, 2009), 163–183.

Van Engen, John. *Learning Institutionalized: Teaching in the Medieval University* (Notre Dame: University of Notre Dame Press, 2000).

Vauchéz, Andre. *Sainthood in the Later Middle Ages* (Cambridge: Cambridge University Press, 1997).

Venarde, B. L. *Women's Monasticism in Medieval Society: Nunneries in France and England (890–1215)* (Ithaca: Cornell University Press, 1997).

Verdon, Jean. *Night in the Middle Ages* (Notre Dame: University of Notre Dame Press, 2002).

Verger, Jacques. "The First French Universities and the Institutionalization of Learning: Faculties, Curricula, Degrees," *Learning Institutionalized: Teaching in the Medieval University*.

Voigts, Linda E. and Michael R. McVaugh, "A

Latin Technical Phlebotomy and Its Middle English Translation," *Transactions of the American Philosophical Society*, New Series, Vol. 74, No. 2 (1984), 1–69.

Wack, Mary Frances. "The *Liber de heros morbo* of *Johannes Afflacius* and Its Implications for Medieval Love Conventions," in Speculum 62 (1987), 324–44.

Walinski-Kiehl, Robert S. "The Devil's Children: Child Witch Trials," in *New Perspectives on Witchcraft, Magic, and Demonology: Witchcraft in Continental Europe*, ed. Brian P. Levack (New York: Routledge, 2001), 413–31.

Wallis, Faith. "Signs and Senses: Diagnosis and Prognosis in Early Medieval Pulse and Urine Tests," in *Society for the Social History of Medicine* (2000).

Wallis, Faith, ed. *Medieval Medicine: A Reader* (Toronto: University of Toronto Press, 2010).

Walter, Brenda Gardenour. "*Phantasmic Science*: Medieval Theology, Victorian Spiritualism, and the Specific Rationality of Twenty-First Century Ghost Hunting," *Jefferson Journal of Science and Culture* 2 (2013), 2–16.

Walter, Brenda Gardenour. "Ghastly Transmissions: The Horror of Connectivity and the Transnational Flow of Fear," in *Horror across Visual Media: Fragmented Bodies*, ed. Dana Och (London: Routledge, Taylor and Francis, 2013).

Walter, Brenda Gardenour. "Corrupt Air, Poisonous Places, and the Toxic Breath of Witches in Late-Medieval Medicine and Theology" in *Toxic Airs: Body, Place, Planet in Historical Perspective* (Pittsburgh: University of Pittsburgh Press, 2014).

Walter, Brenda Gardenour. "Thrust and Probe: The Physician's Phallic Blade" in *Sensational Pleasures in Cinema, Literature, and Visual Culture: The Phallic Eye*, eds. Gilad Padva and Nurit Buchweitz (London: Palgrave MacMillan, 2014).

Walter, Brenda Gardenour. "The Biology of Blood-Lust: Medieval Physiognomy, Physiology, and the Vampire Jew in Twentieth Century Cinema," *Film and History* 41:2 (2011), 51–63.

Ward, Benedicta. *Miracles and the Medieval Mind: Theory, Record, and Event, 1000–1215* (Philadelphia: University of Pennsylvania Press, 1982).

Warner, Marina. *Alone of All Her Sex: The Myth and the Cult of the Virgin Mary* (New York: Vintage, 1976).

Weinstein, Donald and Rudolph M. Bell, *Saints and Society: The Two Worlds of Western Christendom, 1000–1700* (Chicago: University of Chicago Press, 1986).

Weinstein, Sheri. "Technologies of Vision: Spiritualism and Science in Nineteenth-Century America," *Spectral America: Phantoms and the National Imagination*, ed. J. A. Weinstock (Madison: University of Wisconsin Press, 2004), 124–140.

Weiss, Andrea. "The Lesbian Vampire Film: A Subgenre of Horror," *Dracula's Daughters: The Female Vampire on Film*, eds. Douglas Brode and Leah Deyneka (New York: Scarecrow Press, 2014), 21–36

Wells, Charlotte. "Leeches on the Body Politic: Xenophobia and Witchcraft in Early Modern French Political Thought" *French Historical Studies*, 22:3 (1999), 351–377.

Wheatley, Dennis. *To The Devil—A Daughter* (London: Hutchinson, 1953).

Wildberg, Christian. *John Philoponus' Criticism of Aristotle's Theory of Aether.* (Berlin: De Gruyter, 1988).

William of Auvergne, *De Universo*, trans. Roland J. Teske (Milwaukee: Marquette University Press, 1998).

Williams, Wes. *Monsters and Their Meanings in Early Modern Culture: Mighty Magic* (Oxford: Oxford University Press, 2011).

Witches, Devils, and Doctors in the Renaissance: Johann Weyer's Praestigiis Daemonum, ed. George Mora (Binghamton: Medieval and Renaissance Texts and Studies, 1993).

Yates, Frances. *Giordano Bruno and the Hermetical Tradition* (Chicago: University of Chicago Press, 1964).

Young, Robert J. C. *Colonial Desire: Hybridity in Theory, Culture, and Race* (London: Routledge, 2005).

Yuval, Israel. "Vengeance and Damnation, Blood and Defamation: From Jewish Martyrdom to Blood Libel Accusations," *Zion* 58 (1993), 33–90.

Zafran, Eric. "Saturn and the Jews," *Journal of the Warburg and Courtauld Institutes* 42 (1979), 16–27.

Ziegler, Joseph. "*Ut Dicunt Medici*: Medical Knowledge and Theological Debates in the Second Half of the Thirteenth Century" *Bulletin of the History of Medicine*, 73:2,. (1999).

Ziegler, Joseph. "Physiognomy, Science, and Proto-Racism 1200–1500," in *The Origins of Racism in the West*, ed. M. Eliav-Feldon and B. Isaac and J. Ziegler (Cambridge: Cambridge University Press, 2009), 181–99.

Ziegler, Joseph. 'Practitioners and Saints: Medical Men in Canonization Processes in the Thirteenth to Fifteenth Centuries', *Social History of Medicine*, 12 (1999), 191–225.

Zika, Charles. *Exorcizing Our Demons: Magic, Witchcraft, and Visual Culture in Early Modern Europe* (Leiden: Brill, 2010).

Filmography

Abby, William Girdler, American International (1974)
An American Werewolf in London, John Landis, Universal (1981)
Anneliese: The Exorcist Tapes, Jude Gerard Prest, The Asylum (2011)
L'Anticristo, Alberto de Martino, First Line (1974)
The Bad Seed, Mervyn LeRoy, Warner Brothers (1956)
Báthory: Countess of Blood, Juraj Jakubisko, Bonton Film (2008)
Bedknobs and Broomsticks, Robert Stevenson, Walt Disney Productions (1971)
The Believers, John Schlesinger, Orion (1987)
The Black Cat, Edgar G. Ulmer, Universal (1934)
Black Sunday, Mario Bava, American International (1960)
Blackwater Valley Exorcism, Ethan Wiley, Lionsgate Home Entertainment (2006)
Blacula, William Crane, American International (1972)
The Blair Witch Project, Daniel Myrick and Eduardo Sánchez, Haxan Films (1999)
Bless the Child, Chuck Russell, Paramount (2000)
Blessed: Samantha's Child, Simon Fellows, Warner Home Video (2004)
Blood on Satan's Claw, Piers Haggard, Tigon (1971)
Bram Stoker's Dracula, Francis Ford Coppola, Columbia (1992)
The Brotherhood of Satan, Bernard McEveety, Columbia (1971)
Cabin Fever, Eli Roth, Lionsgate (2002)
The Cabin in the Woods, Drew Goddard, Lionsgate (2011)
Cathy's Curse, Eddy Matalon, Jupiter Communications (1977)
The Cat People, Jacques Tourneur, RKO Radio Pictures (1942)
The Children of the Corn, Fritz Kiersch, New World Pictures (1984)
The Children of the Damned, Anton M. Leader, Metro-Goldwyn Mayer (1963)
Children of the Full Moon, Tom Clegg, Hammer (1980)
Chronicles of an Exorcism, Nick G. Miller, Fortune Five Entertainment (2008)
The City of the Dead, John Moxey, Vulcan (1960)
The Company of Wolves, Neil Jordan, Cannon (1984)
The Corridor, Evan Kelley, Cinemavault (2010)
Cosmopolis, David Cronenberg, eOne Films (2012)
Count Dracula, Philip Saville, BBC (1977)
The Countess, Julie Delpy, Bac Films (2009)
Cremaster 3: The Order, Matthew Barney, Glacier Field LLC (2002)
Cry of the Banshee, Gordon Hessler, American International (1970)
Curse of the Crimson Altar, Vernon Sewell, American International (1968)
The Curse of the Werewolf, Terence Fisher, Hammer (1961)
Dark Side of the Moon, D.J. Webster, Trimark (1990)
Daughters of Satan, Hollingswood Morse, United Artists (1972)
The Devil Inside, William Brent Bell, Paramount (2012)
The Devil Rides Out, Terence Fisher, Hammer (1968)
The Devils, Ken Russell, Warner Brothers (1971)
The Devil's Daughter, Jeannot Szwarc, Paramount Television (1973)
The Devil's Hand, William J. Hole, Jr., Crown International (1962)
The Devil's Rain, Robert Fuest, Bryanston (1975)
Dominion, Paul Schrader, Warner Brothers (2005)
Don't Go Into the Woods, Vincent D'Onofrio, Tribeca (2010)
Dracula, Tod Browning, Universal (1931)
Dracula Has Risen from the Grave, Freddie Francis, Hammer (1968)

Dracula: Pages from a Virgin's Diary, Guy Maddin, Zeitgeist (2002)
Dracula: Prince of Darkness, Terence Fisher, Hammer (1966)
End of Days, Peter Hyams, Universal (1999)
Evil Dead, Sam Raimi, New Line (1981)
Evil Dead, Fede Alvarez, Sony (2013)
Exorcism, William A. Baker, York Entertainment (2003)
The Exorcism of Emily Rose, Scott Derrickson, Screen Gems (2005)
Exorcism: The Possession of Gail Bowers, Leigh Scott, The Asylum (2006)
Exorcismo, Juan Bosch, Cinefear (1975)
Exorcismus: La Possession de Emma Evans, Manuel Carballo, Filmax (2010)
The Exorcist, William Friedkin, Warner Brothers (1973)
Exorcist: The Beginning, Renny Harlin, Warner Brothers (2004)
Exorcist II: The Heretic, John Boorman, Warner Brothers (1977)
Exorcist III, William Peter Blatty, 20th Century–Fox (1990)
The Fearless Vampire Killers, Roman Polanski, Metro-Goldwyn Mayer (1969)
Friday the Thirteenth, Sean S. Cunningham, Paramount Pictures (1980)
Ghostbusters, Ivan Reitman, Columbia (1984)
Ginger Snaps, John Fawcett, Motion International (2000)
Guardian of Hell, Bruno Mattei, Film Concept Group (1981)
A Haunting, Discovery Channel, (2005–2007; 2012-present)
The Haunting of Morella, Jim Wynorski, New Horizons (1990)
Häxan, Benjamin Christensen, Criterion (1922)
The Hills Have Eyes, Wes Craven, Vanguard (1977)
Holy Mountain, Alejandro Jodorowsky, ABKCO Music and Records (1973)
Horror of Dracula, Terence Fisher, Hammer (1958)
The House of the Devil, Ti West, MPI Media Group (2009)
The Howling, Joe Dante, Embassy Pictures (1981)
I Drink Your Blood, David E. Durston, Grindhouse (1970)
I Vampiri, Riccardo Freda and Mario Bava, Athena Cinematografica (1956)
The Last Exorcism, Daniel Stamm, Lionsgate (2010)
The Last Exorcism II, Ed Gass-Donnelly, CBS Films (2012)
Let the Right One In, Tomas Alfredson, Magnet (2008)
The Lost Boys, Joel Schumacher, Warner Brothers (1987)
Lucifer Rising, Kenneth Anger, Mystic Fire (1972)
Magdalena: Possessed by the Devil, Walter Boos, Mill Creek Entertainment (1974)
Mark of the Devil, Michael Strong, Hallmark Releasing (1970)
Le Moine et la Sorcière, Suzanne Schiffman, European Classics (1987)
The Naked Witch, Larry Buchanan, Alexander Enterprises (1964)
Necromancy (The Witching), Bert I. Gordon, Cinerama (1972)
Nosferatu: Ein Symphonie des Grauens, F. W. Murnau, Film Arts Guild (1922)
Nosferatu: Phantom der Nacht, Werner Herzog, 20th Century–Fox (1979)
The Omen, Richard Donner, 20th Century–Fox (1976)
Once Bitten, Howard Storm, Samuel Goldwyn (1985)
Paranormal Activity, Oren Peli, Paramount (2009)
Paranormal Activity 2, Tod Williams, Paramount (2010)
Paranormal Activity 3, Henry Joost and Ariel Schulman, Paramount (2011)
Paranormal Activity 4, Christopher B. Landon, Paramount (2012)
Paranormal State, A&E Network (2007–2011)
Plague of the Zombies, John Gilling, Hammer (1966)
The Possession of David O'Reilly, Andrew Cull and Steve Isles, IFC Films (2010)
Prince of Darkness, John Carpenter, Universal (1981)
Pro-Life in *Hammer Masters of Horror*, John Carpenter, Hammer House (2006)
Queen of the Damned, Michael Rymer, Warner Brothers (2002)
Rosemary's Baby, Roman Polanski, Paramount (1968)
Salem's Lot, Tobe Hooper, CBS (1979)
The Satanic Rites of Dracula, Alan Gibson, Hammer (1973)
Satan's Blood, Carlos Puerto, Mondo Macabro (1978)
Satan's Princess, Bert I. Gordon, Paramount Home Video (1990)
Scream Blacula Scream, Bob Kelljan, American International (1973)
Season of the Witch, Tommy Lee Wallace, Universal (1972)
The Sentinel, Michael Winner, Universal (1977)
The Shining, Stanley Kubrick, Warner Brothers (1980)
Storm of the Century, Craig R. Baxley, ABC (1999)
Superstition, James W. Roberson, Anchor Bay (1982)
Tales of Terror (the segment "Morella"), ROger Corman, American International (1962)
Taste the Blood of Dracula, Peter Sasdy, Hammer (1970)

To the Devil a Daughter, Peter Sykes, Hammer (1976)
True Blood, HBO (2008-present)
Twins of Evil, John Hough, Hammer (1971)
The Undying Monster, John Brahm, 20th Century-Fox (1942)
Vamp, Richard Wenk, New World Pictures (1986)
Vampire in Brooklyn, Wes Craven, Paramount (1995)
Vampyr, Carl Th. Dreyer, Vereinigte Star Film (1932)
Vampyros Lesbos, Jesus Franco, Fenix Films (1971)
The Vatican Tapes, Mark Neveldine, Lionsgate (2015)
The Village of the Damned, Wolf Rilla, Metro-Goldwyn Mayer (1960)
The Village of the Damned, John Carpenter, Universal (1995)
Virgin Witch, Ray Austin, Tigon (1972)
WereWolf of London, Stuart Walker, Universal (1935)
White Zombie, Victor Halperin, United Artists (1932)
The Wicker Man, Robin Hardy, British Lion (1973)
Witchboard, Kevin Tenney, Paragon (1986)
Witchboard 2: The Devil's Doorway, Kevin Tenney, Blue Rider (1993)
Witchboard 3: The Possession, Peter Svatek, Artisan (1995)
Witchery, Fabrizio Laurenti, Vidmark (1988)
The Witches, Cyril Frankel, Hammer (1966)
Witchfinder General, Michael Reeves, American International (1968)
The Witching (*Necromancy*), Bert I. Gordon, Cinerama (1972)
The Witchmaker, William O. Brown, Las Cruces-Arrow (1969)
The Wolf Man, George Waggner, Universal (1941)
The X-Files, Fox Network (1993–2002)

Index

Abelard, Peter 18
abjection 106, 126, 128–9, 137, 139, 153, 164, 169
abortion 60–61, 93, 116
adoption 61
Agrippa, Heinrich Cornelius 40
Albertus Magnus 17, 23, 26
Alexander V 34
An American Werewolf in London (1981) 186
Anderl Von Rinn 150, 165
angels 5, 21–22, 27, 29, 34, 56, 59, 68, 181
anti-Catholicism 106, 130, 161–62
Antichrist 6, 34, 55–61, 150
anti-Judaism 137–38, 141–50
Antisemitism 12, 60, 151, 154–59, 165
apocalypse 56–57, 115, 149
Aquinas 5, 10, 62, 17, 28, 37, 56, 143, 169, 174–6, 178, 181
Aristotle (Passim) 5, 16, 19, 62, 137–139, 159, 166, 170–75, 179–81
Arnau de Villanova 73
Ash Wednesday 126
astrology 44, 188
Augustine 10, 18, 27, 37, 77, 88, 167, 181
autumn 9, 11, 125, 138, 152, 169, 182
Avicenna 69
Avignon papacy 34, 55

Bad Moon (1996) 12, 187, 188–89
badges 142, 146
baptism 22, 38–39, 45, 96, 103
Báthory, Elizabeth 163
bats 9, 27
Bauhaus 43, 60
BDSM 116, 128
beauty 8, 95–96, 98, 100, 105, 107–8, 111–113, 118, 121, 131, 134, 163
Beguines 34, 79, 143–44
The Believers (1987) 54
Bible 4, 17, 20, 24, 26, 33, 37, 94, 114, 126, 165
Bisclavret 10, 167, 173
black 5, 24, 27, 47–51, 66–67, 138, 140, 141, 149, 152, 158, 180, 182
black bile 7, 9, 10, 137–141, 147–49, 157–58, 168, 176
The Black Cat (1934) 6, 43–44
Black Mass 6, 39–40, 42–53, 67, 93

Black Sunday (1960) 163
Blackwater Valley Exorcism(2006) 6
Blackula (1972) 10
The Blair Witch Project (1999) 8
Bless the Child (2000) 54
Blessed: Samantha's Child (2004) 6, 60–61
blood (consumption) 8–11, 145–7, 149, 156–65, 169
blood (menstrual) 83, 84–88
blood libel 9, 141–46, 165
Blood on Satan's Claw (1971) 6, 52–53
bloodlust 8, 90, 93, 100, 111, 113, 118, 133, 148, 152, 161, 186
Bodin, Jean 11, 40, 91, 93, 168–9, 177–78, 180
Boguet, Henri 40, 168, 180–81
Boniface VIII 34
Bonum Univerale De Apibus (1260) 152
bowels 7, 26, 27, 28, 63–64, 78, 87–88, 137
brain 7–8, 63, 73–75, 77, 87, 91, 140, 147, 157, 168, 176–77, 188–90
Bram Stoker's Dracula (1992) 162
breath 8, 10, 30, 62, 64, 85, 90–92, 99, 138, 158
broomstick 39, 98, 102–3, 179
The Brotherhood of Satan (1971) 8, 53, 107, 113–15
burning at the stake 34, 95, 117, 117, 118, 124, 128, 130, 181, 186

Caciola, Nancy 87
Caesarius of Heisterbach 27, 147
Calmet, Augustin 136, 151
candlemas 47, 49, 111, 115
candles 49, 57, 92, 132, 169, 178, 184, 191
cannibalism 30, 32, 36–37, 93, 174
Canon Episcopi (9th century) 167, 172
carnality 8, 9, 10, 11, 31, 94–96, 137, 176
The Cat People (1942) 54
Cathars 30–32
Catholicism 49–51, 55–57, 61, 67, 89–90, 92, 101, 102, 106, 129–130, 161
Centriloquium (10th century) 188
changelings 32, 61, 123, 178
chastity 78
children 9, 11, 28, 39, 60–61, 89–90, 92–96, 98, 121
Children of the Full Moon (1980) 186–87, 192

237

238 INDEX

Christina Mirabilis 7, 81–82
Christina of Stommeln 83
Chronicle of an Exorcism (2008) 6
Church (Medieval) 22, 29–30, 38
circumcision 145
City of the Dead (1960) 6, 8, 46–48, 118–19
civil rights movement 110
Clark, Stuart 150
Clavicle of Solomon 45, 116
Clericos Laicos (1296) 34
coldness (passim) 16–19, 24, 27, 64–67
communion 78, 130
Company of Wolves (1984) 12, 193
Compendium Maleficarum (1608) 40, 91
Compendium Medicinae (1250) 176
Condemnations of Paris (1277) 17–18
conservativism 104–6, 110, 114, 115, 128, 131, 133, 154, 164–65
conspiracy 149–50
Constantine the African 69, 72, 157
contagion 8, 10, 12, 92, 105, 137–38, 149, 151, 155, 158, 163, 169, 176, 187, 193
contraception 104
contrareity 18–20, 77; *see also* inversion
conventual life 78–79
corpse 3, 81, 93, 123, 137, 152, 155, 161
Corpus Christi 143
cosmology (Aristotelian) 16, 19, 140
cosmology (Christian) 16, 20–28, 140
Council of Basel (1431–40) 35
Council of Constance (1414–18) 35
Council of Nicaea (325) 30
Council of Pisa (1409) 34
Count Dracula (1977) 162
counter culture 6, 52–53, 56, 104–106, 115, 128–29
coven 47
coven (matriarchal) 117–28
coven (patriarchal) 107–17
The Craft (1989) 133
crucifix 11, 38, 45, 130–31, 144, 159, 161–62, 186
crusade 31, 88, 142, 187
Cry of the Banshee (1970) 8, 121–24
cryptonomy 129–30
The Curse of the Werewolf (1961) 11, 186–87, 192

dance 47, 49, 107–108, 121–22, 180
Daneau, Lambert 92
Daughters of Satan (1972) 8, 124
De Melancholia (10th century) 168, 176
De Secretis Mulierum 84–88, 91
De Universo (13th century) 174–75
decapitation 152
decay 10, 76, 88, 115, 117, 137, 141, 147, 188
Demonmania of Witches (1580) 11, 40, 91, 168, 177–78
Demonolatry (1595) 40, 48, 91, 102, 112
demons 7–8, 27–29, 36–37, 56, 62–67, 78, 79, 83, 87, 91, 94–96, 103, 105, 111, 128, 130, 133, 138, 146, 152, 167–68, 172, 174–75, 178
Descartes 3, 12, 169, 183–82, 189–91
desert 53, 113
The Devil See Satan
The Devil Rides Out (1968) 6, 44–46
The Devil's Daughter (1973) 6, 53

The Devil's Hand (1962) 8, 107–10
diet 62, 148
discernment 62–65, 79–84, 89
Discoverie of Witchcraft (1584) 40, 169
dismemberment 152
doctor 40, 62, 66, 73–75, 102, 113–114, 132, 159–60, 170, 179–80, 184, 188
dog 6, 27, 32, 61, 85, 94, 98, 123–24, 176, 180, 182, 187, 192
Dog Soldiers (2002) 12
doll 108, 110, 119
Dominicans 32, 36, 78–79
double coding 153
Dracula 6, 10, 50–52
Dracula (1931) 159–61
Dracula Has Risen from the Grave (1968) 161–62cat
Dracula Prince of Darkness (1966) 161
duplicity 98, 100, 105, 107–108, 112, 113, 124–125, 128, 137, 147, 158

earth (elemental) 23, 27, 81–82, 88, 103, 115, 117, 126, 138, 147, 139–40, 152, 155, 175
Easter 142, 144, 147
Eastern Europe 136, 151–53, 155–57, 159–60
Ecstatic Union 79–80, 143
Egyptian 43, 49, 115, 127
elements 19, 23–24, 27, 77–78, 174
Elliott, Dyan 89
emasculation 119, 121, 128, 130–31
Empedocles 170–71
Empyrean 5, 20–22, 161
End of Days (1999) 54
Ermine of Rheims 27
Errores Gazariorum (1437) 36, 39
eucharist 9, 31, 36, 47, 50, 62–3, 79–80, 93–94, 130, 143–44, 150–51, 159, 167, 173–74, 178
evil eye 85–86, 90–91
An Examen of Witches (1602) 40, 168, 180–81
excrement 73, 83
exempla 35–36, 81, 84, 89, 91
exorcism 6, 41–42, 64–67, 83, 186
Exorcism (2003) 6
Exorcism of Emily Rose (2005) 6
Exorcism of Gail Bowers (2006) 6
Exorcismus (2010) 6
The Exorcist (1973) 6, 64–65, 105–6
exploitation cinema 106, 154

family (middle class, nuclear) 113–14, 105, 124–28, 131–33, 153
fasting 79–84
fathers (bad) 105, 107–117
Fearless Vampire Killers (1967) 159
female body (construct) 7, 62–65, 77–84, 89–97, 101, 103, 175–76
female sanctity 79–84
feminism 8–9, 104–5, 113, 121, 124–28, 154, 192–94
fetus 57–61, 94, 130
folklore 9, 137, 159, 170
Foucault, Michel (*Discourses of Power*) 4, 41, 46, 101, 103, 125, 138, 152, 154, 162–63, 164–65, 169
Fourth Lateran Council (1215) 23, 32, 78, 141

Franciscans 33–34
freemasonry 46, 127
Freud, Sigmund 169–70, 183–84
Fulda 145

Galen 62, 69–75, 77–78
Garlic 50, 122
Garnier, Gilles 178
Gay Liberation Front 104
gentleman vampire 159–162
Gerald of Wales 10, 172–73, 188
Gervaise of Tillbury 174
Ghostbusters (1984) 54
ghosts 3, 9, 12, 27, 123, 128–33
Gilbertus Anglicus 176
Ginger Snaps (2000) 12, 186–87, 193–94
Glaber, Raoul 27
goat 26, 45, 116, 145
gold 21, 24
gothic 136
graveyard 47, 123, 170, 176
great famine 33
great schism 5, 34–35, 55
Gregory the Great 26, 30
Grenier 182
Guazzo, Francesco Maria 40, 91–92
Guibert of Nogent 27

hagiography 30, 32, 79–84, 88–89
hail 27, 180
Halloween 98
Hand of Glory 120
Haunting of Morella (1990) 8
Häxan (1922) 102
heart 7, 26, 62–65, 74, 77–78, 80–83, 85–88, 131, 143, 148
heaven 20–22
heaviness 23
Hebrew 165
hell 5, 24, 26, 37, 103, 138, 180, 185
hemorrhoids 147
hereditary evil 89, 112, 126, 124, 132, 134, 181, 182, 187, 189
heresy 8, 30–35, 36, 91, 93, 139, 141, 172
Hildegard von Bingen 55
The Hills Have Eyes (1977) 53
Hippocrates 62, 69, 71–72
Hocus Pocus (1993) 134
Homer 170
Horror of Dracula (1958) 161
host desecration 9, 144
House of the Devil (2009) 6, 59
The Howling (1980) 12, 190–91
Hugh of Lincoln 9, 145, 165
humors 7, 70–76, 90, 93, 133, 139–41, 147, 157, 168, 175–
Hussites 33
hylomorphism 143, 174
hypertrichosis 169, 184
hysteria 102

I Drink Your Blood (1970) 6, 52
Ibn-Imran, Ishaq 168, 176
Ibn-Jazzar (al-Qayrawani) 75, 157
Illuminati 44, 46

immortality 49, 53, 131, 158, 171
impotence 9, 75, 96, 114, 131, 137–38, 148, 156–158
in vitro 60
Inquisition 5, 32, 124, 130, 150
Interview with a Vampire (1994) 10
inversion 6, 7, 47, 16, 38, 59, 101, 103, 109–10, 111, 114, 118, 119, 124–25, 128, 151–52, 155, 159–61, 162, 168, 182, 184
irrationality 7–9, 77–78, 94–95, 124, 112, 117–20, 124, 127, 133, 137, 146–50, 159, 175, 186

Jacques de Vitry 7, 78, 79–80, 84
Jesuits 64–65
Jews 5, 9, 137, 142–159, 161–62, 178
Joachim de Fiore 34

Kramer, Heinrich 89, 168, 176–77, 179, 188; see also *Malleus Maleficarum*
Kristeva, Julia 126, 128–9, 137, 139, 169

Lancre, Pierre de 93, 168, 180–82
The Last Exorcism (2010) 6, 59–60
The Last Exorcism II (2013) 6, 59–60
leaky 97, 138, 156
leprosy 37, 91, 130, 137, 139, 149
lesbians 121, 128, 131–32, 164
Let the Right One In (2008) 165
levitation 79, 82
Lewton, Val 54
light 20–21, 23, 24, 35, 158, 161, 166
The Little Mermaid (1989) 134
Lollards 33
Lost Boys (1987) 10
Lovecraft, H.P. 46
lovesickness 157–58, 175–76, 184
Lutgard of Aywières 7, 82–83
Luther, Martin 150
lycanthropy 11–12, 181–191

male body (construct) 7, 64–66, 76–78, 89
male gaze 7–8, 78–89, 90, 101–2, 133, 164
Malleus Maleficarum (1486) 5, 11, 37, 68, 89–91, 93–96, 119, 120, 128, 130, 133, 168
Manson, Charles 52
Marie de France 10, 167, 173–4
Marie d'Oignies 79–80
mark of the devil 38–39, 49, 51, 96, 178, 180, 183, 186
masturbation 65, 126
Mather, Cotton 40
matriarchy 105, 112–113, 117–28, 163–64
Matthew of Paris 145
medicine 40, 69, 77–78, 139–41, 151, 175–76, 185, 187–88
medieval color theory 24, 43, 115, 149, 185
medieval university 17–18
melancholia 168, 175–76, 179
melancholic body 9, 89–97, 101, 103, 112–13, 118–19, 128, 136–66
menopause 87, 96, 99
menstruation 7, 77–78, 83, 84–88, 96, 99, 193
menstruation (male) 9, 137, 147
Metamorphoses 170
metamorphosis 166–94

metempsychosis 167, 171–2
metensomatosis 171–2
middle class status quo 3, 8, 10, 12, 53, 105, 124–28, 138, 158–59, 162, 164–65
midwives 93, 186
milk 82
mirabolitism 82
miracles 21, 63, 144, 168, 173–74, 177
misogyny 9, 90, 121, 122–24, 128, 133–34
Mogen David 46, 165
monstrosity 4–5, 8, 10, 12, 24–26, 150–51
moon 9, 11, 19, 43, 109, 111, 126, 138, 154, 166, 168–170, 174, 180
mothers (bad) 89, 93–94, 121, 125–28, 163
mothers (good) 104–5, 121
multiplicity 17, 23, 28–29, 30, 35, 88–90, 138, 141
mushrooms 8, 82, 140, 155
Muslims 5

natural philosophy 17–19, 27–28, 174
necromancy 116
neo-platonism 17
New Age 50, 112–13, 190–91
New England 46–48, 53, 118, 158–59
New World Order 115
New York 54–55
Nider, Johannes 36, 42
night 9, 27, 43, 138, 169, 180
night flight 36–37, 92, 123, 172
non-naturals 70–71
nose 103, 145, 155, 158
Nosferatu: Eine Symphonie des Grauens (1922) 10, 154–57
Nosferatu: Phantom der Nacht (1979) 10, 157–58
nunsploitation 106

occultism 6, 44–46, 116, 120, 131–32, 145, 191
odor (foul) 138, 149, 152, 155
odor (sweet) 80, 83
ointment 11, , 39, 82, 92–93, 102, 109, 169, 178, 180–81, 193
The Omen (1976) 6, 61
On the Inconstancy of Witches (1602) 168, 180–81
On the Illusions of the Demons and on Spells and Poisons (1563) 40, 169, 179–80
Once Bitten (1985) 10
orgy 30, 45, 50, 52, 116, 121, 122, 169, 178
Otia Imperialia (1211) 174
ouija 64, 106
Ovid 170

pact 11, 36, 38–39, 44, 47, 48, 94, 108, 110, 111, 112, 117, 118, 141, 178, 182
paganism 52, 122, 166, 172
pallid 24, 43, 138, 146–47, 152, 155, 158, 169
Paole, Arnold 9, 136, 151–2
Paranormal State 66–67
passions of the soul 71, 74, 175
patriarchy 7–8, 10, 12, 52, 64–66, 101–2, 104–5, 109–10, 113, 114, 116–18, 124–27, 128–29, 133, 154, 159–61, 164
penis 85, 96, 119, 121, 128, 164
pentagram 43, 46, 51, 67, 116, 184–85

Peter of Dacia 83
Peter of John Olivi 34
Peter of Verona 32
Petronius 170
phallus (Satan) 24
phantasy 8, 10, 40, 96, 107, 167–68, 172, 174–8, 181–82
Philippines 124–25
physiognomy 96–97, 103, 137, 146, 155–56
plague 27, 91–92, 139, 145, 149, 152, 155, 182
Plato 171
pneuma 7–8, 62–65, 74, 77, 85–86, 91, 95, 138, 155, 175
poison 8, 9, 11, 84, 86, 90–93, 141, 149, 155, 178
Pope Clement V 34
possession 7, 28, 62–67, 87–88, 175, 186
Practical Magic (1989) 133
pregnancy 57–61
prime mover 19–20, 23
Prince of Darkness (1987) 6, 58–59
Pro-Life (2006) 60–61
protestantism (mainline) 101, 106, 124, 129, 150
pseudo–Albertus Magnus 84–88, 188
psychology 102, 119, 126, 169–70, 183–84, 189–90
puberty 105–6, 134, 193–94
purgation 63–65, 74–75, 82–83, 88

Queen of the Damned (2002) 10
queer theory 154, 157–58, 164–65, 192–93

race 110, 164
Ralph of Coggeshall 31
rapacity 8, 28, 85–86, 90, 94–96, 100–1, 112, 124, 127–28, 131, 133, 137, 148, 156, 158, 161, 163, 169, 187
rape 122, 126–27, 186, 193
rats 10, 155, 158, 159
"reality" tropes 41–42, 66–67
redemption 48
reform 32, 35–37
reformation 90
Remy, Nicholas 40, 42, 48, 91–93, 112
repression 184–85
reproductive rights 60–61, 104
revenants 137–38, 151–52
revenge 8, 47, 91, 96, 98, 118, 126, 129–33
Rhazes 69
ritual murder (children) 9, 113, 118, 120, 132, 137, 141–46, 165, 163, 178
robes 43, 47, 117, 118, 123, 154
Rosemary's Baby (1968) 6, 54, 56–57, 126

Sabrina the Teenaged Witch (1996–3) 134
sacraments 16, 22, 38, 42, 50, 117
sacred objects 63, 65, 152
sacrifice 31, 49, 128, 130, 132, 161
Salem's Lot (1979) 158–59
Satan (Devil) 5–6, 11, 12, 24–26, 56–59, 89–91, 116, 118, 123, 124, 128, 130, 125–26, 141, 152, 163, 176, 180–81
satanic panic 12, 41, 162
The Satanic Rites of Dracula (1970) 6, 50–52
Satan's Princess (1990) 127–28
Satyricon 170

Index

scholasticism (passim) 5, 9, 12, 17–18, 69, 76, 137–39, 143, 167–8, 174–75
scopophilia 101, 122
Scot, Reginald 40, 169
Season of the Witch (1972) 8
seasons 70–72
The Sentinel (1977) 54
serpents 30, 75, 86, 90, 92, 140, 174
The Seventh Victim (1943) 54
sex (intercourse) 7, 8, 9, 10, 52, 56–59, 75, 85, 126
shaggy 111, 169
shapeshifting 161, 168, 172
Sidhe 123
sign of the cross 29, 30, 95, 159
silver bullets 11, 186, 189, 191
similars (doctrine of) 24, 47, 75
single parents 64–65, 113–14
soul 7, 10, 62, 95, 109, 141, 143, 167, 170–76
spiders 9, 84, 118, 140, 159
spontaneous generation 86, 97, 100, 140, 155
stake 131, 152, 161
Stephen of Bourbon 32
stomach 62, 73, 139–140
storm 27, 107, 130, 160, 170, 180,
Summa Theologica (1274) 5, 17, 143, 175
Superstition (1982) 8, 129
Synagogue of Satan 149–50, 165
"Syzygy" (X-Files, 1996) 133–34

Taste the Blood of Dracula (1973) 6, 50–52, 162
television 3, 4, 10, 66–67, 126, 133–34, 165
Tertullian 167, 171–74
Theriac 75
Thomas of Cantimpré 7, 70, 77, 80–83, 84, 152
Thomas of Monmouth 144–45
To the Devil a Daughter (1976) 6, 57–58
toads 27, 38, 81, 86, 89, 92, 93, 97
Topography of Ireland 10, 172–73
transgression 12, 136–39, 153, 156, 193–94
translation 69–70
transubstantiation 9, 23, 33, 142–44, 150–51, 167
True Blood (2008–present) 4, 10, 165
Twins of Evil (1971) 163
Tyrnau 145

Unam Sanctam (1302) 34
uncanny 4, 129, 131, 184
underground 31, 45, 48, 49, 103, 106, 110, 115, 118, 121, 123–24, 129, 159
The Undying Monster (1942) 185, 187

urine 39, 73, 106
usury 148, 155
uterus *see* womb

Vamp (1986) 10
vampire 9–10, 136–39, 150–66
vampire treatises 151–52
Vampiros Lesbos (1971) 10
vapors 85–88, 91, 140, 157, 176
The Vatican Tapes (2015) 6
Vatican II (1962–68) 49, 162
venesection 74–75
violence against women 121–22, 125
Virgin Mary 21, 58, 94, 142
Virgin Witch (1971) 133
vision (sight) 85–86, 90, 155, 159
Visum et Repertum (1732) 151
vixen 98–99, 105, 107, 111, 128, 131, 134, 186, 190–91, 193–94
voodoo 108, 110, 119

werewolf 10–11, 123, 166–94
Werewolf of London (1935) 185, 187, 189, 192
Weyer, Johann 40, 169, 179–80
Wheatley, Dennis 44, 57
White Zombie (1932) 110
wife 95, 124–27, 173, 186, 193
wilderness 6, 11, 48–49, 52–53, 122, 125, 133, 155, 158, 169, 170, 174, 180, 182, 186–87
William of Auvergne 25, 174–75
William of Norwich 9, 144–45
wind 71–72, 91, 138, 159
windows 92, 154, 157, 158
witchcraft (heresy) 36–40
witchcraft treatises 8, 11, 36–37, 89–97, 176–83
witches 8–9, 10, 46–50, 89–97, 98–99, 163, 176, 182
The Witches (1966) 8, 119
Witches' Sabbath 36–49, 46–49, 89–97, 111, 116, 178, 180
Witchfinder General (1968) 121
The Witching (1972) 8, 116
The Witchmaker (1969) 6, 8, 48–50, 110–13
Wizard of Oz (1939) 102–3
wolf 166, 167, 173, 174–75, 179, 189
wolf skin 173, 180–81, 182
The Wolf Man (1941) 11, 185, 187, 192
wolves 9, 10, 11
womb (uterus) 83, 84–88, 94, 129, 133, 147
women's liberation 8–9, 105, 115, 117, 124–28
worms 9, 27, 76, 97, 100, 138, 140, 142, 188

www.ingramcontent.com/pod-product-compliance
Ingram Content Group UK Ltd.
Pitfield, Milton Keynes, MK11 3LW, UK
UKHW041939140426
5217IPUK00014B/559